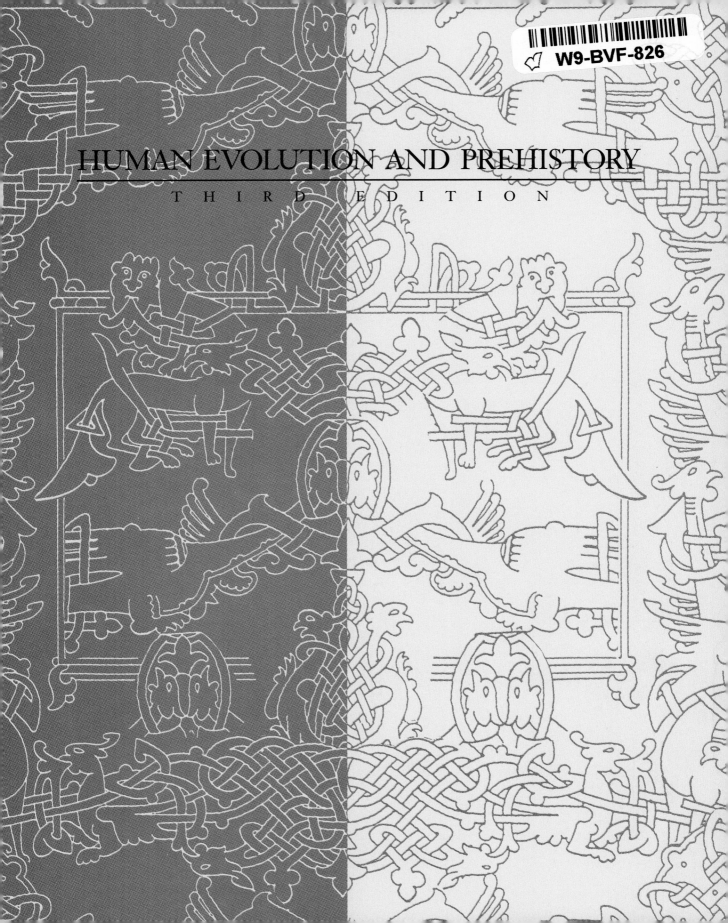

HUMAN EVOLUTION AND PREHISTORY

THIRD EDITION

HUMAN EVOLUTION AND PREHISTORY
THIRD EDITION

WILLIAM A. HAVILAND

University of Vermont

Harcourt Brace College Publishers

Fort Worth Philadelphia San Diego New York Orlando Austin San Antonio
Toronto Montreal London Sydney Tokyo

Editor-in-chief	Ted Buchholz
Acquisitions editor	Chris Klein
Developmental editor	Karee Galloway
Project editor	Steve Norder
Production manager	Kathleen Ferguson
Art directors	Priscilla Mingus/Linda Miller
Picture editor	Sandra Lord
Literary permissions editor	Sheila Shutter

Cover and part opening illustrations by Rebbeca Ruegger

Literary and photo credits appear on p. 306 and constitute an extension of this page.

Library of Congress Catalog Card Number: 93-79950

Address for editorial correspondence: Harcourt Brace College Publishers, 301 Commerce Street, Suite 3700, Fort Worth, TX 76102.

Address for orders: Harcourt Brace & Company, 6277 Sea Harbor Drive, Orlando, FL 32887. 1-800-782-4479 or 1-800-433-0001 (in Florida).

ISBN: 0-15-501259-2

This book is printed on acid-free paper.

Printed in the United States of America

3 4 5 6 7 8 9 0 1 2 048 9 8 7 6 5 4 3 2 1

To my wife, Anita

ABOUT THE AUTHOR

Dr. William A. Haviland is professor of anthropology at the University of Vermont, where he has taught since 1965. He holds a doctoral degree in anthropology from the University of Pennsylvania and has published widely on archaeological, ethnological, and physical anthropological research carried out in Guatemala, Maine, and Vermont. Dr. Haviland is a member of many professional societies, including the American Anthropological Association and the American Association for the Advancement of Science. In 1988, he participated in the project on "Gender and the Anthropology Curriculum" sponsored by the American Anthropological Association.

One of Dr. Haviland's greatest loves is teaching, which originally prompted him to write *Anthropology,* and its companion books *Cultural Anthropology* and *Human Evolution and Prehistory.* He has learned much from his students, as well as from his work with Vermont's Native American Community, about what students need out of their first college course in anthropology.

PREFACE

This textbook is designed for introductory courses at the college level that combine physical anthropology and prehistoric archaeology. It presents the key concepts and terms from these two subfields of anthropology that apply to the interrelated subjects of human biological and cultural evolution.

A book that combines archaeology and physical anthropology cannot by itself hope to be an adequate introduction to either subdiscipline. What this textbook does is to give the student a thorough introduction to selected aspects of each as these bear on the related topics of the origin of humanity, the origin of culture, and the development of human biological and cultural diversity. In the process, the student will come to understand the ways human culture and biology are intertwined, each affecting the other in important ways.

OUTSTANDING FEATURES OF THE BOOK

READABILITY

The major purposes of a textbook are to provide ideas and information, to induce the readers to see old things in new ways, and to cause readers to think about what they see. A book may be the most elegantly written, handsomely designed, lavishly illustrated text available on the subject; but if it is not interesting, clear, and comprehensible to the student, it is valueless as a teaching tool. The trick is not just to present facts and concepts, but to make them memorable.

To aid readability this book has been carefully structured. Each section and each chapter within each section are organized so that the material is presented to the student in segments, each clearly separated from the other. It is easier for the student to grasp and retain material if it is presented as a series of discrete units, rather than as a continuous flow of information.

This book presents even the most difficult concepts in prose that is clear, straightforward, and easy for today's first- and second-year students to understand, without feeling that they are being "spoken down to." Technical terms, which appear in boldface type, are carefully explained in the text itself, then defined again in the running glossary in simple, clear language.

INTEGRATION OF PHYSICAL ANTHROPOLOGY AND ARCHAEOLOGY

A major feature of this textbook is that the findings of physical anthropology and archaeology are presented together, rather than in separate sections. This format explicitly recognizes that no organism can survive unless it is able to adapt to some available environment. Adaptation requires the development of behavior patterns that help the organism utilize the environment to its advantage; in turn, organisms need to have the biological equipment that makes possible the development of such behavior patterns. Obviously, the biology of an organism cannot be understood apart from the way the organism behaves and vice versa. To understand human evolution, then, we must consider biology and behavior patterns together rather than separately. Physical anthropology provides the relevant biological information. Behavioral information, at least since the appearance of the genus *Homo,* is provided by archaeology.

ADAPTABILITY OF THE BOOK

Many colleges now offer separate one-semester courses that combine physical anthropology and archaeology. This book is well adapted for use in such courses. Its eleven chapters fit the one-semester format well, and may easily be supplemented by short modules in physical anthropology and/or archaeological case studies, as the instructor wishes. Moreover, this book is easily adaptable to the traditional full-year course in general anthropology, when used in conjunction with the companion text *Cultural Anthropology,* seventh edition. Together, the two become a single text in general anthropology.

ORIGINAL STUDIES

One of the unique features of this text is the Original Study that is included within each chapter. These studies consist of selections from case studies and other original works of men and women who have done, or are doing, work of importance in physical anthropology and/or archaeology. Each study, integrally related to the material in the text, sheds additional light on some important concept or subject area found in the chapter. The Original Studies help give students a real "feel" for how physical anthropologists and archaeologists work and deal with their material.

ILLUSTRATIONS

Another means of appealing to the nondominant hemisphere of the brain is through the use of numerous illustrations and other graphic materials. The use of such material is important for two other reasons as well. First, as primates, our primary sensual reliance is on visual images, a fact that is not always acknowledged in literate societies. Second, in today's world, people rely primarily on visual, rather than print media for information. Thus, we need to teach students to be thoughtful viewers, just as we teach them to be thoughtful readers. In this book, numerous four-color photos have been used to make important anthropological points by catching the student's eye and mind. Many are unusual in that they are not the "standard" anthropological textbook photographs; each has been chosen because it complements the text in some distinctive way. The line drawings, maps, charts, and tables were selected especially for their usefulness in illustrating, emphasizing, or clarifying certain anthropological concepts and should prove valuable teaching aids.

EMPHASIS ON GEOGRAPHY

It's necessary in any anthropology textbook to refer frequently to places throughout the world. Unfortunately, today's students are far less knowledgeable about world geography than were students even twenty years ago; and most anthropology textbooks have done little to address this problem. In this edition, a consistent effort has been made to help students identify regions, countries, and continents as they are discussed. When appropriate, Original Studies are accompanied by a detailed map that helps students locate the region under discussion. Longer discussions of major archaeological sites are also accompanied by detailed maps. In addition, a new section titled "Putting the World in Perspective" introduces students to some of the landmarks in the history of cartography and deceptions necessarily inherent in any two-dimensional map. This introductory section includes reproductions of several different world maps, each representing a unique view of the world.

PREVIEWS AND SUMMARIES

An old but effective pedagogical technique is repetition: "Tell 'em what you're going to tell 'em, do it, and then tell 'em what you've told 'em." To do this, each chapter begins with preview questions that set up a framework for studying the chapter. Each chapter ends with a summary of the most important ideas presented in the chapter. The summaries provide handy reviews without being so long and detailed as to seduce students into thinking that they can get by without reading the chapter itself.

SUGGESTED READINGS AND BIBLIOGRAPHY

Each chapter also includes a list of suggested readings that will supply the inquisitive student with further information about specific points which may be of interest. In addition, a bibliography at the end of the book lists several hundred books, monographs, and articles from scholarly journals as well as popular magazines on almost every topic covered in the text.

RUNNING GLOSSARY

A running glossary defines key terms on the same or nearby page that they are first introduced, thereby reinforcing the meaning of each new term. It is also useful for chapter review, as the student may readily isolate those terms introduced in one chapter from those introduced in others. Because each term is defined in clear, understandable language, less class time is required to review terms.

LENGTH

This book has deliberately been kept relatively short for two reasons. First, while students must have sufficient detail to be able to understand what we know and how we know, they must not become so immersed in details that they lose sight of "the big picture." Above all, human biological and cultural evolution is a fascinating story, and we ought to use it to "hook" students so that they will come back for more. At that point, they will be more receptive to the nitty gritty details. Second, by keeping the book reasonably short, the instructor is provided the opportunity to supplement the textbook with whatever extra reading he or she may wish, thereby providing greater flexibility.

ADVANTAGES OF THE THIRD EDITION

The planning of the third edition of *Human Evolution and Prehistory* was based on extensive review and criticism by instructors who teach this material. One major change in this edition is the inclusion of important material on gender in every chapter of the book, in order to make it absolutely clear that both sexes played critical roles in the evolution of our species (it wasn't the "evolution of man" alone), as well as to combat common misconceptions as to the nature of gender distinctions, and how these have changed over time and between cultures. In addition to the expansion of gender material, the number of features highlighting important figures in the history of physical anthropology and archaeology have been increased, in order to spotlight the important contributions made by women as well as men. For example, a new biobox, on Adrienne Zihlman, has been added to Chapter 7, and three new Original Studies featuring the work of women in the field have been added to Chapters 2, 4, and 9.

Another innovation is the addition of "Anthropology Applied" boxes to Chapters 1, 2, 4, and 10. These features emphasize the important practical contributions our disciplines have to make in such diverse fields as forensic anthropology (Chapter 1), cultural resource management (Chapter 2), wildlife conservation (Chapter 4), and surgery (Chapter 8).

It goes without saying that in the ten years since the last edition of this book, there have been enormous advances in our understanding of human biological and cultural evolution, requiring substantial updating and rewriting in all chapters. In addition, the Original Studies are all new, as are most of the illustrations. In many respects, it is almost a new book.

SUPPLEMENTS TO THE TEXT

The ancillaries that accompany *Human Evolution and Prehistory*, third edition, have been skillfully prepared by Cynthia Keppley Mahmood of the University of Maine, Orono.

An *Instructor's Manual* offers lecture and class activity suggestions which correspond to every chapter of the textbook. The manual also includes other resources designed to help anthropology instructors.

An extensive *Test Bank,* available in both printed and computerized form, offers a wide selection of carefully constructed multiple-choice and true/false questions.

A set of color transparencies also is available to instructors for use in classroom lectures.

Through common learning and teaching objectives, structured student activities, and careful organization, these supplements are intended to work together as a fully integrated instructional package that is adaptable to different teaching situations. It is my hope that they will encourage interaction between teacher and student as well.

William A. Haviland
1993

ACKNOWLEDGMENTS

The third edition of this book had its beginnings in the seventh edition of my book, *Anthropology,* and so it owes a good deal to those anthropologists who helped in one way or another with that edition. They include: Kathleen J. Reichs, The University of North Carolina at Charlotte; H. Lyn Miles, University of Tennessee; Jim Mielke, The University of Kansas; Lisa Sattenspiel, University of Missouri, Columbia; Sonja O. Solland, Shoreline Community College; and Nancy P. McKee, Washington State University. Their comments were all helpful and carefully considered; how I have made use of them has been determined by my own perspective on the human past, as well as by my experience with undergraduate students. Therefore, the readers cannot be blamed for any shortcomings the book may have.

My own particular perspective on the human past owes a good deal to a number of anthropologists under whom I was privileged to study archaeology and physical anthropology. I learned my archaeology at the University of Pennsylvania from William R. Coe, Carleton S. Coon, Robert Ehrich, J. Louis Gaddings, Ward H. Goodenough, Alfred V. Kidder II, Froelich Rainey, and Linton Satterthwaite; and in the field, first from Warren W. Caldwell in South Dakota and then William R. Coe in Guatemala. My physical anthropology I learned from Carleton S. Coon, Loren Eisley, and especially Wilton M. Krogman, for whom I worked while a graduate student at the Philadelphia Center for Research in Child Growth. My debt to all these people is enormous, and while they may not always recognize the final product, they all contributed to it in important ways.

I have been teaching introductory courses in physical anthropology since 1962 and archaeology from 1964 until the mid-1970s, and I must acknowledge the contribution made by the students who have enrolled in these courses over the years. My experience with them and their reactions to various textbooks have been important in determining what has and what has not gone into this book. Although I no longer teach the introduction to archaeology, I have continued my interest in it, through discussions with my colleague Marjory Power who now teaches it, through review of new textbooks for such courses, and most recently as a member of the national advisory board for an archaeology telecourse funded by the Annenburg/CPB Project.

It has been my great good fortune to be able to work with a supportive, friendly, and knowledgeable group of people at Harcourt Brace. These include acquisitions editor Chris Klein, development editor Karee Galloway, project editor Steve Norder, book designer Priscilla Mingus, production manager Kathleen Ferguson, art editor Sandra Lord, and permissions editor Shiela Shutter. I also owe a special thanks to David Brill for his expertise and artistry in photographing many of the skulls found throughout the book.

The greatest debt of all is owed my wife, Anita de Laguna Haviland, who has had to put up with my preoccupation with this revision, reminding me when it is time to feed the livestock or play midwife to the sheep in the barn. As if that were not enough, it was she who fed revised text into the word processor, bringing me at last into the world of "high tech" and delivering my editors from the frustration of dealing with cut-and-paste copy full of pencilled-in changes. Finally, she has been a source of endless good ideas on things to include, and ways to express things. The book has benefitted enormously from her involvement.

W.A.H.

BRIEF CONTENTS

BRIEF CONTENTS

Preface

CONTENTS

PART I

THE STUDY OF HUMANKIND 1

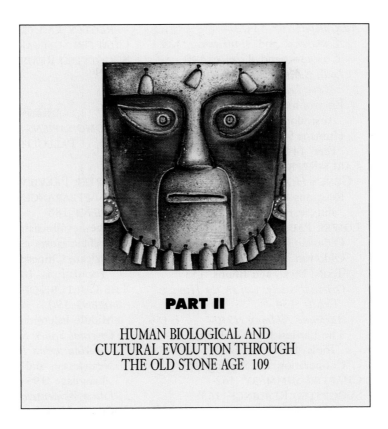

PART II

HUMAN BIOLOGICAL AND CULTURAL EVOLUTION THROUGH THE OLD STONE AGE 109

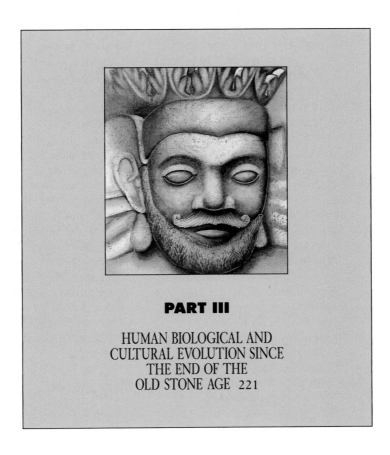

PART III

HUMAN BIOLOGICAL AND CULTURAL EVOLUTION SINCE THE END OF THE OLD STONE AGE 221

PUTTING THE WORLD IN PERSPECTIVE

Although all humans that we know about are capable of producing accurate sketches of localities and regions with which they are familiar, CARTOGRAPHY (the craft of mapmaking as we know it today) had its beginnings in 13th century Europe, and its subsequent development is related to the expansion of Europeans to all parts of the globe. From the beginning, there have been two problems with maps: the technical one of how to depict on a two-dimensional, flat surface a three-dimensional spherical object, and the cultural one of whose world view they reflect. In fact, the two issues are inseparable, for the particular projection one uses inevitably makes a statement about how one views one's own people and their place in the world. Indeed, maps often shape our perception of reality as much as they reflect it.

In cartography, a PROJECTION refers to the system of intersecting lines (of longitude and latitude) by which part or all of the globe is represented on a flat surface. There are more than 100 different projections in use today, ranging from polar perspectives to interrupted "butterflies" to rectangles to heart shapes. Each projection causes distortion in size, shape, or distance in some way or another. A map that shows the shape of land masses correctly will of necessity misrepresent the size. A map that is accurate along the equator will be deceptive at the poles.

Perhaps no projection has had more influence on the way we see the world than that of Gerhardus Mercator, who devised his map in 1569 as a navigational aid for mariners. So well suited was Mercator's map for this purpose that it continues to be used for navigational charts today. At the same time, the Mercator projection became a standard for depicting land masses, something for which it was never intended. Although an accurate navigational tool, the Mercator projection greatly exaggerates the size of land masses in higher latitudes, giving about two-thirds of the map's surface to the northern hemisphere. Thus, the lands occupied by Europeans and European descendents appear far larger than those of other people. For example, North America (19 million square kilometers) appears almost twice the size of Africa (30 million square kilometers), while Europe is shown as equal in size to South America, which actually has nearly twice the land mass of Europe.

A map developed in 1805 by Karl B. Mollweide was one of the earlier equal-area projections of the world. Equal-area projections portray land masses in correct relative size, but, as a result, distort the shape of continents more than other projections. They most often compress and warp lands in the higher latitudes and vertically stretch land masses close to the equator. Other equal-area projections include the Lambert Cylindrical Equal-Area Projection (1772), the Hammer Equal-Area Projection (1892), and the Eckert Equal-Area Projection (1906).

The Van der Grinten Projection (1904) was a compromise aimed at minimizing both the distortions of size in the Mercator and the distortion of shape in equal-area maps such as the Mollweide. Although an improvement, the lands of the northern hemisphere are still emphasized at the expense of the southern. For example, in the Van der Grinten, the Commonwealth of Independent States (the former Soviet Union) and Canada are shown at more than twice their relative size.

The Robinson Projection, which was adopted by the National Geographic Society in 1988 to replace the Van der Grinten, is one of the best compromises to date between the distortion of size and shape. Although an improvement over the Van der Grinten, the Robinson projection still depicts lands in the northern latitudes as proportionally larger at the same time that it depicts lands in the lower latitudes (representing most third-world nations) as proportionally smaller. Like European maps before it, the Robinson projection places Europe at the center of the map with the Atlantic Ocean and the Americas to the left, emphasizing the cultural connection between Europe and North America, while neglecting the geographical closeness of northwestern North America to northeast Asia.

The following pages show four maps that each convey quite different "cultural messages." Included among them is the Peters Projection, an equal-area map that has been adopted as the official map of UNESCO (the United Nations Educational, Scientific, and Cultural Organization), and a map made in Japan, showing us how the world looks from the other side.

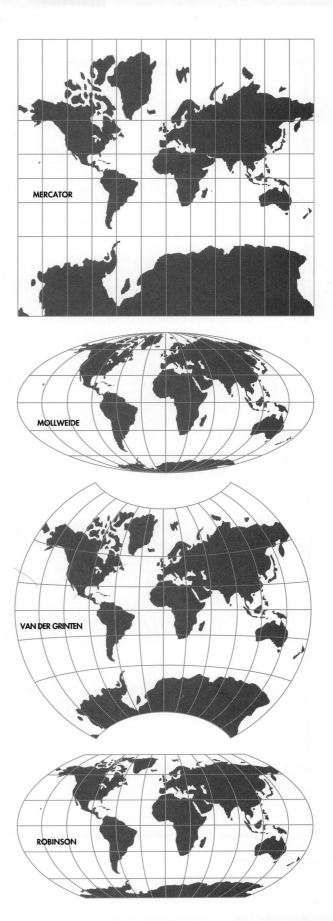

MERCATOR

MOLLWEIDE

VAN DER GRINTEN

ROBINSON

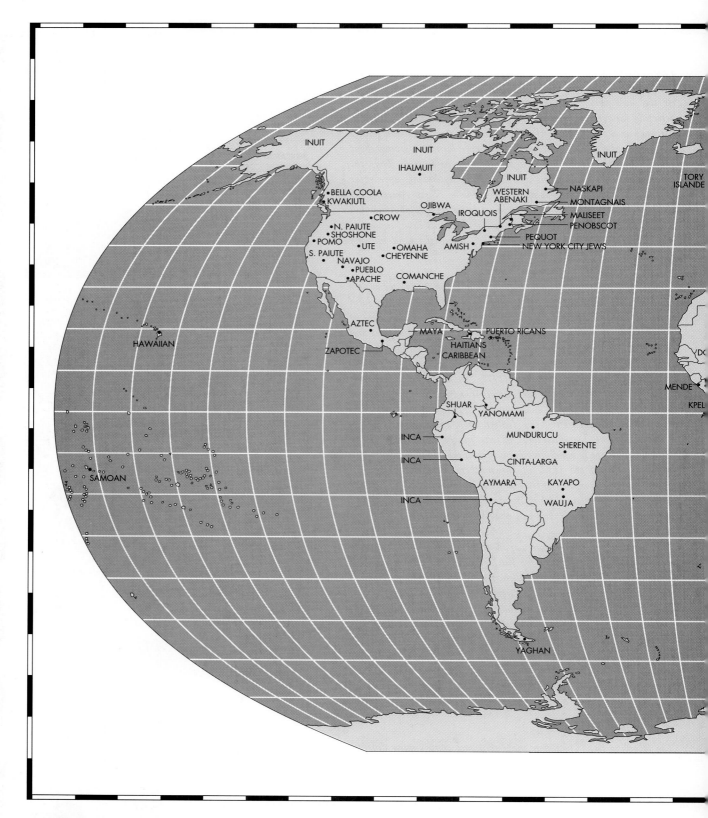

INUIT

INUIT

INUIT

INUIT

IHALMUIT

TORY ISLANDE

•BELLA COOLA
•KWAKIUTL

WESTERN ABENAKI

NASKAPI

OJIBWA

IROQUOIS

MONTAGNAIS

•CROW

MALISEET
PENOBSCOT

N. PAIUTE
•SHOSHONE
•POMO
•UTE
S. PAIUTE
NAVAJO
•PUEBLO
•APACHE

OMAHA
CHEYENNE

AMISH

PEQUOT
NEW YORK CITY JEWS

COMANCHE

AZTEC

MAYA

PUERTO RICANS

HAWAIIAN

ZAPOTEC

HAITIANS
CARIBBEAN

MENDE

KPEL

SHUAR

YANOMAMI

INCA

MUNDURUCU

SHERENTE

INCA

CINTA-LARGA

SAMOAN

AYMARA

KAYAPO

INCA

WAUJA

YAGHAN

THE ROBINSON PROJECTION *The map above is based on the Robinson Projection, which is used today by the National Geographic Society and Rand McNally. Although the Robinson Projection distorts the relative size of land masses, it does so to a much lesser degree than*

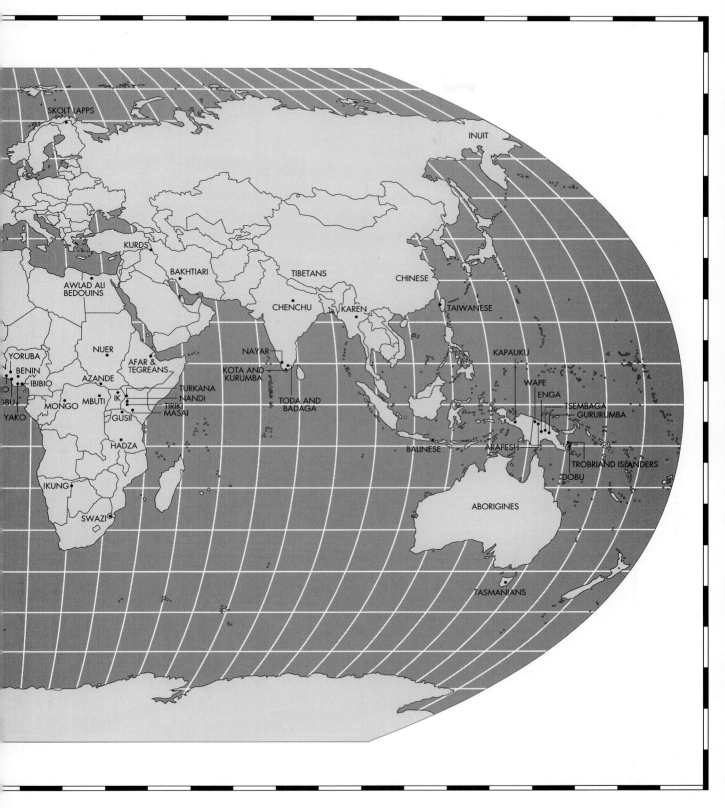

most other projections. Still, it places Europe at the center of the map.
This particular view of the world has been used to identify the location of many of the cultures discussed in this text.

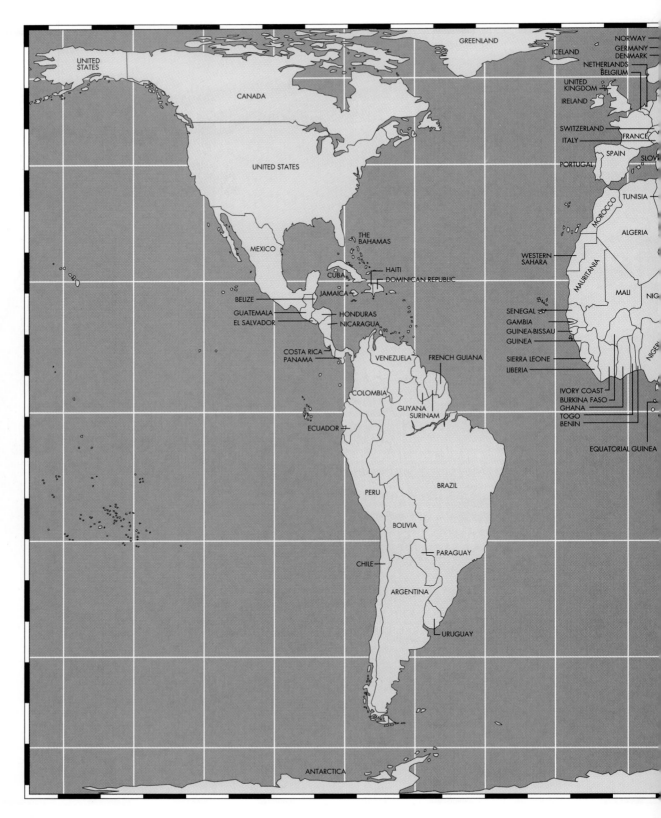

THE PETERS PROJECTION   *The map above is based on the Peters Projection, which has been adopted as the official map of UNESCO. While it distorts the shape of continents (countries near the equator are vertically elongated by a ratio of two to one),*

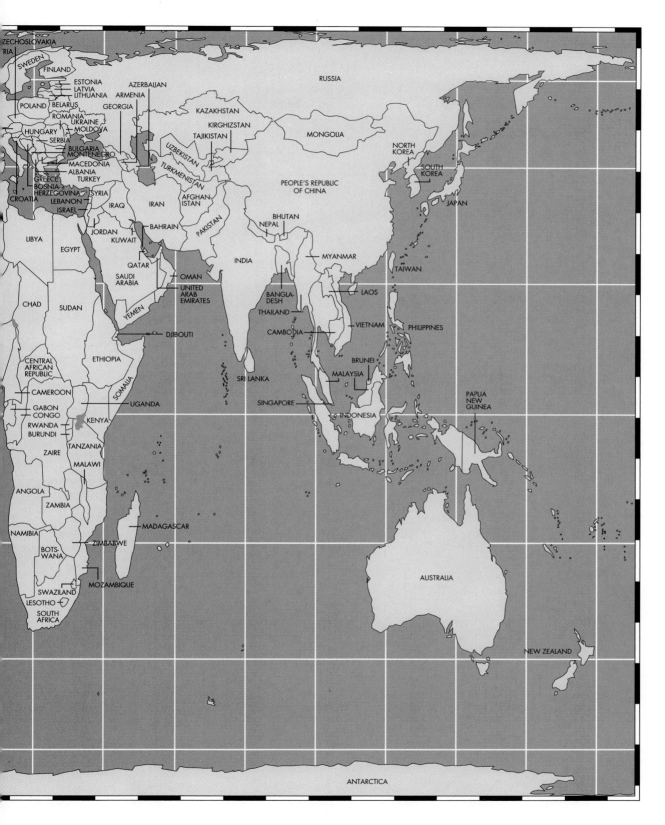

the Peters Projection does show all continents according to their correct relative size. Though Europe is still at the center, it is not shown as larger and more extensive than the third world.

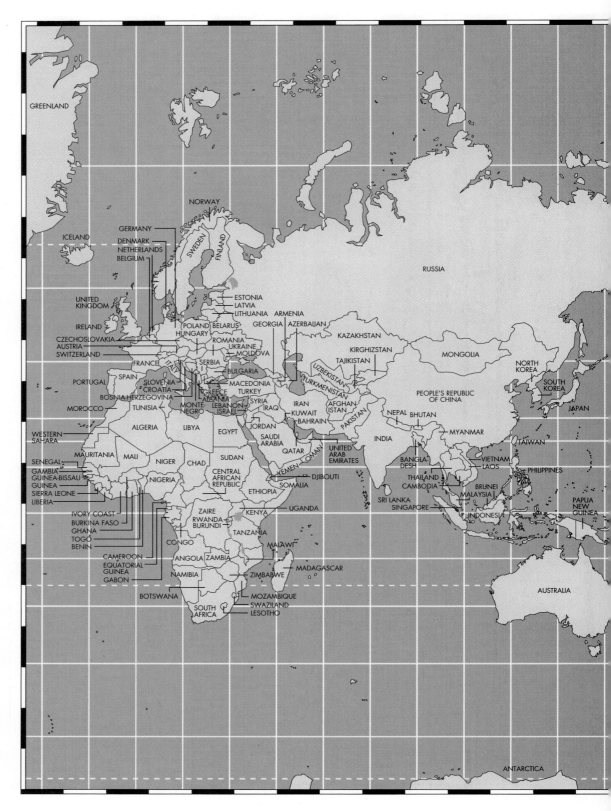

JAPANESE MAP *Not all maps place Europe at the center of the world, as this Japanese map illustrates. Besides reflecting the importance the Japanese attach to themselves in the world, this map has the virtue of showing the*

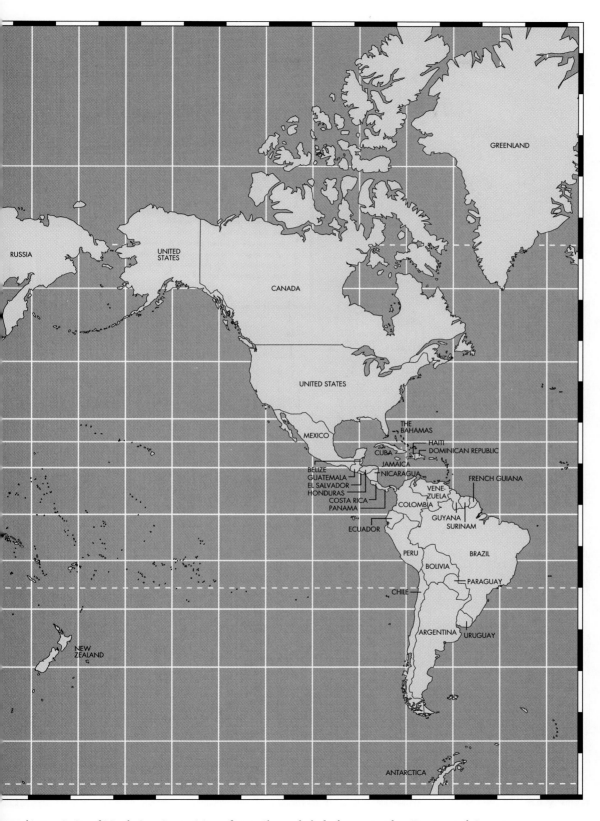

graphic proximity of North America to Asia, a fact easily overlooked when maps place Europe at their center.

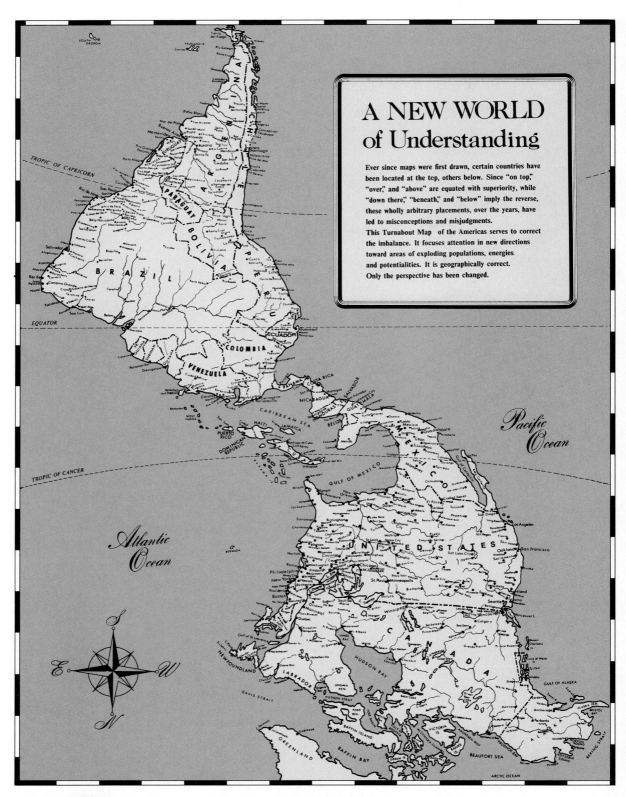

THE TURNABOUT MAP *The way maps may reflect (and influence) our thinking is exemplified by the "Turnabout Map," which places the South Pole at the top and the North Pole at the bottom. Words and phrases such as "on top," "over," and "above" tend to be equated by some people with superiority. Turning things upside down may cause us to rethink the way North Americans regard themselves in relation to the people of Central and South America.* © 1982 by Jesse Levine Turnabout Map™ — Dist. by Laguna Sales, Inc., 7040 Via Valverde, San Jose, CA 95135

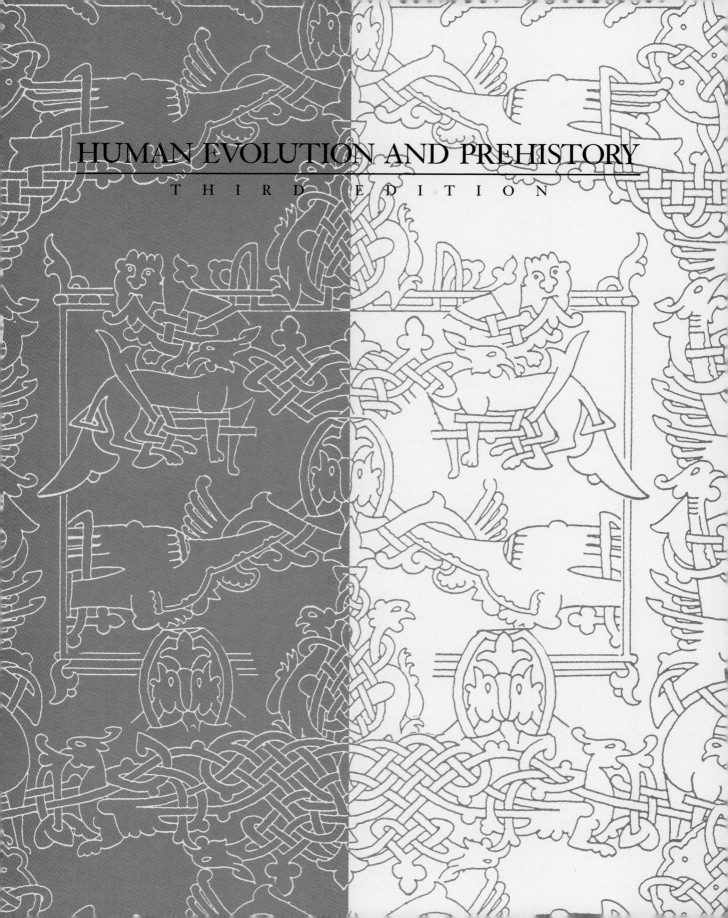

HUMAN EVOLUTION AND PREHISTORY

T H I R D   E D I T I O N

PART I

THE STUDY OF HUMANKIND

INTRODUCTION

ANTHROPOLOGY IS THE MOST LIBERATING OF ALL THE SCIENCES. NOT ONLY HAS IT EXPOSED THE FALLACIES OF RACIAL AND CULTURAL SUPERIORITY, BUT ITS DEVOTION TO THE STUDY OF ALL PEOPLES, REGARDLESS OF WHERE AND WHEN THEY LIVED,

has cast more light on human nature than all the reflections of sages or the studies of laboratory scientists. If this sounds like the assertion of an overly enthusiastic anthropologist, it is not; it was all said by the philosopher Grace de Laguna in her 1941 presidential address to the Eastern Division of the American Philosophical Association.

The subject matter of anthropology is vast, as we shall see in this book: It includes everything that has to do with human beings, past and present. Of course, many other disciplines are concerned in one way or another with human beings. Some, such as anatomy and physiology, study humans as biological organisms. The social sciences are concerned with the distinctive forms of human relationships, while the humanities examine the great achievements of human culture. Anthropologists are interested in all of these things, too, but they try to deal with all of these things together, in all places and times. It is

this unique, broad perspective that equips anthropologists so well to deal with that elusive thing called human nature.

Needless to say, no single anthropologist is able to investigate personally everything that has to do with people. For practical purposes, the discipline is divided into various subfields, and individual anthropologists specialize in one or more of these. Whatever their specialization, though, they retain a commitment to a broader, overall perspective on humankind. For example, cultural anthropologists specialize in the study of human behavior, while physical anthropologists specialize in the study of humans as biological organisms. Yet neither can afford to ignore the work of the other, for human behavior and biology are inextricably intertwined, with each affecting the other in important ways. We can see, for example, how biology affects a cultural practice, color-naming behavior. Human populations differ in the density of pigmentation

within the eye itself, which in turn affects people's ability to distinguish the color blue from green, black, or both. For this reason, a number of cultures identify blue with green, black or both. We can see also how a cultural practice may affect human biology, as exemplified by the sickle-cell trait and related conditions. In certain parts of the Old World, when humans took up the practice of farming, they altered the ecology in a way that, by chance, created ideal conditions for the breeding of mosquitoes. As a result, malaria (a disease carried by mosquitos) became a serious problem, and a biological response to this was the spread of certain genes that, in substantial numbers of people living in malarial areas, produced a built-in resistance to the disease.

To begin our introduction to the study of anthropology, we will look closely at the nature of the discipline. In Chapter 1 we will see how the field of anthropology is subdivided, how the subdivisions relate to one another, and how they relate to the other sciences and humanities. Chapter 1 introduces us as well to the methods anthropologists use to study human cultures, especially those of today, or the very recent past. The very different methods used to find out about the ancient past are the subject of Chapter 2, which discusses the nature of fossils and archaeological materials, where they are found, how they are (quite literally) unearthed, and how they must be treated once unearthed. From this, one can begin to appreciate what the evidence can tell us if handled properly, as well as its limitations.

In order to understand what fossils have to tell us about our past, some knowledge of how biological evolution works is necessary. But fossils, unlike flesh-and-blood people, do not speak for themselves, and so they must be interpreted. If we are to have confidence in an interpretation of a particular fossil, we must be sure the interpretation is consistent with what we know about the workings of evolution; therefore, Chapter 3 is devoted to a discussion of evolution.

The zoological order that gave rise to human beings includes lemurs, lorises, indriids, tarsiers, monkeys, and apes: the Primate order. In Chapter 4 we shall examine the modern primates in order to understand how we humans are like the other primates; in particular we can begin to appreciate that many of the physical characteristics we think of as distinctively human are simply exaggerated versions of characteristics common to other primates. For example, primate brains tend to be large and heavy relative to body size and weight; in humans, this trait is realized to a greater degree than it is in other primates. We can begin to appreciate as well the kind of behavioral versatility of which present-day members of this order are capable. In the range of modern primate behavior patterns, we find clues to patterns that were characteristic of primates that lived in the past, from which humans are descended. With these things done, we will have set the stage for our detailed look at human biological and cultural evolution in Parts Two and Three.

1

THE NATURE

OF

ANTHROPOLOGY

In this sixteenth-century depiction of a meeting between Frenchmen and American Indians, the latter look more like costumed Europeans than aboriginal Americans. The tendency to see other people as one has been conditioned to see them, rather than as they are, is still a major problem throughout the world.

WHAT IS ANTHROPOLOGY?

Anthropology, the study of humankind, seeks to produce useful generalizations about people and their behavior, to arrive at the fullest possible understanding of human diversity, and to understand those things that all humans have in common.

WHAT DO ANTHROPOLOGISTS DO?

Physical anthropologists study humans as biological organisms, tracing the evolutionary development of the human animal and looking at the biological variations within the species today. Cultural anthropologists are concerned with human cultures, or the ways of life in societies. Within the field of cultural anthropology are archaeologists, who seek to explain human behavior by studying material objects, usually from past cultures; linguists, who study languages, by which cultures are maintained and passed on to succeeding generations; and ethnologists, who study cultures as they can be experienced and discussed with persons whose culture is to be understood.

HOW DO ANTHROPOLOGISTS DO WHAT THEY DO?

Anthropologists, in common with other scientists, are concerned with the formulation and testing of hypotheses, or tentative explanations of observed phenomena. In so doing, they hope to arrive at a system of validated hypotheses or theory, although they recognize that no theory is ever completely beyond challenge. In order to frame hypotheses that are as objective and free of cultural bias as possible, anthropologists typically develop them through a kind of total immersion in the field, becoming so familiar with the minute details of the situation that they can begin to recognize patterns inherent in the data. It is also through fieldwork that anthropologists test existing hypotheses.

A common component of the mythology of all peoples is a legend that explains the appearance of humans on earth. For example, the Nez Perce of the American Northwest believe that humanity is the creation of Coyote, one of the animal people that inhabited the earth before humans. Coyote chased the giant beaver monster, Wishpoosh, in an epic chase whose trail formed the Columbia River. When Coyote caught Wishpoosh, he killed him and dragged his body to the river bank. Ella Clark retells the legend:

> With his sharp knife Coyote cut up the big body of the monster.
>
> "From your body, mighty Wishpoosh," he said, "I will make a new race of people. They will live near the shores of Big River and along the streams which flow into it."
>
> From the lower part of the animal's body, Coyote made people who were to live along the coast. "You shall live near the mouth of Big River and shall be traders."
>
> "You shall live along the coast," he said to others. "You shall live in villages facing the ocean and shall get your food by spearing salmon and digging clams. You shall always be short and fat and have weak legs."
>
> From the legs of the beaver monster he made the Klickitat Indians. "You shall live along the rivers that flow down from the big white mountain north of Big River. You shall be swift of foot and keen of wit. You shall be famous runners and great horsemen."
>
> From the arms of the monster he made the Cayuse Indians. "You shall be powerful with bow and arrows and with war clubs."
>
> From the ribs he made the Yakima Indians. "You shall live near the new Yakima River, east of the mountains. You shall be the helpers and the protectors of all the poor people."
>
> From the head he created the Nez Perce Indians. "You shall live in the valleys of the Kookooskia and Wallowa rivers. You shall be men of brains, great in council and in speechmaking. You shall also be skillful horsemen and brave warriors."
>
> Then Coyote gathered up the hair and blood and waste. He hurled them far eastward, over the big mountains. "You shall be the Snake River Indians," said Coyote. "You shall be people of blood and violence. You shall be buffalo hunters and shall wander far and wide."[1]

[1] Ella E. Clark, *Indian Legends of the Pacific Northwest* (Berkeley, Calif.: University of California Press, 1966), p. 174.

For as long as they have been on earth, people have needed answers to questions about who they are, where they came from, and why they act the way they do. Throughout most of their history, though, people had no extensive and reliable body of data about their own behavior and background, and so they relied on myth and folklore for their answers to these questions. Anthropology, over the last 200 years, has emerged as a more scientific approach to answering these questions. Simply stated, **anthropology** is the study of humankind. The anthropologist is concerned primarily with a single species—*Homo sapiens*—the human species, its ancestors, and near relatives. Because anthropologists are members of the species being studied, it is difficult to be completely objective. They have found, however, that the use of the scientific approach produces useful generalizations about humans and their behavior. With the scientific approach, anthropologists are able to arrive at a reasonably reliable understanding of human diversity, as well as those things that all humans have in common.

DEVELOPMENT OF ANTHROPOLOGY

Although works of anthropological significance have a considerable antiquity—among others, the accounts of other peoples by Herodotus the Greek, or the Arab Ibn Khaldun, written in the fifth century B.C. and 14th century A.D.—anthropology as a distinct field of inquiry is a relatively recent product of Western civilization. In the United States, for example, the first course in general anthropology to carry credit in a college or university was offered at the University of Rochester, but not until 1879. If people have always been concerned about themselves and their origins, why then did it take such a long time for a systematic discipline of anthropology to appear?

Anthropology: The study of humankind, in all times and places.

In the United States, anthropology began in the nineteenth century, when a number of dedicated amateurs went into the field to determine whether prevailing ideas about so-called savage peoples were valid. Shown here are Alice Fletcher, who spent the better part of 30 years documenting the ways of the Omaha Indians, and Frank Hamilton Cushing, who lived four and a half years with the Zuni in New Mexico.

The answer to this is as complex as human history. In part, the question of anthropology's late growth may be answered by reference to the limits of human technology. Throughout most of history, people have been restricted in their geographical horizons. Without the means of traveling to distant parts of the world, observation of cultures and peoples far from one's own was a difficult—if not impossible—venture. Extensive travel was usually the exclusive prerogative of a few; the study of foreign peoples and cultures was not likely to flourish until adequate modes of transportation and communication could be developed.

This is not to say that people have always been unaware of the existence of others in the world who look and act differently from themselves. The Old and New Testaments of the Bible, for example, are full of references to diverse peoples, among them Jews, Egyptians, Hittites, Babylonians, Ethiopians, Romans, and so forth. Different though they

may have been, however, these peoples were at least familiar to one another, and familiar differences are one thing, while unfamiliar differences are another. It was the massive encounter with hitherto unknown peoples, which came as Europeans sought to extend their trade and political domination to all parts of the world, that focused attention on human differences in all their glory.

Another significant element that contributed to the slow growth of anthropology was the failure of Europeans to recognize the common humanity that they share with people everywhere. Societies that did not subscribe to the fundamental cultural values of Europeans were regarded as "savage" or "barbarian." It was not until the late eighteenth century that a significant number of Europeans considered the behavior of such people to be at all relevant to an understanding of themselves. This awareness of human diversity, coming at a time when there were increasing efforts to explain things in terms of

ANTHROPOLOGY APPLIED

FORENSIC ANTHROPOLOGY

In the public mind, anthropology is often identified with the recovery of the bones of remote human ancestors, the uncovering of ancient campsites and "lost cities," or the study of present-day tribal peoples whose way of life is erroneously seen as being something "out of the past." What people are often unaware of are the many practical applications of anthropological knowledge. One field of applied anthropology—known as **forensic anthropology**—specializes in the identification of human skeletal remains for legal purposes. Forensic anthropologists are routinely called upon by police and other authorities to identify the remains of murder victims, missing persons, or people who have died in disasters such as plane crashes. From skeletal remains, the forensic anthropologist can establish the age, sex, race, and stature of the deceased, and often whether they were right or left handed, exhibited any physical abnormalities, or evidence of trauma (broken bones and the like). In addition, some details of an individual's health and nutritional history can be read from the bones.

One well-known forensic anthropologist is Clyde C. Snow, who has been practicing in this field for 35 years, first for the Federal Aviation Administration and more recently as a free-lance consultant. In addition to the usual police work, Snow has studied the remains of George Armstrong Custer and his men from the battlefield at Little Big Horn, and in 1985, he went to Brazil where he identified the remains of the notorious Nazi war criminal Josef Mengele. He also has been instrumental in establishing the first forensic team devoted to

documenting cases of human rights abuses around the world. This began in 1984, when he went to Argentina at the request of a newly elected civilian government as part of a team to help with the identification of remains of the *desaparecidos*, or "disappeared ones," the 9000 or more people who were eliminated by government death squads during seven years of military rule. A year later, he returned to give expert testimony at the trial of nine junta members, and to teach Argentineans how to recover, clean, repair, preserve, photograph, x-ray, and analyze bones.

Besides providing factual accounts of the fate of victims to their surviving kin, and refuting the assertions of "revisionists" that the massacres never happened, the work of Snow and his Argentinean associates was crucial in convicting several military officers of kidnapping, torture, and murder. Subsequently, Snow and two of his Argentine associates were invited to the Philippines to look into the disappearance of 600 or more suspected victims of the Marcos regime. Similar requests from other South American countries, from Guatemala to Chile, in addition to work for regular clients in the United States such as the medical examiners' offices of Oklahoma, Cook County, Illinois, and the Federal Bureau of Investigation, keep Snow busy. Although not all cases he investigates involve abuse of police powers, when this is an issue, it is often the investigators who bring the culprits to justice. To quote Snow: "Of all the forms of murder, none is more monstrous than that committed by a state against its own citizens. And of all murder victims, those of the state are the most helpless and vulnerable since the very entity to which they have entrusted their lives and safety becomes their killer."* Thus, it is especially important that states be called to account for their deeds.

Forensic Anthropology: Field of applied physical anthropology that specializes in the identification of human skeletal remains for legal purposes.

*Christopher Joyce, *Witnesses from the Grave: The Stories Bones Tell*. Boston: Little, Brown, 1991.

natural laws, cast doubts on the traditional biblical mythology, which no longer adequately "explained" human diversity. From the reexamination that followed came the awareness that "savages"

were just as human as anyone else, and no less worthy of study than Europeans. Indeed, neglect of their study would result in a seriously distorted understanding of humanity.

ANTHROPOLOGY AND THE OTHER SCIENCES

It would be incorrect to infer from the foregoing that serious attempts were never made to analyze human diversity before the eighteenth century. Anthropology is, after all, not the only discipline that studies people. In this respect it shares its objectives with the other social and natural sciences. Anthropologists do not think of their findings as something quite apart from those of psychologists, economists, sociologists, or biologists; rather, they welcome the contributions these other disciplines have to make to the common goal of understanding humanity, and they gladly offer their own findings for the benefit of these other disciplines. Anthropologists do not expect, for example, to know as much about the structure of the human eye as anatomists, or as much about the perception of color as psychologists. As synthesizers, however, they are better prepared to understand these things, in analyzing color-naming behavior in different human societies, than any of their fellow scientists. Because they look for the broad basis of human behavior without limiting themselves to any single social or biological aspect of that behavior, anthropologists can acquire an especially extensive overview of the complex biological and cultural organism that is the human being.

THE DISCIPLINE OF ANTHROPOLOGY

Anthropology is traditionally divided into four fields: physical anthropology and the three branches of cultural anthropology, which are archaeology, linguistic anthropology, and ethnology. **Physical anthropology** is concerned primarily with humans as biological organisms, while **cultural anthropology** deals with humans as cultural animals. Both, of course, are closely related; we cannot understand

Physical anthropology: The systematic study of humans as biological organisms.

Cultural anthropology: The branch of anthropology that focuses on human behavior.

what people do unless we know what people are. And we want to know how biology does and does not influence culture, as well as how culture affects biology.

PHYSICAL ANTHROPOLOGY

Physical anthropology (or, alternatively, biological anthropology) is the branch of anthropology that focuses on humans as biological organisms, and one of its many interests is human evolution. Whatever distinctions people may claim for themselves, they are mammals—specifically, primates—and, as such, they share a common ancestry with other primates, most specifically apes and monkeys. Through the analysis of fossils and the observation of living primates, the physical anthropologist tries to trace the ancestry of the human species in order to understand how, when, and why we became the kind of animal we are today.

Another major concern of physical anthropology is the study of present-day human variation. Although we are all members of a single species, we differ from each other in many obvious and not so obvious ways. We differ not only in such visible traits as the color of our skins or the shape of our noses, but also in such biochemical factors as our blood types and our susceptibility to certain diseases. Drawing as well on the findings of allied disciplines such as genetics and biochemistry, the modern physical anthropologist seeks to achieve fuller understanding of human variation and the ways in which it relates to the different environments in which people have lived.

CULTURAL ANTHROPOLOGY

Because the capacity for culture is rooted in our biological natures, the work of the physical anthropologist provides a necessary background for the cultural anthropologist. In order to understand the

Physical anthropologists do not just study fossil skulls. Shown here is Clyde Snow whose specialty is forensic anthropology, and who is well known for his work identifying the victims of state sponsored terrorism. Here he holds the skull of a Kurdish youth who was executed by Saddam Hussein's Iraqi security forces.

work of the cultural anthropologist, we must clarify what we mean when we refer to culture. For our purposes here, we may think of culture as the often unconscious standards by which societies—groups of people—operate. These standards are learned, rather than acquired through biological inheritance. Since they determine, or at least guide, the day-to-day behavior of the members of a society, human behavior is above all cultural behavior. The manifestations of culture may vary considerably from place to place, but no person is "more cultured" in the anthropological sense than any other.

Just as physical anthropology is closely related to the other biological sciences, cultural anthropology is closely related to the other social sciences. The one to which it has most often been compared is sociology, since the business of both is the description and explanation of behavior of people within a social context. Sociologists, however, have concentrated heavily on studies of people living in modern

Sociologists interview and administer questionnaires to *respondents*, while psychologists experiment with *subjects*. Anthropologists, by contrast, learn from *informants*.

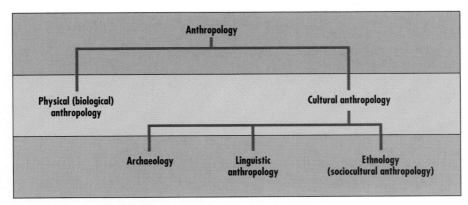

Figure 1.1 Anthropology can be divided into four subfields.

—or at least recent—North American and European societies, thereby increasing the probability that their theories of human behavior will be **culture–bound**: that is, based on assumptions about the world and reality that are part of the sociologists' Western culture, usually the middle-class version most typical of professional people. Cultural anthropologists, while not immune to culture–bound theorizing, constantly seek to minimize the problem by studying the whole of humanity in all times and places, and do not limit themselves to the study of recent Western peoples; anthropologists have found that to fully understand human behavior, all humans must be studied. More than any other feature, this unique cross–cultural and evolutionary perspective distinguishes cultural anthropology from the other social sciences. It provides anthropology with a far richer body of data than that of any other social science, and it can also be applied to any current issue. As a case in point, two different anthropologists have tested independently the validity of the argument that a high degree of military sophistication acts as a deterrent to war. By comparing the frequency of war in a number of different types of cultures, both found that the more sophisticated a community is militarily, the more frequently it engages in aggressive war and is attacked in turn. Thus, it should come as no

surprise that, since 1950, an era of unprecedented weapons development and expansion of its arsenal, the United States has gone to war more often than any other country.

The emphasis cultural anthropology places on studies of prehistoric as well as more recent non-Western cultures has often led to findings that dispute existing beliefs arrived at on the basis of Western studies. Thus, cultural anthropologists were the first to point out "that the world does not divide into the pious and the superstitious; that there are sculptures in jungles and paintings in deserts; that political order is possible without centralized power and principled justice without codified rules; that the norms of reason were not fixed in Greece, the evolution of morality not consummated in England. . . . We have, with no little success, sought to keep the world off balance; pulling out rugs, upsetting tea tables, setting off firecrackers. It has been the office of others to reassure; ours to unsettle."[2] Although the findings of cultural anthropologists have often challenged the conclusions of sociologists, psychologists, and economists, anthropology is absolutely indispensable to them as the testing ground for their theories. It is to these disciplines what the laboratory is to physics and chemistry.

Cultural anthropology may be divided into the areas of archaeology, linguistic anthropology, and ethnology (often called sociocultural anthropology; Fig.1.1). Although each has its own special interests and methods, all deal with cultural data. The

Culture–bound: Theories about the world and reality based on the assumptions and values of one's own culture.

[2] Clifford Geertz, "Distinguished Lecture: Anti Anti-Relativism," *American Anthropologist*, 86 (June 1984):275.

archaeologist, the anthropological linguist, and the ethnologist take different approaches to the subject, but each gathers and analyzes data that are useful in explaining similarities and differences between human cultures, as well as the ways that cultures everywhere develop, adapt, and continue to change.

ARCHAEOLOGY

Archaeology is the branch of cultural anthropology that studies material remains in order to describe and explain human behavior. Most often, it has focused on the human past, for material products of behavior, rather than behavior itself are all that survive of that past. The archaeologist studies the tools, pottery, and other enduring relics that remain as the legacy of extinct cultures, some of them as much as 2.5 million years old. Such objects, and the way they were left in the ground, reflect certain aspects of human behavior. For example, shallow, restricted concentrations of charcoal, that include oxidized earth, bone fragments, and charred plant remains as well, and near which are pieces of fire-cracked rock, pottery, and tools suitable for food preparation, indicate cooking and associated food processing. From such remains much can be learned about a people's diet and subsistence activities. Thus the archaeologist is able to find out about human behavior in the past, far beyond the mere 5000 years to which historians are limited, by their dependence upon written records. Indeed, in few parts of the world are written records even that old. By contrast, archaeologists are not limited to the study of prehistoric societies, but may also study those for which historic documents are available to supplement the material remains that people left behind them. In most literate societies, written records are associated with governing elites, rather than with people at the "grass roots." Thus, while they can tell archaeologists much that they might not know from archaeological evidence alone, it is equally true that archaeological remains can tell historians much about a society that is not apparent from its written documents.

Archaeology: The study of material remains, usually from the past, to describe and explain human behavior.

Archaeologists study material remains to learn about human behavior. Shown here is an exposed burial at the ancient Maya site of Cuello in Belize.

Although archaeology began as a study of the human past, archaeologists have recently become involved in the study of material objects in contemporary settings. One well-known example is the University of Arizona's "Garbage Project," which, by a carefully controlled study of household waste, continues to produce information about contemporary social issues. One aim of this project has been to test the validity of interview-survey techniques, upon which sociologists, economists, other social scientists and policymakers rely heavily for their data. The tests clearly show a significant difference between what people say they do and what garbage analysis shows they actually do. For example, in 1973, conventional techniques were used to construct and administer a questionnaire to find out about the rate of alcohol consumption in Tucson. In one part of town, 15 percent of respondent households admitted consuming beer, and no household reported consumption of more than eight cans a week. Analysis of garbage from the same area, however, demonstrated that some beer was consumed in over 80 percent of households, and 50 percent discarded more than eight empty cans a week. Another interesting finding of the Garbage Project is that when beef prices reached an all-time high in 1973, so did the amount of beef wasted by households (not just in Tucson, but other parts of the country as well). Although common sense would lead us to suppose just the opposite, high prices and scarcity correlate with more, rather than less, waste. Obviously, such findings are important, for they suggest that ideas about human behavior based on conventional interview-survey techniques alone may be seriously flawed.

In 1987, the Garbage Project began a program of test excavations in landfills in various parts of the United States. From this work has come the first reliable data on what materials actually go into landfills and what happens to them once there. And once again, we are finding that our existing beliefs are at odds with the actual situation. For example, biodegradable materials, like newspapers, take a much longer time to decay when buried in deep compact landfills than anyone previously expected. Needless to say, this kind of information is vital if the United States is ever to solve its waste disposal problems.

LINGUISTIC ANTHROPOLOGY

Perhaps the most distinctive human feature is the ability to speak. Humans are not alone in the use of symbolic communication. Studies have shown that the sounds and gestures made by some other animals—especially by apes—may serve functions comparable to those of human speech; yet no other animal has developed so complex a system of symbolic communication as have humans. Ultimately, language is what allows people to preserve and transmit their culture from generation to generation.

The branch of cultural anthropology that studies human languages is called **linguistic anthropology**. Linguists may deal with the description of a language (the way a sentence is formed or a verb conjugated) or with the history of languages (the way languages develop and influence each other with the passage of time). Both approaches yield valuable information, not only about the ways in which people communicate but about the ways in which they understand the world around them as well. The "everyday" language of English-speaking North Americans, for example, includes a number of slang words, such as "dough," "greenback," "dust," "loot," "cash," "bucks," "change," and "bread," to identify what a Papuan would recognize only as "money." Such phenomena help identify things that are considered of special importance to a culture. Through the study of linguistics the anthropologist is better able to understand how people perceive themselves and the world around them.

Anthropological linguists may also make a significant contribution to our understanding of the human past. By working out the genealogical relationships among languages, and examining the distributions of those languages, they may estimate how long the speakers of those languages have lived where they do. By identifying those words in related languages that have survived from an ancient ancestral tongue, they can also suggest where the speakers of the ancestral language lived, as well as how they lived.

ETHNOLOGY

As the archaeologist has traditionally concentrated on cultures of the past, so the **ethnologist**, or sociocultural anthropologist, concentrates on cultures of the present. While the archaeologist focuses on the study of material objects to learn about human behavior, the ethnologist concentrates on the study of human behavior as it can be seen, experienced, and discussed with those whose culture is to be understood.

Fundamental to the ethnologist's approach is descriptive **ethnography**. Whenever possible, the ethnologist becomes ethnographer by going to live

Linguistic anthropology: The branch of cultural anthropology that studies human language.

Ethnologist: An anthropologist who studies cultures from a comparative or historical point of view.

Ethnographers—such as Marjory Shostak, shown here with the !Kung of Aftica's Kalahari Desert—learn about the cultures of other people by actually living among them.

Ethnography: The systematic description of a culture based on firsthand observation.

among the people under study. Through **participant observation**—eating a people's food, speaking their language, and personally experiencing their habits and customs—the ethnographer is able to understand their way of life to a far greater extent than any non-participant anthropologist ever could; one learns a culture best by learning how to behave acceptably in the society in which one is

Participant observation: In ethnography, the technique of learning a people's culture through direct participation in their everyday life over an extended period of time.

Holistic perspective: A fundamental principle of anthropology, that things must be viewed in the broadest possible context, in order to understand their interconnections and interdependence.

doing fieldwork. To become a participant observer in the culture under study does not mean that the ethnographer must join in a people's battles in order to study a culture in which warfare is prominent, but by living among a warlike people, the ethnographer should be able to understand the role of warfare in the overall cultural scheme. He or she must be a meticulous observer in order to be able to get a broad overview of a culture without emphasizing one of its parts to the detriment of another. Only by discovering how all cultural institutions—social, political, economic, religious —relate to one another can the ethnographer begin to understand the cultural system. Anthropologists refer to this as the **holistic perspective**, and it is one of the fundamental principles of anthropology. Robert Gordon, an anthropologist from Namibia, speaks of it in this way: "Whereas the sociologist or the political scientist might examine the beauty of a flower petal by petal, the anthropologist is the person that stands on the top of the mountain and looks at the beauty of the field. In other words, we try and go for the wider perspective."[3]

So basic is ethnographic fieldwork to ethnology that the British anthropologist C. G. Seligman once asserted, "Field research in anthropology is what the blood of the martyrs is to the church."[4] Something of its flavor is conveyed by the experience of one young anthropologist working in Thailand.

---

[3] Robert Gordon, Interview for Coast Telecourses, Inc., Los Angeles, December 4, 1981.

[4] I. M. Lewis, *Social Anthropology in Perspective* (Harmondsworth, England: Penguin, 1976), p. 27.

ORIGINAL STUDY

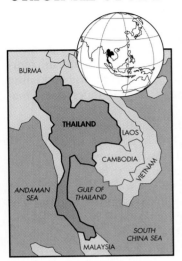

PARTICIPANT OBSERVATION ON A MOTORCYCLE [5]

A short while after arriving in the field in southern Thailand, I managed to acquire a motorcycle. While I did not actually possess a licence to ride it, some kind words to those in high places by patrons who had taken me under their wing had cleared the way for me to be turned loose on the roads of Thailand without hindrance unless, it was sharply stressed, I was foolish enough to get involved in an accident. At an early stage I had wondered whether I should mention that my licence at home had been repossessed by a couple of incredulous policemen who took a very dim view of creative driving, but I felt that to try and explain this in Thai would probably lead to misunderstandings, and might well have caused my hosts unnecessary anxiety.

Come St. David's Day, the inevitable accident occurred. I had been on an afternoon jaunt on my freshly-cleaned motorcycle, merrily weaving through the traffic, and thinking how interesting it was that Thai motorists actually lived out the theory of loose structure in their driving. During this course of musing I decided to make a right-hand turn, and still being rather set in my Western ways, slowed down to do so. This was an ethnocentric mistake. As I began to turn, another motorcyclist, complete with an ice chest full of fish and a large basket of oranges on the pillion seat, decided that this was the ideal moment to overtake. I was much too slow, he was far too fast, and our subjective constructions of existence spectacularly collided with the limits of the material world.

What followed was actually quite pleasurable for the brief but slow-motion moments it lasted. A massive surge of metal, flesh, fish, and disintegrating oranges swept me from behind, then passed overhead in a surrealistic collage as my body easily performed a series of gymnastic stunts that I had been totally unable to master at school. As always in life, the brief pleasure had to be repaid with an extended flood of unwelcome pain, relieved only by the happy realization that I, and the other motorist who had flown so gracefully above me, had narrowly but successfully avoided truncating our skulls on a Burmese ebony tree.

Anxious to reassure myself that nothing was broken, I got quickly to my feet, dusted myself off, and walked over to switch off my motorcycle engine, which by now was making a maniacal noise without its exhaust pipe. Then I walked back to the other rider, who was still lying rigidly on his back and wondering whether he should believe what was happening. I politely asked him if he was all right, but the hypothesis that in a crisis everyone reverts to speaking English clearly required some revision. Months of Thai lessons began to trickle back, but far too slowly, and in the meantime he had also stood up. It was only then that I realized the pair of us had been surrounded by a rather large crowd of onlookers.

Television in Thailand does not commence broadcasting until 4:30 p.m. so our little accident had a good audience, with local residents coming out of their houses and shops, and cars, motorcycles, and trucks stopping to take in the scene. The other rider began talking to some people near him, and a shopkeeper who knew me came and asked if I was all right. From that moment, I never had a chance to speak to the other rider again. We were slowly but surely separated, each of us in the centre of a group, the two groups gathering slightly apart from one another. I had a sudden and horrible realization that I was in the middle of one of those dispute settlement cases that I had intermittently dozed through as an undergraduate. With an abrupt and sickening shock, participant observation had become rather too much participation and too little cosy observation.

Some of the other rider's newly-acquired entourage came over to ask the fringes of my group what exactly had happened. I pleaded my version to those standing close to me, and it was then relayed—and, I should add, suitably amended—back through the throng to be taken away and compared with the other rider's tale of woe. While this little contest was going on, a number of people from both groups were inspecting the rather forlorn wreckages of our motorcycles and debating over which one appeared to be more badly damaged. "Look at this!" someone cried, lifting a torn section of the seat and helpfully making the tear more ostentatious in the process. "But look at this!" came the reply, as someone else wrenched a limply hanging indicator light completely off its mounting. After a series of such exchanges, the two groups finally agreed that both motorcycles were in an equally derelict state, though I could not help feeling, peering from the little prison within my group of supporters, that those judging the damage to the machines had played a more than passive role in ensuring a parity of demolition.

Physical injuries were the next to be subjected to this adjudication process. I found my shirt being lifted up, and a chorus of oohs and aahs issuing from the crowd, as someone with jolly animation prodded and pinched the large areas of my back which were now bravely attempting to stay in place without the aid of skin. My startled eyes began looking in opposite directions at the same time, while somewhat less than human groans gargled out of my mouth. From similar sounds in the distance I deduced that the other poor rider was being subjected to similar treatment. He frankly looked rather the worse for wear than I did, but whenever his group claimed this, my supporters would proceed to show just what excruciating pain I was suffering by prodding me in the back and indicating my randomly circumambulating eyes as if to say "see, we told you so."

On issues of damage, both mechanical and physical, we were adjudged by the two groups to be fairly evenly scored. Fault in relation to road rules had never been an issue. Then came a bit of a lull, as if something serious was about to happen. A senior person from the other group came over and spoke to me directly, asking if I wanted to call the police. A hush fell over everyone. I, of course, was totally terrified at the prospect—no licence, visions of deportation, and so far only one meagre book of field notes to my name. I put on my best weak pathetic smile and mumbled that I thought it was not really necessary unless the other chap insisted. A culturally appropriate move: everyone looked happily relieved, and the other rider's spokesman said generously that it would only be a waste of time and cause unnecessary bother to bring the police out on an errand like this. It was to be a few months before I realized that, like many other motorcyclists, the other rider was also probably roaming the roads without a licence, and that in this part of the country calling the police was generally regarded as a last, and unsporting, resort.

The final agreement was that we should settle our own repairs—to both body and vehicle—and let the matter rest. A visible sigh of relief passed through the two groups that had gathered, and they slowly began to disperse. For the first time since the collision, I saw the other rider face to face, so I walked towards him to offer my apologies. I never managed to reach him. The dispersing groups froze in horror, then quickly regathered around me. "What is wrong now?" I was interrogated on all sides. Was I not happy with the result? I had clearly made a serious blunder, and it took a while to settle things down once more. A perceptive shopkeeper from nearby grabbed my arm and dragged me off to his shop for coffee, explaining to me that the matter had been settled and that further contact for any reason with the other rider or his group would only prolong an unpleasant situation that could now be forgotten by all involved.

So it was that later that evening I was able to start my second book of field notes with an entry on dispute settlement, though painful twinges up my back and throbbing between the ears made me wish I had relied on some other informant to provide the ethnographic details. I made a silent vow to myself to discontinue this idiosyncratic method of participant observation, and managed to some extent to keep the vow for the rest of my stay. Thereafter I successfully steered clear of motorcycle accidents, and instead got shot at, electrocuted, and innocently involved in scandal and otherwise abused. But all that, as they say, is another story.

[5] Andrew Cornish, "Participant Observation on a Motorcycle," *Anthropology Today*, 3(6) (December 1987):15–16. By permission of the Royal Anthropological Institute of Great Britain and Ireland.

The popular image of ethnographic fieldwork is that it takes place among far-off, exotic peoples. To be sure, a lot of ethnographic work has been done in places like Africa, the islands of the Pacific Ocean, the deserts of Australia, and so on. One very good reason for this is that non-western peoples have been too often ignored by other social scientists. Still, anthropologists have recognized from the start that an understanding of human behavior depends upon knowledge of all cultures and peoples, including their own. During the years of the Great Depression and World War II, for example, many anthropologists in the United States worked in settings ranging from factories to whole communities. One of the landmark studies of this period was W. Lloyd Warner's study of "Yankee City" (Newburyport, Massachusetts). Less well known is that it was an anthropologist, Philleo Nash, who worked at the time in the White House under presidents Franklin Roosevelt and Harry Truman,

Anthropolgists carry out fieldwork at home as well as abroad. Known on the road as "Dr. Truck," Michael Agar spends much of his time in the cabs of the eighteen-wheelers studying the culture of independent truckers.

who was instrumental in desegregating the armed forces and moving the federal government into the field of civil rights.

In the 1950s, the availability of large amounts of money for research in foreign lands diverted attention from work at home. Later on, as political unrest in many parts of the world made fieldwork increasingly difficult to carry out, there was renewed awareness of important anthropological problems that needed to be dealt with in North American society. Many of these problems involve people that anthropologists have studied in other settings. Thus, as Hispanic Americans have moved into the cities of the United States, or as refugees have arrived from southeast Asia, anthropologists have been there not just to study them, but to help them adjust to their new circumstances. Simultaneously, anthropologists are applying the same research techniques that served them so well in the study of non-western peoples to the study of such diverse things as street gangs, corporate bureaucracies, religious cults, health care delivery systems, schools, and how people deal with consumer complaints.

An important discovery from such research is that it produces knowledge that usually does not emerge from the kinds of research done by other social scientists. For example, the theory of cultural deprivation arose during the 1960s as a way of explaining the educational failure of many children of minorities. In order to account for their lack of achievement, some social scientists proposed that such children were "culturally deprived." They then proceeded to "confirm" this idea by studying children, mostly from Native-American, African-American, and Hispanic populations, interpreting the results through the protective screen of their theory. By contrast, ethnographic research on the cultures of "culturally deprived" children reveals a different story. Far from being culturally deprived, they have elaborate, sophisticated, and adaptive cultures that are simply different from the ones espoused by the educational system. Although some still cling to it, the cultural–deprivation theory is culture–bound, and is merely a way of saying that people are "deprived" of "my culture." One cannot argue that such children do not speak adequate Spanish, black English, or whatever; that they do not do well the things that are considered rewarding in *their* cultures.

Much though it has to offer, the anthropological study of one's own culture is not without its own special problems. Sir Edmund Leach, a distinguished British anthropologist, put it in the following way:

> Surprising though it may seem, fieldwork in a cultural context of which you already have intimate first-hand experience seems to be much more difficult than fieldwork which is approached from the naive viewpoint of a total stranger. When anthropologists study facets of their own society their vision seems to become distorted by prejudices which derive from private rather than public experience.[6]

Probably the most successful anthropological studies of their own culture by North Americans have been done by those who first worked in some other culture. Lloyd Warner, for example, had studied the Murngin of Australia before he tackled Newburyport. In addition to getting outside of one's

[6] Edmund Leach, *Social Anthropology* (Glasgow, Scotland: Fontana Paperbacks, 1982), p. 124.

own culture before trying to study it, much is to be gained by encouraging anthropologists from outside—from Africa, Asia, and South America, for example, to do fieldwork in North America. From their outsiders' perspective come insights all too easily overlooked by an insider. Nonetheless, the special difficulties of studying one's own culture can be overcome; what it requires is the development of an outsider's perspective.

Although ethnographic fieldwork is basic to ethnology, it is not the sole occupation of the ethnologist. What it provides is the basic data the ethnologist may then use to study one particular aspect of a culture by comparing it with that same aspect in others. Anthropologists constantly make such cross-cultural comparisons, and this is another hallmark of the discipline. Interesting insights into the practices of North Americans may come from cross-cultural comparisons, as when one compares the time that people devote to what North Americans consider to be "housework." In the United States, people generally believe that the ever-increasing output of household appliance consumer goods has resulted in a steady reduction in housework, with a consequent increase in leisure time. Thus, consumer appliances have become principal indicators of a high standard of living. Anthropological research among food foragers (people who rely on wild plant and animal resources for subsistence), however, has shown that they work far less at household tasks, and indeed less at all subsistence pursuits, than do people in industrialized societies. Aboriginal Australian women, for example, devote an average of approximately 20 hours per week to collecting and preparing food, as well as other domestic chores, whereas women in the rural United States in the 1920s, without the benefit of laborsaving appliances, devoted approximately 52 hours a week to their housework. Some 50 years later, contrary to all expectations, urban U.S. women who were not working for wages outside their homes were putting 55 hours a week into their housework, in spite of all their "laborsaving" dishwashers, washing machines, clothes dryers, vacuum cleaners, food processors, and microwave ovens.[7]

Cross-cultural comparisons highlight alternative ways of doing things, and so have much to offer North Americans, increasing numbers of whom, opinion polls show, doubt the effectiveness of their own ways of doing things. In this sense, one may think of ethnology as the study of alternative ways of doing things. At the same time, by making systematic cross-cultural comparisons of cultures, ethnologists seek to arrive at valid conclusions concerning the nature of culture in all times and places.

ANTHROPOLOGY AND SCIENCE

The chief concern of all anthropologists is the careful and systematic study of humankind. Anthropology has been called a social or a behavioral science by some, a natural science by others, and one of the humanities by still others. Can the work of the anthropologist properly be labeled scientific? What exactly do we mean by the term "science"?

Science is a powerful and elegant way people have hit upon to understand the workings of the visible world and universe. Science seeks testable explanations for observed phenomena in terms of the workings of hidden but universal and immutable principles, or laws. Two basic ingredients are essential for this: imagination and skepticism. Imagination, though capable of leading us astray, is required in order that we may imagine the ways in which phenomena might be ordered, and think of old things in new ways. Without it, there can be no science. Skepticism is what allows us to distinguish fact from fancy, to test our speculations, and to prevent our imaginations from running away with us.

In their search for explanations, scientists do not assume that things are always as they appear on the surface. After all, what could be more obvious than that the earth is a stable entity, around which the sun travels every day? And yet, it isn't so. Supernatural explanations are rejected, as are all explanations and appeals to authority that are not supported by strong observational evidence. Because explanations are constantly challenged by new observations and novel ideas, science is self-correcting; that is, inadequate explanations are sooner or later shown

[7] John H. Bodley, *Anthropology and Contemporary Human Problems* (Palo Alto, Calif.: Mayfield, 1985), p. 69.

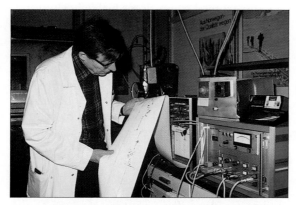

To many people, a scientist is someone who works in a laboratory, carrying out experiments with the aid of specialized equipment. Contrary to such a stereotypical image, not all scientists are white men in lab coats, not all work in laboratories, and experimentation is not the only technique they use.

up as such, and are replaced by more reliable explanations.

The scientist begins with an **hypothesis**, or tentative explanation of the relationship between certain phenomena. By gathering various kinds of data that seem to support such generalizations, and, equally important, by showing why alternative hypotheses may be falsified, or eliminated from consideration, the scientist arrives at a system of validated hypotheses, or **theory**. Although a theory is actually a well-supported body of knowledge, no theory is acknowledged to be beyond challenge. Truth, in science, is not considered to be absolute, but rather a matter of varying degrees of probability; what is considered to be true is what is most probable. This is true of anthropology, just as it is true of biology or physics. As our knowledge expands, the odds in favor of some theories over others are generally increased, but sometimes old "truths" must be discarded as alternative theories are shown to be more probable.

Hypothesis: A tentative explanation of the relation between certain phenomena.

Theory: A system of validated hypotheses that explains phenomena systematically.

DIFFICULTIES OF THE SCIENTIFIC APPROACH

Straightforward though the scientific approach may appear to be, there are serious difficulties in its application in anthropology. One of them is that once one has stated a hypothesis, one is strongly motivated to verify it, and this can cause one unwittingly to overlook negative evidence, not to mention all sorts of other unexpected things. This is a familiar problem in science; as paleontologist Stephen Jay Gould puts it, "The greatest impediment to scientific innovation is usually a conceptual lock, not a factual lock."[8] In the fields of cultural anthropology there is a further difficulty: In order to arrive at useful theories concerning human behavior, one must begin with hypotheses that are as objective and as little culture–bound as possible. And here lies a major—some people would say insurmountable—problem: It is difficult for someone who has grown up in one culture to frame objective hypotheses about another that are not culture–bound.

As one example of this sort of problem, we may look at attempts by archaeologists to understand the nature of settlement in the Classic period of Maya civilization. This civilization flourished between A.D. 250 and 900 in what is now northern Guatemala, Belize, and adjacent portions of Mexico and Honduras. Today much of this region is covered by a dense tropical forest of the sort that people of European background find difficult to deal with. In recent times this forest has been inhabited by few people, who sustain themselves through slash-and-burn farming. (After cutting and burning the natural vegetation, crops are grown for two years or so before fertility is exhausted, and a new field must be

[8] Stephen Jay Gould, *Wonderful Life* (New York: Norton, 1989), p.226.

The Japanese surrender came less than a week after the August 9, 1945, atomic bomb blast over Nagasaki. Late in World War II, however, anthropologists and other social scientists working for the U.S. government predicted a Japanese surrender without the need to drop nuclear bombs. Since this conflicted with preconceived notions, these scientists' prediction was not heeded, but evidence found after the war confirmed its correctness.

cleared.) Yet numerous archaeological sites, featuring temples sometimes as tall as a modern 20-story building, other sorts of monumental architecture, and carved monuments are to be found there. Because of their cultural bias against tropical forests as places to live, and against slash-and-burn farming as a means of raising food, North American and European archaeologists asked the question: How could the Maya have maintained large, permanent settlements on the basis of slash-and-burn farming? The answer seemed self-evident—they couldn't; therefore, the great archaeological sites must have been ceremonial centers inhabited by few, if any, people. Periodically a rural peasantry, living scattered in small hamlets over the countryside, must have gathered in these centers for rituals, or to provide labor for their construction and maintenance.

This view was the dominant one for several decades, and it was not until 1960 that archaeolo-

gists working at Tikal, one of the largest of all Maya sites, decided to ask the simplest and least biased questions they could think of: Did anyone live at this particular site on a permanent basis; if so, how many, and how were they supported? Working intensively over the next decade, with as few preconceived notions as possible, the archaeologists were able to establish that Tikal was a huge settlement inhabited by tens of thousands of people, who were supported by intensive forms of agriculture. It was this work at Tikal that paved the way for a new understanding of Classic Maya civilization totally at odds with the older, culture–bound ideas.

Recognizing the problem of framing hypotheses that are not culture–bound, anthropologists have relied heavily on a technique that has proved successful in other fields of the natural sciences. As did the archaeologists working at Tikal, they immerse themselves in the data to the fullest extent possible. By doing so, they become so thoroughly

The unique character of anthropology among the social sciences in North America owes a great deal to these three men, all educated in the natural sciences: Franz Boas (1858–1942), in physics; Frederic Ward Putnam (1839–1915), in zoology; and John Wesley Powell (1834–1902), in geology. Although not the first to teach anthropology, Boas (and his students) made such courses a common part of college and university curricula. Similarly, Putnam established anthropology in the museum world, as did Powell in government.

familiar with the minute details that they can begin to see patterns inherent in the data, many of which might otherwise have been overlooked. These patterns are what allow the anthropologist to frame hypotheses, which then may be subjected to further testing.

This approach is most easily seen in ethnographic fieldwork, but it is just as important in archaeology. Unlike many social scientists, the ethnographer usually does not go into the field armed with prefigured questionnaires; rather, the ethnographer recognizes that there are probably all sorts of unguessed things, to be found only by maintaining as open a mind as one can. This is not to say that anthropologists never use questionnaires, for sometimes they do. Generally, though, they use them as a means of supplementing or clarifying information gained through some other means. As the fieldwork proceeds, ethnographers sort their complex observations into a meaningful whole, sometimes by formulating and testing limited or low-level hypotheses, but as often as not by making use of intuition and playing hunches. What is important is that the results are constantly scrutinized for consistency, for if the parts fail to fit together in a manner that is internally consistent, then the ethnographer knows that a mistake has been made and that further work is necessary.

The contrast between the anthropological and other social–science approaches is dramatically illustrated by the following example—one of several—presented by Robert Chambers in his book, *Rural Development*. Since Chambers is a highly respected professional in the field of international development, and not an anthropologist, he can scarcely be accused of trying to promote his own discipline at the expense of others.

> Sean Conlin lived as a social anthropologist in a village in Peru. While he was there a sociologist came and carried out a survey. According to the sociologist's results, people in the village invariably worked together on each others' individually owned plots of land. That was what they told him. But in the period of over a year during which Conlin lived in the village, he observed the practice only once. The belief in exchange relations was, he concludes, important for the people's understanding of themselves, but it was not an economic fact.[9]

This does not mean that all sociological research is bad and all anthropological research is good;

9 Robert Chambers, *Rural Development: Putting the Last First* (New York: Longman, 1983), p. 51.

merely that reliance on questionnaire surveys is a risky business, no matter who does it. Robert Chambers sums up the difficulties:

Unless careful appraisal precedes drawing up a questionnaire, the survey will embody the concepts and categories of outsiders rather than those of rural people, and thus impose meanings on the social reality. The misfit between the concepts of urban professionals and those of poor rural people is likely to be substantial, and the questions asked may construct artificial chunks of "knowledge" which distort or mutilate the reality which poor people experience. Nor are questionnaire surveys on their own good ways of identifying causal relationships—a correlation alone tells us nothing definite about cause—or of exploring social relationships such as reciprocity, dependence, exploitation, and so on. Their penetration is usually shallow, concentrating on what is measurable, answerable, and acceptable as a question, rather than probing less tangible and more qualitative aspects of society. For many reasons—fear, prudence, ignorance, exhaustion, hostility, hope of benefit—poor people give information which is slanted or false.

For these and many other reasons, conventional questionnaire surveys have many drawbacks if the aim is to gain insight into the lives and conditions of the poorer rural people. Other methods are re-

quired, either alone, or together with surveys. But extensive questionnaire surveys pre-empt resources, capturing staff and finance, and preventing other approaches.[10]

The end result of archaeological or ethnographic fieldwork, if properly carried out, is a coherent account of a culture, which provides an explanatory framework for understanding the behavior of the people who have been studied. And this, in turn, is what permits the anthropologist to frame broader hypotheses about human behavior. Plausible though such hypotheses may be, however, the consideration of a single society is generally insufficient for their testing. Without some basis for comparison, the hypothesis grounded in a single case may be no more than an historical coincidence. A single case may be adequate, however, to cast doubt on, if not refute, a theory that had previously been held to be valid. The discovery in 1948 that aborigines living in Australia's Arnhem Land put in an average work day of less than six hours, while living well above a level of bare sufficiency, was enough to call into question the widely accepted notion that food-for-

[10] Ibid., p. 51.

!Kung family members relax in their Kalahari Desert home. Like most food foragers, these people spend only a small percentage of their time working—in this case, no more than about 20 hours a week.

aging peoples are so preoccupied with finding food that they lack time for any of life's more pleasurable activities. Even today, economists are prone to label such peoples as "backward" (some examples will be given in Chapter 15 and the Introduction to Part Seven), even though the observations made in the Arnhem Land study have since been confirmed many times over in various parts of the world.

Hypothetical explanations of cultural phenomena may be tested by the comparison of archaeological and/or ethnographic data for several societies found in a particular region. Nonhistorical, controlled comparison provides a broader context for understanding cultural phenomena than does the study of a single culture. The anthropologist who undertakes such a comparison may be more confident that the conditions believed to be related really are related, at least within the region that is under investigation; however, an explanation that is valid in one region is not necessarily so in another.

Ideally, theories in cultural anthropology are generated from worldwide comparisons. The cross-cultural researcher examines a worldwide sample of societies in order to discover whether or not hypotheses proposed to explain cultural phenomena seem universally applicable. Because the sample is selected at random, it is probable that the conclusions of the cross-cultural researcher will be valid; however, the greater the number of societies being examined, the less likely it is that the investigator will have a detailed understanding of all the societies encompassed by the study. The cross-cultural researcher depends upon other ethnographers for data. It is impossible for any single individual personally to perform in-depth analyses of a broad sample of human cultures throughout the world.

In anthropology, cultural comparisons need not be restricted to ethnographic data. Anthropologists can, for example, turn to archaeological data to test hypotheses about culture change. Cultural characteristics thought to be caused by certain specified conditions can be tested archaeologically by investigating situations where such conditions actually occurred. Also useful are data provided by the ethnohistorian. **Ethnohistory** is a kind of historic ethnography that studies cultures of the recent past through the accounts of explorers, mission-

Ethnohistory: The study of cultures of the recent past through oral histories, accounts left by explorers, missionaries, and traders, and through the analysis of such records as land titles, birth and death records, and other archival materials.

aries, and traders and through the analysis of such records as land titles, birth and death records, and other archival materials. The ethnohistorical analysis of cultures, like archaeology, is a valuable approach to understanding change. By examining the conditions believed to have caused certain phenomena, we can discover whether or not those conditions truly precede those phenomena.

Ethnohistorical research, like the field studies of archaeologists, is valuable for testing and confirming hypotheses about culture. And like much of anthropology, it has practical utility as well. In the United States, ethnohistorical research has flourished, for it often provides key evidence necessary for deciding legal cases involving Native American land claims.

ANTHROPOLOGY AND THE HUMANITIES

Although the sciences and humanities are often thought of as mutually exclusive approaches to learning, they both come together in anthropology. That is why, for example, anthropological research is funded not only by such "hard science" agencies as the National Science Foundation, but also by such organizations as the National Endowment for the Humanities. The humanistic side of anthropology is perhaps most immediately evident in its concern with other cultures' languages, values, and achievements in the arts and literature (oral literature, among peoples who lack writing). Beyond this, anthropologists remain committed to the proposition that one cannot fully understand another culture by observing it; one must *experience* it as

Like the ethnologist, the religious missionary lives among an unfamiliar people. However, where the ethnologist seeks, through participant observation, to investigate and comprehend people just as they are, the missionary seeks to change the very beliefs that make life meaningful to them.

well. Thus, ethnographers spend prolonged periods of time living with the people whom they study, sharing their joys and suffering their deprivations, including sickness and, sometimes, premature death. They are not so naive as to believe that they can be, or even should be, dispassionate about the people whose trials and tribulations they share. As Robin Fox puts it, "our hearts, as well as our brains, should be with our men and women."[11] Nor are anthropologists so self-deceived as to believe that they can avoid dealing with the moral and political consequences of their findings.

Given their intense encounters with other peoples, it should come as no surprise that anthropologists have amassed as much information about human frailty and nobility—the stuff of the humanities—as any other discipline. Small wonder, too, that above all, they intend to avoid allowing a "coldly" scientific approach to blind them to the fact that human societies are made up of individuals with rich assortments of emotions and aspirations that demand respect. Anthropology has sometimes been called the most human of the sciences, a designation in which anthropologists take considerable pride.

QUESTIONS OF ETHICS

The kinds of research carried out by anthropologists, and the settings within which they work, raise a number of important questions concerning ethics. Who will make use of the findings of anthropologists, and for what purposes? In the case of a militant minority, for example, will others use anthropological data to suppress that minority? And what of traditional communities around the world? Who is to decide what changes should, or should not, be introduced for community "betterment"? By whose definition is it betterment—the community's or that of a remote national government? Then there is the problem of privacy. Anthropologists deal with people's private and sensitive matters, including things that people would not care to have generally known about them. How does one write about such matters and at the same time protect the privacy of informants? Not surprisingly, because of these and other questions, there has been much discussion among anthropologists over the past two decades on the subject of ethics.

The present consensus among anthropologists about the ethics of their profession was summed up by Laura Nader in an interview:

> Anthropologists have obligations to three different sets of people. First, to the people that we study; secondly, to the profession which expects us to report back our findings; and thirdly, to the organizations that fund the research. Some people would order them differently—one, two, three; three, two, one, or whatever—but those three are in the minds of most anthropologists. Now, sometimes the obligations conflict. If I do fieldwork among a group of people and I learn certain things that, if revealed, might come back to hurt them, then reporting my findings back to the profession is going to be secondary because first and foremost I have to protect my informants because they trusted me. In the case of the Zapotec, I was dealing with very sensitive materials about law and disputes and conflicts and so forth. And I was very sensitive about how much of that to report while people were still alive and while things might still be warm, so I waited on that. I'm just finishing my Zapotec monograph now. I've written certain things, but I waited for the most part, and I feel comfortable now releasing that information. With regard to a funder in that case, it was the Mexican government, and I feel that I have written enough to have paid off the $1200 which they gave me to support that work for a year. So, I've not felt particularly strained for my Zapotec work in those three areas. On energy research that I've done, it's been another story. Much of what people wanted me to do energy research for was . . . to tell people in decision-making positions about American consumers in such a way that they could be manipulated better, and I didn't want to do that. So what I said was I would be willing to study a vertical slice. That is, I would never study the consumer without studying the producer. And once you take a vertical slice like that, then it's fair because you're telling the consumer about the producer and the producer about the consumer. But just to do a study of consumers for producers, I think I would feel uncomfortable.[12]

---

[11] Robin Fox, *Encounter with Anthropology* (New York: Dell, 1968), p. 290.

[12] Laura Nader, Interview for Coast Telecourses, Inc., Los Angeles, December 3, 1981.

ANTHROPOLOGY AND CONTEMPORARY LIFE

Anthropology, with its long-standing commitment to understanding people in all parts of the world, coupled with its holistic perspective, is better equipped than any other discipline to grapple with a problem of overriding importance for all of humanity as the twentieth century draws to a close. An inescapable fact of life is that North Americans live in a global community in which all the world's people are interdependent upon one another. Although there is widespread awareness of this in the business community, which relies on foreign sources for raw materials, sees the non-Western world as its major area for market expansion, and is more and more making its products abroad, citizens of the United States are on the whole as ignorant about the cultures of the rest of the world as they have ever been. As a result, they are poorly equipped to handle the demands of living in the modern world.

Anthropologist Dennis Shaw sums up the implications of this state of affairs:

> Such provinciality raises questions about the welfare of our nation and the global context in which it is a major force. We have, as a nation, continued to interpret the political actions of other nations in terms of the cultural and political norms of our own culture and have thus made major misinterpretations of global political affairs. Our economic interests have been pursued from the perspective of our own cultural norms, and thus, we have failed to keep up with other nations that have shown a sensitivity to cultural differences. Domestically, a serious question can be raised about the viability of a democracy in which a major portion of the electorate is basically ignorant of the issues which our political leaders must confront. Internationally, one can speculate about the well-being of a world in which the citizens of one of the most powerful nations are seriously deficient in their ability to evaluate global issues.[13]

Former ambassador Edwin Reischauer put it more tersely: "Education is not moving rapidly enough in the right directions to produce the knowledge about the outside world and attitudes toward other peoples that may be essential for human survival."[14] What anthropology has to contribute to contemporary life, then, are an understanding of, and way of looking at, the world's peoples, which are nothing less than basic skills for survival in the modern world.

---

[13] Dennis G. Shaw, "A Light at the End of the Tunnel: Anthropological Contributions Towards Global Competence," *Anthropology Newsletter*, 25 (November 1984):16.

[14] Quoted in Susan L. Allen, "Media Anthropology: Building a Public Perspective," *Anthropology Newsletter*, 25 (November 1984):6.

Chapter Summary

Throughout human history, people have needed to know who they are, where they came from, and why they behave as they do. Traditionally, myths and legends provided the answers to these questions. Anthropology, as it has emerged over the last 200 years, offers another approach to answering the questions people ask about themselves.

Anthropology is the study of humankind. In employing a scientific approach, anthropologists seek to produce useful generalizations about humans and their behavior and to arrive at a reasonably objective understanding of human diversity. The two major fields of anthropology are physical and cultural anthropology. Physical anthropology focuses on humans as biological organisms. Particular emphasis is given by physical anthropologists to tracing the evolutionary development of the human animal and studying biological variation within the species today. Cultural anthropologists study humans in terms of their cultures, the often unconscious standards by which societies operate.

Three areas of cultural anthropology are archaeology, anthropological linguistics, and ethnology. Archaeologists study material objects, usually from past cultures, in order to explain human behavior. Linguists, who study human languages, may deal with the description of a language or with the history of languages. Ethnologists concentrate on cultures of the present or recent past; in doing comparative studies of culture, they may also focus on a particular aspect of culture, such as religious or economic practices, or as ethnographers, they may

go into the field to observe and describe human behavior as it can be seen, experienced, and discussed with persons whose culture is to be understood.

Anthropology is unique among the social and natural sciences in that it is concerned with formulating explanations of human diversity based on a study of all aspects of human biology and behavior in all known societies, rather than in European and North American societies alone. Thus anthropologists have devoted much attention to the study of non-Western peoples.

Anthropologists are concerned with the objective and systematic study of humankind. The anthropologist employs the methods of other scientists by developing a hypothesis, or assumed explanation, using other data to test the hypothesis, and ultimately arriving at a theory—a system of validated hypotheses. The data used by the cultural anthropologist may be field data of one society or comparative studies of numerous societies.

In anthropology, the humanities and sciences come together into a genuinely human science. Anthropology's link with the humanities can be seen in its concern with people's values, languages, arts, and literature—oral as well as written—but above all in its attempt to convey the experience of living as other people do. As both science and humanity, anthropology has essential skills to offer the modern world, where understanding the other people with whom we share the globe has become a matter of survival.

Suggested Readings

de Vita, Philip R. *The Naked Anthropologist: Tales From Around the World.* Belmont, Calif.: Wadsworth, 1992.
What is it like for an outsider to try to learn something of what it is to be an insider in another culture? Read this delightful book and find out; it consists of essays by various anthropologists on their attempts to make sense of other cultures: their trials, tribulations, and the unexpected surprises they found in the process.

Lett, James. *The Human Enterprise: A Critical Introduction to Anthropological Theory.* Boulder, Col., Westview, 1987.
Part 1 examines the philosophical foundations of anthropological theory, paying special attention to the nature of scientific inquiry and the mechanisms of scientific progress. Part 2 deals with the nature of social science as well as the particular features of anthropology.

Peacock, James L. *The Anthropological Lens: Harsh Light, Soft Focus.* New York: Cambridge University Press, 1986.
This lively and innovative book manages to give the reader a good understanding of the diversity of activities undertaken by anthropologists, while at the same time identifying the unifying themes that hold the discipline together.

Spradley, James P. *The Ethnographic Interview.* New York: Holt Rinehart and Winston, 1979.
This book contains one of the best discussions of the nature and value of ethnographic research to be found. The bulk of the book is devoted to a step-by-step, easy-to-understand account of how one carries out ethnographic research with the assistance of "informants." Numerous examples drawn from the author's own research in such diverse settings as Skid Row, courtrooms, and bars make for interesting reading. A companion volume, *Participant Observation* is also highly recommended.

2

METHODS

OF STUDYING

THE HUMAN PAST

CHAPTER PREVIEW

This excavation is taking place in New York City's oldest slum, the Five Point Site. Because excavation of remains destroys the site in which they are found, meticulous records must be kept. Without such records, the finds tell us nothing about the human past.

WHAT ARE ARCHAEOLOGICAL SITES AND FOSSIL LOCALITIES AND HOW ARE THEY FOUND?

Archaeological sites are places containing the remains of past human activity. They are revealed by the presence of artifacts—objects fashioned or altered by humans—as well as certain kinds of soil marks, changes in vegetation, irregularities of the surface, and the like. Fossil localities are places containing the actual remains of organisms that lived in the past. They are revealed by the presence of fossils—any trace or impression of an organism of past geological time that has been preserved in the earth. Although fossils are sometimes found in archaeological sites, not all archaeological sites contain fossils, and localities are often found apart from archaeological sites. Though often discovered by accident, sites and localities are generally located by systematically surveying a region.

HOW ARE SITES AND LOCALITIES INVESTIGATED?

Archaeologists and paleoanthropologists face something of a dilemma. The only way to thoroughly investigate a site or locality is by excavation, which results in its destruction. Thus, every attempt is made to excavate in such a way that the location of everything found, no matter how small, is precisely recorded. Without such records little sense can be made of the data, and the potential of the site or locality to contribute to our knowledge of the past would be lost forever.

HOW ARE ARCHAEOLOGICAL OR FOSSIL REMAINS DATED?

Remains can be dated in relative terms by noting their stratigraphic position, by measuring the amount of fluorine contained in fossil bones, or by associating them with different floral or faunal remains. More precise dating is achieved by counting the tree rings in wood from archaeological contexts, by measuring the amount of Carbon 14 remaining in organic materials, or by measuring the percentage of potassium that has decayed to argon in volcanic materials. Some other techniques are less commonly used, but they are often expensive, are not always as widely available, or else they have not yet been proved as reliable.

A common misconception of anthropologists is that they are concerned exclusively with the human past, but as should now be evident, this is not the case. Not even archaeologists and physical anthropologists, those most likely to be engaged in the study of the past, devote all of their time to such pursuits. As we have seen, some archaeologists study the refuse of modern peoples, and many physical anthropologists carry out research into such issues as present-day human variation and adaptation. Nevertheless, the study of the human past is an important *part* of anthropology, given its concern with peoples in all places and times. Moreover, an understanding of the human past is essential if we are to understand what it was that made us distinctively human, as well as how the processes of change—both biological and cultural—affect the human species. Indeed, given the radical changes taking place in the world today, one may say that an understanding of the nature of change has never been more important.

Although it is not their exclusive concern, archaeology and physical anthropology are the two branches of anthropology most involved in the study of the human past. Archaeologists (apart from those engaged in the analysis of modern garbage) study things left behind by people who lived in historic or prehistoric times—tools, trash, traces of shelters, and the like. Most of us are familiar with some kind of archaeological material: the coin dug out of the earth, the fragment of an ancient jar, the spear point used by some ancient hunter. The finding and cataloging of such objects is often thought by nonprofessionals to be the chief goal of archaeology. While this was true in the last century, the emphasis today is on using archaeological remains to reconstruct human societies that can no longer be observed firsthand, in order to understand and explain human behavior.

The actual remains of our ancestors, as opposed to the things they lost or discarded, are the concern of physical anthropologists. Those physical anthropologists engaged in the recovery and study of the fossil evidence for human evolution, as opposed to those who study present-day peoples, are generally known as **paleoanthropologists**. Just as the finding and cataloging of objects was once

Paleoanthropologist: An anthropologist who studies human evolution from fossil remains.

the chief concern of the archaeologist, so the finding and cataloging of fossils was once the chief concern of the paleoanthropologist. But, again, there has been a major change in the field; while recovery, description, and organization of fossil materials are still important, the emphasis now is on what those fossils can tell us about the processes at work in human biological evolution.

In Chapter 1, we surveyed at some length just what it is that anthropologists do, and why they do it. We also looked briefly at the ethnographic methods used by anthropologists to study living peoples. Other methods are required, however, when studying peoples of the past—especially those of the prehistoric past. Since the next two parts of this book are about the prehistoric past, in this chapter, we shall look at how archaeologists and paleoanthropologists go about their study of the human past.

METHODS OF DATA RECOVERY

Archaeologists, one way or another, work with **artifacts**, by which we mean any object fashioned

Artifact: Any object fashioned or altered by humans.

or altered by humans—a flint chip, a basket, an axe, a pipe, or such nonportable things as house ruins or walls. An artifact expresses a facet of human culture. Because it is something that someone made, archaeologists like to say that an artifact is a product of human behavior or, in more technical words, that it is a material representation of an abstract ideal.

Just as important as the artifacts themselves is the way they were left in the ground. What people do with the things they have made, how they dispose of them, and how they lose them also reflect important aspects of human behavior. Furthermore, it is the context in which the artifacts were found that tells us which objects were contemporary with which other objects, which are older, and which are younger. Without this information, the archaeologist is in no position at all to even identify, let alone understand, specific cultures of the past. This importance of context cannot be overstated; without context, the archaeologist in effect knows nothing! Unfortunately, such information is easily lost if the materials have been disturbed, whether by bulldozers or by the activities of relic collectors.

While archaeologists work with artifacts, paleoanthropologists work with fossils—the remains of past forms of life. And just as the context of a find is as important to the archaeologist as is the find itself, so is the context of a fossil absolutely critical to the paleoanthropologist. Not only does it tell which fossils are a product of earlier or later time than other fossils, but by noting the association of human fossils with other nonhuman remains, the paleoanthropologist may also go a long way toward reconstructing the environmental setting in which the human lived.

THE NATURE OF FOSSILS

Broadly defined, a **fossil** is any trace or impression of an organism of past geologic time that has been preserved in the earth's crust. Fossilization typically involves the hard parts of an organism; bones, teeth, shells, horns, and the woody tissues of plants are the most successfully fossilized materials. Al-

Fossil: The preserved remains of plants and animals that lived in the past.

though the soft parts of an organism are rarely fossilized, the casts of footprints, and even whole bodies, are sometimes found.

An organism or part of an organism may be preserved in a number of ways. The whole animal may be frozen in ice, like the famous mammoths found in Siberia, safe from the actions of predators, weathering, and bacteria. Or it may be enclosed in a fossil resin such as amber. Specimens of spiders and insects dating back millions of years have been preserved in the Baltic Sea area, which is rich in resin-producing conifers. It may be preserved in the bottoms of lakes and sea basins, where the accumulation of chemicals renders the environment antiseptic. The entire organism may also be mummified or preserved in tar pits, peat, oil, or asphalt bogs, in which the chemical environment prevents the growth of decay-producing bacteria. Such **unaltered fossils**, although not common, are often quite spectacular and may be particularly informative.

Unaltered fossil: Remains of plants and animals that lived in the past that have not been altered in any significant way.

ORIGINAL STUDY

**PEAT HOLDS CLUES
TO EARLY
AMERICAN LIFE**[1]

Tenderly buried in a shallow pond in central Florida, the dead of an early American Indian society lay under an ever-deepening shroud of peat for more than 7000 years. Recently resurrected, the bones and artifacts speak poignantly of a little-understood culture and reveal levels of craft previously undocumented in the New World during that era. The site is a genetic gold mine as well—brains preserved in this peat environment have yielded the oldest known human DNA.

Excavation directed by Florida State University began in 1984, two years after a construction crew turned up skulls in a Titusville housing development called Windover Farms. By late 1986 the Windover Archaeological Research Project had uncovered more than a hundred burials dating from 7000 to 8000 years ago. Few sites of this age in the Americas have held so large and diverse a group—nearly equally divided between male and female, adult and subadult.

In life they were hunter–gatherers, making seasonal rounds through this region today known for Walt Disney World and the Kennedy Space Center. At death they were placed in the foot-deep pond. Often laid on their side in a flexed position, they were wrapped in grass mats, then covered with peat and wood. A frame of branches secured the grave.

Fabric, perhaps from a blanket or poncho, clung to some skeletons. Analysis by Dr. James Adovasio at the University of Pittsburgh unraveled five distinct types of weaving more sophisticated than any known in the Americas from that time. Made without a loom, one weave is nearly as tight as a modern T-shirt. "There are lots of simpler ways to make durable cloth," says archaeologist Dr. Glen Doran, director of the excavation. "It challenges our traditional model of hunter-gatherer societies. These people had taken care of the basic necessities of life and had enough time to devote to a very complex nonessential activity." Further evidence comes from the skeleton of a teenager who suffered from a degenerative chronic spinal disorder. "It tells us they could support a nonproductive person for a long time," explains archaeologist and co-director Dr. David Dickel.

"They seem to have been oriented toward doing things for children," says Dickel, noting that the most bountiful grave offerings lie with children and teenagers. Artifacts found include a wooden pestle and a paddle, perhaps used to pound plant fibers for weaving. Antler from deer and bone from manatee, rabbit, and fish were shaped into awls and needles, a small hammer, devices to accelerate spear throwing, and tools of unknown function.

Under a tarpaulin shielding the drained pond, field archaeologist John Ricisak (upper left) slices peat from the skeleton of a child who died at about the age of the observing schoolchildren. Even at about 12 years, teeth (upper right) show wear from a diet of rough vegetation such as nuts and cabbage palm.

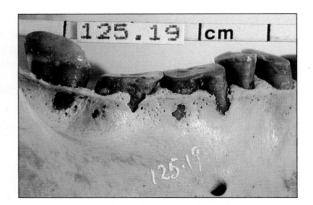

About ten feet of peat was cleared to reach the burials. Sealed from oxygen and saturated with minerals from Florida peatland waters, the preserved bones contain protein that may reveal diseases this population encountered. Unprotected soft tissue dissolved, but, locked in the skull, a shrunken brain often survived, as seen in this X ray of a middle-aged woman (below). The water's almost neutral pH balance also saved brain DNA. "One of this find's most significant aspects is that human DNA can be preserved," says Dr. William Hauswirth, a microbiologist at the University of Florida who, in collaboration with biochemist Dr. Philip Laipis, has extracted this genetic-coding molecule from the Windover site brains. They are trying to clone it. "There are not many things we can

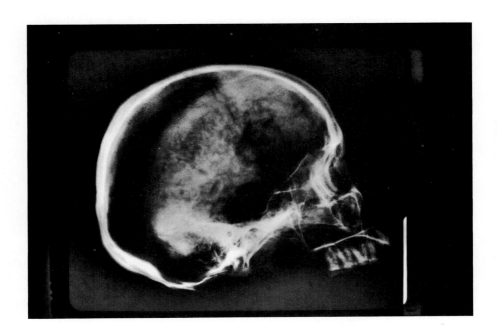

do with it now, but it will be a resource for the future when we understand more about human genes."

In anticipation of such advances, the site was not totally excavated. Reflooded, it awaits archaeologists of another generation.

[1] Louise E. Levathes, "Mysteries of the Bog," *National Geographic*, 171(1987):406–407.

Cases in which an entire organism is preserved in a relatively unaltered state are rare and comprise possibly less than 1 percent of all fossil finds. The majority of **fossils** have been **altered** in some way. They generally consist of such things as scattered teeth and fragments of bones and are found embedded in the earth's crust as part of rock deposits. Thousands, and even millions, of years ago, the organisms died and were deposited in the earth; they may then have been covered by sediments and silt, or sand. These materials gradually hardened, forming a protective shell around the skeleton of the organism. The internal cavities of bones or teeth and other parts of the skeleton are generally filled in with mineral deposits from the sediment immediately surrounding the specimen. Then the external walls of the bone decay and are replaced by calcium carbonate or silica.

Fossilization is most apt to occur among marine animals and other organisms that live near water, because their remains accumulate on shallow sea or river bottoms, away from waves and tidal action. These concentrations of shells and other parts of organisms are covered and completely enclosed by the soft marine sediments that eventually harden into shale and limestone.

Terrestrial animals, however, are not so successfully fossilized unless they happened to die in a cave, or their remains were dragged there by some other meat-eating animal. In caves, conditions are often excellent for fossilization, as minerals contained in water dripping from the ceiling may

harden over bones left on the cave floor. In northern China, for example, many fossils of *Homo erectus* (discussed in Chapter 7) and other animals were found in a cave at a place called Zhoukoudian, in deposits consisting of consolidated clays and rock that had fallen from the cave's limestone

Fossils are not always found in the ground. In this picture, paleoanthropologist Donald Johanson searches for fossils in a gully in Ethiopia. The fossils in the foreground were once buried beneath sediments on an ancient lake bottom, but rains in more recent times have eroded the sediments from around them so that they lie exposed on the surface.

Altered fossils: Remains of plants and animals that lived in the past that have been altered, as by the replacement of organic material by calcium carbonate or silica.

ceiling. The cave had been frequented by both humans and predatory animals, who left remains of many a meal there.

Outside of caves, the bones of a landdweller, having been picked clean and often broken by predators and scavengers, are then scattered and exposed to the deteriorating influence of the elements. The fossil record for many primates, for example, is poor, because the acid soil of the tropical forests in which they lived decomposes the skeleton rather quickly. The records are much more complete in the case of primates that lived on the grassy plains, or savannas, where conditions are much more favorable to the formation of fossils. This is particularly true in places where ash falls from volcanic eruptions, or waterborne sediments along lakes and streams, could quickly cover over the skeletons of primates that lived there. At several localities in Ethiopia, Kenya, and Tanzania in East Africa, numerous fossils important for our understanding of human evolution have been found near ancient lakes and streams, often "sandwiched" between layers of volcanic ash.

SITES AND FOSSIL LOCALITIES

Places containing archaeological remains of previous human occupation are known as **sites**. There are many kinds of sites, and sometimes it is difficult to define the boundaries of a site, for remains may be strewn over large areas. Some examples of sites are hunting campsites, in which hunters waited for game to pass; kill sites, in which game was killed and butchered; village sites, in which domestic activities took place; and cemeteries, in which the dead, and sometimes their belongings, were buried.

Sometimes human fossil remains are present at archaeological sites. This is the case, for example, at certain early sites in East Africa. Sometimes, though, they are found at other localities. For example, in South Africa the fossil remains of early

Site: In archaeology, a place containing remains of previous human occupants.

Fossil locality: In paleoanthropology, a place where fossils are found.

hominines have been found in rock fissures, where their remains were dropped by predators. Such places are usually referred to as **fossil localities**.

SITE AND LOCALITY IDENTIFICATION

Archaeological sites, particularly very old ones, frequently lie buried underground, and therefore the first task for the archaeologist is actually finding sites to investigate. Most sites are revealed by the presence of artifacts. Chance may play a beneficial role in the discovery of artifacts and sites, but usually the archaeologist will have to survey a region in order to plot the sites available for excavation. A survey can be made from the ground, but nowadays more and more use is being made of remote sensing techniques, many of them byproducts of space-age technology. Aerial photographs have been used off and on by archaeologists since the 1920s and are widely used today. Among other things, they were used for the discovery and interpretation of the huge geometric and zoomorphic markings on the coastal desert of Peru. More recently, use of high-resolution aerial photographs, including satellite imagery, resulted in the astonishing discovery of more than 200 miles of prehistoric roadways connecting sites in the four-corners region (where Arizona, New Mexico, Colorado, and Utah meet) with other sites in ways that archaeologists had never suspected. This has led to a whole new understanding of prehistoric Pueblo Indian economic, social, and political organization. Evidently, large centers like Pueblo Bonito were able to exercise political control over a number of satellite communities, mobilize labor for large public works, and see to the regular redistribution of goods over substantial distances.

On the ground, sites can be spotted by **soil marks**, or stains, that often show up on the surface of recently plowed fields. From soil marks, many Bronze Age burial mounds were discovered in

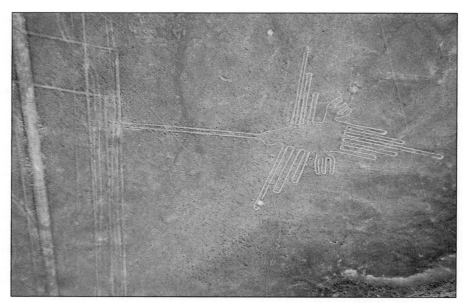

Some archaeological features are best seen from the air, such as this figure of a hummingbird made in prehistoric times on the Nazca Desert of Peru.

Soil marks: Stains that show up on the surface of recently plowed fields that reveal an archaeological site.

northern Hertfordshire and southwestern Cambridgeshire, England. The mounds hardly rose out of the ground, yet each was circled at its core by chalky soil marks. Sometimes the very presence of certain chalky rock is significant. A search for Stone Age cave sites in Europe would be simplified with the aid of a geological map showing where limestone—a mineral necessary in the formation of caves—is found.

Some sites may be spotted by the kind of vegetation they grow. For example, the topsoil of ancient storage and refuse pits is often richer in organic matter than that of the surrounding areas, and so it grows a distinct vegetation. At Tikal, an ancient Maya site in Guatemala (Chapter 10), breadnut trees usually grow near the remains of ancient houses, so that an archaeologist looking for the remains of houses at Tikal would do well to search where these trees grow. In England, a wooden monument of the Stonehenge type at Darrington, Wiltshire, was discovered from an

aerial photograph showing a distinct pattern of vegetation growing where the ancient structure stood.

Documents, maps, folklore—ethnohistorical data—are also useful to the archaeologist. Heinrich Schliemann, the famous (and controversial) nineteenth-century German archaeologist, was led to the discovery of Troy after a reading of Homer's *Iliad*. He assumed that the city described by Homer as Ilium was really Troy. Place names and local lore often are an indication that an archaeological site is to be found in the area. Archaeological surveys in North America depend a great deal upon amateur collectors who are usually familiar with local history.

Sometimes sites in eastern North America are exposed by natural agents, such as soil erosion or droughts. Many prehistoric Indian shell refuse mounds have been exposed by the erosion of river banks. A whole village of stone huts was exposed at Skara Brae in the Orkney Islands by the action of wind as it blew away sand. And during the long drought of 1853-1854, a well-preserved prehistoric village was exposed when the water level of Lake Zurich, Switzerland, fell dramatically. In 1991, the mummified body of a late Neolithic man was found in the Tyrolean Alps, where it had been released by glacial melting.

Shown here is the body of a Neolithic man who froze to death in the Tyrolean Alps; not until 1991 were his remains released by the melting of a glacier.

Often, archaeological remains are accidentally discovered in the course of some other human activity. Ploughing sometimes turns up bones, fragments of pots, and other archaeological objects. Stone quarrying revealed one of the most important sites of the Old Stone Age in England—at Swanscombe, Kent, in which human remains thought to be about 250,000 years old were found. In 1965, ground breaking for a new apartment complex in Nice, France, uncovered the remains of a campsite of *Homo erectus* (Chapter 7) 400,000 years old. So frequently do construction projects uncover archaeological remains that in many countries, including the United States, projects that require government approval will not be authorized unless measures are first taken to identify and protect archaeological remains on the construction sites. Archaeological surveys in the United States are now regularly carried out as part of the environmental review process for federally funded or licensed construction projects.

Conspicuous sites such as the great mounds or **tells** of the Middle East are easy to spot, for the country is open. But it is difficult to locate ruins, even those that are well above ground, where there is a dense forest cover. Thus, the discovery of archaeological sites is strongly affected by local geography.

While archaeological sites may be found just about anywhere, the same is not true for fossil localities. One will find fossils only in geological contexts where conditions are known to have been right for fossilization. Once the paleoanthropologist has identified such regions, specific localities are identified in much the same ways as archaeological sites. Indeed, the discovery of ancient stone tools may lead to the discovery of human fossil remains. For example, it was the presence of very crude stone tools in Olduvai Gorge, East Africa, which prompted Mary and Louis Leakey to search there for the human fossils they eventually found.

SITE AND LOCALITY EXCAVATION

Before the archaeologist or paleoanthropologist plans an excavation, he or she must ask the question: "Why am I digging?" Then must be considered the amount of time, money, and labor that can be committed to the enterprise. The recovery of archaeological and fossil material has long since ceased to be the province of the enlightened amateur, as it once was when any enterprising collector went out to dig for the sake of digging. A modern excavation is carefully planned and rigorously conducted; not only should it shed light on the human

ANTHROPOLOGY APPLIED

CULTURAL RESOURCE MANAGEMENT

In June 1979, on a knoll next to a river not far from Lake Champlain, a survey crew working for Peter A. Thomas of the University of Vermont discovered archaeological materials unlike any found before in the region. The following June, Thomas returned to the site with a crew of five, in order to excavate a portion of it. What they found were the remains of an 8000-year-old hunting and fishing camp that had been occupied for up to a few months in the spring or fall by perhaps one or two families. From the site they recovered a distinctive tool inventory never recognized before, as well as data related to hunting and fishing subsistence practices, butchery or hide processing, cooking, tool manufacture, and a possible shelter. Since many archaeologists had previously believed the region to be devoid of human occupation 8000 years ago, recovery of these data was especially important.

What sets this work apart from conventional archaeological research is that it was conducted as part of cultural resource management activities required by state and federal laws to preserve important aspects of the country's prehistoric and historic heritage. In this case, the Vermont Department of Highways planned to replace an inadequate bridge with a new one. Since the project was partially funded by the U.S. government, steps had to be taken to identify and protect any significant prehistoric or historic resources that might be adversely affected. To do so, the Vermont Agency of Transportation hired Thomas, first to see if such resources existed in the project area, and then to retrieve data from the endangered portions of the one site that was found. As a result, an important contribution was made to our knowledge of the prehistory of northeastern North America.

Since passage of the Historic Preservation Act of 1966, the National Environmental Policy Act of 1969 and the Archaeological and Historical Preservation Act of 1974, the field of cultural resource management has undergone something of a boom. Consequently, many archaeologists have been employed by such agencies as the National Park Service, The U.S. Forest Service, and the U.S. Soil and Conservation Service to assist in the preservation, restoration, and salvage of archaeological resources. Archaeologists are also employed by state historic preservation agencies. Finally, they do a considerable amount of consulting work for engineering firms, to help them prepare environmental impact statements. Some of these archaeologists, like Thomas, operate out of universities and colleges, while others are on the staffs of independent consulting firms.

past but it should also help us to understand cultural and evolutionary processes in general.

ARCHAEOLOGICAL EXCAVATION

After a site is chosen for excavation, on the basis of its potential contribution to the solution of some important research problem, the land is cleared and the places to be excavated are plotted. This is usually done by means of a **grid system**. The surface of the site is divided into squares, and then each square is numbered and marked with stakes. Each object found may then be located precisely in the square from which it came. (Remember, in archaeology, context is everything!) The starting point of a grid system may be a large rock, the edge of a stone wall, or an iron rod sunk into the ground. The starting point is also known as the reference or **datum point**. At a large site covering several square miles, this kind of grid system is not feasible

Grid system: A system for recording data from an archaeological excavation.

Datum Point: Starting, or reference, point for a grid system.

Sometimes archaeological sites are marked by dramatic ruins, as shown here. This temple stands at the heart of the ancient Maya city of Tikal. Built by piling up rubble and facing it with limestone blocks held together with mortar, it served as the funerary monument of a king, whose body was placed in a tomb beneath the pyramidal base.

because of the large size of the ruins. In such cases, the plotting may be done in terms of individual structures, numbered according to the square of a "giant grid" in which they are found (Figure 2.1).

In a gridded site, each square is dug separately with great care. Trowels are used to scrape the soil, and screens are used to sift all the loose soils so that even the smallest artifacts, such as flint chips or beads, are recovered.

A technique employed when looking for very fine objects, such as fish scales or very small bones, is called **flotation**. Flotation consists of immersing soil in water, causing the particles to separate. Some will float, others will sink to the bottom, and the remains can be easily retrieved. If the site is **stratified**—that is, if the remains lie in layers one upon the other—each layer, or stratum, will be dug separately (see Figure 2.2 for an example of stratigraphy). Each layer, having been laid down during a particular span of time, will contain artifacts deposited at the same time and belonging to the same culture. Culture change can be traced through the order in which artifacts were deposited. But, say archaeologists Frank Hole and Robert F. Heizer, "because of difficulties in analyzing stratigraphy, archaeologists must use the greatest caution in

Flotation: An archaeological technique employed to recover very tiny objects by immersion of soil samples in water to separate heavy from light particles.

Stratified: Layered; said of archaeological sites where the remains lie in layers, one upon another.

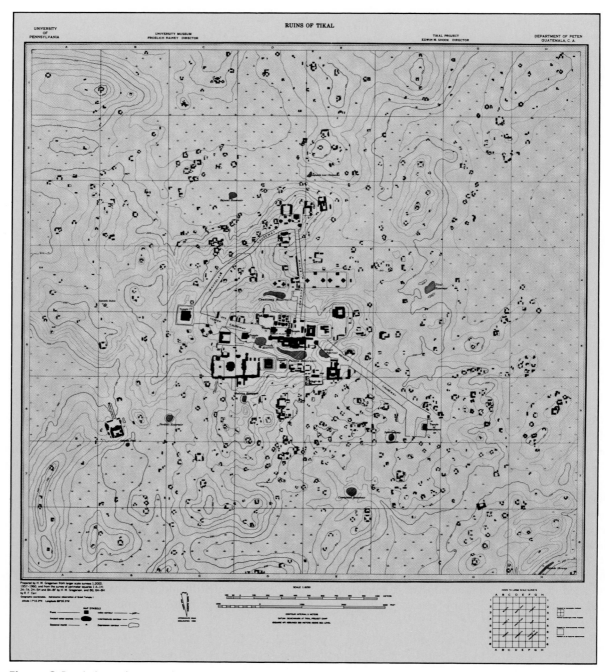

Figure 2.1   At large sites covering several square miles, a giant grid is constructed, as shown in this map of the center of the ancient Maya city of Tikal. Each square of the grid is one quarter of a square kilometer; individual structures are numbered according to the square in which they are found. The temple shown on page 41 can be located near the center of the map, on the east edge of the Great Plaza.

This photo is of the stratigraphy associated with one of the structures (5D-26) shown schematically in Figure 2.2.

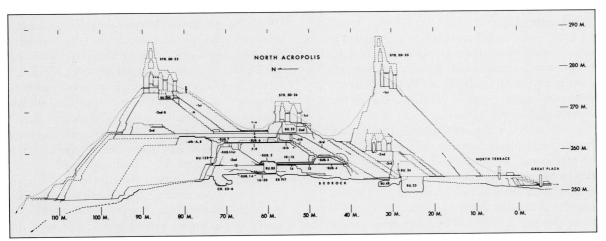

Figure 2.2   This drawing shows the strata (layers) uncovered on the North Acropolis of Tikal. The remains of at least twenty-two structures were found at this one location. The North Acropolis is shown near the center of the map in Figure 2.1, just north of the Great Plaza.

drawing conclusions. Almost all interpretations of time, space, and culture contexts depend on stratigraphy. The refinements of laboratory techniques for analysis are wasted if archaeologists cannot specify the stratigraphic position of their artifacts."[2] If no stratification is present, then the

archaeologist digs by arbitrary levels. Each square must be dug so that its edges and profiles are straight; walls between squares are often left standing to serve as visual correlates of the grid system.

EXCAVATION OF FOSSILS

Excavating for fossils is in many ways like archaeological excavation, although there are some

[2] Frank Hole and Robert F. Heizer, *An Introduction to Prehistoric Archeology* (New York: Holt, Rinehart and Winston, 1969), p. 113.

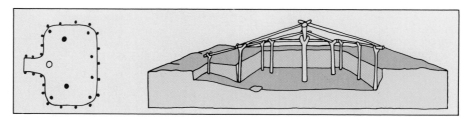

Figure 2.3   Although the wooden posts of a house may have long since decayed, their positions may still be marked by discoloration of the soil. The plan shown on the left, of an ancient posthole pattern and depression at Snaketown, Arizona, permits the hypothetical house reconstruction on the right.

differences. The paleoanthropologist must be particularly skilled in the techniques of geology, or else have ready access to geological expertise, because a fossil is of little use unless its temporal place in the sequence of rocks that contain it can be determined. In addition, the paleoanthropologist must be able to identify the fossil-laden rocks, their deposition, and other geological details. In order to provide all the necessary expertise, paleoanthropological expeditions these days generally are made up of teams of experts in various fields in addition to physical anthropology.

A great deal of skill and caution is required to remove a fossil from its burial place without damage. An unusual combination of tools and materials is usually contained in the kit of the paleoanthropologist—pickaxes, enamel coating, burlap for bandages, and plaster of paris.

To remove newly discovered bones, the paleoanthropologist begins uncovering the specimen, using pick and shovel for initial excavation, then small camel hair brushes and dental picks to remove loose and easily detachable debris surrounding the bones. Once the entire specimen has been uncovered (a process that may take days of back-breaking, patient labor), the bones are covered with shellac and tissue paper to prevent cracking and damage during further excavation and handling.

Both the fossil and the earth immediately surrounding it, or the matrix, are prepared for removal as a single block. The bones and matrix are cut out of the earth (but not removed), and more shellac is applied to the entire block to harden it. The bones are covered with burlap bandages dipped in plaster of paris. Then the entire block is enclosed in plaster and burlap bandages, perhaps splinted with tree branches, and allowed to dry overnight. After it has hardened, the entire block is carefully removed from the earth, ready for packing and transport to a laboratory. Before leaving the discovery area, the investigator makes a thorough sketch map of the terrain and pinpoints the find on geological maps to aid future investigators.

STATE OF PRESERVATION OF ARCHAEOLOGICAL AND FOSSIL EVIDENCE

Just what is recovered in the course of excavation depends upon the nature of the remains as much as upon the excavator's digging skills. Inorganic materials such as stone and metal are more resistant to decay than organic ones such as wood and bone. Often an archaeologist comes upon an assemblage—a collection of artifacts made of durable inorganic materials, such as stone tools, and traces of organic ones long since decomposed, such as woodwork (Figure 2.3), textiles, or food.

State of preservation is affected by climate; under favorable climatic conditions, even the most perishable objects may survive over vast periods of time. For example, predynastic Egyptian burials consisting of shallow pits in the sand often yield well-preserved corpses. Since these bodies were buried long before mummification was ever practiced, their preservation can only be the result of rapid desiccation in the very warm, dry climate. The tombs of dynastic Egypt often contain wooden furniture, textiles, flowers, and papyri barely touched by time seemingly as fresh looking as they were when deposited in the tomb 3000 years ago—a consequence of the dryness of the atmosphere.

The dryness of certain caves is also a factor in the preservation of fossilized human or animal

At the Maya site of Ceren, the remains of a corn crib and ears of corn were recovered by pouring dental plaster into a cavity in the soil, left when the original organic remains decayed.

feces. Human feces are a source of information on prehistoric foods and can be analyzed for dietary remains. From such analysis can be determined not only what the inhabitants ate but also how the food was prepared. Because so many sources of food are available only in certain seasons, it is even possible to tell the time of year in which the food was eaten and the excrement deposited.

Certain climates can soon obliterate all evidence of organic remains. Maya ruins found in the very warm and moist tropical rain forests of Mesoamerica are often in a state of collapse—notwithstanding the fact that many are massive structures of stone—as a result of the pressure exerted upon them by the heavy forest vegetation. The rain and humidity soon destroy almost all traces of woodwork, textiles, or basketry. Fortunately, wood, textile and basketry impressions are sometimes preserved in plaster, and some objects made of these materials are depicted in stone carvings and pottery figurines. Thus, even in the face of complete decay of organic substances, something may still be learned about them.

The cultural practices of ancient humans may also account for the preservation of archaeological remains. The ancient Egyptians believed that eternal life could be achieved only if the dead person were buried with his or her worldly possessions. Hence, their tombs are usually filled with a wealth of artifacts. Many skeletal remains of Neandertals (Chapter 8) are known because they practiced burial, probably because they too believed in some sort of afterlife. By contrast, skeletal remains of pre-Neandertal peoples are rare and when found usually consist of mere fragments rather than complete skeletons.

SORTING OUT THE EVIDENCE

It cannot be stressed too strongly that the value of archaeological materials is virtually destroyed if an accurate and detailed record of the excavations has not been kept.

> The fundamental premise of excavation is that all digging is destructive, even that done by experts. The archaeologist's primary responsibility, therefore, is to record a site for posterity as it is dug because there are no second chances.[3]

[3] Brian M. Fagan, *People of the Earth*, 7th ed. (New York: HarperCollins, 1992), p. 29.

The records include a scale map of all the features, the stratification of each excavated square, a description of the exact location and depth of every artifact or bone unearthed, and photographs and scale drawings of the objects. This is the only way archaeological evidence can later be pieced together in order to arrive at a plausible reconstruction of a culture. Although the archaeologist may be interested only in certain kinds of remains, every aspect of the site must be recorded, whether it is relevant to the particular investigation or not, because such evidence may be useful to others and would otherwise be permanently lost. One must remember that archaeological sites are nonrenewable resources, and that their destruction, whether by proper excavation or by looting, is permanent.

After photographs and scale drawings are made, the materials recovered are processed in the laboratory. In the case of fossils, the block in which they have been removed from the field is cut open, and the fossil is separated from the matrix. Like the initial removal from the earth, this is a long, painstaking job involving a great deal of skill and special tools. This task may be done with hammer and chisel, dental drills, rotary grinders or pneumatic chisels, and, in the case of very small pieces, with awls and tiny needles under a microscope.

Chemical means, such as hydrochloric and hydrofluoric acid, are also used in the separation process. Some fossils require processing by other methods. For example, precise identification can be obtained by examining thin, almost transparent strips of some fossils under a microscope. Casts of the insides of skulls are made by filling the skull wall with an acid-resistant material, then removing the wall with acid. A skull may be cleaned out and the inside painted with latex. After the latex hardens, it is removed in a single piece, revealing indirect evidence of brain shape and nerve patterns. Such a cast of the skull's interior is helpful in determining the size and complexity of the specimen's brain.

Archaeologists, as a rule of thumb, generally plan on at least three hours of laboratory work for each hour of fieldwork. In the lab, artifacts which have been recovered must first be cleaned and cataloged—often a tedious and time-consuming job—before they are ready for analysis. From the shapes of the artifacts and from the traces of manufacture and wear, archaeologists can usually determine their function. For example, the Russian archaeologist S. A. Semenov devoted many years to the study of prehistoric technology.[4] In the case of a flint tool used as a scraper, he was able to determine, by examining the wear patterns of the tool under a microscope, that the prehistoric individuals who used it began to scrape from right to left and then scraped from left to right, and in so doing avoided straining the muscles of the hand.

Analysis of vegetable and animal remains provides clues about the environment and the economic activities of the occupants of a site (see Figure 2.4). Such analysis may help clarify peoples' relationship to their environment and its influence upon the development of their **technology**—the knowledge they employ to make and use objects. For example, we know that the inhabitants of Serpent Mound, in Ontario, Canada (a mound consisting of burials and a shell midden) were there only in the spring and early summer, when they came to collect shellfish and perform their annual burial rites; apparently they moved elsewhere at the beginning of summer to pursue other seasonal subsistence activities. Archaeologists have inferred that the mound was unoccupied in winter, because this is the season when deer shed their antlers, yet no deer antlers were found on the site. Nor were duck bones found, and so archaeologists conclude that the mound was also unoccupied in the fall, when ducks stopped on their migratory route southward to feed on the wild rice which was growing in the region.

Analysis of human skeletal material also provides important insights into ancient peoples' diets. Microscopic wear patterns on teeth, for example, may reveal whether abrasive plants were important foods. Similarly, people who eat more plants than meat will have a higher ratio of strontium to

---

[4] A. Semenov, *Prehistoric Technology* (New York: Barnes & Noble, 1964).

Technology: The knowledge people employ to make and use objects.

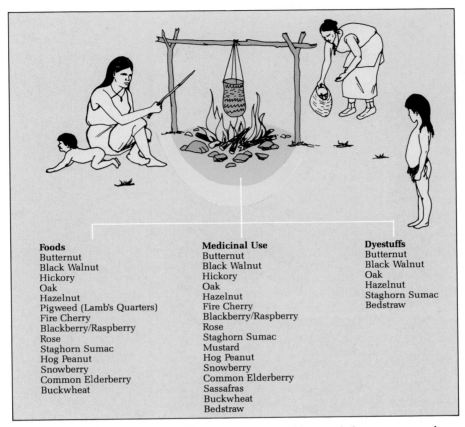

Foods
Butternut
Black Walnut
Hickory
Oak
Hazelnut
Pigweed (Lamb's Quarters)
Fire Cherry
Blackberry/Raspberry
Rose
Staghorn Sumac
Hog Peanut
Snowberry
Common Elderberry
Buckwheat

Medicinal Use
Butternut
Black Walnut
Hickory
Oak
Hazelnut
Fire Cherry
Blackberry/Raspberry
Rose
Staghorn Sumac
Mustard
Hog Peanut
Snowberry
Common Elderberry
Sassafras
Buckwheat
Bedstraw

Dyestuffs
Butternut
Black Walnut
Oak
Hazelnut
Staghorn Sumac
Bedstraw

Figure 2.4   Plant remains recovered from hearths used by people between one and two thousand years ago at an archaeological site in Vermont may have been utilized as shown here, based on our knowledge of how some plants were used by Indians in the region when first encountered by Europeans. Occupation of the site must have been in the summer and fall, the seasons when these plants are available.

calcium in their bones. At the ancient Maya city of Tikal, analysis of human skeletons showed that elite members of society had access to better diets than lower ranking members of society, allowing them to reach their full growth potential with greater regularity. Important insights into life expectancy, mortality, and health status also emerge from the study of human skeletal remains. Unfortunately, such studies have become more difficult to carry out, especially in the United States, as Native-American communities demand the return of skeletons from archaeological excavations for reburial. Archaeologists find themselves in something of a quandary over this; as scientists, they know the importance of the information that can be gleaned

from studies of human skeletons, but as anthropologists, they are bound to respect the feelings of those whose ancestors those skeletons represent. Currently, archaeologists are working with representatives of Native-American communities to work out procedures with which both parties can live.

DATING THE PAST

Reliable methods of dating objects and events are necessary if archaeologists and paleoanthropologists are to know the sequence of events in the situation under study. But since archaeologists and paleoanthropologists deal mostly with peoples and

Some ancient societies devised precise ways of recording dates that archaeologists have been able to correlate with our own calendar. Here is the tomb of the important ruler Stormy Sky, at the ancient Maya city of Tikal. The glyphs painted on the wall give the date of the burial in the Maya calendar, which is the same as March 18, A.D. 457, in our calendar. The tomb, Burial 48, is shown in Figure 2.2 above the 30-meter mark.

events in times so far removed from our own, the calendar of historic times is of little use to them. So they must rely on two kinds of dating: relative and "absolute." **Relative dating** consists simply of finding out if an event or object is younger or older than another. **"Absolute"** or (more properly) **chronometric dates** are dates based upon solar

years and are reckoned in "years before the present" (B.P., with "present" defined as A.D. 1950) or years before or after Christ (B.C. and A.D.). Many relative and chronometric techniques are available; here, there is space to discuss only the ones most often used. Ideally, archaeologists try to utilize as many methods as are appropriate, given the materials available to work with and the funds at their disposal. By doing so, they significantly reduce the risk of arriving at erroneous dates.

METHODS OF RELATIVE DATING

Of the many relative dating techniques available, **stratigraphy** is probably the most reliable. Stratigraphy is based on the simple principle that the oldest layer, or stratum, was deposited first (it is the deepest) while the newest layer was deposited last (in undisturbed situations, it lies at the top). Therefore, in an archaeological site the evidence is usually deposited in chronological order. The lowest stratum contains the oldest artifacts and/or fossils, whereas the uppermost stratum contains the most recent ones. Thus, even in the absence of precise dates, one knows the *relative* age of objects in one stratum compared with the ages of those in other strata.

Another method of relative dating is the **fluorine test**. It is based on the fact that the amount of fluorine deposited in bones is proportional to their age. The oldest bones contain the greatest amount of fluorine, and vice versa. The fluorine test is useful in dating bones that cannot be ascribed with certainty to any particular stratum and cannot be dated according to the stratigraphic method. A

Relative dating: In archaeology and paleoanthropology, designating an event, object, or fossil as being older or younger than another.

Absolute, or chronometric, dates: In archaeology and paleoanthropology, dates for archaeological materials based on solar years, centuries, or other units of absolute time.

Stratigraphy: In archaeology and paleoanthropology, the most reliable method of relative dating by means of strata.

Fluorine test: In archaeology or paleoanthropology, a technique for relative dating based on the fact that the amount of fluorine in bones is proportional to their age.

Palynology: In archaeology and paleoanthropology, a method of relative dating based on changes in fossil pollen over time.

shortcoming of this method is that the rate of fluorine formation is not constant, but varies from region to region.

Relative dating can also be done on the evidence of botanical and animal remains. A common method, known as **palynology**, involves the study of pollen grains. The kind of pollen found in any geologic stratum depends on the kind of vegetation that existed at the time that stratum was deposited. A site or locality can therefore be dated by determining what kind of pollen was found associated with it. In addition, palynology is also an important technique for reconstructing past environments in which people lived.

Another method relies on our knowledge of paleontology. Sites containing the bones of extinct animal species are usually older than sites in which the remains of these animals are absent. Very early North American Indian sites have yielded the remains of mastodons and mammoths—animals now extinct—and on this basis the sites can be dated to a time before these animals died out, roughly 10,000 years ago.

METHODS OF CHRONOMETRIC DATING

One of the most widely used methods of "absolute" or chronometric dating is **radiocarbon analysis**. It

Radiocarbon analysis: In archaeology and paleoanthropology, a technique for chronometric dating based on measuring the amount of radioactive carbon (C-14) left in organic materials found in archaeological sites.

is based on the fact that all living organisms absorb radioactive carbon (known as Carbon 14), which reaches equilibrium with that in the atmosphere, and that this absorption ceases at the time of death. It is possible to measure in the laboratory the amount of radioactive carbon left in a given organic substance, because radioactive substances break down or decay slowly over a fixed period of time. Carbon 14 begins to disintegrate, returning to Nitrogen 14, emitting radioactive (beta) particles in the process. At death, about 15 beta radiations per minute per gram of material are emitted. The rate of decay is known as "half-life," and the half-life of Carbon 14 is 5730 years. This means that it takes 5730 years for one-half of the original amount of Carbon 14 to decay into Nitrogen 14. Beta radiation will be about 7.5 counts per minute per gram. In another 5730 years, one-half of this amount of Carbon 14 will also have decayed. In other words, after 11,460 years, only one-fourth of the original amount of Carbon 14 will be present. Thus the age of an organic substance such as charcoal, wood, shell, or bone can be measured by counting the beta rays emitted by the remaining Carbon 14. The radiocarbon method can adequately date organic materials up to 70,000 years old. Of course, one has to be sure that the association between organic remains and archaeological materials is valid. For example, charcoal found on a site may have gotten there from a recent forest fire, rather than more ancient activity, or wood used to make something by the people who lived at a site may have been retrieved from some older context.

Because there is always a certain amount of error involved, radiocarbon dates are not as "absolute" as is sometimes thought. This is why any stated date always has a ± factor attached to it. For example, a date of 5200±120 years ago means that there is a two out of three chance that the true date falls somewhere within the 240 years between 5080 and 5320 radiocarbon years ago. The qualification "radiocarbon" years ago is necessary, because we have discovered that radiocarbon years are not precisely equivalent to calendar years.

The discovery that radiocarbon years are not precisely equivalent to calendar years was made possible by another method of "absolute" dating, **dendrochronology**. Originally devised for dating Pueblo Indian sites in the North American

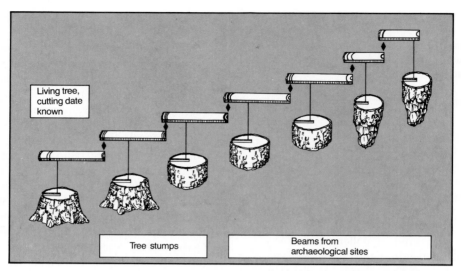

Figure 2.5 Chronometric dating based on tree rings is called dendrochronology. Starting with a sample of known age, ring patterns toward the inner part are matched with those from the outer part of the older sample, and so on, back in time.

Dendrochronology: In archaeology, a method of chronometric dating based on the number of rings of growth found in a tree trunk.

Potassium–argon analysis: In archaeology and paleoanthropology, a technique for chronometric dating which measures the ratio of radioactive potassium to argon in volcanic debris associated with human remains.

southwest, this method is based on the fact that in the right kind of climate, trees add one (and only one) new growth ring to their trunks every year (see Figure 2.5). The rings vary in thickness, depending upon the amount of rainfall received in a year, so that climatic fluctuation is registered in the growth ring. By taking a sample of wood, such as a beam from a Pueblo Indian house, and by comparing its pattern of rings with those in the trunk of a tree known to be as old as the artifact, archaeologists can date the archaeological material. Dendrochronology is applicable only to wooden objects. Furthermore, it can be used only in regions in which trees of great age, such as the giant sequoias and the bristlecone pine, are known to grow. On the other hand, radiocarbon dating of wood from

bristlecone pines that have been dated by dendrochronology allows us to "correct" Carbon 14 dates so as to bring them into agreement with calendar dates.

Potassium–argon analysis, another method of absolute dating, is based on a technique similar to that of radiocarbon analysis. Following intense heating, as from a volcanic eruption, radioactive potassium decays at a known rate to form argon, any previously existing argon having been released by the heating. The half-life of radioactive potassium is 1.3 billion years. Deposits that are millions of years old can now be dated by measuring the ratio of potassium to argon in a given rock. Volcanic debris, such as at Olduvai Gorge and other localities in East Africa, can be dated by potassium–argon

Amino acid racemization dating: In archaeology and paleoanthropology, a technique for chronometric dating which measures the ratio of right- to left-handed amino acids.

Electron spin resonance: In archaeology and paleoanthropology, a technique for chronometric dating which measures the number of trapped electrons in bone or shell.

analysis; thus we know when the volcanic eruption occurred. If fossils or artifacts are found sandwiched between layers of volcanic ash, as they are at Olduvai and other sites in East Africa, they can therefore be dated with some precision. But as with radiocarbon dates, there are limits to that precision, and potassium–argon dates are always stated with a ± margin of error attached.

Amino acid racemization dating, yet another chronometric technique, is of potential importance because it bridges a time gap between the effective ranges of the radiocarbon and potassium–argon methods. It is based on the fact that amino acids trapped in organic materials gradually change, or "racemize" after death, from left-handed forms to right-handed forms. Thus, the ratio of left- to right-handed forms should indicate the specimen's age. Unfortunately, in substances like bone, moisture and acids in the soil can leach out the amino acids, thereby introducing a serious source of error. However, ostrich eggshells have proven immune to this problem, the amino acids being so effectively locked up in a tight mineral matrix that they are preserved for thousands of years. Because ostrich eggs were widely used as food, and the shells as containers in Africa and the Middle East, they provide a powerful means of dating sites of the Middle Stone Age, between 40,000 and 180,000 years ago.

Radiocarbon, potassium–argon, and amino acid racemization dating are only three of the several "high tech" dating methods developed in the past few decades. Radiocarbon and potassium–argon, in particular, are the chronometric methods most heavily relied upon by archaeologists and paleoanthropologists; nevertheless, other methods are increasingly used as a check on the accuracy and to supplement dates determined by other means. To cite one example, a new technique called **electron spin resonance**, measures the trapped electron population in bone or shell (the number of trapped electrons indicates the specimen's age). Because electron spin resonance dates derived from an important Middle Stone Age skull from Qafzeh, Israel (discussed in Chapter 8) agree with those based on amino acid racemization, we can have confidence that the dating is correct. Because other methods of chronometric dating are often quite complicated to carry out, they tend to be expensive; many can be carried out only on specific kinds of materials, and in the case of some, are so new that their reliability is not yet unequivocally established. It is for these reasons that they have not been as widely used as radiocarbon and potassium–argon.

CHANCE AND THE STUDY OF THE PAST

It is important to understand the imperfect nature of the archaeological record. It is imperfect, first of all, because the chance circumstances of preservation have determined what has and what has not survived the ravages of time. Thus, cultures must be reconstructed on the basis of incomplete and, possibly, unrepresentative samples of artifacts. The problems are further compounded by the large role chance continues to play in the discovery of prehistoric remains. Thus, one must always be cautious when trying to interpret the human past. No matter how elegant a particular theory may be about what happened in the past, new evidence may at any time force its reexamination and modification, or even rejection in favor of some better theory.

Chapter Summary

Archaeology and physical anthropology, though they do not neglect the present, are the two branches of anthropology most involved in the study of the human past. Archaeologists study material remains to describe and explain human behavior; physical anthropologists called paleoanthropologists study fossil remains to understand and explain the processes at work in human biological evolution.

Artifacts are objects fashioned or altered by humans, such as a flint chip, a pottery vessel, or even a house. A fossil is any trace of an organism of past geological time that has been preserved in the earth's crust. Fossilization typically involves the hard parts of an organism and may take place through freezing in ice, preservation in bogs or tar pits, immersion in water, or inclusion in rock deposits. Fossilization is most apt to occur among marine animals and other organisms that live near water because of the favorable chances that their corpses will be buried and preserved on sea and river bottoms. On the land, conditions in caves, or where there is active volcanic activity, may be conducive to fossilization.

Places containing archaeological remains of previous human occupation are known as sites. Sometimes human fossils are present at archaeological sites, but they may occur by themselves at fossil localities. Sites and localities are generally located by means of a survey of a region. While fossil localities are revealed by the presence of fossils, archaeological sites are revealed by the presence of artifacts. Irregularities of the ground surface, unusual soil discoloration, and unexpected variations in vegetation type and coloring may also indicate the location of a site. Ethnohistorical data—maps, documents, and folklore—may provide further clues to the location of archaeological sites. Sometimes both fossils and archaeological remains are discovered accidentally, for example, in plowing, quarrying, or in building construction.

Once a site or locality has been selected for excavation, the area is divided and carefully marked with a grid system; the starting point of the dig is called the datum point. Each square within the grid is carefully excavated, and any archaeological or fossil remains are recovered through employment of various tools and screens; for very fine objects, the method of flotation is employed. The location of each artifact when found must be carefully noted. Once excavated, artifacts and fossils undergo further cleaning and preservation in the laboratory with the use of specialized tools and chemicals.

The durability of archaeological evidence depends upon climate and the nature of the artifacts. Inorganic materials are more resistent to decay than organic ones. However, given a very dry climate, even organic materials may be well preserved. Warm, moist climates as well as thick vegetation act to decompose organic material quickly, and even inorganic material may suffer from the effects of humidity and vegetation growth. The durability of archaeological evidence is also dependant upon the social customs of ancient people.

Because excavation in fact destroys a site, the archaeologist must maintain a thorough record in the form of maps, descriptions, scale drawings, and photographs of every aspect of the excavation. All artifacts must be cleaned and classified before being sent to the laboratory for analysis. Often the shape and markings of artifacts can determine their function, and the analysis of vegetable and animal remains may provide information.

There are two types of methods for dating archaeological and fossil remains. Relative dating is a method of determining the age of objects relative to each other and includes the method of stratigraphy, based upon the position of the artifact or fossil in relation to different layers of soil deposits. The fluorine test is based upon the determination of the amount of fluorine deposited in the bones. The analysis of floral remains (including palynology) and faunal deposits is also widely employed. Methods of "absolute," or chronometric, dating include radiocarbon analysis, which measures the amount of Carbon 14 that remains in organic objects; potassium–argon analysis, which measures the percentage of radioactive potassium which has decayed to argon in volcanic material; dendrochronology, dating based upon tree rings; and amino acid racemization, based upon changes from left- to right-handed amino acids in organic materials, especially egg shells. Other chronometric methods exist, such as electron spin resonance, but are not as widely used, owing to limited applicability, difficulty of application, expense, or their reliability is as yet unproven.

Suggested Readings

Cole, Sonia. *Leakey's Luck: The Life of Louis Seymour Bazett Leakey, 1903–1972.* New York: Harcourt Brace Jovanovich, 1975.
No one accomplished and promoted more work dealing with human origins than Leakey. This is an honest and thorough account of the man and his work by an early protegee and friend of more than a quarter century.

Fagan, Brian M. *People of the Earth: An Introduction to World Prehistory*, 7th ed. New York: HarperCollins, 1992.
There are a number of good texts that, like this one, try to summarize the findings of archaeologists on a worldwide scale. This book, being one of the more recent ones, is reasonably up to date.

Joukowsky, Martha. *A Complete Field Manual of Archaeology: Tools and Techniques of Field Work for Archaeologists.* Englewood Cliffs, N.J.: Prentice-Hall, 1980.
This book, encyclopedic in its coverage, explains for the novice and professional alike all of the methods and techniques used by archaeologists in the field. Two concluding chapters discuss fieldwork opportunities and financial aid for archaeological research.

Sharer, Robert J., and Wendy Ashmore. *Archaeology: Discovering Our Past*, 2nd ed. Palo Alto, Calif.: Mayfield, 1993.
One of the best presentations of the body of method, technique, and theory that most archaeologists accept as a foundation for their discipline. The authors confine themselves to the operational modes, guiding strategies, and theoretical orientations of anthropological archaeology in a manner well designed to lead the beginner into the discipline.

Thomas, David H. *Archaeology.* 2nd ed. New York: Holt, Rinehart and Winston, 1989.
Some books tell us how to do archaeology, some tell us what archaeologists have found out, but this one tells us why we do archaeology. It does so in a coherent and thorough way, and Thomas' blend of ideas, quotes, biographies, and case studies makes for really interesting reading.

White, Peter. *The Past Is Human*, 2nd ed. New York: Maplinger, 1976.
This book, written for a nonprofessional audience, is a response to those advocating extraterrestrial interference and other mystical "explanations" of the human past.

CHAPTER

3

BIOLOGY

AND

EVOLUTION

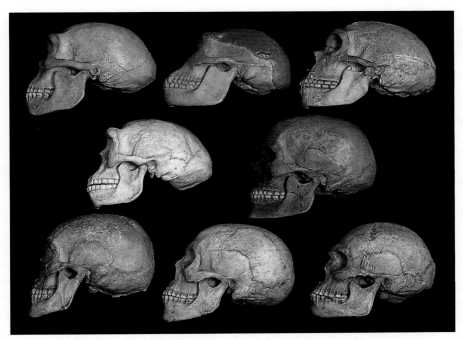

Human evolution has resulted in a number of skull variations. Such variation is not the result of progressive change, but rather the adaptation of organisms to conditions as they are. Once those conditions change, new adaptations are required.

WHAT FORCES ARE RESPONSIBLE FOR THE DIVERSITY OF PRIMATES IN THE WORLD TODAY?

Although all primates—lemurs, lorises, indriids, tarsiers, monkeys, apes, and humans—share a common ancestry, they have come to differ through the operation of evolutionary forces which have permitted them to adapt to a variety of environments, in a variety of ways. Although biologists are agreed upon the fact of evolution, they are still unraveling the details of how it has proceeded.

WHAT ARE THE PROCESSES OF EVOLUTION?

Evolution works through mutation, which produces genetic variation, which is then acted upon by drift (accidental changes in gene frequencies in a population), gene flow (the introduction of new genes from other populations), and natural selection. Natural selection is the adaptive mechanism of evolution, and works through differential reproduction as individuals with genes for adaptive traits produce more offspring than those without.

HOW DO THESE PROCESSES PRODUCE NEW FORMS OF ORGANISMS?

Populations may evolve in a linear manner, as small changes from one generation to another improve that population's adaptation. Through the accumulation of such changes over many generations, an older species may evolve into a new one. Or evolution may proceed in a branching manner, in response to isolating mechanisms. These serve to separate populations, preventing gene flow between them so that drift and selection may proceed in different ways. This may lead to the appearance first of divergent races and then of divergent species.

Humans have long had close contact with other animals. Some, such as dogs, horses, and cows, have lived close to people for so long that little attention is paid to their behavior. We are interested only in how well they do what they were bred for—companionship, racing, milk-giving, or whatever. Domestic animals are so dependent on humans that they have lost many of the behavioral traits of their wild ancestors. Except to a small child, perhaps, and a dairy farmer, a cow is not a very interesting animal to watch.

By contrast, wild animals, especially exotic ones, have always fascinated people; circuses and zoos attest to this fascination. In cultures very different from those of the industrialized countries of the world, like those of some American Indians, people can have a special relationship with animals, believing themselves to be descended from them; such animals represent their "totems."

A curious feature of this interest is the desire of humans to see animals as mirror images of themselves, a phenomenon known as **anthropomorphism**. Stories in which animals talk, wear clothes, and exhibit human virtues and vices go back to antiquity. Many children learn of Mickey Mouse, Garfield the Cat, or Kermit the Frog and Miss Piggy; the animals created by Walt Disney, Jim Hensen, and others have become an integral part of contemporary North American culture. Occasionally one sees on television trained apes dressed like humans eating at a table, pushing a stroller, or riding a tricycle. They are amusing because they look so "human."

Over the ages, people have trained animals to perform tricks, making them mimic human behavior. But never did people suspect the full extent of the relationship they have with animals. The close biological tie between humans and the other **primates**—the group of animals which, besides humans, includes lemurs, lorises, indriids, tarsiers, monkeys, and apes—is now better understood. The diversity of primates seen today is the result of the

Primate order: The group of mammals which include lemurs, lorises, indriids, tarsiers, monkeys, apes, and humans.

operation of evolutionary forces which have permitted them to adapt to environments in a variety of ways. These evolutionary processes are the subject of this chapter.

HEREDITY

In order to understand how evolution works, one must first have some understanding of the mechanisms of heredity, because heritable variation constitutes the raw material for evolution. Our knowledge of the mechanisms of heredity is fairly recent; most of the fruitful research into the molecular level of inheritance has taken place in the past four decades. Although certain aspects remain puzzling, the outlines by now are reasonably clear.

THE TRANSMISSION OF GENES

Biologists call the actual units of heredity **genes**, a term that comes from the Greek word for "birth." The presence and activity of genes were originally deduced rather than observed by an Austrian monk, Gregor Mendel, in the nineteenth century. Working shortly after publication of Darwin's theory of evolution, Mendel sought to answer some of the riddles posed by that theory by experimenting with garden peas to determine how various traits are inherited. Specifically, he discovered what Darwin never knew: how variation, so important to his

Anthropomorphism: The ascription of human attributes to nonhuman beings.

Genes: Portions of DNA molecules that direct the development of observable or identifiable traits.

Gregor Mendel performed carefully controlled breeding experiments with garden peas that led to the discovery, in 1865, of the basic laws of heredity.

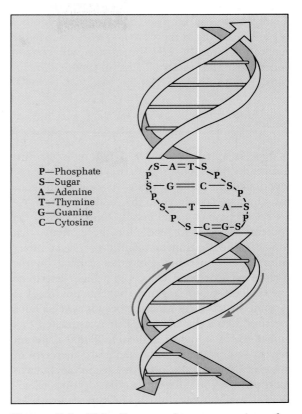

P—Phosphate
S—Sugar
A—Adenine
T—Thymine
G—Guanine
C—Cytosine

Figure 3.1 This diagrammatic representation of a portion of a deoxyribonucleic acid (DNA) molecule represents the double helix strands and the connecting nitrogenous base pairs. The helix strands are formed by alternating sugar and phosphate groups. The connection is produced by complementary bases—adenine, cytosine, guanine, and thymine—as shown for a section of the molecule.

theory, was produced. Interestingly, Mendel's work was generally ignored until it was rediscovered at the turn of the century. Since then, the function of genes has been fairly well known, even though no one really knew what genes were until quite recently.

DNA

In 1953, James Watson and Francis Crick discovered that genes are actually portions of molecules of deoxyribonucleic acid, or **DNA**. DNA is a complex

DNA: The genetic material—deoxyribonucleic acid; a complex molecule with information to direct the synthesis of proteins. DNA molecules have the unique property of being able to produce exact copies of themselves.

molecule with an unusual shape, rather like two strands of a rope twisted around one another (Figure 3.1). The way that smaller molecules are arranged in this giant molecule is actually a code that contains information to direct the production of proteins. It is at this level that the development of certain traits occurs. The code directs the formation of such things as the protein that colors the iris of the eye (thereby determining eye color) or the hemoglobin molecule in red blood cells. Recently there has been great progress in cracking the genetic code, in a series of events as fascinating as any spy story.

DNA molecules have the unique property of being able to produce exact copies of themselves.

Thus a copy can be made and passed to another organism; as long as there are no errors made in the replication process, new organisms will contain genetic material exactly like that in ancestral organisms.

GENES

A gene is a segment of the DNA molecule that directs the development of particular observable or identifiable traits. Thus, when we speak of the gene for a human blood type in the A–B–O system, we are referring to the portion of a DNA molecule that contains the genetic code for the proteins that result in the attachment of different sugar molecules to certain other molecules carried on the surface of red blood cells, and which determine one's blood type. A gene, then, is not really a separate structure, as had once been imagined, but a location, like a dot on a map. It is estimated that human DNA contains at least 100,000 different genes. Interestingly, only about 10 percent of human DNA encodes proteins. As Jerold Lowenstein puts it, our DNA, ". . . like daytime television, is nine-tenths junk."[1] The genes themselves are split by long stretches of this "junk" DNA which, in the course of producing proteins, is metaphorically "snipped out" and left on the "cutting room floor."

CHROMOSOMES

DNA molecules do not float freely about in our bodies; they are located on structures called **chromosomes** found in the nucleus of each cell. Chromosomes are probably nothing more than long

[1] Jerold M. Lowenstein, "Genetic Surprises," *Discover* 13(12), December, 1992, p. 86.

Alleles: Alternate forms of a single gene.

strands of DNA combined with protein to produce structures that can actually be seen under a conventional light microscope. Each kind of organism has a characteristic number of chromosomes, which are usually found in pairs. For example, the body cells of the fruit fly each contain four pairs of chromosomes, those of humans contain 23 pairs, those of some brine shrimp have as many as 160 pairs. The two chromosomes in each pair contain genes for the same traits. The gene for eye color, for instance, will be found on each chromosome of a particular pair, but there may be variant forms of these genes. One might be for brown and the other for blue eyes. Forms of genes that are located on paired chromosomes and that code for different versions of the same trait are called **alleles.**

CELL DIVISION

In order to grow and maintain good health, the body cells of an organism must divide and produce new cells. Cell division is initiated when the chromosomes, and hence the genes, replicate, forming a second pair that duplicates the original pair of chromosomes in the nucleus. This new pair then separates from the original pair, is surrounded by a membrane, and becomes the nucleus that directs the activities of a new cell. This kind of cell division is called **mitosis,** and it produces new cells that have exactly the same number of chromosome pairs, and hence genes, as did the parent cell.

When new individuals are produced through sexual reproduction, the process involves the merging of two cells, one from each parent. If two regular body cells, each containing 23 pairs of chromosomes, were to merge, the result would be a

Chromosome: In the cell nucleus, long strands of DNA combined with a protein which can be seen under the microscope.

Mitosis: A kind of cell division which produces new cells having exactly the same number of chromosome pairs, and hence genes, as the parent cell.

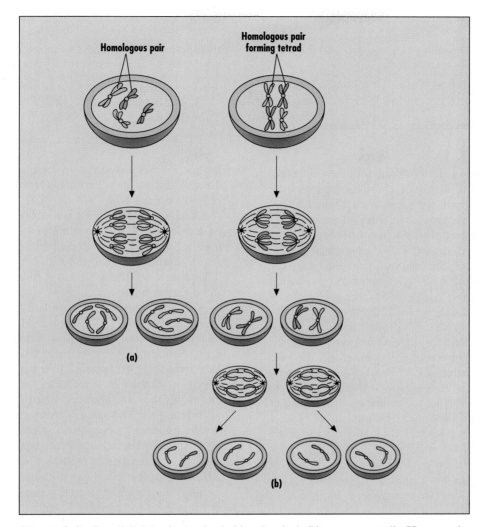

Figure 3.2 In cell division both mitosis (a) and meiosis (b) create new cells. However, in mitosis the new cell has the same number of chromosomes as the parent cell, while in meiosis there are half of the chromosomes. Chromosomes in blue originally came from one parent, those in pink from the other.

new individual with 46 pairs of chromosomes; such an individual, if it lived at all, would surely be a monster. But this increase in chromosome number never occurs, because the sex cells that join to form a new individual are the product of a different kind of cell division, called **meiosis.**

Although meiosis begins like mitosis, with the replication and doubling of the original genes and chromosomes, it proceeds to divide that number into four new cells rather than two (Figure 3.2). Thus each new cell has only half the number of chromosomes with their genes found in the parent cell. Human eggs and sperm, for example, have only

23 single chromosomes (half of a pair), whereas body cells have 23 pairs, or 46 chromosomes.

The process of meiotic division has important implications for genetics. Since paired chromosomes are separated, two different types of new

Meiosis: A kind of cell division which produces the sex cells, each of which has half the number of chromosomes, and hence genes, as the parent cell.

Homozygous: Describing a chromosome pair that bears identical alleles for a single gene.

Heterozygous: Describing a chromosome pair that bears different alleles for a single gene.

Phenotype: The physical appearance of an organism which may or may not reflect its genotype because the latter may include recessive alleles.

Genotype: The actual genetic composition of an organism.

cells will be formed; two of the four new cells will have one half of a pair of chromosomes, and the other two will have the second half of the original chromosome pair. Of course, this will not make any difference if the original pair was **homozygous**, or identical in genetic material. For example, if in both chromosomes of the original pair the gene for blood type in the A–B–O system was represented by the allele for Type A blood, then all new cells will have the "A" allele. But if the original pair was **heterozygous**, with the "A" allele on one chromosome and the allele for Type O blood on the other, then half of the new cells will contain only the "O" allele; the offspring have a 50–50 chance of getting either one. It is impossible to predict any single individual's genotype, or genetic composition, but statistical probabilities can be established.

What happens when a child inherits the allele for Type O blood from one parent and that for Type A from the other? Will the child have blood of Type A, O, or some mixture of the two? Many of these questions were answered by Mendel's original experiments.

Mendel discovered that certain alleles are able to mask the presence of others; one allele is dominant, whereas the other is recessive. Actually, it is the traits that are dominant or recessive, rather than the alleles themselves; geneticists merely speak of dominant and recessive alleles for the sake of convenience. Thus, one might speak of the allele for Type A blood as being dominant to the one for Type O. An individual whose blood type genes are heterozygous, with one "A" and one "O" allele, will have Type A blood. Thus the heterozygous condition (AO) will show exactly the same physical characteristic, or **phenotype**, as the homozygous AA, even though the two have a somewhat different genetic composition, or **genotype**. Only the homozygous recessive genotype (OO) will show the phenotype of Type O blood.

The dominance of one allele does not mean that

the recessive one is lost or in some way blended. A Type A heterozygous parent (AO) will produce sex cells containing both "A" and "O" alleles. Recessive alleles, such as that for albinism in humans, can be handed down for generations before they are matched with another recessive in the process of sexual reproduction and show up in the phenotype. The presence of the dominant allele simply renders the recessive allele inactive.

All of the traits Mendel studied in garden peas showed this dominant–recessive relationship, and so for some years it was believed that this was the only relationship possible. Later studies, however, have indicated that patterns of inheritance are not always so simple. In some cases, neither allele is dominant; they are both codominant. An example of codominance in human heredity can be seen also in the inheritance of blood types. Type A is produced by one allele, Type B by another. A heterozygous individual will have a phenotype of AB, since neither allele can dominate the other.

The inheritance of blood types points out another complexity of heredity. The number of alleles is by no means limited to two; certain traits seem to have three or more allelic genes. Of course, only one allele can appear on each of the pairs of chromosomes, so each individual is limited to two alleles.

Another relatively recent discovery is the fact that dominance need not always be complete. This is the case with the alleles for normal **hemoglobin** (the protein that carries oxygen in the red blood cells) and the abnormal hemoglobin that is respon-

Hemoglobin: The protein that carries oxygen in the red blood cells.

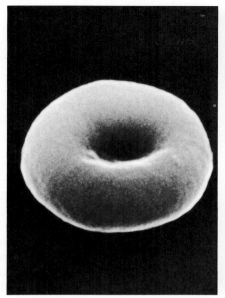 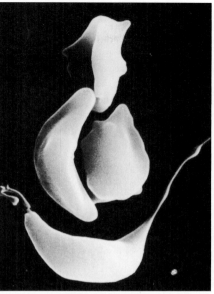

Sickle-cell anemia is caused by an abnormal hemoglobin, called "hemoglobin S." Those afflicted by the disease are homozygous for the allele S; heterozygotes are not afflicted. Shown are a normal red blood cell (left) and the sickle-shaped cells of the abnormal hemoglobin (right).

sible for **sickle-cell anemia** in humans. Sickle-cell anemia occurs in individuals who are homozygous for a particular allele. In those with two such alleles, the red blood cells take on a characteristic sickle shape which, because they are more rapidly removed from circulation than normal cells, leads to anemia. To compound the problem, the sickle cells tend to clump together, blocking the capillaries and causing tissue damage. Such individuals normally die before reaching adulthood. The homozygous dominant condition ($Hb^A Hb^A$; normal hemoglobin is known as hemoglobin A, not to be confused with blood type A) produces only normal molecules of hemoglobin while the heterozygous condition ($Hb^A Hb^S$) produces some normal and abnormal molecules; except under low-oxygen conditions, such individuals suffer no ill effects. The normal seems dominant to the abnormal, but the dominance is incomplete, and therefore the other allele is not completely inactive. It is now believed that many instances in which phenotypes appear to indicate complete dominance may show incomplete dominance on the molecular level. We shall return to the sickle-cell condition later, for we now know that under certain conditions the heterozygous condition is actually more advantageous than is the "normal" homozygous condition.

POLYGENES

So far, we have spoken as if the traits of organisms are single-gene traits; that is, the alleles of one particular gene determine one particular trait. Certainly this is the case with the A–B–O blood groups and some other things, but in humans, the most obvious traits are usually not single-gene traits. Skin color, for example, is programmed by the action of many genes, each of which produces a small effect. Such genes are called **polygenes**, two or more genes (as opposed to just two or more alleles) that work together to affect some phenotypic character. Because so many genes are involved, each of which may have alternative alleles, it is difficult to unravel the genetic underpinnings of a trait like skin color. Theoretically, the observed

Sickle-cell anemia: An inherited form of anemia caused by the red blood cells assuming a sickled shape.

Polygenes: Two or more genes that work together to affect some phenotypic character.

range of variation in human skin color seems to require the presence of at least three, if not as many as six, separate genes, each of which produces a small additive effect.

POPULATION GENETICS

At the level of the individual, the study of genetics indicates the way that traits are transmitted from one generation to the next and enables a prediction about the chances that any given individual will display some phenotypic characteristic. At the level of the group, the study of genetics takes on additional significance, revealing mechanisms that support evolutionary interpretations of the diversity of life.

A key concept in genetics is that of the **population**, or a group of individuals that can and does interbreed. It is on the population level that natural selection takes place, as some members of the population produce more than their share of the next generation, while others produce less than their share. Thus, over a period of generations, the population shows a measure of adaptation to its environment due to this evolutionary mechanism.

THE STABILITY OF THE POPULATION

In theory, the characteristics of any given population should remain remarkably stable. And indeed, generation after generation, the bullfrogs in my farm pond, for example, look much alike, have the

Population: In biology, a group of similar individuals that can and do interbreed.

Gene pool: The total genes of a population.

same calls, exhibit the same behavior when breeding. Another way to look at this remarkable consistency is to say that the **gene pool** of the population —the total number of different genes and alleles— seems to remain the same.

The theoretical stability of the gene pool of a population is not only easy to observe; it is also easy to understand. Mendel's experiments with garden peas, and all subsequent genetic experiments as well, have shown that, although some alleles may be dominant to others, the recessive alleles are not just lost or destroyed. Statistically, a heterozygous individual has a 50 percent chance of passing on to the next generation the dominant allele; he or she also has a 50 percent chance of passing on the recessive allele. The recessive allele may again be masked by the presence of a dominant allele in the next generation, but it is there nonetheless, and will be passed on again.

Since alleles are not just "lost" in the process of reproduction, the frequency with which certain ones occur in the population should remain exactly the same from one generation to the next. The **Hardy–Weinberg Principle**, named for the English mathematician and German physician who worked it out in 1908, demonstrates algebraically that the percentage of individuals that are homozygous for the dominant allele, homozygous for the recessive allele, and heterozygous will remain the same from one generation to the next provided that certain specified conditions are met. These are that mating is entirely random, that the population is sufficiently large for statistical averages to express themselves, that no new variants will be introduced

Hardy–Weinberg Principle: Demonstrates algebraically that the percentage of individuals that are homozygous for the dominant allele, homozygous for the recessive allele, and heterozygous should remain constant from one generation to the next, provided that certain specified conditions are met.

Evolution: A heritable change in genotype which becomes effective in the gene pool of a population.

---

into the population's gene pool, and that all individuals are equally successful at surviving and reproducing. In real life, however, these conditions are rarely met, as geographical, physiological, or behavioral factors may favor matings between certain individuals over others, as populations—on islands, for example—may be quite small, as new genetic variants may be introduced through mutation or gene flow, and as natural selection may favor the carriers of some alleles over others. Thus, changes in the gene pools of populations, without which there could be no evolution, can and do take place. Formally defined, **evolution** is a heritable change in genotype which becomes effective in the gene pool of a population.

FACTORS FOR CHANGE

MUTATION

The ultimate source of change is **mutation** of genes. This amounts to an alteration of a gene that produces a new allele, one not inherited from an ancestor, but that is heritable by descendants. Although mutation rarely occurs, the large number of genes in each individual sex cell, the large number of sex cells produced (the human male ejaculates hundreds of millions of sperm cells at a single time), and the large number of individuals in a population mean that there will always be new mutant genes.

Geneticists have calculated the rate at which various types of mutant genes appear. In the human

---

Mutation: Chemical alteration of a gene that produces a new allele.

---

population, they run from a low of about five mutations per million sex cells formed, in the case of a gene abnormality that leads to the absence of an iris in the eye, to a high of about 100 per million, in the case of a gene involved in a form of muscular dystrophy. The average is about 30 mutants per million. Although mutations sometimes produce marked abnormalities, the great majority of them produce more subtle effects.

Research with viruses and bacteria indicates that certain factors increase the rate at which mutations occur. These include certain chemicals, such as some dyes and also some antibiotics; some chemicals used in the preservation of food also have this property. Another important cause of increased mutation rates is irradiation. The ultraviolet rays of sunshine are capable of producing mutations, as are X-rays. Radioactive rays have the same mutation-causing effect, as was so sadly demonstrated by the high rates of mutation found in the children of survivors of the bombings of Hiroshima and Nagasaki.

In humans, as in all multicelled animals, the very nature of the genetic material itself ensures that mutations will occur. For instance, the fact that genes are split by stretches of "junk" DNA increases the chances that a simple editing mistake in the process of copying DNA will cause significant gene mutations. To cite one example, the gene for collagen (the main structural protein of the skin, bones, and teeth) is fragmented by no less than 50 segments of "junk" DNA. As a consequence, there are 50 chances for error each time the gene is copied. One result of this seemingly inefficient, if not dangerous state of affairs, is that it becomes possible to shuffle the gene segments themselves like a deck of cards, putting together new proteins with new functions. Although individuals may suffer as a result (the French artist Henri Toulouse-Lautrec's growth abnormality resulted from a mutation of the collagen gene), it does make it possible for an evolving species to adapt more quickly to a new environment. Another source of genetic remodeling from within is the movement of whole DNA sequences from one locality or chromosome to another. This may disrupt the function of other genes or, in the case of so-called "jumping genes," carry important functional messages of their own.

It is important to realize that mutations do not arise out of need for some new adaptation. Indeed, there is no tendency for the frequency of a particular mutation to correlate with the direction in which a population is evolving. They are purely chance events; what happens once they appear depends on whether or not they happen (by chance) to enhance the survival and reproductive success of the individuals who carry them.

GENETIC DRIFT

Each individual is subject to a number of chance events that determine life or death. For example, an individual squirrel in good health and possessed of a number of advantageous traits may be killed in a forest fire; a genetically superior baby cougar may not live longer than a day if its mother gets caught in an avalanche, whereas the weaker offspring of a mother that does not may survive. In a large population, such accidents of nature are unimportant; the accidents that preserve individuals with certain genes will be balanced out by the accidents that destroy them. However, in small populations, such averaging out may not be possible. Since human populations are so large, we might suppose that human beings are unaffected by chance events. While it is true that a rock slide which kills five campers whose home community has a total population of 100,000 is not statistically significant, a rock slide which killed five hunters from a small group of food foragers could significantly alter frequencies of alleles in the local gene pool. The average size of local groups of modern food foragers (people who hunt, fish, and gather other wild foods for subsistence) varies between about 25 and 50.

Another sort of chance event may occur when an existing population splits up into two or more new ones, especially if one of these new populations is founded by a particularly small number of individuals. What this amounts to is a sampling error; in such cases, it is unlikely that the gene frequencies of the smaller population will duplicate those of the larger population.

The effect of chance events on the gene pool of small populations is called **genetic drift**. Genetic drift plays an important role in causing the sometimes bizarre characteristics found in animals in isolated island populations. It is also likely to have been an important factor in human evolution,

Genetic drift, in the form of "sampling error," is responsible for the appearance of many exotic forms of life on oceanic islands, such as these marine iguanas on the Galapagos Islands.

Genetic drift: Chance fluctuations of allele frequencies in the gene pool of a population.

because until 10,000 years ago all humans were food foragers, who probably lived in relatively small, self-contained populations.

GENE FLOW

Another factor that brings change to the gene pool of a population is **gene flow**, or the introduction of new genes from nearby populations. Gene flow occurs when previously separated groups are once again able to interbreed, as, for example, when a river that once separated two populations of small mammals changes course. Migration of individuals or groups into the territory occupied by others may also lead to gene flow. This has been observed in several North American rodents that have been forced to leave their territory due to changes in

Gene flow: The introduction of alleles from the gene pool of one population into that of another.

In Central America, gene flow between Native Americans (upper left), Spaniards (upper right), and Africans (lower left) has led to the emergence of a new phenotype (lower right).

environmental conditions. Gene flow has been an important factor in human evolution, both in terms of early hominine groups and in terms of current racial variation. For example, the last 400 years have seen the establishment of a new phenotype throughout much of Central and South America as a result of the introduction into the gene pool of Indians native to the area of genes from both the Spanish colonists and the Africans whom Europeans imported as slaves.

NATURAL SELECTION

Although the factors listed above may produce change in a population, that change would not necessarily make the population better adapted to its biological and social environment. By **adaptation** is meant both a process, by which organisms achieve a beneficial adjustment to an available environment, and the results of that process, the characteristics of organisms that fit them to the particu-

Adaptation: A process by which organisms achieve a beneficial adjustment to an available environment, and the results of that process, the characteristics of organisms that fit them to the particular set of conditions of the environment in which they are generally found.

lar set of conditions of the environment in which they are generally found. Genetic drift, for example, often produces strange characteristics that have no survival value; mutant genes may be either helpful or harmful to survival, or just plain neutral. It is the action of natural selection that makes evolutionary change adaptive.

Natural selection refers to the evolutionary process through which the environment exerts pressure that selects some individuals and not others to reproduce the next generation of the

CHARLES R. DARWIN

(1809–1882)

Grandson of Erasmus Darwin (a physician, scientist, poet, and originator of a theory of evolution himself), Charles Darwin began the study of medicine at the University of Edinburgh. Finding himself unfitted for this profession, he then went to Christ's College, Cambridge, to study theology. On completion of his studies there, he took the position of naturalist and companion to Captain Robert Fitzroy on the HMS *Beagle,* which was about to embark on an expedition to various poorly mapped parts of the world. The voyage lasted almost five years, taking Darwin along the coasts of South America, over to the Galapagos Islands, across the Pacific to Australia, and then across the Indian and Atlantic Oceans back to South America before returning to England.

The observations he made on this voyage, and the arguments he had with the orthodox and dogmatic Fitzroy, had a powerful influence on the development of the ideas which culminated in Darwin's most famous book, *On the Origin of Species*, which was published in 1859.

Contrary to what a lot of people seem to think, Darwin did not "discover" or "invent" evolution. The general idea of evolution had been put forward by a number of writers, including his grandfather, long before Darwin's time. Nor is evolution a single theory, as some people seem to think, any more than gravity is a single theory. To be sure, there are competing theories of gravity—the Newtonian and Einsteinian—that seek to explain its workings; nevertheless,

the evidence in favor of gravity is overwhelming, even though there ar[e] competing theories that seek to expl[ain] how it works.

Darwin's contribution was one s[uch] theory, that of evolution through natural selection. His was the theory that was best able to account both fo[r] changes within species and for the emergence of new species in purely naturalistic terms. As is usually the c[ase] with pioneering ventures, there wer[e] flaws in Darwin's original theory. Today, we can say that Darwin's bas[ic] idea has stood the test of scientific scrutiny remarkably well, and that [the] evidence in its favor is about as goo[d as] we had for the theory that the earth [is] spherical, until we were able to put [up] an astronaut who could see with his own eyes that this is indeed the case[.]

Natural selection: The evolutionary process through which factors in the environment exert pressure that favors some individuals over others to produce the next generation.

---

group. In other words, instead of a completely random selection of individuals whose traits will be passed on to the next generation, there is selection by the forces of nature. In the process, the frequency of genetic variants for harmful or maladaptive traits within the population is reduced while the frequency of genetic variants for adaptive traits is increased.

In popular writing, natural selection is often equated with the "survival of the fittest," in which the weak and the unfit are eliminated from the population by disease, predation, or starvation. Obviously, the survival of the fittest has some bearing on natural selection; one need hardly point out that the dead do not reproduce. But there may be many cases in which individuals survive but do not reproduce. They may be incapable of attracting mates, or they may be sterile, or they may produce offspring that do not survive after birth. For example, among the Uganda Kob, a kind of antelope

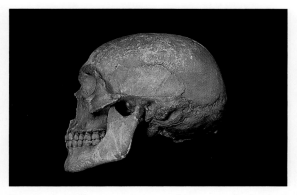 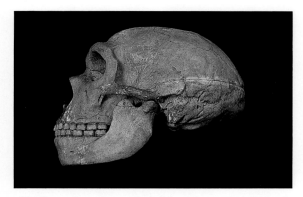

Despite the different appearance of these two skulls, the brain housed in the modern one on the left is no larger than the brain in the ca. 50,000-year-old skull on the right.

native to east Africa, males that are unable to attract females form all-male herds in which they live out their lives. As members of a herd, they are reasonably well protected against predators, and so they may survive to relatively ripe old ages. They do not, however, pass their genes on to succeeding generations. This is an instance of natural selection at work, leading to different rates of reproduction for different types of individuals within a population. Change brought about by natural selection in the frequency with which certain genes appear in a population is actually a very slow process. For example, the present frequency of the sickle-cell allele is .05 percent in the entire U.S. population. A 5 percent reduction per generation (about 25 years) would take about 2000 years to reach a frequency of .01, assuming complete selection against those homozygous for the allele. Yet given the great time span involved—life on earth has existed for three to four billion years—even such small and slow changes will have a significant cumulative impact on both the genotypes and phenotypes of any population.

Natural selection, as it acts to promote change in gene frequencies, is referred to as **directional selection.** Another form it may take is **stabilizing**

Directional selection: Natural selection as it acts to promote change in a population's gene pool.

Stabilizing selection: Natural selection as it acts to promote stability, rather than change in a population's gene pool.

selection, in which it acts to promote stability, rather than change. This occurs in populations which are already well adapted, or at least where change would be disadvantageous. In humans, for instance, there has been no significant increase in brain size for the last 100,000 years or so. Stabilizing selection seems to be operating here, as the human birth canal is not adequate for the birth of larger-brained offspring. In cases where change is disadvantageous, natural selection will favor the retention of gene frequencies as they are. For this reason, the evolutionary history of most forms of life is not one of constant change, proceeding as a steady, stately progression over vast periods of time; rather, it is one of prolonged periods of stability punctuated by shorter periods of change (or extinction) when altered conditions require new adaptations.

Discussions of the action of natural selection typically focus on anatomical or structural changes, such as the evolutionary change in the types of teeth found in primates; ample evidence (fossilized teeth, for example) exists to interpret such changes. By extrapolation, biologists assume that the same mechanisms work on behavioral traits as well. It seems reasonable that a hive of bees capable of

The moths shown in these two pictures are varieties of a single species. While the mottled brown variant is well camouflaged on relatively clean tree trunks, it is readily visible on sooty tree trunks. The reverse is true for the black variant, which became especially common when coal fueled British industry.

communicating the location of nectar-bearing flowers would have a significant survival advantage over those that must search for food by trial and error. Natural selection of behavioral and social traits was probably a particularly important influence on hominid evolution, since in the primates, social mechanisms began to replace physical structures for foodgetting, defense, and mate attraction.

Many anthropologists point out the close parallel between biological and cultural evolution, and therefore they postulate that a process of natural selection continues to work on cultural traits within a society. By inventing better tools, more efficient means of organization, and the like, humans may make life significantly easier for themselves. As a result, selective pressures are reduced, reproduction becomes easier, more offspring survive than before, and so populations grow. Because culture is learned rather than biologically inherited, cultural evolution can take place much more rapidly than biological evolution.

ADAPTATION

As a consequence of the process of natural selection, those populations that do not become extinct generally become well adapted to their environments. Anyone who has ever looked carefully at the plants and animals that survive in the deserts of the western United States can cite many instances of adaptation. For example, members of the cactus family have extensive root networks close to the

surface of the soil, enabling them to soak up the slightest bit of moisture; they are able to store large quantities of water whenever it is available; they are shaped so as to expose the smallest possible surface to the dry air and are generally leafless as adults, thereby preventing water loss through evaporation, and a covering of spines discourages animals from chewing into the juicy flesh of the plant.

Desert animals are also adapted to their environment. The kangaroo rat can survive without drinking water; many reptiles live in burrows where the temperature is lower; most animals are nocturnal, or active only in the cool of the night. Many of the stories traditionally offered to explain observable cases of adaptation rely heavily on the purposeful acts of a world creator. The legend of Coyote and Wishpoosh (Chapter 1) is one such example; the belief popular among Europeans early in the nineteenth century that God created each animal separately to occupy a specific place in a hierarchical ladder of being is another.

The adaptability of organic structures and functions, no matter how much a source of wonder and fascination, nevertheless falls short of perfection. This is so because natural selection can only work with what the existing store of genetic variation provides; it cannot create something entirely new. That exquisite design is often not the rule is illustrated by the pains of aching backs and the annoyances of hernias that we humans must put up with because the body of a four-footed vertebrate, designed for horizontal posture, has been "jury rigged" to be held vertically above the two hind limbs. Furthermore, the structural alterations that

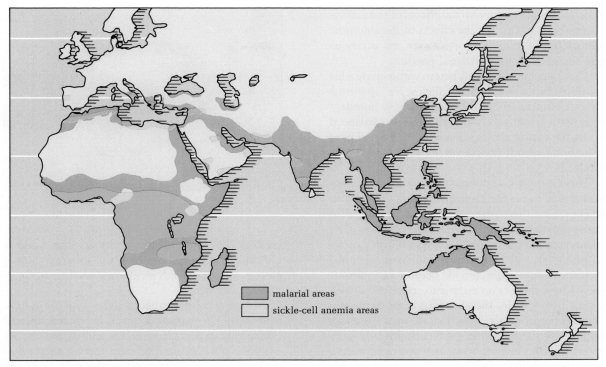

Figure 3.3   The allele that, in homozygotes, causes sickle-cell anemia makes heterozygotes resistant to the ill effects of falciparum malaria. Thus, the allele is most common in populations native to regions where this form of malaria is common.

enable us to walk erect have made it more difficult than it is for any other species of mammal to bear offspring. Yet, these defects have been perpetuated by natural selection, because they are outweighed by other aspects of human adaptation that enhance the reproductive success of the species as a whole.

THE CASE OF SICKLE-CELL ANEMIA

Among human beings, a particularly well-studied case of an adaptation paid for by the misery of many individuals brings us back to the case of sickle-cell anemia. Sickle-cell anemia first came to the attention of geneticists when it was observed that most North Americans who suffer from it are black. Investigation traced the abnormality to populations that live in a clearly defined belt throughout central Africa (although brought to North America from central Africa, the abnormality also exists in some non-African populations, as will be noted below).

Geneticists were curious to know why such a deleterious hereditary disability persisted in these populations. According to the theory of natural selection, any alleles that are harmful will tend to disappear from the group, since the individuals who are homozygous for the abnormality generally die —are "selected out"—before they are able to reproduce. Why, then, had this seemingly harmful condition remained in populations from central Africa?

The answer to this mystery began to emerge when it was noticed that the areas in which sickle-cell anemia is prevalent are also areas in which falciparum malaria is common (Figure 3.3). This severe form of malaria causes high fevers which significantly interfere with the reproductive abilities of those who do not actually die from the disease. Moreover, it was discovered that the same hemoglobin abnormalities are found in residents of parts of the Arabian Peninsula, Greece, Algeria, and Syria, as well as in certain East Indians, all of whom also live in regions where falciparum malaria is common. Further research established that the abnormal hemoglobin was associated with an increased ability to survive the effects of the malarial parasite; it seems that the effects of the abnormal hemoglobin in limited amounts were less injurious than the effects of the malarial parasite.

Thus, selection favored heterozygous individuals ($Hb^A Hb^S$). The loss of alleles for abnormal hemoglobin caused by the death of those homozygous for it (from sickle-cell anemia) was balanced out by the loss of alleles for normal hemoglobin, as those homozygous for it experienced reproductive failure.

This example also points out how specific adaptations tend to be; the abnormal hemoglobin was an adaptation to the particular parts of the world in which the malarial parasite flourished. When Africans adapted to that region moved to North America, where falciparum malaria is unknown, what had been an adaptive characteristic became an injurious one. Where there is no malaria to attack those with normal hemoglobin, the abnormal hemoglobin becomes comparatively disadvantageous. Although the rates of sickle-cell trait are still relatively high among North American blacks—about 9 percent show the sickling trait—this represents a significant decline from the approximately 22 percent who are estimated to have shown the trait when the first slaves were brought from Africa. A further decline over the next several generations is to be expected, as selection pressure continues to work against it.

This example also points out the important role culture may play even with respect to biological adaptation. In West Africa, falciparum malaria was not a significant problem until humans abandoned food foraging for farming a few thousand years ago. In order to farm, they had to clear areas of the natural forest cover. In the forest, decaying vegetation on the forest floor had imparted an absorbent quality to the ground so that the heavy rainfall of the region rapidly soaked into the soil. But once stripped of its natural vegetation, the soil lost this quality. Furthermore, the forest canopy was no longer there to break the force of the rainfall, and so the impact of the heavy rains tended to compact the soil further. The result was that stagnant puddles commonly formed after rains, and these were perfect for the breeding purposes of mosquitoes. Mosquitoes then began to flourish, and it is mosquitoes that carry the malarial parasite and inflict it on humans. Thus, humans unwittingly

This X ray illustrates the unusually large size of a Kiwi's egg.

created the kind of environment that made a hitherto disadvantageous trait, the abnormal hemoglobin associated with sickle-cell anemia, advantageous.

Although it is true that all living organisms have many adaptive characteristics, it is not true that all characteristics are adaptive. All male mammals, for example, possess nipples, even though they serve no useful purpose. To female mammals, however, nipples are essential to reproductive success, which is why males have them. The two sexes are not separate entities, shaped independently by natural selection, but are variants upon a single ground plan, elaborated in later embryology. Precursors of mammary glands are built in all mammalian fetuses, enlarging later in the development of females, but remaining small and without function in males.

Nor is it true that current utility is a reliable guide to historical origin. For one thing, nonadaptive characters may be coopted for later utility following origins as developmental consequences of changing patterns in embryonic and postnatal growth. The unusually large size of the Kiwi egg, for example, enhances the survivability of Kiwi chicks, in that they are particularly large and capable when hatched. Nevertheless, Kiwi eggs probably did not evolve because they are adaptive. Kiwis evolved from large, Moa-sized ancestors, and in birds, egg size reduces at a slower rate than does body size. Therefore, the out-sized eggs of Kiwi birds seem to be no more than a developmental byproduct of a reduction in body size.[2] Similarly,

[2] Stephen Jay Gould, *Bully for Brontosaurus* (New York: W.W. Norton, 1991), pp. 109–123.

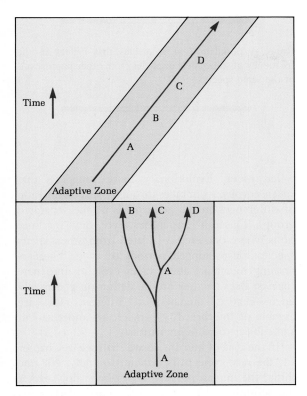

Figure 3.4 Linear evolution (top) occurs when relatively small-scale changes accumulate over time gradually transforming an old species into a new one. Divergent evolution (bottom) occurs as different populations became reproductively isolated resulting in an increase in the number of species.

an existing adaptation may come under strong selective pressure for some new purpose, as did insect wings. These did not arise that insects might fly, but rather as devices useful in regulating body temperature. Later, the larger ones by chance proved useful for purposes of flight.

EVOLUTION OF POPULATIONS

One consequence of the process of natural selection is that a population may become increasingly well adapted to its environment. This kind of evolutionary change can be thought of as a refinement of the organism. As it moves from the rather generalized prototype to more and more specialized versions, the organism becomes better and better adapted; each new "model" replaces the old, in a process somewhat analogous to the changes that

have been made to automobiles since their first appearance. Still, a car remains a car, no matter how "improved" the latest model may have become; it has not been transformed into something radically different. The same principle holds for **linear evolution** (Fig. 3.4 top). Ultimately, stabilizing selection is likely to take over, as available alleles reach their most adaptive frequencies in a species' gene pool.

Alternatively, a species may become extinct if it becomes too well adapted. If the environment changes for some reason, those organisms most highly adapted to the old environment will have the greatest difficulty surviving in a new one. It appears that such changes took place a number of times during the course of vertebrate evolution; one of the most dramatic examples was the sudden extinction of the dinosaurs. In such cases, it is usually the more generalized organisms that survive; later they may give rise to new lines of specialists.

But not all evolution is a linear progression from one form to more specialized forms of the same type. Evolution is also **divergent**, or branching (Figure 3.4 bottom). This happens when a single ancestral species gives rise to two or more descendant species. Divergent evolution is probably responsible for much of the diversity of life observed today. Evolution may also be **convergent**, when two dissimilar forms develop greater similarities, birds and bats, for example. Convergent evolution takes place in circumstances where an environment exerts similar pressures on different organisms, so that unrelated species become more like one another. Because evolution can take so many different courses, it is often difficult to reconstruct the sequence of events that led to the emergence of any

Linear evolution: The gradual transformation of an old species into a new one, as small-scale changes accumulate over time.

Divergent evolution: An evolutionary process in which an ancestral population gives rise to two or more descendant populations that differ from one another.

Convergent evolution: A process in which two phylogenetically unrelated organisms develop greater similarities.

given group or species, especially when that evidence, such as fossil remains, is often fragmentary and incomplete. We are fortunate, though, in that the fossil record for human evolution is particularly rich.

SPECIATION

Both linear and divergent evolution can result in the establishment of a new **species**. The term "species" is usually defined as a population or group of populations that is mechanically capable of interbreeding and reproductively isolated from other such populations. Thus the bullfrogs in my farm pond are the same species as those in my neighbor's pond, even though the two populations may never actually interbreed; in theory, they are capable of it if they are brought together. This definition is not altogether satisfactory, because isolated populations may be in the process of evolving into different species, and it is hard to tell exactly when they become separate. For example, all dogs belong to the same species, but a male Saint Bernard and a female Chihuahua are not capable of producing offspring; even if they could somehow manage the feat of copulation, the Chihuahua would die trying to give birth to such large pups. On the other hand, Alaskan sled dogs are able to breed with wolves, even though they are of different species. In nature, however, wolves most often mate with their own kind. Although all species definitions are relative rather than absolute, the modern concept of species puts more stress on the question of whether breeding actually takes place in the wild than on the more academic question of whether breeding is technically feasible.

Populations within species that are quite capable of interbreeding but may not regularly do so are

Race: A population of a species that differs in the frequency of some allele or alleles from other populations of the same species.

called **races**. Evolutionary theory suggests that species evolve from races through the accumulation of differences in the gene pools of the separated groups. This can happen, however, only in situations where one race is isolated from others of its species for prolonged periods of time. There is nothing inevitable about races evolving into new species. Because they are by definition genetically open—that is, members of different races are capable of interbreeding—races are impermanent and subject to reamalgamation.

In the case of humans, as we shall see in Chapter 11, the race concept is difficult to apply. For one thing, the human propensity for gene flow makes the definition of biological races particularly arbitrary; for another, there has been a deplorable tendency to mix cultural with biological phenomena under the heading of "race."

ISOLATING MECHANISMS

Certain factors, known as **isolating mechanisms**, separate breeding populations, leading to the appearance first of divergent races and then divergent species. This happens as mutations may appear in one of the isolated populations but not in the other, as genetic drift affects the two populations in different ways, and as selective pressures may come to differ slightly in the two places. Because isolation prevents gene flow, changes that affect the gene

Species: In biology, a population or group of populations that is capable of interbreeding, but that is reproductively isolated from other such populations.

Isolating mechanisms: Factors that separate breeding populations, creating divergent races and then divergent species.

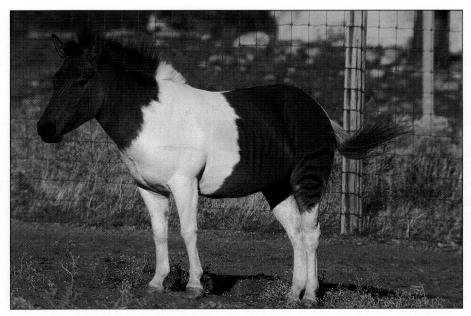

Although zebras and ponies can produce live offspring like the one shown here, sterility of the offspring maintains the reproductive isolation of the parental species.

pool of one population cannot be introduced into the gene pool of the other.

Some isolating mechanisms are geographical, preventing gene flow between members of separated populations as a result of traveling individuals or bands. Anatomical structure can also serve as an isolating mechanism, as we saw in the case of the Saint Bernard and the Chihuahua. Other physical isolating factors include early miscarriage of the offspring, weakness or presence of maladaptive traits that cause early death in the offspring, or, as in the case of horses and asses, sterility of the hybrid offspring (mules).

Although physical barriers to reproduction may develop in geographical isolation, as genetic differences accumulate in the gene pools of separate populations, they may also result from accidents in the course of meiosis. In the course of such accidents genetic material may be broken off, transposed, or transferred from one chromosome to another. Even a relatively minor mutation, if it involves a gene that regulates the growth and development of an organism, may have a major effect on its adult form.

Isolating mechanisms may also be social rather than physical. Speciation due to this mechanism is particularly common among birds. For example, cuckoos (birds that do not build nests of their own but lay their eggs in other birds' nests) attract mates by mimicking the song of the bird species whose nests they borrow; thus cuckoos that are physically capable of mating may have different courtship behavior, which effectively isolates them from others of their kind.

Social isolating mechanisms are thought to have been important factors in human evolution. They continue to play a part in the maintenance of so-called racial barriers. Although mating is physically possible between any two mature humans of the opposite sex, the awareness of social and cultural differences often makes the idea distasteful, perhaps even unthinkable; in India, for example, someone of an upper caste would not think of marrying an "untouchable." This isolation results from the culturally implanted concept of a significant difference between "us" and "them." Yet, as evidenced by the blending of human populations that has so often taken place in the world, people are also capable of reasoning away social isolating mechanisms that would, in the case of other animals, lead separate races to evolve into separate species. Such speciation is very unlikely in *Homo sapiens.*

THE NONDIRECTEDNESS OF EVOLUTION

In the popular mind, evolution is often seen as leading in a predictable and determined way from one-celled organisms, through various multicelled forms, to humans, who occupy the top rung of a "ladder of progress." The fallacy of this notion is neatly made clear by paleontologist Stephen Jay Gould:

ORIGINAL STUDY

EVOLUTION AND THE IMPROBABILITIES OF HISTORY [3]

Classical determination and complete predictability may prevail for simple macroscopic objects subject to a few basic laws of motion (balls rolling down inclined planes in high school physics experiments), but complex historical objects do not lend themselves to such easy treatment. In the history of life, all results are products of a long series of events, each so intricately dependent upon particular environments and previous histories that we cannot predict their future course with any certainty. The historical sciences try to explain unique situations —immensely complex historical accidents. Evolutionary biologists, as historical scientists, do not expect detailed repetition and cannot use the actual results of history to establish probabilities for recurrence (would a Caesar again die brutally in Rome if we could go back to Australopithecus in Africa and start anew?). Evolutionists view the origin of humans (or any particular butterfly, roach, or starfish) as a historical event of such complexity and improbability that we would never expect to see anything exactly like it again (or elsewhere)— hence our strong opposition to the specific argument about humanoids on other worlds. Consider just two of the many reasons for uniqueness of complex events in the history of life.

1. Mass extinction as a key influence upon the history of life on earth. Dinosaurs died some 65 million years ago in the great worldwide Cretaceous extinction that also snuffed out about half the species of shallow water marine invertebrates. They had ruled terrestrial environments for 100 million years and would probably reign today if they had survived the debacle. Mammals arose at about the same time and spent their first 100 million years as small creatures inhabiting the nooks and crannies of a dinosaur's world. If the death of dinosaurs had not provided their great opportunity, mammals would still be small and insignificant creatures. We would not be here, and no consciously intelligent life would grace our earth. Evidence gathered since 1980 indicates that the impact of an extraterrestrial body triggered this extinction. What could be more unpredictable and unexpected than comets or asteroids striking the earth literally out of the blue. Yet without such impact, our earth would lack consciously intelligent life. Many great extinctions (several larger than the Cretaceous event) have set basic patterns in the history of life, imparting an essential randomness to our evolutionary pageant.

2. **Each species as a concatenation of improbabilities.** Any animal species—human, squid, or coral—is the latest link of an evolutionary chain stretching through thousands of species back to the inception of life. If any of these species had become extinct or evolved in another direction, final results would be markedly different. Each chain of improbable events includes adaptations developed for a local environment and only fortuitously suited to support later changes. Our ancestors among fishes evolved a peculiar fin with a sturdy, central bony axis. Without a structure of this kind, land-bound descendants could not have supported themselves in a nonbuoyant terrestrial environment. (Most lineages of fishes did not and could not evolve terrestrial descendants because they lacked fins of this form.) Yet these fins did not evolve in anticipation of future terrestrial needs. They developed as adaptations to a local environment in water, and were luckily suited to permit a new terrestrial direction later on. All evolutionary sequences include such a large set of *sine quibus non*, a fortuitous series of accidents with respect to future evolutionary success. Human brains and bodies did not evolve along a direct and inevitable ladder, but by a circuitous and tortuous route carved by adaptations evolved for different reasons, and fortunately suited to later needs.

[3] Stephen Jay Gould, *The Flamingo's Smile: Reflections in Natural History* (New York: W.W. Norton, 1985), pp. 408–410.

The history of life is not one of progressive advancement in complexity; if anything, it is one of proliferation of enormously varied designs which subsequently have been restricted to a few highly successful forms. Even at that, imperfections remain. As Gould so aptly puts it:

> Our world is not an optimal place, fine tuned by omnipotent forces of selection. It is a quirky mass of imperfections, working well enough (often admirably); a jury-rigged set of adaptations built of curious parts made available by past histories in different contexts.[4]

[4] Ibid, p. 54.

Chapter Summary

Evolution may be defined as a heritable change in genotype which becomes effective in the gene pool of a population. Genes, the actual units of heredity, are portions of molecules of DNA (deoxyribonucleic acid), a complex molecule resembling two strands of rope twisted around one another. The way that smaller molecules are arranged in this giant molecule is actually a code that contains information to direct the synthesis of proteins. DNA molecules have the unique property of being able to produce exact copies of themselves. As long as no errors are made in the process of replication, new organisms will contain genetic material exactly like that in ancestral organisms.

A gene is a unit of the DNA molecule that directs the development of observable traits, for example, blood type. Human DNA is believed to contain at least 100,000 different genes.

DNA molecules are located on chromosomes, structures found in the nucleus of each cell. Each kind of organism has a characteristic number of chromosomes, which are usually found in pairs. Humans have 23 pairs. Genes that are located on paired chromosomes and coded for different versions of the same trait are called alleles.

Mitosis, one kind of cell division, begins when the chromosomes (hence the genes) replicate, forming a second pair that duplicates the original pair of chromosomes in the nucleus. It results in new cells with exactly the same number of chromosome pairs as the parent cell. Meiosis, a different kind of cell division, results from sexual reproduction. It begins with the replication of original chromosomes, but these are divided into four cells, each containing 23 single chromosomes.

The Austrian monk Gregor Mendel studied the mechanism of inheritance with garden peas. He discovered that some alleles are able to mask the presence of others. They are called dominant. The allele which is not expressed is recessive. The allele for Type A blood in humans, for example, is dominant to the allele for Type O blood.

Phenotype refers to the physical characteristics of an organism, whereas genotype refers to its genetic composition. Two organisms may have the same phenotype, but different genotypes.

A key concept is that of population, or a group of similar individuals within which most breeding takes place. It is populations, rather than individuals, that evolve. The total number of different genes and alleles available to a population is called its gene pool. The frequency with which certain genes occur in the same gene pool theoretically remains the same from one generation to another; this is known as the Hardy–Weinberg Principle. Nonetheless, change does take place in gene pools as a result of several factors.

The ultimate source of genetic change is mutation. These are accidents that cause changes in sequences of DNA. Normally mutation is a rare occurrence, but some factors, such as certain chemicals or radioactive substances, can increase the mutation rate.

The effects of chance events (other than mutations) on the gene pool of a small population is called genetic drift. Genetic drift may have been an important factor in human evolution because until 10,000 years ago all humans probably lived in relatively small populations. Another factor that brings change to the gene pool of a population is gene flow, or the introduction of new variants of genes from nearby populations. Gene flow occurs when previously separated groups are able to breed once again.

Natural selection is the force that makes evolutionary change adaptive. It reduces the frequency of alleles for harmful or maladaptive traits within a population and increases the frequency of alleles for adaptive traits. By adaptation is meant the process by which organisms achieve a beneficial adjustment to an available environment, and the results of the process, the characteristics of organisms that fit them to the particular set of conditions of the environment in which they are generally found. A well-studied example of adaptation through natural selection in humans is inheritance of the trait for sickling red blood cells. The sickle-cell trait, caused by the inheritance of an abnormal form of hemoglobin, is an adaptation to life in regions in which falciparum malaria is common. In these regions, the sickle-cell trait plays a beneficial role, but in other parts of the world, the sickling trait is no longer advantageous, while the associated sickle-cell anemia remains injurious. Geneticists predict that as malaria is brought under control, within several generations, there will be a decline in the number of individuals who carry the allele responsible for the sickle-cell anemia.

Evolution is the process whereby organisms change into a new form from a previous form. Evolution is not necessarily a linear progression. It may be divergent (branching) or convergent, where two dissimilar forms develop similarities.

A species is a population or a group of populations that is mechanically capable of interbreeding. The concept of species is relative rather than absolute; whether breeding takes place in the wild or not is more important than the academic question of whether it is technically feasible or not. Populations within species that are quite capable of interbreeding but do so to a limited extent are called races. While species are reasonably discreet and stable units in nature, races are impermanent and subject to reamalgamation.

Isolating mechanisms serve to separate breeding populations, creating first divergent races and then (if isolation continues) divergent species. Isolating mechanisms can be geographical; physical, as in the differing anatomical structures of the Saint Bernard and Chihuahua; or social, such as in the caste system of India.

Evolution is not a "ladder of progress" leading in a predictable and determined way to ever more complex forms. Rather, it has produced, through a series of accidents, a diversity of enormously varied designs which subsequently have been restricted to a lesser number of still less-than-perfect forms.

Suggested Readings

Cavalli-Sforza, L. L. *Elements of Human Genetics*. Menlo Park, CA: Benjamin, 1977.
A short book for those who want to know something about genetics, and who would like basic genetic principles discussed from a "human" angle.

Edey, Maitland A., and Donald Johanson. *Blueprints: Solving the Mystery of Evolution*. Boston: Little, Brown, 1989.
This book is about the evolution of the idea of evolution, told as a scientific detective story. As much about the discoverors of evolution as it is about their discoveries, the book provides insights into the workings of science and gives readers the information they need to ponder the significance of our newfound ability, through genetic engineering, to actually direct the evolution of living things, including ourselves.

Gould, Stephen Jay. *Bully for Brontosaurus: Reflections in Natural History*. New York: Norton, 1991.
A collection of Gould's essays from Natural History magazine, in which he ranges over various issues in evolutionary biology. No one is better at explaining how evolution works, or exposing common fallacies, than Gould. Collections of his earlier essays, also highly recommended, are *Ever Since Darwin*, *The Panda's Thumb*, *Hens' Teeth and Horses' Toes* and *The Flamingo's Smile*.

Miller, Johnathan, and Brian Van Loon. *Darwin for Beginners*. New York: Pantheon, 1982.
Witty, clever, yet informative and sophisticated, this is a "fun" introduction to Darwin's life and thought.

Stanley, Stephen M. *Macroevolution*. San Francisco: Freeman, 1979.
Evolution, according to what is called the Modern Synthesis, proceeds as relatively small-scale changes accumulate over many generations. Not all biologists agree that this is the whole story, however, and Stanley feels that the fossil record tells us things about evolution that the Modern Synthesis does not.

Woodward, Val. *Human Heredity and Society*, St. Paul, Minn.:West, 1992.
Written for college students, this book discusses the implications of our knowledge of modern genetics for public policy. Concerned with the rise of interest in genetic engineering for the fixing of social ills, Woodward's premise is that it is as important to know what genes *aren't*, as what they are.

4

MONKEYS, APES, AND HUMANS: THE MODERN PRIMATES

From studying those primates most closely related to us, as well as those (like baboons) that live in environments similar to those faced by our own early ancestors, we can reconstruct much of what life was like for our ancestors.

WHAT IS THE PLACE OF HUMANITY AMONG THE OTHER ANIMALS? Humans are classified by biologists as belonging to the primate order, a group that also includes lemurs and indriids, lorises, tarsiers, monkeys, and apes. They are so classified on the basis of shared characteristics of anatomy, physiology, protein structure, and even the genetic material itself. Among the primates, humans resemble monkeys, but most closely resemble apes.

WHAT ARE THE IMPLICATIONS OF THE SHARED CHARACTERISTICS BETWEEN HUMANS AND THE OTHER PRIMATES? The similarities on which the modern classification of animals is based are indicative of evolutionary relationships. Therefore, by studying the anatomy, physiology, and molecular structure of the other primates, we can gain a better understanding of what human characteristics we owe to our general primate ancestry, and what traits are uniquely ours, as humans. Such studies indicate that many of the differences between apes and humans are differences of degree, rather than kind.

WHY DO ANTHROPOLOGISTS STUDY THE SOCIAL BEHAVIOR OF MONKEYS AND APES? By studying the behavior of apes and monkeys living today— especially those most closely related to us, and those which have adapted to life on savannas to which our earliest ancestors adapted—we may find essential clues in the reconstruction of adaptations and behavior patterns involved in the emergence of our earliest ancestors.

All living creatures, be they great or small, fierce or timid, active or inactive, face a fundamental problem in common, that of survival. Simply put, unless they are able to adapt themselves to some available environment, they cannot survive. Adaptation requires the development of behavior patterns that will help an organism to utilize the environment to its advantage—to find food and sustenance, avoid hazards, and, if the species is to survive, reproduce its own kind. In turn, organisms need to have the biological equipment that makes possible the development of appropriate patterns of behavior. For the hundreds of millions of years that life has existed on earth, biological adaptation has been the primary means by which the problem of survival has been solved. This is accomplished as those organisms of a particular kind, whose biological equipment is best suited to a particular way of life, produce more offspring than those whose equipment is not. In this way, advantageous characteristics become more common in succeeding generations, while less advantageous ones become less common.

In this chapter, we will look at the biological equipment possessed by the primates, the group of animals to which humans belong. By doing so, we will gain a firmer understanding of those characteristics we share with other primates, as well as those that distinguish us from them, and make us distinctively human. We shall also sample the behavior made possible by the biological equipment possessed by primates. The study of that behavior is important to help us understand something of the origins of human culture and the origin of humanity itself.

THE CLASSIFICATION SYSTEM

In order to understand the exact place of humanity among the animals, it is helpful to describe briefly the system used by biologists to classify living things. The basic system was devised by the eighteenth-century Swedish naturalist Karl von Linné. The purpose of the Linnaean system was simply to create order in the great mass of confusing biological data that had accumulated by that time. Von Linné—or Linnaeus, as he is generally called—classified living things on the basis of overall

Analogies: In biology, structures that are superficially similar; the result of convergent evolution.

Homologies: In biology, structures possessed by two different organisms which arise in similar fashion and pass through similar stages during embryonic development. May or may not be similar in adults, but have evolved from a common ancestral stock.

similarities into small groups, or species. Modern classification has gone a step further by distinguishing superficial similarities between organisms—called **analogies**—from basic ones—called **homologies**. The latter are possessed by organisms that share a common ancestry; even though homologous structures may serve different functions (the arm of a human and the forefoot of a dog, for instance), they arise in similar fashion and pass through similar stages in embryonic development prior to their ultimate differentiation. On the basis of homologies, groups of like species were organized into larger, more inclusive groups, called **genera** (the singular term is "genus"). The characteristics on which Linnaeus based his system were:

1. Body structure: A Guernsey cow and a Holstein cow are of the same species because they have identical body structure. A cow and a horse do not.
2. Body function: Cows and horses bear their young in the same way. Although they are of different species, they are closer than either cows or horses are to chickens, which lay eggs, and have no mammary glands.
3. Sequence of bodily growth: Both cows and chickens give birth to—or hatch out of the egg—fully formed young. They are therefore more closely related to each other than either one is to the frog, whose tadpoles undergo a series of changes before attaining adult form.

Genus: In the system of plant and animal classification, a group of like species.

Table 4.1   Classification of Humans

Kingdom	Animals	Do not make their own food, but depend on intake of living food.
Phylum	Chordata	Have at some stage gill slits as well as **notochord** (a rodlike structure of cartilage) and a nerve cord running along the back of the body.
Subphylum*	Vertebrata	Notochord replaced by veterbral column ("backbone") to form internal skeleton along with skull, ribs, and limb bones.
Class	Mammalia	Maintain constant body temperature; young nourished after birth by milk from mother's mammary glands.
Order	Primates	Hands and feet capable of grasping; tendency to erect posture with head balanced on spinal colulmn; acute development of vision rather than sense of smell; tendency to larger brains.
Family	Hominidae	More rigid bodies, longer arms than other primates, ability to hang vertically from arms; 98 percent identical at the genetic level.
Subfamily	Homininae	Ground-dwelling with bidepal locomotion; more reliance on learned, as opposed to biologically determined, behavior.
Genus	*Homo*	Larger brains; reliance on cultural, as opposed to biological, adaptation.
Species	*sapiens*	Brains of modern size; relatively small faces.

*Most categories can be expanded or narrowed by adding the prefix "sub" or "super." A family could thus be part of a super family, and in turn contain two or more subfamilies.

Modern taxonomy (scientific classification) is based on more than body structure, function, and growth. Now, one must also compare chemical reactions of blood, protein structure, and even the genetic material itself. Even comparison of parasites is useful, for they tend to show the same degree of relationship as the forms they infest.

Through careful comparison and analysis, Linnaeus and those who have come after him have been able to classify specific animals into a series of larger and more inclusive groups up to the largest and most inclusive of all, the animal kingdom. In Table 4.1 are the main categories of the Linnaean system applied to the classification of the human species, with some of the more important distinguishing features noted for each category. (Other categories of primates will be dealt with later in this chapter.)

Notochord: A rodlike structure of cartilage which, in vertebrates, is replaced by the vertebral column.

THE PRIMATE ORDER

The primate order is only one of several mammalian orders, such as rodents, carnivores, ungulates (hoofed mammals), and so on. As such, primates share a number of features with other mammals. Generally speaking, mammals are intelligent animals, having more in the way of brains than reptiles or other kinds of vertebrates. In most species, the young are born live, the egg being retained within

Table 4.2   The Primate Order

Order	Suborder	Infraorder	Superfamily	Family
Primates	Strepsirhini	Lemuiformes	(lemurs, lorises, and indriids)	
	Haplorhini	Tarsii		
		Platyrrhini	(New World monkeys)	
		Catarrhini	Cercopithecoidea (Old World monkeys)	
			Hominoidea	Hylobatidae (small apes)
				Pongidae (Asian great apes)
				Hominidae (African apes, humans, and near humans)

the womb of the female until it achieves an advanced state of growth. Once born, the young are nourished by their mothers with milk provided from the mammary glands, from which the class Mammalia gets its name. During this period of infant dependency, young mammals are able to learn some of the things that they will need for survival as adults.

Mammals are also active animals. This is made possible by their maintenance of a relatively constant body temperature, an efficient respiratory system featuring a separation between the nasal and mouth cavities, a diaphragm to assist in drawing in and letting out breath, and an efficient four-chambered heart that prevents mixing of oxygenated and deoxygenated blood. It is facilitated as well by a skeleton in which the limbs are positioned beneath the body, rather than out at the sides, for ease and economy of movement. The bones of the limbs have joints that are constructed in such a way as to permit growth in the young, while at the same time providing strong, hard joint surfaces that will stand up to the stresses of sustained activity.

The skeleton of most mammals is simplified, compared to that of most reptiles, in that it has fewer bones. For example, the lower jaw consists of a single bone, rather than several. The teeth, however, are another matter. Instead of the relative-ly simple, pointed, peglike teeth of reptiles, mammals have special teeth for special purposes: incisors for nipping, gnawing, and cutting; canines for ripping, tearing, killing, and fighting; premolars that may either slice and tear or crush and grind (depending on the kind of animal); and molars for crushing and grinding. This enables mammals to make use of a wide variety of food—an advantage to them, since they require more food than do reptiles to sustain their high activity. But they pay a price: Reptiles have unlimited tooth replacement, whereas mammals are limited to two sets. The first set serves the immature animal, and is replaced by the "permanent" or adult dentition.

The primate order is divided into two suborders (Table 4.2), of which one is the **Strepsirhini,** (from the Greek for "turned nose") which include lemurs, lorises, and indriids (all members of the infraorder **Lemuriformes**). On the whole, strep-

Strepsirhini: A primate suborder that includes the single infraorder, Lemuriformes.

Lemuriformes: A strepsirhine infraorder that includes lemurs, indriids, and lorises.

Haplorhini: A primate suborder that includes tarsiers, monkeys, apes, and humans.

sirhines are cat-sized or smaller, although there have been some larger forms in the past. Generally, they do not exhibit the characteristics of their order to as great a degree as do the members of the other suborder, the **Haplorhini** (from the Greek for "simple nose"). The Strepsirhines also retain certain features common among non-primate mammals, such as claws and moist, naked skin on their noses, that have not been retained by the haplorhines.

The haplorhine suborder is divided into three infraorders; the **Tarsii**, or tarsiers; the **Platyrrhini**, or New World monkeys; and the **Catarrhini**, consisting of the superfamilies Cercopithecoidea (Old World monkeys) and Hominoidea. Within the latter are the families Hylobatidae (small apes, like the gibbon), Pongidae (orangutans), and Hominidae (gorillas, chimpanzees, and humans). Only at the level of subfamily are humans (Homininae) separated from gorillas and chimps.[1]

PRIMATE CHARACTERISTICS

Although the living primates are a varied group of animals, they do share a number of features in common. These features are, however, displayed in varying degree by the different kinds of primate; in

[1] The classification utilized here, which differs from the traditional ones dividing primates into prosimians and anthropoids, is the one favored by most primatologists today.

Tarsii: A haplorhine infraorder that includes tarsiers.

Platyrrhini: A haplorhine infraorder that includes the New World monkeys.

Catarrhini: A haplorhine infraorder that includes Old World monkeys, apes, and humans.

Arboreal: Tree-dwelling.

some they are barely detectable, while in others they are greatly elaborated. All are useful in one way or another to **arboreal**, or tree-dwelling animals, although (as any squirrel knows) they are not essential to life in the trees. For animals preying upon the many insects living on the fruit and flowers of trees and shrubs, however, such primate characteristics as manipulative hands and keen vision would have been enormously adaptive. Probably, it was as arboreal animals relying on visual predation of insects that primates got their start in life.

PRIMATE SENSE ORGANS

The primates' adaptation to their way of life in the trees coincided with changes in the form and function of their sensory apparatus: The senses of sight and touch became highly developed, and the sense of smell declined. When primates took to the trees in search of insects, they no longer needed to live a "nose-to-the-ground" existence, sniffing close to the ground in search of food. The haplorhines have the least-developed sense of smell of all land animals.

Catching insects in the trees, as the early primates did and many still do, demands quickness of movement and the ability to land in the right place without falling. Thus, they had to be adept at judging depth, direction, distance, and the relationships of objects in space, abilities that remain useful to animals that travel through the trees (as most primates still do today), even though they may have given up most insect eating in favor of fruits and leaves. In the haplorhines, these abilities are provided by their **stereoscopic vision**, the ability to see the world in three dimensions—height, width, and

Stereoscopic vision: Three-dimensional vision.

Hands that grasp and eyes that see in three dimensions enable primates, like this South American squirrel monkey, to live effectively in the trees.

depth. It requires two eyes set apart from one another on the same plane. Each eye thus views an object from a slightly different angle, and the object assumes a three-dimensional appearance, indicating spatial relationships. Stereoscopic vision is one of the most important factors in primate evolution, for it is believed to have led to increased brain size in the visual area and a great complexity at nerve connections.

Visual acuity, however, varies throughout the primate order. Lemuriformes, for example, are the most visually primitive of the primates. Lacking stereoscopic vision, their eyes look out from either side of their muzzle or snout, much like those of a cow or a rabbit. Nor do they possess color vision. All other primates possess both color and stereoscopic vision, as well as a unique structure called the **fovea centralis,** or central pit in the retina of each eye. Like a camera lens, this remarkable feature enables the animal to focus on a particular object for acutely clear perception, without sacrificing visual contact with the object's surroundings.

Fovea centralis: A shallow pit in the retina of the eye that enables an animal to focus on an object while maintaining visual contact with its surroundings.

Primate sense of touch also became highly developed as a result of arboreal living. Primates found useful an effective feeling and grasping mechanism to grab their insect prey, and to prevent them from falling and tumbling while moving through the trees. The primitive mammals from which primates descended possessed tiny tactile hairs that gave them extremely sensitive tactile capacities. In primates, these hairs were replaced by informative pads on the tips of the animals' fingers and toes.

THE PRIMATE BRAIN

By far the most outstanding characteristic of primate evolution has been the enlargement of the brain among members of the order. Primate brains tend to be large, heavy in proportion to body weight, and very complex. The cerebral hemispheres (the areas of conscious thought) have enlarged dramatically and, in catarrhines, completely cover the cerebellum, which is the part of the brain that coordinates the muscles and maintains body equilibrium.

The reasons for this important change in brain size are many, but it may have begun as the earliest primates, along with many other mammals, began to carry out their activities in the daylight hours. Prior to 65 million years ago, mammals seem to have been nocturnal in their habits, but with the extinction of the dinosaurs, inconspicuous, nighttime activity was no longer the key to survival. With the change to diurnal, or daytime, activity the sense of vision took on greater importance, and so visual acuity was favored by natural selection. Unlike reptile vision, where the information–processing neurons are in the retina, mammalian vision is processed in the brain, permitting integration with information received by hearing and smelling.

If the evolution of visual acuity began the trend to larger brains, it is likely that the primates' arboreal existence played a major role in furthering that trend. Paleontologist Alfred S. Romer states:

> Locomotion in the trees requires great agility and muscular coordination, which in itself demands development of the brain centers; and it is of interest that much of the higher mental faculties are apparently developed in an area alongside the motor centers of the brain.[2]

An interesting hypothesis that may help account for primate brain development involves the use of the hand as a tactile organ to replace the teeth and jaws or snout. The hands assumed some of the grasping, tearing, and dividing functions of the snout, again requiring development of the brain centers for more complete coordination. Thus, while the skull and brain expanded, the teeth and jaws grew smaller. Certain areas of the brain became more elaborate and intricate. One of these areas is the cortex, generally considered to be the center of an animal's intelligence; it receives impressions from the animal's various sensory receptors, analyzes them, and sends responses back down the motor nerves to the proper receptor.

An animal living in the trees is constantly acting on and reacting to the environment. Messages from the hands, feet, eyes and ears, as well as from the sensors of balance, movement, heat, touch, and pain, are relayed to the cortex, individually and simultaneously. The cortex, then, must be developed to a considerable degree of complexity to receive and coordinate these impressions and to transmit the appropriate responses back. It is assumed that such development must have occurred early in the history of the primates.

The enlarged cortex not only provided the primates with a greater degree of efficiency in the daily struggle for survival but it also gave them the basis for more sophisticated cerebration, or thought. The ability to think probably played a decisive role in the evolution of the primates from which human beings emerged.

PRIMATE DENTITION

Although they have added other things than insects to their diets, primates have retained less-specialized teeth than other mammals. According to primatologist W. E. LeGros Clark:

> An arboreal life obviates the necessity for developing highly specialized grinding teeth, since the diet available to most treeliving mammals in the tropics, consisting of leaves, shoots, soft fruits and insects, can be adequately masticated by molar teeth of relatively simple structure.[3]

In most primates, on each side of each jaw, in front, are two straight-edged, chisellike broad teeth called incisors (Figure 4.1). Behind the incisors is a canine, which in many mammals is large, flaring, and fanglike and is used for defense as well as for tearing and shredding food. Among some catarrhines the canine is reduced in size somewhat, especially in females, though it is still large in males. In humans, though, incisors and canines are practically indistinguishable, although the canine has an oversized root, suggestive of larger canines some time back in our ancestry. Behind the canines are

---

[2] Alfred S. Romer, *Vertebrate Paleontology* (Chicago: University of Chicago Press, 1945), p. 103.

[3] W. E. LeGros Clark, *History of the Primates* 5th ed. (Chicago: University of Chicago Press, 1966), p. 271.

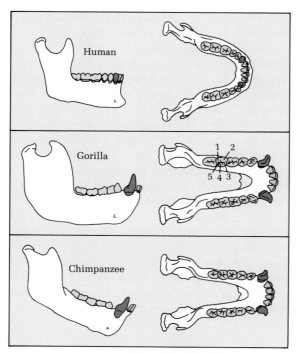

Figure 4.1 In this depiction of the lower jaws of a human, a gorilla, and a chimpanzee incisors are shown in green, canines in red, and premolars and molars in yellow. On one of the gorilla molars, the cusps are numbered to enhance their identification.

the premolars. Last come the molars, usually with four or five cusps, used mostly for crushing or grinding food. This basic pattern of dentition contrasts sharply with that of nonprimate mammals.

On the evidence of comparative anatomy and the fossil record, LeGros Clark postulated the existence of an early primate ancestor that possessed three incisors, one canine, four premolars, and three molars on each side of the jaw, top and bottom, for a total of 44 teeth. In the early stages of primate evolution, four incisors (one on each side of each jaw) were lost. This change differentiated the primates, with their two incisors on each side of each jaw, from other mammals. The canines of most primates develop into long, daggerlike teeth that enable them to rip open tough husks of fruit and other foods. In a combat situation, male baboons, apes, and other primates flash these formidable teeth at their enemy, hoping to scare it off. Only on rare occasions, when this bluffing action fails, are teeth used to inflict bodily harm.

Other evolutionary changes in primate dentition involve the premolar and molar teeth. Over the millennia, the first and second premolars became smaller and eventually disappeared altogether, while the third and fourth premolars grew larger with the addition of a second pointed projection, or cusp, thus becoming "bicuspid." The molars, meanwhile, evolved from a three-cusp pattern to one with four and even five cusps. This kind of molar economically combined the functions of grasping, cutting, and grinding in one tooth.

The evolutionary trend for primate dentition has generally been toward economy, with fewer, smaller, more efficient teeth doing more work. Thus our own 32 teeth are fewer in number than those of some, and more generalized than those of most primates. Indeed, the absence of third molars in many individuals indicates that the human dentition is undergoing further reduction.

THE PRIMATE SKELETON

The skeleton gives an animal its basic shape or silhouette, supports the soft tissues, and helps protect the vital internal organs. In primates (Figure 4.2), for example, the skull protects the brain and the eyes. A number of factors are responsible for the shape of the primate skull as compared with those of most other mammals: changes in dentition, changes in the sensory organs of sight and smell, and increased brain size. The primate brain case, or **cranium**, tends to be high and vaulted. A solid partition exists in most primate species between the eye and the temple, affording maximum protection to the eyes in their vulnerable forward position.

The **foramen magnum** (the large opening in the skull through which the spinal cord passes and connects to the brain) is an important clue to evolutionary relationships. In primates, the evolutionary trend has been for this to shift forward, toward the center of the skull's base, so that it faces

Cranium: The brain case of the skull.
Foramen magnum: A large opening in the skull through which the spinal cord passes and connects to the brain.

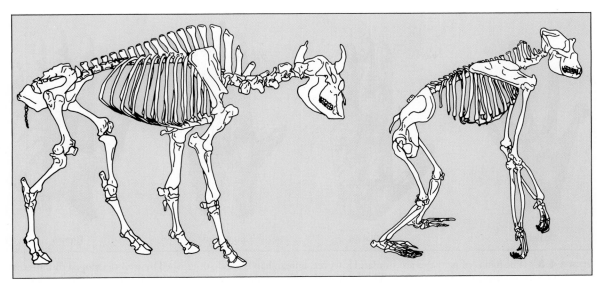

Figure 4.2 Note where the skulls and vertebral columns are joined in these skeletons of a bison (left) and gorilla (right). In the bison (as in most mammals) the skull projects forward from the vertebral column, but in the semierect gorilla, the vertebral column is well down beneath the skull.

downward, as in humans, rather than directly backward, as in dogs, horses, and other mammals. Thus, the skull does not project forward from the vertebral column. Instead, the vertebral column joins the skull toward the center of its base, thereby placing the skull in a balanced position in animals which frequently assume upright posture.

In most primates, the snout or muzzle portion of the skull has grown smaller as the acuity of the sense of smell declined. The smaller snout offers less interference with stereoscopic vision; it also enables the eyes to be placed in the frontal position. As a result, primates have more of a humanlike face than other mammals. Below the primate skull and the neck is the **clavicle**, or collarbone, a holdover from primitive mammal ancestors. This serves as a strut that prevents the arm from collapsing inward when brought across the front of the body. It allows greater maneuverability of the arms, permitting them to swing sideways and outward from the trunk of the body. The clavicle also supports the **scapula** and allows for the muscle development that

is required for flexible, yet powerful, arm movement. This shoulder and limb structure is associated with considerable acrobatic agility and, in the case of all apes and some New World monkeys, the ability to **brachiate**—use their arms to swing and hang among the branches of trees with the body in a vertical (upright) position.

Primates have also retained the characteristic, found in early mammals, of **pentadactyly**. Pentadactyly, which means possessing five digits, is a primitive characteristic found in many nonarboreal animals, but it proved to be of special advantage to tree-dwelling primates. Their grasping feet and hands (Figure 4.3) have sensitive pads at the tips of their digits, backed up (except in some strepsirhines) by flattened nails. This unique combination of pad and nail provides the animal with an excellent **prehensile** (grasping) device for use when moving from tree to tree. The structural

Clavicle: The "collar bone."

Scapula: The "shoulder blade."

Brachiate: To use the arms to move from branch to branch, with the body hanging suspended from them.

Pentadactyly: Possessing five digits (fingers and toes).

Prehensile: Having the ability to grasp.

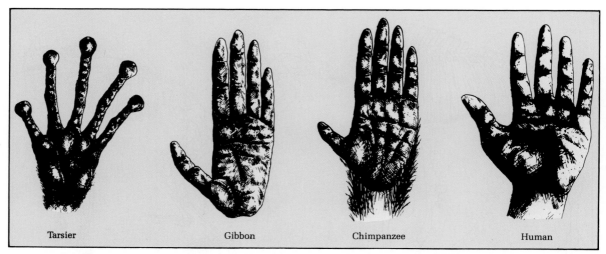

Figure 4.3   The hands of primates are similar. However, human hands are distinguished by well-developed thumbs that can be used in opposition to the fingers. The highly specialized hands of brachiators (gibbons and chimpanzees) are characterized by long fingers and weakly developed thumbs.

characteristics of the primate foot and hand make grasping possible; the digits are extremely flexible, the big toe is fully opposable to the other digits in most species, and the thumb is opposable to the other digits to varying degrees.

Hindsight indicates that the flexible, unspecialized primate hand was to prove a valuable asset for future evolution of this group. Had they not had generalized grasping hands, early hominines would not have been able to manufacture and utilize tools, and thus embark on the new and unique evolutionary pathway that led to the revolutionary ability to adapt through culture.

REPRODUCTION AND CARE OF YOUNG

The breeding of most mammals occurs once or twice a year, but most primate species are able to breed at any time during the course of the year. Generally, the male is ready to engage in sexual activity whenever females are in **estrus**, around the

---

Estrus: In primate females, the time of sexual receptivity during which ovulation takes place.

---

time of ovulation. The female's receptivity is cyclical, corresponding to her period of estrus which occurs once each month.

This is not to say that females are receptive regularly each month. Rather, the average adult female monkey or ape spends most of her time either pregnant or nursing, at which times she is not sexually receptive. But after her infant is weaned, she will come into estrus for a few days each month, until she becomes pregnant again. Since this can happen at any time, it is advantageous to have males present throughout the year. Thus, sex plays a role in keeping both sexes constantly together, except among orangutans, among whom adults only come together when females are in estrus. In most species, however, sex is not the only, or even the most important, cause of males and females remaining together.

One of the most noticeable adaptations to arboreal life among primates is a trend toward reduction in the number of offspring born at one time to a female. The most primitive primates—lemurs and marmosets—produce two or three young at each birth. Catarrhines, however, usually produce only a single offspring at a time. Natural selection may have favored single births among primate tree-dwellers because the primate infant, which has a highly developed grasping ability (the grasping reflex can also be seen in human infants), must be transported about by its mother, and more than one

A young baboon clings to its mother. Since her hands are used in locomotion, she cannot herself carry her infant. Consequently, it must be able to hold on for itself.

Swelling of her sexual skin indicates that this baboon is in estrus. Females of most primates come into estrus once a month until pregnant; thereafter they will not come into estrus until their infant is weaned.

clinging infant would seriously encumber her as she moved about the trees. Moreover, a female pregnant with a large litter would be unable to lead a very active life as a tree-dweller.

Primates bear fewer young at a time, and so they must devote more time and effort to their care if the species is to survive. This usually means a longer period during which the infant is dependent upon its mother. As a general rule, the more closely related to humans the species is, the smaller, more

helpless, and more immature the newborn offspring tend to be. For example, a lemur is dependent upon the mother for only a few months after birth; an ape, for four or five years; and a human for more than a decade. Longer infancy is typically associated with an increase in longevity (see Figure 4.4). If the breeding life of primates had not extended, the lengthened infancy could have led to a decrease in numbers of individuals. Something approaching

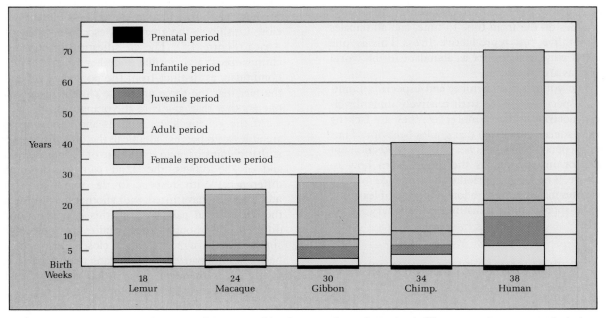

Figure 4.4   Primates are born at earlier stages of development than other animals. Humans are born at a particularly early stage because of their larger brain size; later, the baby's head would be too large for the mother's pelvis.

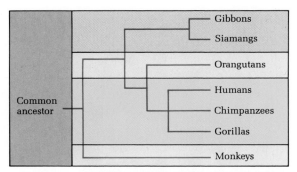

Figure 4.5 Based on molecular similarities and differences, a relationship can be established among various catarrhine primates. It is difficult to take seriously any date in excess of 8 million years for the origin of the separate lineages for chimpanzees and humans.

this can be seen in the great apes: A female chimpanzee, for example, does not reach sexual maturity until about the age of ten, and once she produces her first live offspring, there is a period of about 5.6 years before she will bear another. Furthermore, a chimpanzee infant cannot survive if its mother dies before it reaches the age of four at the very least. Thus, assuming that none of her offspring die before adulthood, a female chimpanzee must survive for at least 20 or 21 years just to maintain the size of chimpanzee populations at their current levels. In fact, chimpanzee infants and juveniles do die from time to time, and all females do not live full reproductive lives. This is one reason why apes are not as abundant in the world today as are monkeys.

The young of catarrhine, and especially hominoid, species are born with relatively underdeveloped nervous systems; moreover, they are lacking in the social knowledge that guides behavior. Thus they depend upon adults not only for protection but also for instruction, as they must learn how to survive. The longer period of dependence in these primates makes possible a longer period of learning, which appears to be a distinct evolutionary advantage.

ESTABLISHING EVOLUTIONARY RELATIONSHIPS

Most of the primate characteristics so far discussed are present at least in a rudimentary sort of way in the strepsirhines, but all are seen to a much greater

degree in the haplorhines. The differences between humans and the other haplorhines, especially catarrhines, are rather like those between strepsirhines and haplorhines. In humans most of the characteristic primate traits are developed to a degree not realized by any other species. Among some strepsirhines, some of the distinctive primate traits are missing, while others are clearly present, so that the borderline between primate and nonprimate becomes blurred, and the difference is one of degree rather than kind. All of this is fully expectable, given an evolutionary history in which primitive primates having a rough resemblance to today's strepsirhines, developed out of some other mammalian order, and eventually gave rise to primitive haplorhines; from these emerged the catarrhines and, ultimately, hominids.

Just how close our evolutionary relationship is to other primates is indicated by molecular evidence. There is a striking similarity in blood and protein chemistry among the hominoids especially, indicating close evolutionary relationships. On the basis of tests with blood proteins, it has been shown that the chimpanzee and gorilla are closest to humans; next comes the orangutan; then the smaller apes (gibbons and siamangs), Old World monkeys, New World monkeys, and finally the strepsirhines. Measurements of genetic affinity confirm these findings, providing further evidence of humanity's close kinship to the great apes, especially those of Africa (Figure 4.5). The classification of humans, chimpanzees, and gorillas together in the family hominidae, as distinct from the pongidae, reflects the fact that the three are more closely related to one another than any is to the orangutan.

At the genetic level, humans and chimpanzees are at least 98 percent identical; the only difference is that chimps have an extra pair of chromosomes, and of the others, the 22nd pair shows some difference. With respect to the extra pair, in humans these have fused with another pair to form the single 22nd pair, so even this is not a major difference. Although some studies of molecular similarities have suggested a closer relationship between chimpanzees and humans than either has to gorillas, subsequent research has not supported such a conclusion.[4] On present evidence, all three hominids show an equal degree of relationship.

[4] Russell L. Ciochon and John G. Fleagle, *The Human Evolution Source Book* (Englewood Cliffs, N.J.: Prentice-Hall, 1993), pp. 1, 37.

MODERN PRIMATES

The modern primates are mostly restricted to warm areas of the world. As already noted, they are divided into two suborders, Strepsirhini and Haplorhini. Strepsirhines are small, mostly quadrupedal Old World animals; haplorhines include tarsiers, monkeys, apes, and humans.

STREPSIRHINES

The strepsirhines are considered to be the most primitive primates. They are represented by the single infraorder Lemuriformes, within which are the lemurs, indriids, and lorises. Although lemurs and indriids are restricted to the island of Madagascar, off the east coast of Africa, lorises range from Africa to southern and eastern Asia. All are small, with none larger than a good-sized dog. In general body outline, they resemble rodents and insectivores, with short pointed snouts, large pointed ears, and big eyes. In the anatomy of the upper lip and snout, lemuriformes resemble nonprimate mammals, in that the upper lip is bound down to the gum and the naked skin on the nose around the nostrils is moist. They also have long tails, with that of a ring-tail lemur somewhat like the tail of a raccoon.

In brain structure, lemuriformes are clearly primates, and they have characteristically primate "hands," which they use in pairs, rather than one at a time. They move on all fours, with the forelimbs in a "palms down" position, and also cling in near-vertical positions to branches. Although they retain a claw on their second toe, which they use for scratching and grooming, all other digits are equipped with flattened nails. With their distinctive mix of characteristics, strepsirhine primates appear to occupy a place between the haplorhines and insectivores.

HAPLORHINES

The suborder Haplorhini is divided into three infraorders: the Tarsii (tarsiers), the Platyrrhini (New World monkeys), and Catarrhini (Old World monkeys, apes, and humans). Most haplorhines are bigger than the strepsirhines, and are strikingly human-like in appearance. Actually, it is more

Lemur

Indriid

Loriser

Modern strepsirhines represent highly evolved variants of an early primate model. In them, primate characteristics are not as prominant as they are in monkeys, apes, and humans.

accurate to say that humans are remarkably like monkeys, but even more like apes, in appearance. The defining traits of the strepsirhines—large cranium, well-developed brain, acute vision, chisel–like incisors, prehensile digits—are even more apparent in the haplorhines. Most haplorhines generally move on all four limbs, but many stand erect to reach fruit hanging in trees; some apes occasionally walk on two feet. Monkeys are often highly arboreal, and New World species have prehensile tails that wrap around a tree branch, freeing the forelimbs to grasp food. Some New World monkeys brachiate; Old World monkeys almost never do.

All apes may once have been fully arboreal brachiators, but among modern apes, only the gibbon and siamang still are. The chimpanzee and the gorilla spend most of their time on the ground, but sleep in the trees and may also find food there. Orangutans, too, spend time down on the ground, but are somewhat more arboreal than the African apes. When on the ground, they move mostly on all fours.

TARSIERS

Tarsiers are the haplorhine primates most like the lemuriformes, and in the past they were usually classified in the same suborder with them. The head, eyes, and ears of these kitten-sized arboreal creatures are huge in proportion to the body. They have the remarkable ability to turn their heads 180 degrees, so they can see where they have been as well as where they are going. The digits end in platelike, adhesive discs. Tarsiers are named for the elongated tarsal, or foot bone, that provides leverage for jumps of six feet or more. Tarsiers are mainly nocturnal insect eaters. In the structure of the nose and lips, and the part of the brain governing vision, tarsiers resemble monkeys.

NEW WORLD MONKEYS

New World monkeys live in forests and swamps of South and Central America. They are characterized by flat noses with widely separated, outward-flaring nostrils, from which comes their name of platyrrhine monkeys. All are arboreal, and some have long, prehensile tails by which they hang from trees. These and the presence of three, rather than

In tarsiers, primate characteristics are somewhat more prominent than among strepsirhines.

two, premolars on each side of each jaw distinguish them from the Old World monkeys, apes, and humans. Platyrrhines walk on all fours with their palms down and scamper along tree branches in search of fruit, which they eat sitting upright. Spider monkeys are accomplished brachiators as well. Although other New World monkeys spend much of their time in the trees, they do not often hang or swing from limb to limb by their arms and have not developed the extremely long forelimbs characteristic of brachiators.

OLD WORLD MONKEYS

Old World, or catarrhine, monkeys are characterized by noses with closely spaced, downward-pointing nostrils, the presence of two, rather than three, premolars on each side of each jaw, and their lack of prehensile tails. They may be either arboreal or terrestrial. The arboreal species include the guereza monkey, the Asiatic langur, and the strange-looking proboscis monkey. Some are equally at home on the ground and in the trees, such as the macaques, of which there are some nineteen species ranging from Gibraltar (the "Barbary Ape") to Japan.

Several species of baboons are largely terrestrial, living in the savannas, deserts, and highlands of Africa. They have long, fierce faces and move quadrupedally, with all fours in the palms-down position. Their diet consists of leaves, seeds, insects, and lizards, and they live in large, well-

organized troops. Because baboons have abandoned trees (except for sleeping) and live in environments like that in which humans may have originated, they are of great interest to primatologists.

SMALL AND GREAT APES

The apes are the closest living relatives we humans have in the animal world. Their general appearance and way of life are related to their semierect posture. In their body chemistry, the position of their internal organs, and even their diseases, they are remarkably close to humans. They are arboreal to varying degrees, but their generally greater size and weight are obstacles to their swinging and jumping as freely as monkeys. The small, lithe gibbon can both climb and swing freely through the trees and so spends virtually all of its time in them. At the opposite extreme are gorillas, who climb trees, using their prehensile hands and feet to grip the trunk and branches. Their swinging is limited to leaning outward as they reach for fruit, clasping a limb for support. Most of their time is spent on the ground.

The apes, like humans, have no external tail. But, unlike humans, their arms are longer than their legs, indicating that their ancestors remained arboreal brachiators long after our own had become

Gibbons and orangutans are Southeast Asian apes. Gibbons are brachiators who use their long arms and hands to swing through the trees. Although orangutans sometimes brachiate, their legs move like arms and their feet are like hands; thus, much of their movement is by "four-handed" climbing.

Chimpanzees and gorillas are African apes.

terrestrial. In moving on the ground, the African apes "knuckle-walk" on the backs of their hands, resting their weight on the middle joints of the fingers. They stand erect when reaching for fruit, looking over tall grass, or in any activity where they find the erect position advantageous. The semierect position is natural in apes when on the ground because the curvature of their vertebral column places their center of gravity, which is high in their bodies, in front of their hip joint. Thus, they are both "top heavy" and "front heavy." Furthermore, the structure of the ape pelvis is not well suited to support the weight of the torso and limbs easily. Nor do apes have the arrangement of leg muscles that enables humans to stand erect and swing their legs freely before and behind.

Gibbons and siamangs, which are found in Southeast Asia and Malaya, have compact, slim bodies and disproportionately long arms and short legs, and stand about three feet high. Although their usual form of locomotion is brachiation, they can run erect, holding their arms out for balance. Gibbons and siamangs resemble monkeys in size and general appearance more than the other apes.

Orangutans are found in Borneo and Sumatra. They are somewhat taller than gibbons and siamangs and are much heavier, with the bulk characteristic of apes. In the closeness of the eyes and facial prominence, an orangutan looks a little like a chimpanzee, except that its hair is reddish. Orangs walk with their forelimbs in a fists-sideways, or a palms-down, position. Of the apes, they are the most solitary in their habits, and somewhat more arboreal than the African apes.

Gorillas, found in equatorial Africa, are the largest of the apes; an adult male can weigh more than 400 pounds. The body is covered with a thick coat of glossy black hair, and mature males have a silvery gray upper back. There is a strikingly human look about the face, and like humans, gorillas focus on things in their field of vision by directing the eyes rather than moving the head. Gorillas are mostly ground dwellers, but may sleep in trees in carefully constructed nests. Because of their weight, brachiation is limited to raising and lowering themselves among the tree branches when searching for fruit. They "knuckle-walk," using all four limbs with the fingers of the hand flexed,

ANTHROPOLOGY APPLIED

PRIMATE CONSERVATION

At present, no less than 76 species of primates are recognized as being in danger of extinction. Included among them are all of the great apes, as well as such formerly widespread and adaptable species as rhesus macaques. In the wild, they are threatened by destruction of their habitat in the name of "development," by hunting for food and trophies, and by trapping for pets and research. Because monkeys and apes are so closely related to humans, they are regarded as essential for biomedical research in which humans cannot be used. It is ironic that trade in live primates to supply laboratories can be a major factor in their local extinction.

Because of their vulnerability, the conservation of primates has become a matter of urgency. Two approaches to the problem may be taken, both of which require application of knowledge gained from studies of free-ranging animals. One is to maintain some populations in the wild, either by establishing preserves where animals are already living, or by moving populations to localities where suitable habitat exists. In either case, constant monitoring and management are necessary to assure that sufficient space and resources remain available. The other approach is to maintain breeding colonies in captivity, in which case care must be taken to provide the kind of physical and social environment that will encourage reproductive success. Without such amenities as things to climb, materials to use for nest building, others to socialize with, and places to withdraw not only from humans but from each other, primates in zoos and laboratories do not successfully reproduce.

The value of field studies for effective wild animal management is illustrated by Shirley Strum's relocation in 1984 of three troops of free-ranging baboons in Kenya. The troop she had been studying for 15 years had become a problem, raiding peoples' crops and garbage. Accordingly, it was decided to move this and two other local troops—130 animals in all—to more sparsely inhabited country 150 miles away. Knowing their habits, Strum was able to trap, tranquilize, and transport the animals to their new home in such a way as not to disrupt their social relationships, cause them to abandon their new home, or block the transfer into their troops of new males, with their all-important knowledge of local resources. The success of her effort, which had never been tried with baboons before, proves that relocation is a realistic technique for saving endangered primate populations.

---

placing the knuckles instead of the palm of the hand on the ground. They will stand erect to reach for fruit, to see something more easily, or to threaten perceived sources of danger with their famous "chest beating" displays. Although gorillas are gentle and tolerant, bluffing is an important part of their behavioral repertoire.

Chimpanzees are widely distributed throughout Africa. They are probably the best known of the apes, and have long been favorites in zoos and circuses. Although thought of as particularly quick and clever, all three great apes are of equal intelligence, despite some differences in cognitive styles. More arboreal than gorillas, but less so than orangs, chimpanzees forage on the ground much of the day, "knuckle-walking" like gorillas. At sunset, they return to the trees, where they build their nests.

THE SOCIAL BEHAVIOR OF PRIMATES

The physical resemblance of human beings to the other catarrhines is striking, but the most startling resemblance of all is in their social behavior. Because of their highly developed brains, monkeys and apes behave in a manner far more complex than most other animals except humans. Only over the past three decades have primatologists made prolonged close-range observations of catarrhines in their natural habitats, and we are discovering much about social organization, learning ability, and communication among our closest relatives in the animal kingdom. In particular, we are finding that a number of behavioral traits that we used to think of as distinctively human are found to one degree or

Catarrhine primates, like these baboons, spend a lot of time grooming one another. Such behavior is important in maintaining group cohesion.

another among other primates, reminding us once again that many of the differences between us and them are differences of degree, rather than kind.

The range of behavior shown by living primates is great—too great to be adequately surveyed in this book. Instead, we shall look primarily at the behavior of those species most closely related to humans—chimpanzees and gorillas—or that which has adapted to an environment somewhat like the one to which our own ancestors adapted millions of years ago—savanna baboons.

THE GROUP

Primates are social animals, living and traveling in groups that vary in size from species to species. In most species, females and their offspring constitute the core of the social system. Among baboons, these females are all related, in that they remain for life in the group into which they were born, whereas males generally move to other groups as adolescents. Among chimpanzees, females sometimes leave their natal group to join another, but their sons, and often their daughters, remain in their mother's group for life. Among gorillas, either

sex may or may not leave its natal group for another.

Savanna baboons live in large troops which may number more than 100 animals. They have male and female status hierarchies, and males dominate females, unless a female is supported by another male (males are twice as big as females). Each animal knows its place, and the hierarchies are maintained by the self-assertiveness of dominant animals and their success in securing the support of other animals, as well as by the deference of subordinates. High dominance brings with it priority of access to choice food, water, and (sometimes) mates; moreover, high-ranking females are more often groomed by others of their sex as well as by juveniles, and are less vulnerable to harassment by others when caring for young infants. Although adult females tend to avoid one another when foraging, closely related females sit together and groom each other when at rest. They will also support one another during aggressive encounters with other troop members. Males, by contrast, rarely associate with members of their own sex. Instead, they strike up friendships with one or more females.

Among chimps, the largest organizational unit is the community, composed of 50 or more individuals. Rarely, however, do all these animals come together at a single time. Instead, they are usually found ranging singly or in small subgroups consisting of adult males together, females with their young, or males and females together with the young. In the course of their travels, subgroups may join forces and forage together, but sooner or later these will break up again into smaller units. When they do, members are often exchanged, so that new subunits are different in their composition from the ones that initially came together.

Although relationships between individuals within the community are relatively harmonious, dominance hierarchies do exist. Generally, males outrank females, although high-ranking females may dominate low-ranking males. Physical strength and size are important determinants of an animal's rank, as are the rank of its mother, its effectiveness at enlisting the aid of other individuals, and, in the case of the male, its motivation to achieve high status. Highly motivated males may bring considerable intelligence and ingenuity to bear in their quest for high rank. For example, one chimp in the community studied by Jane Goodall, a pioneer in the study of primate behavior, was able to figure out how to incorporate noisy kerosene cans into his charging displays, thereby intimidating all the other males.[5] As a result, he rose from relatively low status to the number one (alpha) position.

The gorilla group is a "family" of five to twenty individuals led by a mature, silver-backed male and includes younger, black-backed males, females, the young, and sometimes other silver-backs. Subordinate males, however, are usually prevented by the dominant male from mating with the group's females, although he may occasionally allow access to lower-ranking ones. Thus, young silver-backs often leave their natal family to start their own families by winning outside females. If the dominant male is weakening with age, however, one of his sons may remain with the group to succeed to his father's position. Unlike chimpanzees, gorillas rarely fight over food, territory, or sex, but will fight fiercely to maintain the cohesiveness of the group.

INDIVIDUAL INTERACTION

One of the most notable primate activities is grooming, the ritual cleaning of another animal's coat to remove parasites, shreds of grass, or other matter. The grooming animal deftly parts the hair of the one being groomed with two fingers, and with the thumb and forefinger of the other hand removes any foreign object, often eating it. Among gorillas, grooming is mainly hygienic, but among chimpanzees and baboons it is a gesture of friendliness, submission, appeasement, or closeness. Embracing, touching, and jumping up and down are forms of greeting behavior among chimpanzees. Touching is also a form of reassurance.

Gorillas, though gentle and tolerant, are also aloof and independent, and individual interaction among adults tends to be quite restrained. Friendship or closeness between adults and infants is more evident. Among baboons, chimpanzees, gorillas, and most other primates, the mother–infant bond is the strongest and most long-lasting in the group. A new infant baboon is an object of tremendous interest to the group, and shortly after birth, mother and infant are surrounded by attention. The adults lipsmack and touch the infant with their fingers or mouths, and young females may even try to take it to practice "mothering" on their own. The new mother aligns herself with a male friend, who protects her from animals that may threaten her or her infant. Two incidents reported by primatologist Barbara Smuts are indicative of the care males may invest in their friends' offspring: Two infants of the group she was studying lost their mothers while they were still quite young. In each case, their bond with the mother's male friend intensified, and was probably critical in the youngsters' survival.[6] Although such friends are not always the fathers, this grouping of adult males, adult females, and juveniles suggests the kind of situation that may have been a forerunner of human family organization.

Among gorillas and chimpanzees, the mother–infant bond is especially strong and may last for many years, commonly for the lifetime of the mother. Gorilla infants and young juveniles share their mothers' nests and have been seen sharing

[5] Jane Goodall, *The Chimpanzees of Gombe: Patterns of Behavior.* (Cambridge, Mass.: Belknap Press, 1986), p. 424.

[6] Barbara Smuts, "What Are Friends For?" *Natural History* (1987), 96(2):41.

Among chimpanzees, as among most primates, the mother–infant bond is strong. This mother is playfully tickling her offspring.

nests with mature, childless females. Both chimpanzee and gorilla males are attentive to juveniles, and may share in parental responsibilities. Male chimpanzees, however (as among human food foragers), may wander apart from the females and juveniles. Thus, it is the females who provide stability in the chimpanzee group, whereas it is the dominant silver-back who provides this in the gorilla family.

SEXUAL BEHAVIOR

Among the three forgoing species, as with humans, there is no fixed breeding season. Sexual activity, however—initiated by either the male or the female—occurs only during the period each month when the female is receptive to impregnation. Once impregnated, females are not sexually receptive until their offspring are weaned (at about age four among chimps and gorillas, sooner among baboons). Baboon females typically mate with several different males, but exercise choice as to whom they mate with, and clearly prefer those with whom they have a prior friendship. Thus, friendship often precedes, rather than follows, a sexual relationship. When they are at the height of estrus, females commonly spend most of their time in proximity to males with whom they maintain exclusive mating relationships.

To a degree, chimps are promiscuous in their sexual behavior, and twelve to fourteen males have been observed to have as many as fifty copulations in one day with a single female. Nor do females appear to show preference for known over strange males. Generally, dominant males try to monopolize females in full estrus, although cooperation from the female is usually required for this to succeed. By making herself scarce, she may be able to exercise some choice in the matter. An alpha male, however, is able to monopolize the females to some extent, and some alphas have been seen to monopolize several estrus females at the same time.

In gorilla families, the dominant silver-back has exclusive breeding rights with the females, although he may allow a young silver-back occasional access to a low-ranking female. Otherwise, the young silver-back must leave "home" in order to find sexual partners, usually by luring them away from other established groups.

Sexual dimorphism: Within a single species, the presence of marked anatomical differences between males and females.

Although the vast majority of primate species are not "monogamous" in their mating habits, many smaller species of New World monkeys, a few island-dwelling populations of leaf-eating Old World monkeys, and all of the smaller apes (gibbons and siamangs) do mate for life with a single individual of the opposite sex. None of these species is closely related to human beings, nor do "monogamous" species ever display the degree of **sexual dimorphism**—anatomical differences between males and females—that is characteristic of our closest primate relatives, or that was characteristic of our own ancient ancestors.

PLAY

Frequent play activity among primate infants and juveniles is a means of learning about the environment, testing strength (rank in dominance hierarchies is based partially—but only partially—on size and strength), and generally learning how to behave as adults. Chimpanzee infants mimic the food-getting activities of their mothers, "attack" dozing adults, and "harass" adolescents.

Observers have watched young gorillas do somersaults, wrestle, and play tug-of-war, follow the leader, and king of the mountain. One juvenile, becoming annoyed at repeated harassment by an infant, picked it up, climbed a tree, and deposited it on a branch from which it was unable to get down on its own. Its mother had to retrieve it.

COMMUNICATION

Primates, like many animals, vocalize. They have a great range of calls that are often used together with movements of the face or body to convey a message. Observers have not yet established the meaning of all the sounds, but a good number have been distinguished, such as warning calls, threat calls, defense calls, and gathering calls; the behavioral reactions of other animals hearing the call have also been studied. Among chimpanzees and gorillas, vocalizations are mainly emotional rather than propositional. Much of their communication takes place by the use of specific gestures and postures. Indeed, some of these, such as kissing and embracing, are in virtually universal use today among humans, as well as apes.

Primatologists have classified numerous kinds of chimpanzee vocalization and visual communication (see Figure 4.6). Together, these facilitate group protection, coordination of group efforts, and social interaction in general. Experiments with captive apes, discussed later in this chapter, reveal that their communicative abilities exceed what they make use of in the wild. From such experiments, we may learn something about the origin of human language.

HOME RANGES

Primates usually move about within circumscribed areas, or **home ranges**, which are of varying sizes, depending on the size of the group and on ecological factors such as availability of food. Ranges are often moved seasonally. The distance traveled by a group in a day varies; baboons may travel as many as twelve miles in a day. Some areas of a range, known as "core areas," are used more often than others; they may contain water, food sources, resting places, and sleeping trees. The ranges of different groups may overlap, and often a tree-dwelling species will share a range with ground dwellers. In such cases, the two species are not necessarily competing for the same resources; they may be using the range at different times and eating somewhat different foods.

Neither baboons nor gorillas defend their home ranges against incursions of others of their kind,

Home range: The area within which a group of primates usually move.

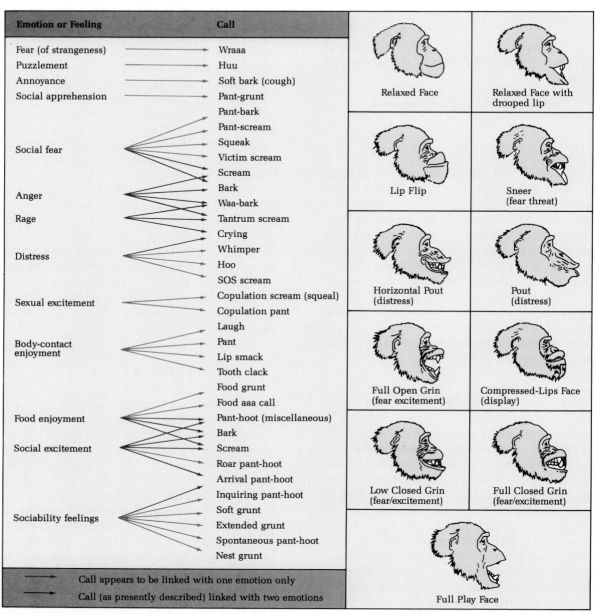

Figure 4.6   Chimpanzee communication combines a number of distinctive calls with different facial expressions.

although they certainly will defend their group if it is in any way threatened. Thus, they may be said to be nonterritorial. Chimpanzees, by contrast, have been observed patrolling their territories to ward off potential trespassers. Moreover, Goodall recorded the destruction of one chimpanzee community by another which invaded the first one's turf. Although Goodall interpreted this as territorial behavior,[7] another interpretation is possible. In Africa today, human encroachment is squeezing chimpanzees into ever smaller pockets of forest. This places considerable stress on animals whose levels of violence tend to increase in the absence of sufficient space. Perhaps the violence that Goodall witnessed was a response to crowding as a consequence of human encroachment. Among primates in general, the clearest territoriality appears in forest species, rather than in those that are more terrestrial in their habits.

[7] Goodall, p. 525.

LEARNING

Observation of monkeys and apes has shown that their learning abilities are remarkably humanlike. In an experiment carried out by some Japanese primatologists, a group of Japanese macaques was fed wheat; within four hours, wheat eating had spread to the entire group of macaques living in the valley. Inventive behavior has also been observed among Japanese macaques. A group living on an island off the Japanese coast learned to clean sweet potatoes by dipping them in water after observing the young macaque who had first done it. From this youngster, the behavior spread to its playmates and some of their mothers. Once a mother had learned to wash sweet potatoes, this skill was always passed on to her offspring.

The more we learn about catarrhines in general, and apes in particular, the more we become aware of a degree of intelligence and capacity for conceptual thought hitherto unsuspected for any nonhuman primate.

ORIGINAL STUDY

THE INTELLECTUAL ABILITIES OF CHIMPANZEES[8]

The mid-sixties saw the start of a project that, along with other similar research, was to teach us a great deal about the chimpanzee mind. This was Project Washoe, conceived by Trixie and Allen Gardner. They purchased an infant chimpanzee and began to teach her the signs of ASL, the American Sign Language used by the deaf. Twenty years earlier another husband and wife team, Richard and Cathy Hayes, had tried, with an almost total lack of success, to teach a young chimp, Vikki, to talk. The Hayes's undertaking taught us a lot about the chimpanzee mind, but Vikki, although she did well in IQ tests, and was clearly an intelligent youngster, could not learn human speech. The Gardners, however, achieved spectacular success with their pupil, Washoe. Not only did she learn signs easily, but she quickly began to string them together in meaningful ways. It was clear that each sign evoked, in her mind, a mental image of the object it represented. If, for example, she was asked, in sign language, to fetch an apple, she would go and locate an apple that was out of sight in another room.

Other chimps entered the project, some starting their lives in deaf signing families before joining Washoe. And finally Washoe adopted an infant, Loulis. He came from a lab where no thought of teaching signs had ever penetrated. When he was with Washoe he was given no lessons in language acquisition—not by humans, anyway. Yet by the time he was eight years old he had made fifty-eight signs in their correct contexts. How did he learn them? Mostly, it seems, by imitating the behaviour of Washoe and the other three signing chimps, Dar, Moja, and Tatu. Sometimes, though, he received tuition from Washoe herself. One day, for example, she began to swagger about bipedally, hair bristling, signing *food! food! food!* in great excitement. She had seen a human approaching with a bar of chocolate. Loulis, only eighteen months old, watched passively. Suddenly Washoe stopped her swaggering, went over to him, took his hand, and moulded the sign for food (fingers pointing towards mouth). Another time, in a similar context, she made the sign for *chewing gum* but with *her* hand on *his* body. On a third occasion Washoe, apropos of nothing, picked up a small chair, took it over to Loulis, set it down in front of him, and very distinctly made the *chair* sign three times, watching him closely as she did so. The two food signs became incorporated into Loulis's vocabulary but the sign for chair did not. Obviously the priorities of a young chimp are similar to those of a human child!

When news of Washoe's accomplishments first hit the scientific community it immediately provoked a storm of bitter protest. It implied that chimpanzees were capable of mastering a human language, and this, in turn, indicated mental powers of generalization, abstraction and concept-formation as well as an ability to understand and use abstract symbols. And these intellectual skills were surely the prerogatives of *Homo sapiens*. Although there were many who were fascinated and excited by the Gardners' findings, there were many more who denounced the whole project, holding that the data was suspect, the methodology sloppy, and the conclusions not only misleading, but quite preposterous. The controversy inspired all sorts of other language projects. And, whether the investigators were sceptical to start with and hoped to disprove the Gardners' work, or whether they were attempting to demonstrate the same thing in a new way, their research provided additional information about the chimpanzee's mind.

And so, with new incentive, psychologists began to test the mental abilities of chimpanzees in a variety of different ways; again and again the results confirmed that their minds are uncannily like our own. It had long been held that only humans were capable of what is called "cross-modal transfer of information"—in other words, if you shut your eyes and someone allows you to feel a strangely shaped potato, you will subsequently be able to pick it out from other differently shaped potatoes simply by looking at them. And vice versa. It turned out that chimpanzees can "know" with their eyes what they "feel" with their fingers in just the same way. In fact, we now know that some other non-human primates can do the same thing. I expect all kinds of creatures have the same ability.

Then it was proved, experimentally and beyond doubt, that chimpanzees could recognize themselves in mirrors—that they had, therefore, some kind of self-concept. In fact, Washoe, some years previously, had already demonstrated the ability when she spontaneously identified herself in the mirror, staring at her image and making her name sign. But that observation was merely anecdotal. The proof came when chimpanzees who had been allowed to play with mirrors were, while anaesthetized, dabbed with spots of odourless paint in places, such as the ears or the top of the head, that they could see only in the mirror. When they woke they were not only fascinated by their images, but immediately investigated, with their fingers, the dabs of paint.

The fact that chimpanzees have excellent memories surprised no one. Everyone, after all, has been brought up to believe that an elephant never forgets, so why should a chimpanzee be any different? The fact that Washoe spontaneously gave the name-sign of Beatrice Gardner, her surrogate mother, when she saw her after a separation of eleven years was no greater an accomplishment than the amazing memory shown by dogs who recognize their owners after separations of almost as long—and the chimpanzee has a much longer life span than a dog. Chimpanzees can plan ahead, too, at least as regards the immediate future. This, in fact, is well illustrated at Gombe, during the termiting season: Often an individual prepares a tool for use on a termite mound that is several hundred yards away and absolutely out of sight.

This is not the place to describe in detail the other cognitive abilities that have been studied in laboratory chimpanzees. Among other accomplishments chimpanzees possess premathematical skills: They can, for example, readily differentiate between *more* and *less*. They can classify things into specific categories according to a given criterion— thus they have no difficulty in separating a pile of food into *fruits* and *vegetables* on one occasion, and, on another, dividing the same pile of food into *large* versus *small* items, even though this requires putting some vegetables with some fruits. Chimpanzees who have been taught a language can combine signs creatively in order to describe objects for which they have no symbol. Washoe, for example, puzzled her caretakers by asking, repeatedly, for a *rock berry*. Eventually it transpired that she was referring to Brazil nuts which she had encountered for the first time a while before. Another language-trained chimp described a cucumber as a *green banana*, and another referred to an Alka-Seltzer as a *listen drink*. They can even invent signs. Lucy, as she got older, had to be put on a leash for her outings. One day, eager to set off but having no sign for *leash*, she signalled her wishes by holding a crooked index finger to the ring on her collar. This sign became part of her vocabulary. Some chimpanzees love to draw, and especially to paint. Those who have learned sign language sometimes spontaneously label their works, "This [is] apple"—or bird, or sweetcorn, or whatever. The fact that the paintings often look, to our eyes, remarkably unlike the objects depicted by the artists either means that the chimpanzees are poor draughtsmen or that we have much to learn regarding ape-style representational art!

People sometimes ask why chimpanzees have evolved such complex intellectual powers when their lives in the wild are so simple. The answer is, of course, that their lives in the wild are not so simple! They use—and need—all their mental skills during normal day-to-day life in their complex society. They are always having to make choices where to go, or with whom to travel. They need highly developed social skills—particularly those males who are ambitious to attain high positions in the dominance hierarchy. Low-ranking chimpanzees must learn deception—to conceal their intentions or to do things in secret—if they are to get their way in the presence of their superiors. Indeed, the study of chimpanzees in the wild suggests that their intellectual abilities evolved, over the millennia, to help them cope with daily life. And now, the solid core of data concerning chimpanzee intellect collected so carefully in the lab setting provides a background against which to evaluate the many examples of intelligent, rational behaviour that we see in the wild.

[8] Jane Goodall, *Through a Window: My Thirty Years with the Chimpanzees of Gombe* (Boston: Houghton Mifflin, 1990), pp. 19–23.

USE OF OBJECTS AS TOOLS

In the wild, neither baboons nor gorillas make or use tools in any significant way, but chimpanzees do. For our purposes, a **tool** may be defined simply as an object used to facilitate some task or activity. Here, a distinction must be made between simple tool *use*, as when one pounds something with a convenient stone when a hammer is not available, and tool *making*, which involves deliberate modification of some material for its intended use. Thus, otters that use unmodified stones to crack open clams may be tool users, but they are not tool makers. Not only do chimpanzees modify objects to make them suitable for particular purposes, but chimps can to some extent modify them to regular and set patterns. They can also pick up, and even prepare, objects for future use at some other location, and they can use objects as tools to solve new and novel problems. For example, chimps have

been observed using stalks of grass, twigs that they have stripped of leaves, and even sticks up to three feet long that they have smoothed down, to "fish" for termites. They insert the modified stick into a termite nest, wait a few minutes, pull the stick out, and eat the insects clinging to it, all of which requires considerable dexterity. Chimpanzees are equally deliberate in their nest building. They test the vines and branches to make sure they are usable. If they are not, the animal moves to another site.

Tool: An object used to facilitate some task or activity. While toolmaking involves intentional modification of the material of which it is made, tool use may consist of the use of either made tools or unmodified objects for some particular purpose.

The chimpanzee is using a tool to "fish" for termites.

Other examples of chimpanzee use of objects as tools involve leaves, used as wipes, or as sponges to get water out of a hollow to drink. Large sticks may serve as clubs or as missiles (as may stones) in aggressive or defensive displays. Stones or rocks are also used as hammers and anvils to open palm nuts and hard fruits. Interestingly, tool use to fish for termites or to crack open nuts is most often exhibited by females, whereas aimed throwing of rocks and sticks is most often exhibited by males. Such tool-using behavior, which young animals learn from their mothers and other adults in their group, may reflect one of the preliminary adaptations that, in the past, led to human cultural behavior.

Although the other large apes do not display the same tool use in the wild as do chimpanzees, captive apes have shown themselves to be just as adept. Indeed, the most extensive tool use in captivity is displayed not by chimps, but by orangutans. Clearly, the ability is there in other apes; it is just that under natural conditions, their tool-using potential is not utilized.

HUNTING

The hunting, killing, and eating of small to medium-sized mammals, something that is unusual among primates, has been observed among baboons and chimps, but not among gorillas. Such behavior is exhibited less often by baboons than by chimps, who are less opportunistic in their meat eating. Although chimpanzee females sometimes hunt, males do so far more frequently. When on the hunt, they may spend up to two hours watching, following, and chasing intended prey. Moreover, in contrast to the usual primate practice of each animal finding its own food for itself, hunting frequently involves teamwork to trap and kill prey. The most sophisticated examples of this occur when hunting baboons; once a potential victim has been partially isolated from its troop, three or more adults will carefully position themselves so as to block off escape routes while another climbs toward the prey for the kill. Once a kill has been made, it is common for most of those present to get a share of the meat, either by grabbing a piece as the chance affords, or by sitting and begging for a piece.

Perhaps limited predation is a very old pattern among chimps. Equally possible, it may be a recent development on the part of chimpanzees living at the edge of the savanna; they may just be starting to exploit a food source that our own ancestors tapped in similar circumstances millions of years earlier. Consistent with this behavior, when out on the savanna, chimps are known to increase their predation on eggs and vertebrate animals, probably because they cannot so easily satisfy their amino acid requirements (necessary for growth and tissue replacement) from the plants there as they can in the forest.[9] In any case, it is interesting to note that, in primates, more cooperation seems to go hand in hand with predation and meat eating.

PRIMATE BEHAVIOR AND HUMAN EVOLUTION

Studies of monkeys and apes living today—especially gorillas and chimpanzees, which are so closely related to us, and baboons, which have adapted to life on savannas like those to which our earliest ancestors adapted—afford essential clues in the reconstruction of adaptations and behavior patterns involved in the emergence of our earliest ancestors. At the same time, we must be careful about how we reconstruct this development. Primates have changed in various ways from earlier times, and undoubtedly certain forms of behavior that they now exhibit were not found among their ancestors. Furthermore, it is important to remember that present-day primate behavior shows considerable variation, not just from one species to another but also from one population to another of a single species. To ignore such variation is to run the risk of faulty generalization—something often seen in the popular literature.

---

[9] Ann Brower Stahl, "Hominid Dietary Selection Before Fire," *Current Anthropology*, 25 (1984):155.

Chapter Summary

The Linnaean system classifies living things on the basis of overall similarities into small groups, or species. The characteristics on which Karl von Linné based his system were body structure, body function, and sequence of bodily growth. Modern taxonomy also utilizes such characteristics as chemical reactions of blood, protein structure, and the makeup of the genetic material itself.

The modern primates, like most mammals, are intelligent animals that bear their young live and then nourish them with milk from their mothers. Like other mammals, they maintain constant body temperature and have respiratory and circulatory systems that will sustain high activity. Their skeleton and teeth also resemble those of other mammals, although there are differences of detail.

Modern primates are divided into two suborders. The strepsirhines include lemurs, indriids, and lorises, which resemble small rodents in body outline. The haplorhines include tarsiers, New and Old World monkeys, apes, and humans. To a greater degree among the haplorhines, and a lesser degree among the strepsirhines, primates show a number of characteristics that developed as adaptations to insect predation in the trees. These adaptive characteristics include a generalized set of teeth, suited to insect eating but also a variety of fruits and leaves as well. These teeth are fewer in number and set in a smaller jaw than in most mammals. Other evolutionary adaptations in the primate line include stereoscopic vision, or depth perception, and an intensified sense of touch. Each of these developments had an effect upon the primate brain, resulting in a general trend toward larger size and greater complexity. There were also changes in the primate skeleton; in particular, a reduction of the snout, larger brain case, and numerous adaptations for upright posture and flexibility of limb movement. In addition, changes in the reproductive pattern took place such that fewer offspring were born

to each female, and there was a longer period of infant dependency.

The apes are the closest relatives humans have. These include gibbons, siamangs, orangutans, gorillas, and chimpanzees. In genetic structure, biochemistry, and anatomy, chimpanzees and gorillas are closest to humans, and thus must share a common ancestry.

The social life of primates is very complex. Primates are social animals, and most species live and travel in groups. Among savanna baboons, females remain for life in the group of their birth, whereas males transfer at adolescence to another. Among chimpanzees, it is females that may transfer, though not all do so; their sons and often their daughters remain with their mothers for life. Among gorillas, either males or females may transfer. In all three species, both males and females are organized into dominance hierarchies. In the case of females, the better food and reduced harassment that are a consequence of high rank enhance reproductive success.

A characteristic primate activity is grooming, which is a sign of closeness between individuals. Among baboons, gorillas, and chimpanzees, sexual interaction generally takes place only when a female is in estrus. Although dominant males try to monopolize females while they are in estrus, the cooperation of the females is usually required for this to succeed. Among baboons, females clearly prefer as sex partners males with whom they already have a friendship. Primates have elaborate systems of communication based on vocalizations and gestures. Usually primates move about within home ranges, rather than defended territories.

The diet of most primates is made up of a variety of fruits, leaves, and insects, but baboons and chimpanzees sometimes hunt, kill, and eat animals as well. Among chimps, most hunting is done by males, and may require considerable teamwork. Once a kill is made, most animals present get a share of the meat.

Suggested Readings

Fossey, Dian. *Gorillas in the Mist*. Burlington, Mass.: Houghton Mifflin, 1983.
Dian Fossey is to gorillas what Jane Goodall is to chimpanzees. Up until the time of her death, Fossey had devoted years to study gorilla behavior in the field. This book is about the first 13 years of her study; as well as being readable and informative, it is well illustrated.

Goodall, Jane. *Through a Window*. Boston: Houghton Mifflin, 1990.
This fascinating book is a personal account of Goodall's experience over 30 years of studying wild chimpanzees in Tanzania. A pleasure to read and a fount of information on the behavior of these apes, the book is profusely illustrated as well.

Jolly, Allison. *The Evolution of Primate Behavior*, 2nd ed. New York: Macmillan, 1985.
The first edition of this book was the standard text on primate behavior for 13 years. In this as in the original edition, the author surveys current knowledge about primate behavior and its relevance for human behavior. Comprehensive and up-to-date, the book is also exciting, amusing, and well illustrated.

LeGros Clark, W. E. *History of the Primates*, 5th ed. Chicago: University of Chicago Press, 1966.
An old classic, this remains a fine introduction to the comparative anatomy of the primates.

Patterson, Francine, and Eugene Linden. *The Education of Koko*. New York: Holt, Rinehart and Winston, 1981.
Several experiments with captive apes have sought to investigate the full potential of their communicative abilities, and one of the most interesting is that involving Koko the gorilla. This is a particularly readable account of those experiments and their results.

PRE-COLUMBIAN
MASK,
PERU

PART II

HUMAN BIOLOGICAL AND CULTURAL EVOLUTION THROUGH THE OLD STONE AGE

INTRODUCTION

N CHAPTER 1, WE SAW HOW THE NEZ PERCE INDIANS OF NORTH AMERICA EXPLAINED THEIR EXISTENCE IN THE WORLD. INDEED, ALL HUMAN CULTURES OF WHICH WE HAVE RECORD HAVE GRAPPLED WITH SUCH AGE-OLD QUESTIONS AS WHERE DO WE COME FROM AND WHAT IS

our place in the overall scheme of things? Each culture has answered these questions in its own way, through bodies of myth and folklore, as did the Nez Perce. It was not really until the twentieth century that hard scientific evidence could be brought to bear on these questions. In particular, as physical anthropologists and archaeologists have unearthed the bones and tools of our earliest ancestors, we have begun to glimpse the outline of a fantastic saga in which a tropical-dwelling apelike creature is transformed into a creative being capable of inventing solutions to problems of existence, rather than passively accepting what the environment and its own biology dictate.

We begin our discussion of this transformation, in Chapter 5, with a review of the fossil evidence for primate evolution, interpreting the important fossils in light of evolutionary theory, our understanding of the biological variation of modern primates, and the behavioral correlates of that variation. This brings us to the apelike creatures of 8 to 16 million years ago, from some of which human ancestors evolved. These early apelike ancestors seem to have spent more and more time on the ground, and probably possessed mental abilities more or less equivalent to those of a modern chimpanzee. Because they were rather small and vulnerable, we think that the greatest measure of reproductive success came to those who were able to rear up on their hind limbs and scan the savanna, threaten predators with their forelimbs, transport food to a tree or other place where it could be eaten in relative safety, and transport offspring instead of relying on them to hang on by themselves.

Chapter 6 continues the saga of the human transformation by showing how improved mental abilities came to play an important role in human survival. The stage was set for this with the appearance some 4 to 6 million years ago of *Australopithecus*, the first undoubted hominine. *Australopithecus* may best be thought of as an

apelike human; it walked bipedally in a fully human manner, but its mental abilities do not seem to have differed greatly from those of its ancestors of a few million years earlier. By 2.4 million years ago, however, some hominines were beginning to manipulate the physical world, inventing solutions to the problems of existence. These earliest members of the genus *Homo* had far smaller brains than ours, but they were significantly larger than those of *Australopithecus*. Their appearance is associated with a new way of surviving. Instead of foraging, as do most primates, on a more or less individualistic basis for vegetables and fruits, supplemented by eggs, grubs, lizards, and similar sources of animal protein, our earliest ancestors invented stone tools with which they could butcher the carcasses of larger animals. This made possible a degree of economic specialization; males scavenged for meat, and females gathered a wide variety of other wild foods. It also made possible new patterns of social interaction; females and males began sharing the results of their food-getting activities on a regular basis.

Over the next nearly 2 million years, a period known as the Paleolithic, or Old Stone Age, the evolving genus *Homo* relied increasingly on improved mental abilities for survival, as we shall see in Chapters 7 and 8. In the process, hunting replaced scavenging as the main means by which meat was procured, and other improvements of this food-foraging way of life took place. As a consequence, the human species, essentially a tropical one, was able to free itself from its tropical habitat and, through invention, adapt itself to colder climates. By 100,000 years ago, humans had acquired essentially modern brains. Shortly thereafter, they achieved the ability to survive under true arctic conditions. To invent ways of surviving under such forbidding and difficult conditions ranks as no less an achievement than sending the first man to the moon.

FOSSIL PRIMATES

CHAPTER PREVIEW

Our knowledge of the earliest catarrhine primates is based primarily on fossils from Egypt's Fayum Depression in the desert west of Cairo. Here, winds and flash floods have uncovered sediments more than 22 million years old, exposing the remains of a tropical rain forest that was home to a variety of monkey-like animals.

WHEN DID THE FIRST PRIMATES APPEAR, AND WHAT WERE THEY LIKE? The earliest primates had developed by 60 million years ago and were small, arboreal insect eaters. Their initial adaptation to life in the trees set the stage for the subsequent appearance of other primate models.

WHEN DID THE FIRST MONKEYS AND APES APPEAR, AND WHAT WERE THEY LIKE? By the Oligocene Epoch, which began about 34 million years ago, monkeys and apes about the size of modern house cats were living in Africa. By about 20 million years ago, they had proliferated and soon spread over many parts of the Old World. Some forms remained relatively small, while others became quite large, comparable to present-day chimpanzees and gorillas.

WHAT GROUP OF PRIMATES GAVE RISE TO THE HUMAN LINE OF EVOLUTION? Present evidence suggests that our own ancestors are found among the "sivapithecines," which lived between approximately 17 and 8 million years ago. Small versions of these apelike primates seem to have had the right kind of anatomy, and at least some of them lived in situations in which the right kind of selective pressures existed to transform them into primitive hominines.

A little more than a century ago, Charles Darwin shattered the surface calm of the Victorian world with his startling theory that humans are cousins of the living apes and monkeys and are descended from their prehistoric ancestors. What would have been the public reaction, one wonders, if they had known, as we do, that even earlier ancestors were small, mouse-sized creatures that subsisted chiefly on insects and worms? Such primitive creatures date back about 60 million years. These ancient forebears of ours evolved over time into different species as mutations produced variation, which was acted upon by natural selection and genetic drift.

Although many of the primates discussed in this chapter no longer exist, their descendants, which were reviewed in Chapter 4, are found living throughout the world. The successful adaptation of the primates is believed to be due largely to their intelligence, a characteristic that reaches its culmination in human beings and which provides for adaptive flexibility. Other physical traits, such as stereoscopic vision and a grasping hand, have also been instrumental in the success of the primates.

What is the justification for studying a form of life whose history is, at best, fragmentary, and which existed millions of years ago? The study of these prehistoric primates tells us something we can use to interpret the evolution of the entire primate line, including ourselves. It gives us a better understanding of the physical forces that caused these primitive creatures to evolve into today's primates. Ultimately, the study of these ancient ancestors gives us a fuller knowledge of the processes through which insect-eating, small-brained animals evolved into a toolmaker and thinker that is recognizably human.

PRIMATE FOSSILS

Considering that primates have shown a tendency through the ages to live in environments where the conditions for fossilization are generally not good, we have a surprising number of fossils to work with. While some nearly complete skeletons of ancient primates do exist, more often what we have are specimens of teeth and jawbones, because these structures are durable and are often the only remains of an animal to be found. Thus a whole branch of fossil study based on tooth structures, or dentition, has arisen. Dentition is most important in helping to identify and classify different fossil forms; often investigators are able to infer a good deal about the total animal on the basis of only a few teeth found lying in the earth. For example, knowledge of the way the teeth fit together indicates much about the operation of the jaws, suggesting the types of muscles needed. This in turn indicates how the skull must have been shaped to provide accommodation for the musculature. The shape of the jaws and details of the teeth also define the type of food that they were suited to deal with, indicating the probable diet of the specimen.

MAMMALIAN EVOLUTION AND PRIMATE ORIGINS

An interesting fact about the evolution of the mammals is that the diverse forms with which we are familiar today, including the primates, are the products of an **adaptive radiation** that did not begin until after mammals had been present on the earth for more than 100 million years. Actually, the story of mammalian evolution starts as long ago as 230 to 280 million years ago (Figure 5.1). From deposits of this period, which geologists call the Permian, we have the remains of reptiles with features pointing in a distinctly mammalian direction. These mammal-like reptiles were slimmer than most other reptiles, and were flesh eaters. In a series of graded fossils, we can see in them a reduction of bones to a more mammalian number, the shifting of limbs underneath the body, development of a separation between the mouth and nasal cavity, differentiation of the teeth, and so forth.

By 180 million years ago—the end of what geologists call the Triassic period—true mammals were on the scene. We know these and the mammals from the succeeding Jurassic and Cretaceous

Adaptive radiation: Rapid diversification of an evolving population, as it adapts to a variety of available niches.

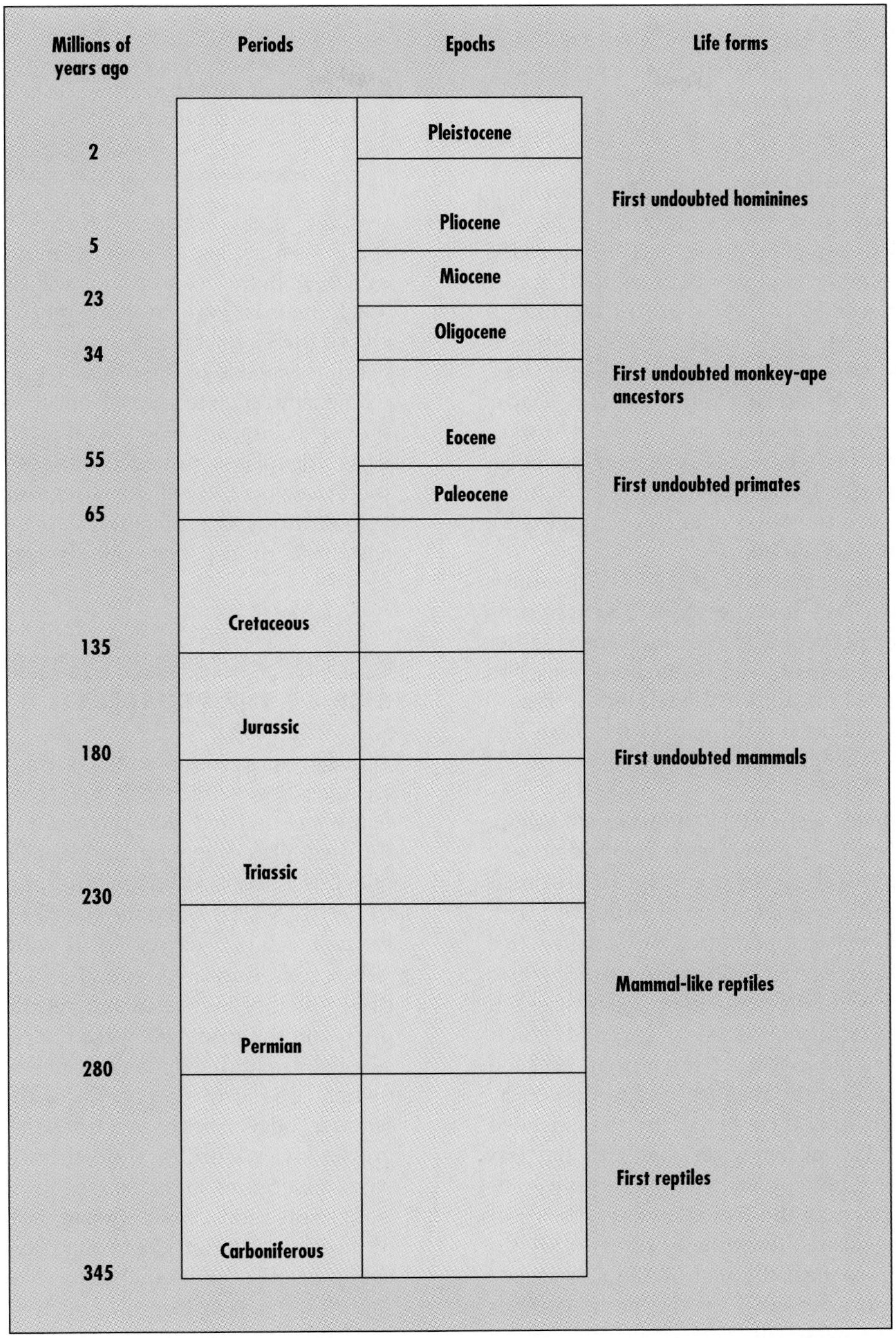

Millions of years ago	Periods	Epochs	Life forms
		Pleistocene	
2			First undoubted hominines
5		Pliocene	
23		Miocene	
34		Oligocene	
			First undoubted monkey-ape ancestors
55		Eocene	
65		Paleocene	First undoubted primates
135	Cretaceous		
180	Jurassic		First undoubted mammals
230	Triassic		
280	Permian		Mammal-like reptiles
345	Carboniferous		First reptiles

Figure 5.1 This timeline highlights major "milestones" in the evolution of mammals.

periods (180 to 75 million years ago) from hundreds of finds of mostly teeth and jaw parts. All of these creatures were small and flesh eaters—such things as insects, worms, and eggs. They seem to have been nocturnal in their habits, which is probably why the senses of smell and hearing became so developed in mammals. Although things cannot be seen as well in the dark as they can in the light, they can be heard and smelled just as well. Both sound and smell are more complex than sight. If something can be seen it is right there in the line of vision. By contrast, it is possible to smell and hear things around corners and in other hidden places, and in addition to figuring out what it is that is smelled or heard and how far away it is, the animal must also figure out where it is. A further complication is the fact that smells linger, and so the animal must figure out if the cause of an odor is still there or, if not, how old the odor is.

As the hearing and sense of smell of mammals became keener, they lost the ability (possessed by reptiles) to see in color. But the new keener senses and the importance of outwitting both prey and predators served to improve their information-processing capacities and the part of the brain that handles this—the cerebral cortex—over that of reptiles.

Since mammals were developing as such bright, active creatures, it may seem puzzling at first why reptiles continued to be the dominant land animals for over 100 million years. After all, mammals, with their constant body temperature, can remain active at any time, whereas reptiles become more sluggish unless the surrounding temperature is just right. Furthermore, mammals provide care for their young, whereas most reptiles leave theirs to fend for themselves. But the mammals were limited by two things. For one, their high activity demanded more in the way of nutrition than did the less constant activity of reptiles. Such high-quality nutrition is provided by the fruits, nuts, and seeds of the flowering plants, but these plants did not become common until the end of the Cretaceous period. It is also provided by the flesh of other animals, but the mammals were small, and dependent particularly on insects and worms. These were limited in numbers until flowers and fruits provided them with a host of new **ecological niches**, or functional positions in their habitats, to exploit.

The second limitation that affected the mammals

Ecological niche: A species' way of life considered in the context of its environment, including other species found in that environment.

was the slight temporal priority enjoyed by the reptiles—they had preempted most available niches, which therefore were not available to mammals. With the mass extinction of so many reptiles at the end of the Cretaceous, a number of existing niches became available to the mammals; at the same time, whole new niches opened up as the new grasses provided abundant food in arid places, and the other flowering plants provided abundant, high-quality food elsewhere. By chance, the mammals had what it took in the way of biological equipment to take advantage of the new opportunities available to them.

RISE OF THE PRIMATES

The early primates emerged during a time of great change all over the world. The separation of continents was under way as the result of movement of the great plate-like segments of the earth's crust on which they rest. Although Europe was still joined to North America, South America and India were isolated, while a narrow body of water separated Africa from Eurasia (Figure 5.2). On the land itself the great dinosaurs had but recently become extinct, and the mammals were undergoing the great adaptive radiation which ultimately led to the development of the diverse forms with which we are familiar today. At the same time, the newly evolved grasses, ivies, shrubs, and other flowering plants were undergoing an enormous proliferation. This, along with a new, mild climate, favored the spread of dense, lush tropical and subtropical forests over much of the earth, including North and South America, much of Eurasia and Africa.

With the spread of these huge belts of forest, the stage was set for the evolution of some mammals from a rodent-like ground existence to the arboreal primate condition. Forests would provide our early ancestors with the ecological niches in which they would flourish.

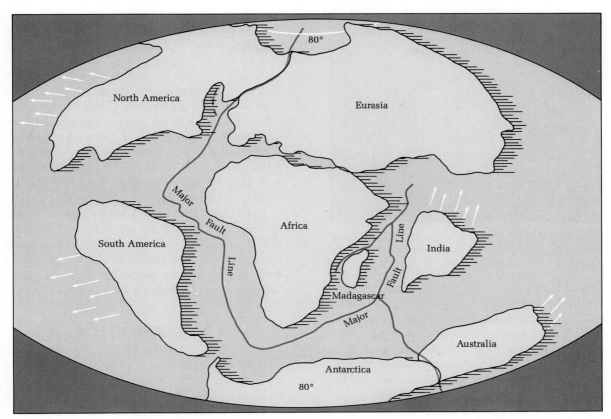

Figure 5.2   The separation of the continents was a result of massive shifting in the plate-like segments of the earth's crust as illustrated by the position of the continents at the end of the Cretaceous period (ca. 65 million years ago).

The move to an arboreal existence brought a combination of the problems of earthbound existence with those of flight. In their move into the air, birds developed highly stereotyped behavior; tree-dwelling primates, on the other hand, exhibit flexible behavior in response to decision making. The initial forays into the trees must have produced many misjudgments and errors of coordination, leading to falls that injured or killed the individuals badly adapted to arboreal life. Natural selection favored those that judged depth correctly and gripped the branches strongly. It is quite likely that the early primates that took to the trees were in some measure preadapted, with better vision and more dexterous fingers than their contemporaries.

The relatively small size of the early primates allowed them to make use of the smaller branches of trees; larger, heavier competitors, and most preda-

tors, could not follow. The move to the smaller branches also opened up a more abundant food supply; the primates were able to gather leaves, flowers, fruits, and insects directly rather than waiting for them to fall to the ground.

The utilization of a new environment led to an acceleration in the rate of change of primate characteristics. Paradoxically, these changes eventually made possible a return to the ground on the part of some primates, including the ancestors of the genus *Homo*.

PALEOCENE PRIMATES

Far back in the reaches of geologic time, small, squirrel-like animals resembling today's tree shrews scampered along the branches of trees in tropical forests. Members of the now-extinct suborder

The ability to judge depth correctly and grasp branches strongly are of obvious use to animals as active in the trees as this South American squirrel monkey.

Plesiadapiformes, these creatures appeared during the Paleocene Epoch, about 65 million years ago. They lived mostly on seeds and insects; their muzzles were long and pointed, their ears were small, their wrists and ankles were capable of turning toward each other, enabling them to climb trees, and their digits were flexible and suitable for grasping in spite of the presence of claws.

Since their survival depended on catching live food, these animals had to be quick and intelligent; the latter characteristic was reflected in their brains, which were larger than those of the tree shrews they otherwise resembled. Plesiadapiformes, of which there were a number of species, are known from a series of fossils from North America and Europe. Clearly, they were successful animals in their day, for in North America they account for a bit over a third of late Paleocene mammalian fossils.

Up until 1990, plesiadapiformes were generally considered to be very primitive primates. The recent discovery of a particularly well-preserved fossil from Wyoming, however, has revealed that they are not; rather, they are related to the Colugos —gliding mammals that are represented today by two species of "flying lemurs" (which aren't lemurs, nor do they fly; like flying squirrels, they glide). Flying lemurs are found today only in Borneo and the Philippines. Since Colugos and primates show a close genetic relationship, both likely shared a common ancestry among the insectivores, probably going their separate evolutionary ways by 60 million years ago. Thus, primates would have arisen as part of the great Paleocene adaptive radiation of mammals.

In fact, the earliest surely known primate fossils, ten teeth from a site in Morocco, are about 60 million years old. These cheek teeth (molars and premolars) are very similar to the corresponding teeth of the modern mouse lemur, a tiny strepsirhine primate weighing a mere two ounces.

EOCENE PRIMATES

The Eocene Epoch, which lasted from about 55 to 34 million years ago, began with an abrupt warming trend, at which time many older forms of mammals became extinct, to be replaced by recognizable progenitors of many of today's forms. Among the latter were numerous forms of lemur-like and tarsier-like primates, of which over 50 genera are known. Fossils of these creatures have been found in North America, Europe and Asia, where the warm, wet conditions of the Eocene sustained extensive rain forests (Figure 5.3).

Eocene primates are usually classified into two families, the **Adapidae** and the **Omomyidae**. The former were mostly diurnal (active during daylight) and generally ate fruit and leaves. Generally small, some were a bit larger than the smallest of today's monkeys. In many ways they were remarkably

Plesiadapiformes: Now-extinct mammals once considered to be primates, now known to be related to colugas (gliding mammals) which share a common ancestry with primates.

Adapidae: Extinct family of lemur-like primates.

Omomyidae: Extinct family of haplorhine primates, probably ancestral to platyrhine and possibly catarhine monkeys.

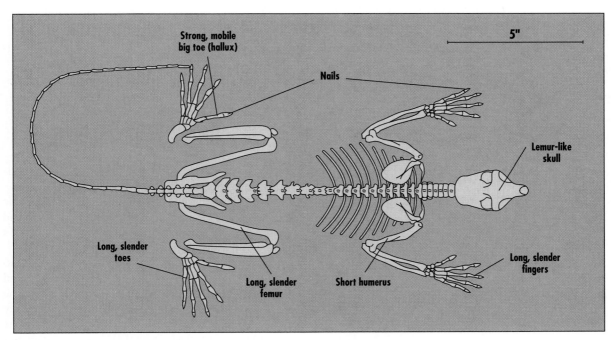

Figure 5.3   The Eocene genus *Notharctus* represents the Omomyidae.

similar to modern lemurs, lorises, and indriids, which likely are their descendants. Smaller than Adapids are the Omomyids, which were nocturnal eaters of fruits and insects. Tarsier-like in their anatomy, they are thought to have given rise to today's tarsier.

What these early primates have in common are somewhat enlarged brain cases, slightly reduced snouts, and a somewhat forward position of the eye orbits, which are surrounded by a complete bony ring (Figure 5.4). Their dentition, however, was primitive and unlike that of modern forms. In their limb skeleton, they were well adapted to grasping, leaping and perching. Moreover, nails, rather than claws, may be seen on some digits.

A third group of Eocene primates may be represented by fossils recently discovered in Algeria.[1] Unfortunately, they consist of only a few teeth, possibly of several distinct species. The teeth of at least one species, however, resemble those of the Oligocene hominoid *Aegyptopithecus*, making it the leading candidate for the oldest known ancestor of the monkeys and apes. Probably weighing between 150 and 300 grams, the animal was not very large—no more than three times the size of a modern chipmunk, at most. Whether this group of primates arose at the same time as the Adapids and Omomyids, or from some early form of one or the other of these two families is so far not known; what we need to settle the matter are more fossils.

With the end of the Eocene, substantial changes took place among the primates, as among other mammals. In North America, primates became extinct and elsewhere their range seems to have

[1] Elizabeth Culatto, "A New Take on Anthropoid Origins," *Science*, 256 (1992):1516–1517.

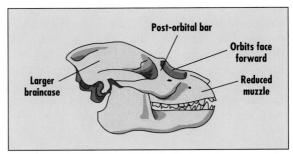

Figure 5.4   The Eocene genus *Adapis* represents the Adapidae.

been reduced considerably. A driving force in all this was probably climatic change. Already, through the late Eocene, climates were becoming somewhat cooler and drier, but at the very end temperatures took a sudden dive, sufficient to trigger formation of a substantial ice cap over Antarctica. The result was a marked reduction of the environment to which early primates were adapted. At the same time, some early primate niches may have been more effectively utilized by newly evolved rodent forms. Finally, the precursors of monkeys and apes, up to then overshadowed by Adapids and Omomyids, may have been able to take over some other niches formerly occupied by the early Adapids and Omomyids.

OLIGOCENE MONKEYS AND APES

The Oligocene Epoch began about 34, and ended about 23, million years ago. Primate fossils that have thus far been discovered and definitely placed in the Oligocene are not common, but enough exist to prove that haplorhines were becoming quite prominent and diverse by this time. The scarcity of Oligocene primate fossils stems from the reduced habitat available to them, and from the arboreal nature of primates then living, which restricted them to damp forest environments where conditions are exceedingly poor for fossil formation.

Fortunately, Egypt's Fayum depression has yielded sufficient fossils (over 1000) to reveal that, by 31 million years ago, haplorhine primates existed in considerable diversity. Moreover, the "cast of characters" is growing, as new fossils continue to be found in the Fayum, as well as in newly discovered localities in Algeria and Oman.[2] At present, we have evidence of at least 60 genera included in two families, **Parapithecidae** and **Propliopithecidae**. Both show a combination of monkey-like and ape-like features, but the parapithecids are generally smaller than the propliopithecids. The origins of both families probably lie in the third, less numerous group of Eocene primates just discussed; but in the Oligocene the tables have been turned; now lemur-like

---

Parapithecidae: Extinct family of small, haplorphine primates, possibly includes ancestors of monkeys.

Propliopithecidae: Extinct family of haplorhine primates, probably ancestral to hominoids.

---

and tarsier-like forms have become far less prominent than the monkey-like–ape-like forms.

Included among the parapithecids may be the ancestors of monkeys. In their dental formula and limb bones, these small primates (about the size of a modern squirrel monkey) resemble platyrhine monkeys. Some of them could easily have gotten to South America via exposed oceanic ridges and islands between the two continents which, in the Oligocene, were far closer to each other than they are today. The earliest surely known catarhine monkey fossil comes from the Miocene epoch, but its molars look as if they evolved from an earlier pattern much like one seen in parapithecids.

Far more ape-like in their dentition are a number of other genera, of which the best known is *Aegyptopithecus* (the "Egyptian ape"). Its lower molars have the five cusps of an ape, and the upper canine and lower first premolar provide a shearing mechanism such as is found in apes. Its skull possesses eye sockets that are in a forward position and completely protected by a bony wall, as is typical of modern monkeys and apes. Evidently *Aegyptopithecus*, and probably the other propliopithecids and parapithecids as well, possessed vision superior to that of the Eocene Adapids and Omomyids and their descendants, the lemurs and tarsiers. In fact, the inside of the skull of *Aegyptopithecus* reveals that its brain had a larger visual cortex and smaller olfactory lobes than do lemurs or tarsiers. Although the brain of *Aegyptopithecus* was smaller relative to body size than that of more recent catarrhines, this primate seems to have had a larger brain than any lemur or tarsier, past or present.

Aegyptopithecus, besides being the best-known Oligocene primate, is also of particular interest to us, for its teeth suggest that it belongs in the ancestry of those Miocene forms that gave rise to both humans and today's African apes. Although no

---

[2] John G. Fleagle, "Early Anthropoid Evolution." Paper presented at the 91st Annual Meeting of the American Anthropological Association, December 1992.

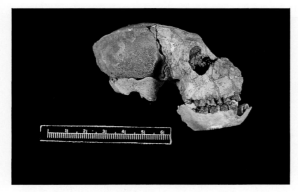

This *Aegyptopithecus* skull dates to the Oligocene Epoch. The enclosed eye sockets and dentition mark it as a catarrhine primate, probably ancestral to *Proconsul*.

bigger than a modern house cat, *Aegyptopithecus* was nonetheless one of the larger Oligocene primates. Possessed of a monkey-like skull and body, it evidently moved about in a quadrupedal monkey-like manner. Differences between males and females include more formidable canine teeth and deeper mandibles (lower jaws) in the males. In modern catarrhines, species with these traits generally live in groups that include several adult females with one or more adult males.

MIOCENE APES

The beginning of the Miocene Epoch, which succeeded the Oligocene about 23 million years ago, saw the catarhine primates still restricted to Africa, where they had originated. Around 17 million years ago, however, Africa came into contact with the Eurasian land mass, permitting the spread and proliferation of apes in the forests that existed in many parts of the Old World.

East Africa is an area particularly rich in the fossils of apes from the early through the middle part of the Miocene. The earliest of these apes, *Proconsul*, is one of the best known, owing to the preservation of much of its skeleton. Species of *Proconsul* varied considerably in size, the smallest being no larger than a modern female baboon, while the largest was the size of a chimpanzee. That they were apes is clearly shown by their dentition, particularly the five-cusped lower molars. Moreover their skull, compared to that of the Oligocene proto-apes, shows a reduced snout and a fuller,

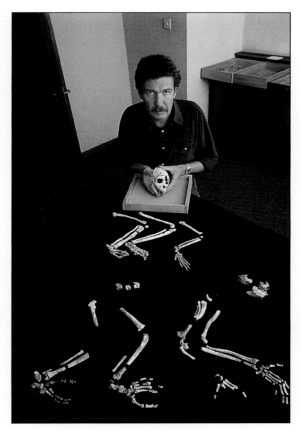

Paleoanthropologist Alan Walker displays bones of *Proconsul*, an unspecialized tree-dwelling, fruit-eating hominoid of the early Miocene.

more rounded brain case. Still, some features are reminiscent of monkeys, particularly the forward thrust and narrowness of the face.

Although its overall configuration is not quite like any living monkey or ape, the elbow, hip, knee, and foot anatomy of *Proconsul* is similar to what one sees in a chimpanzee, while the wrist is monkey-like and the lumbar vertebrae are intermediate between those of a gibbon and a monkey. The consensus is that *Proconsul* represents an unspecialized tree-dwelling, fruit-eating **hominoid** (the catarrhine superfamily to which modern apes and

Hominoid: A catarrhine primate superfamily that includes apes and humans.

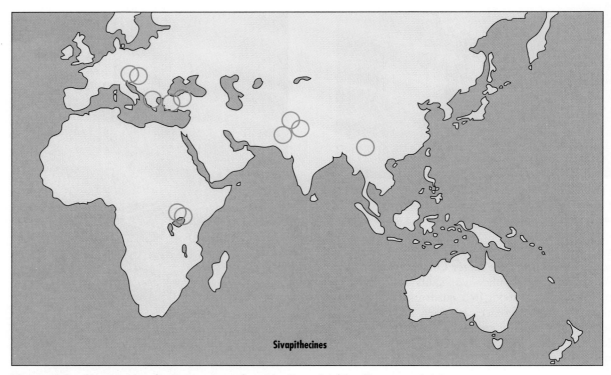

Figure 5.5 Sivapithecine fossils have been found in Central Africa, Europe, and Asia.

humans belong). Easily derivable from an animal like *Aegyptopithecus*, it was almost certainly ancestral to the hominoids of the middle Miocene. Like its probable ancestor as well as its descendants, all species of *Proconsul* were sexually dimorphic, the males being the larger sex, with more formidable canine teeth.

Hominoids of the middle and late Miocene (from roughly 16 million to 5 million years ago) can be divided into two broad groups, informally labeled dryopithecines and sivaphithecines. In the former group are several species of forest-dwelling primates having teeth and jaws very much like those of the earlier *Proconsul*. They seem to have become somewhat more ape-like, rather than monkey-like in their overall appearance, however. Dryopithecines ranged over a remarkably wide geographical area: Their fossils have been found in Europe, Asia, and Africa. Such abundance and wide distribution indicates that these primates were very successful animals.

SIVAPITHECINES

Also living in parts of Africa, Asia, and Europe were the various hominoids lumped together as **sivapithecines** (sometimes called "ramamorphs" and sometimes "ramapithecines") (Figure 5.5). Closely related to the dryopithecines, they too may be descendants of the earlier *Proconsul*. According to David Pilbeam, who has made the study of Miocene hominoids his life work: "Any of [the sivapithecines] would make excellent ancestors for the living hominoids: human bipeds, chimpanzee and gorilla knucklewalkers, orangutan contortion-

---

Sivapithecines: A group of hominoids ancestral to orangutans, and probably to chimpanzees, gorillas, and humans as well.

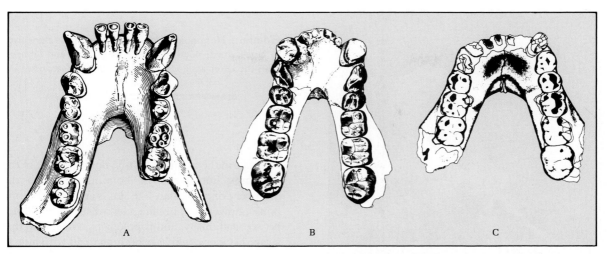

Figure 5.6   The lower jaws of *Dryopithecus* (A), *Sivapithecus* (B), and early *Australopithecus* (C), a hominine who lived nearly 4 million years ago, demonstrate some important similarities and differences between the three hominoids. Relative to the cheek teeth, all have comparably small teeth at the front of the jaw. There is a general similarity between A and B, as well as between B and C. The major difference between *Sivapithecus* and *Australopithecus* is that the rows of cheek teeth are farther apart in the hominine.

ists."[3] For many years, sivapithecines were known exclusively from the remains of teeth and jaws. Relative to the size of the cheek teeth (premolars and molars), their incisor teeth are comparable in size to those of the dryopithecines, although they are placed a bit more vertically in the mouth. The canines are far larger in males than in females, but even in males they are significantly smaller relative to the cheek teeth than the canines of any dryopithecine. Still, they do project beyond adjacent teeth so that, when closed, the jaws of sivapithecines interlock. Furthermore, the shearing function of the upper canine with the first lower premolar is retained. The molars, which show the same five-cusp pattern as the dryopithecines, have noticeably thicker enamel. The shape of the tooth row tends to be slightly V-shaped, while that of the dryopithecines is more like a U, with the rows of cheek teeth parallel to one another (Figure 5.6). The palate, or roof of the mouth, is high and arched. Finally, the lower facial region of the sivapithecines is narrow, short, and deep. Overall, the dental apparatus was built for powerful chewing, especially on the back teeth.

[3] David Pilbeam. *Human Origins.* David Skamp Distinguished Lecture in Anthropology, Indiana University, 1986, p. 6.

In the past decade, our dependence on teeth and jaws for our knowledge of the sivapithecines has lessened as a number of their skull and limb bone fragments have been found in China, Hungary, and Pakistan. In many respects, the face is remarkably orangutan-like, even down to small details of the palate. The mandible, however, is only broadly rather than specifically similar to that of an orang, nor are the upper arm bones quite the same.

SIVAPITHECINES AND HUMAN ORIGINS

As long as sivapithecines were known only from fossils of teeth and jaws, it was easy to postulate some sort of relationship between them and ourselves. This was because a number of features—the position of the incisors, the reduced canines, the thick enamel of the molars, and the shape of the tooth row—seemed to point in a somewhat human direction. Some fossils (notably one from Africa) even show a shallow concavity above the position of the canine tooth, a feature not found in any ape, but often found in humans. Indeed, some even went so

This *Sivapithecus* skull is remarkably similar to skulls of modern orangutans, so much so that an ancestor-descendant relationship is probable. The last common ancestor of chimpanzees, gorillas and humans may not have differed greatly from *Sivapithecus*.

Hominid: Hominoid family to which humans alone used to be assigned; now includes African apes and humans, with the latter assigned to the subfamily *Homininae*.

together in the hominid family; humans alone in the subfamily homininae, or hominines). With the discovery of orangutan-like skulls and ape-like limb bones, however, it became clear that this could not be so, and many anthropologists concluded that sivapithecines could have nothing to do with human origins. Rather, orangutans were seen as the sole modern survivors of an ancient group that had branched off of the evolutionary line that led to the African apes and humans some 12 to 18 million years ago.

Recently, opinion has begun to shift back to a middle position. While the link between Miocene sivapithecines and modern orangutans seems undeniable, this does not rule out the possibility of a link with African apes and humans as well.[4] How anthropologists are reassessing the sivapithecines is illustrated in the following Original Study by Roger Lewin, who at the time it was written reported on developments in paleoanthropology for *Science*, a publication of the American Association for the Advancement of Science.

far as to label sivapithecines as definitely **hominid**, a term then restricted to humans and near humans, excluding all apes (as opposed to current practice which is to classify African apes and humans

[4] Russell L. Ciochon and John G. Fleagle, "Ramapithecus and Human Origins," in *Primate Evolution and Human Origins*. ed. Russell L. Ciochon and John G. Fleagle (Hawthorne, N.Y.: Aldine de Gruyter, 1987), p. 208.

Although not identical, the modern ape most like *Sivapithecus* is the orangutan. Chimpanzees and gorillas, like humans, have come to differ more from the ancestral condition than have these Asian apes.

ORIGINAL STUDY

TOOTH ENAMEL TELLS A COMPLEX STORY[5]

The thickness of the enamel layer on teeth once assumed an especially pertinent diagnostic significance in paleoanthropology: Thick enamel permitted entry to the human family (the hominids), thin enamel betokened an ape. This simple equation has crumbled in recent years, and a current publication by Lawrence Martin, of University College, London, reveals something of the true complexity of enamel morphology.

Tooth enamel in modern humans is thick, which contrasts with the thin coating on chimpanzee and gorilla teeth. The anthropocentric interpretation was that thick enamel represented the specialized, or derived, condition, whereas thin enamel was primitive. The discovery of thick enamel in the australopithecines, fossil hominids that lived in south and east Africa between 4 and 1 million years ago, fitted this preconception. And thick enamel was one of the supposed human attributes of *Ramapithecus*, an ape-like creature that lived in Africa and Asia between 15 and 8 million years ago. *Ramapithecus* is no longer considered by most to be a hominid. Just recently enamel thickness was adduced in support of a proposed ancestral relationship between humans and orangutans, which, unlike their African cousins, have a relatively thick tooth cap.

Martin's work shows, however, that thickness is only one property of enamel that must be examined in taxonomic comparisons: Details of enamel formation are also diagnostic. But, most important, thick enamel turns out to be a primitive, not derived, character for the great ape and human group and therefore cannot be used to define hominids, according to Martin's interpretation.

Enamel is deposited in two basic patterns in the teeth of hominoids, the group to which apes and humans belong. The first is a fast mode, which produces a characteristic appearance known as pattern 3 and is primitive for hominoids. The second is a slow mode, whose product is pattern 1 and is derived within the hominoid group.

In gibbons, for instance, a relatively short-lived burst of pattern 3, fast enamel deposition leaves a thin tooth cap. A longer period of maturation in humans builds up thick enamel by the same, pattern 3, growth. Now, chimpanzees and gorillas, like gibbons, have thin enamel, but deposition proceeds in two stages. The bulk (60 percent) of the initial phase is fast growth, but there is an abrupt switch to slow deposition for the remainder. Martin terms this pattern thin, slowed growth, which is developmentally and phylogenetically distinct from the thin, fast pattern in gibbons.

Orangutans, which have intermediate thick enamel, also go through a two-stage deposition, but again it is not homologous with that in the African apes. After the initial fast phase (80 percent of the total), deposition slows to $2.5\mu m$ per day for about $200\mu m$, and then slows again to the African apes' lower rate for the final $50\mu m$.

A phylogenetic picture begins to emerge, into which the data for the fossil ape *Sivapithecus* fit very neatly. This creature, which existed in Eurasia and Africa 15 to 8 million years ago and represents the group to which Ramapithecus belongs, turns out to have thick, fast-forming enamel, like humans. On the basis of facial morphology, this fossil is considered to be related to the orangutan. Overall, then, the hominoids' primitive dental structure is with thin fast-forming enamel, which is represented today by gibbons. An increase in deposition time produced a derived state of thick, fast-forming enamel, as displayed by, the extinct *Sivapithecus*, possibly via intermediate stages. The orangutan evolved a secondary slowing.

The scheme, as interpreted by Martin, now shows that the common ancestor of the African great apes and humans had thick, fast-forming enamel. He considers that the African apes shared a common ancestor, in which the characteristic slowing process developed: both then derived from this ancestor, which had thin, slow-forming enamel. Once again, there may have been transitional forms with intermediate thick and intermediate thin, slow-forming enamel. If true, the identification of putative African great ape ancestors in the fossil record will be facilitated.

Martin's version of the hominoid family tree runs counter to a newly emerging notion, based, among other things, on DNA-DNA hybridization studies: to wit, that gorillas diverged first, leaving humans and chimpanzees briefly to share a common ancestor. This interpretation would require that chimpanzees and gorillas developed their identical slow enamel deposition process independently. Martin considers this to be possible but unlikely. In a recent study of 125 morphological characters in humans and the African apes, he concluded that chimpanzees and gorillas form an ancestral group, with humans having split off separately, which is in accord with the enamel data. [Recent reanalysis of molecular data, discussed in Chapter 3, also has failed to sustain the idea of a closer link between humans and chimps, as opposed to chimps and gorillas.]

[5] Roger Lewin, "Tooth Enamel Tells a Complex Story," *Science*, 228(May 10, 1985):707. Copyright 1985 by the AAAS.

That the ancestry of humans may ultimately be among the ape-like sivapithecines, then, is consistent with dental evidence. It is consistent as well with resemblances between the shoulder girdle of the earliest undoubted hominine, *Australopithecus* (discussed in the next chapter), and that of orangutans. This suggests that humans evolved from a primate capable of arm movements like those of orangutans, and the sivapithecines were capable of just such arm movements. Finally, the opinion that sivapithecines are ancestral to humans as well as today's great apes (Figure 5.7) is in accord with estimates based on molecular similarities and differences between humans, chimpanzees, and gorillas that they could not have separated from a common ancestral stock more than 10 million years ago. We know from the fossils that the sivapithecines survived until 8 million years ago, and also that our own human ancestors were going their separate evolutionary way by at least 4 million, if not 6 million, years ago.

SIVAPITHECINE ADAPTATIONS

Molar teeth like those of the sivapithecines, having low crown relief, thick enamel, and surfaces poorly developed for cutting, are found in a number of modern primates.[6] Some of these species are terrestrial and some are arboreal, but all have one thing in common: They eat very hard nuts, fruits with very

tough rinds, and some seeds. This provides them with a rich source of easily digested nutrients that are not accessible to species with thin molar enamel incapable of standing up to the stresses of tough rind removal or nutcracking. Thus the sivapithecines probably ate food similar to that eaten by these latter-day nut crackers.

Analysis of other materials from deposits in which sivapithecine fossils have been found suggests utilization of a broad range of habitats, including tropical rain forests as well as drier bush country. Of particular interest to us, from the standpoint of human origins, are those populations that lived on the edge of open country, where food could be obtained through foraging on the ground out in the open, as well as in the trees of the forests. As it happened, there was a climatic shift under way, causing a gradual but persistent breaking up of forested areas, with a consequent expansion of open savanna country. Under such circumstances, it seems likely that those populations of sivapithecines living at the edge of the forests were obliged to supplement food from the forest more and more with other foods readily available on the open savannas. Consistent with this theory, late sivapithecine fossils are typically found in association with greater numbers of the remains of animals adapted to grasslands than are earlier ones.

Because sivapithecines already had large, thickly enameled molars, those that had to were capable of dealing with the tough and abrasive foods available on the savanna. What they lacked, however, were canine teeth of sufficient size to have served as effective "weapons" of defense. By contrast, most modern monkeys and apes that spend much time down on the ground rely heavily for defense on the

[6] Richard F. Kay, "The Nut-Crackers—A New Theory of the Adaptations of the Ramapithecinae," *American Journal of Physical Anthropology*, 55 (1981):141–151.

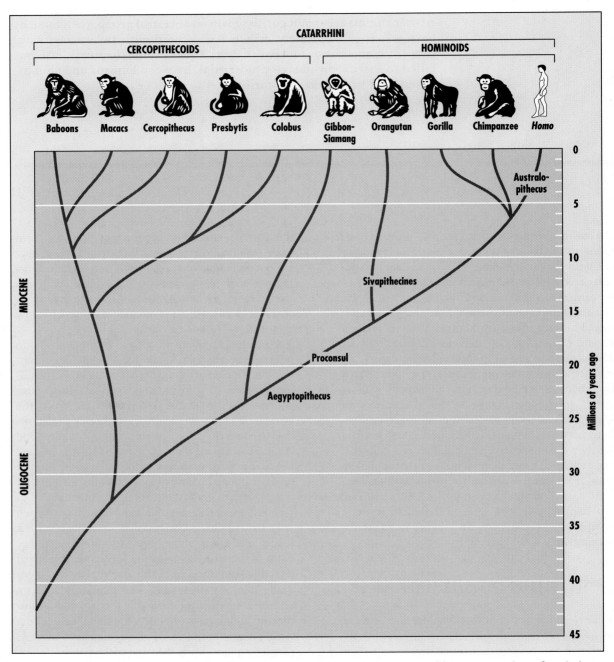

Figure 5.7   Although debate continues over details, this chart presents a reasonable reconstruction of evolutionary relationships among the catarrhine primates.

Ground-dwelling primates, like this male baboon, depend heavily on their massive canine teeth for protection from other animals. *Sivapithecus,* by contrast, lacked such massive weapons of defense.

massive, fang-like canines possessed by the males. Since cat-like predators were even more numerous on the savanna than now, sivapithecines, especially the smaller ones (which probably weighed no more than about 40 pounds[7]), would seem to have been very vulnerable primates indeed. Probably the forest fringe was more than just a source of foods

---

[7] D. R. Pilbeam, "Rethinking Human Origins," Ciochon and Fleagle, p. 217.

different from those of the savanna; its trees would have provided refuge when danger threatened. Yet, with continued expansion of savanna country, trees for refuge would have become fewer and farther between.

Slowly, however, physical and behavioral changes must have improved these primates' chances for survival on the savanna. For one thing, those that were able to gather food on the ground and then carry it to the safety of a tree probably had a better rate of survival than those that did not. Although many species of monkeys have cheek pouches in which to carry food, apes do not. Occasionally, modern apes will assume a bipedal stance in order to transport food in their arms, but they are quite awkward about it. The center of gravity, however, is higher in the body of modern apes than it seems to have been in their earlier ancestors, so that bipedal food transport may not have been quite so awkward for the sivapithecines, especially the smaller ones.

Food may not have been the only thing transported. Among modern primates, infants must be able to cling to their mothers in order to be transported; since the mother is using her forelimbs in locomotion, either to walk or swing by, she can't very well carry her infant. Chimpanzee infants, for example, must cling for themselves to their

A young baboon clings to its mother's back. The ability of apes as well as monkeys to carry their infants is limited by their need to use their arms in locomotion.

mothers, and even at the age of four, they make long journeys on her back. Injuries caused by falling from the mother are a significant cause of infant mortality.[8] Thus, females able to carry their infants would have made a significant contribution to the survivorship of their offspring.

Other advantages of at least the occasional assumption of a bipedal stance would have been the ability to scan the savanna, so that predators could be spotted before they got too close. Such scanning can be seen from time to time among baboons and chimps today when out on the savanna, even though their anatomy is less suited for this than the sivapithecines' was. Another advantage of bipedalism would have been the ability to use the hands to wield and throw things at predators. Among primates, "threat gestures" typically involve shaking branches and large sticks, while on the ground, chimpanzees have been observed throwing rocks at leopards. Lacking the large body size and formidable canines of chimps, there is every reason to suppose that the sivapithecines, when away from the trees and faced by a predator, fell back on the same kind of intimidating displays.

One final incentive to stand bipedally would be to make use of one of the more abundant food sources on the savanna[9]—the thorn bushes that provide edible seeds, leaves, and pods that would have been too high to pick while standing on four (or three) feet; yet, they are too spiny and are not sturdy enough to be climbed. Moreover, by using two hands (rather than one) to feed on seeds, the time necessary for such feeding would be cut in half, thereby reducing the period of vulnerability.

[8] C. Owen Lovejoy, "The Origin of Man," *Science*, 211 (1981):344, 349.

[9] Clifford J. Jolly and Fred Plog, *Physical Anthropology and Archaeology*, 4th ed. (New York: Knopf, 1986), p. 216.

Hominine: Member of the *Homininae*, the subfamily of hominids to which humans belong.

EARLY APES AND HUMAN EVOLUTION

Although the sivapithecines display a number of features from which **hominine** characteristics may be derived, and may occasionally have walked bipedally, they were much too ape-like to be considered hominines. No matter how much some of them may have resorted to bipedalism, they had not yet developed the anatomical specializations for this mode of locomotion that are seen in the earliest known hominines. Nevertheless, existing evidence allows the hypothesis that apes and humans separated from a common evolutionary line sometime during the late Miocene, and some fossils, particularly the smaller African sivapithecines, do possess traits associated with humans. Moreover, the Miocene apes possessed a limb structure less specialized for brachiation than modern apes; this structure could well have provided the basis for the development of human as well as ape limb types.

Clearly not all sivapithecines evolved into hominines. Those that remained in the forests and woodlands continued to develop as arboreal apes, although, ultimately, some of them took up a more terrestrial life. These are the chimpanzees and gorillas, who have changed far more from the ancestral condition than have the still arboreal orangutans.

Chapter Summary

Although the study of comparative anatomy and biochemistry of living animals indicates much about their evolution, the most direct evidence comes from fossils. For animals that have often lived where conditions for fossilization are generally poor, we do have a substantial number of primate fossils. Some are relatively complete skeletons, while most are teeth and jaw fragments.

The primates arose as part of a great adaptive radiation that began more than 100 million years after the appearance of the first mammals. The reason for this late diversification of mammals was that most ecological niches that they have since occupied were not available until the flowering plants became widespread beginning about 75 million years ago, and the reptiles had already preempted most other niches.

The first primates were arboreal insect eaters, and the characteristics of all primates developed as an adaptation to the initial tree-dwelling environment. While some primates no longer inhabit the trees, it is certain that those adaptations which evolved to a life in the trees were preadaptive to the adaptive zone now occupied by the hominines.

The earliest primates had developed by 60 million years ago in the Paleocene Epoch and were small arboreal creatures. Lemur-like adapids were common in the Eocene, as were species of tarsier-like omomyids. By the Oligocene Epoch, beginning about 34 million years ago, small primates combining features of both monkeys and apes were on the scene. In the Miocene Epoch apes proliferated and spread over many parts of the Old World. Among them were the sivapithecines, which appeared by 16 million years ago and remained until perhaps as recently as 8 million years ago. Although remarkably similar to orangutans in some respects, details of dentition suggest that hominines, as well as the modern apes, arose from the sivapithecines. At least some populations of sivapithecines lived where the right kind of selective pressures existed to transform a creature just like it into a primitive hominine. Other populations remained in the forests, developing into today's chimpanzee, gorilla, and orangutan. Of these, the orangutan has changed less from the ancestral condition than have the chimp and the gorilla.

Suggested Readings

Ciochon, Russell L., and John Fleagle, eds. *Primate Evolution and Human Origins*. Hawthorne, N.Y.: Aldine de Gruyter, 1987.
Articles in Part IV of this book summarize current knowledge of early catarrhine evolution, while those in Part V examine the sivapithecines and their possible significance with respect to human origins. Editors' introductions to each section provide the necessary overall perspective on the issues discussed in the articles.

France, Diane L., and Arthur D. Horn. *Lab Manual and Workbook for Physical Anthropology*, 2nd ed. New York: West, 1992.

Two chapters of this useful manual are devoted to a review of early primate fossils through the Miocene. Included are excellent drawings and photos.

Lasker, Gabriel W., and Robert Tyzzer. *Physical Anthropology*. New York: Holt, Rinehart and Winston, 1982.
This is a highly readable textbook in physical anthropology. The chapter on fossil primates is particularly good, with one of the best descriptions of the Fayum deposits from which so many fossils have come.

6

THE EARLIEST

HOMININES AND

CULTURAL ORIGINS

Amini Mturi, head paleoanthropologist for the government of Tanzania, holds a 1.5 million-year-old tool at Natron. Though the recovery of evidence for human evolution was once the preserve of white Europeans and North Americans, a number of Africans have entered the field and are responsible for the discovery of many new specimens crucial for our understanding of how humans evolved.

WHEN DID THE FIRST HOMININES APPEAR, AND WHAT WERE THEY LIKE? By at least 4 million years ago, the first undoubted hominines, known as *Australopithecus*, had appeared. *Australopithecus* was remarkably human from the waist down and had become fully adapted for moving about on the open savanna on its hind legs in the distinctive human manner. But from the waist up, *Australopithecus* was still remarkably ape-like, with a brain suggesting intellectual abilities roughly comparable to those of a modern-day chimpanzee or gorilla.

WHY HAD *AUSTRALOPITHECUS* BECOME A BIPEDAL WALKER? Present evidence suggests that the ancestors of *Australopithecus* were small and vulnerable creatures on an open savanna teeming with predators. Bipedal locomotion would have enabled them to scan the savanna for danger, carry their food to places where it could be consumed in safety, transport their offspring, and grab hold of objects with which to threaten predators.

WHEN AND HOW DID HUMAN CULTURE DEVELOP? Human culture appears to have developed as some populations of early hominines began making stone tools with which they could butcher animals for their meat. Actually, the earliest stone tools and evidence of significant meat eating date to about 2.5 million years ago, just prior to the appearance of the genus *Homo*.

WHEN DID REORGANIZATION AND EXPANSION OF THE HUMAN BRAIN BEGIN? Reorganization and expansion of the human brain did not begin until at least 1.5 million years after the development of bipedal locomotion. It began in conjunction with scavenging and the making of stone tools. This marks the appearance of the genus *Homo*, an evolutionary offshoot of *Australopithecus* . The two forms appear to have coexisted for a million years or so, during the course of which *Australopithecus* emphasized a vegetarian diet while developing a massive chewing apparatus. In contrast, *Homo* ate more meat and became brainier.

The period between about 7.5 and 4.5 million years ago was one of change; climates became dramatically drier than before and in Africa, as many species of forest or bush-loving mammals became extinct, several new groups made their appearance. Among the latter was the first undoubted hominine, known as *Australopithecus*. Several of its fossils have been found in Tanzania that are almost 4 million years old, and fragments of mandibles from two localities in Kenya suggest that *Australopithecus* may have appeared as early as 6 million years ago. What is certain is that *Australopithecus* walked about on the ground on two (rather than four) feet and possessed manipulative and dexterous hands capable of using objects as tools. In spite of its ability to walk in a human manner, its behavior patterns otherwise were probably more ape-like than human. For one thing, it spent more time in trees than later hominines, probably even sleeping in them. Nonetheless, by 2.4 million years ago, it had given rise to a new kind of hominine that could not only use tools, but make them as well. The beginnings of brain expansion and stone toolmaking both date from about this time, probably along with some kind of social organization featuring a greater degree of group cooperation and division of labor.

Until recently, the fossil evidence of the early stages of human evolution was both sparse and tenuous. In the 1960s, however, there began a rush of paleoanthropologists into the field. Numerous international expeditions, including more than 100 researchers from Belgium, Great Britain, Canada, France, Israel, Kenya, the Netherlands, and the United States, swarmed over parts of East Africa, where they have now unearthed more fossil remains in thirty years than had been unearthed in the previous forty. So much material, coming fast and furiously, has been difficult to digest, and our ideas of early human evolution are constantly being revised. Nonetheless, there is widespread agreement over the broad outline, even though debate continues over details. What is clear is that the course of human evolution has not been a simple, steady "advance" in the direction of modern humanity. Rather, it appears that at least three divergent hominine lines evolved in the past.

AUSTRALOPITHECUS

In 1924, an unusual fossil was brought to the attention of Professor Raymond Dart of the University of Witwatersrand in Johannesburg; it was the cranium of an animal unlike any he had ever seen before in South Africa. Recognizing in this unusual fossil an intriguing mixture of simian and human characteristics, anatomist Dart named his discovery *Australopithecus africanus*, or southern ape of Africa. Based on the position of the foramen magnum, the large hole in the skull where the spinal cord enters, Dart claimed that *Australopithecus* was probably a biped.

Since this original find, hundreds of other fossils of *Australopithecus* have been found, first in South Africa and later in Tanzania, Kenya, and Ethiopia (Figure 6.1). As they were discovered, many were given a number of different specific and generic names, but usually all are now considered to belong to the single genus *Australopithecus*. Most anthropologists recognize at least four species of the genus: *A. afarensis*, *A. africanus*, *A. boisei* and *A. robustus*. The latter two, from eastern and southern Africa respectively, are notable for having jaws that are massive, relative to the size of the brain case. *A. afarensis* and *A. africanus*, also from eastern and southern Africa respectively, are slightly smaller on average, and lack such massive jaws.

A. afarensis AND A. africanus

Included in the species *A. africanus* are numerous fossils found in the 1930s and 1940s at Sterkfontein and Makapansgat in South Africa, in addition to Dart's original find from Taung. All date between 3.0 and 2.3 million years ago. Included in *A. afarensis* are parts of between thirty-five and

---

Australopithecus: The first undoubted hominine; lived between one and four or six million years ago. Characterized by bipedal locomotion when on the ground, but with an ape-like brain; includes at least four species: *afarensis*, *africanus*, *boisei*, and *robustus*.

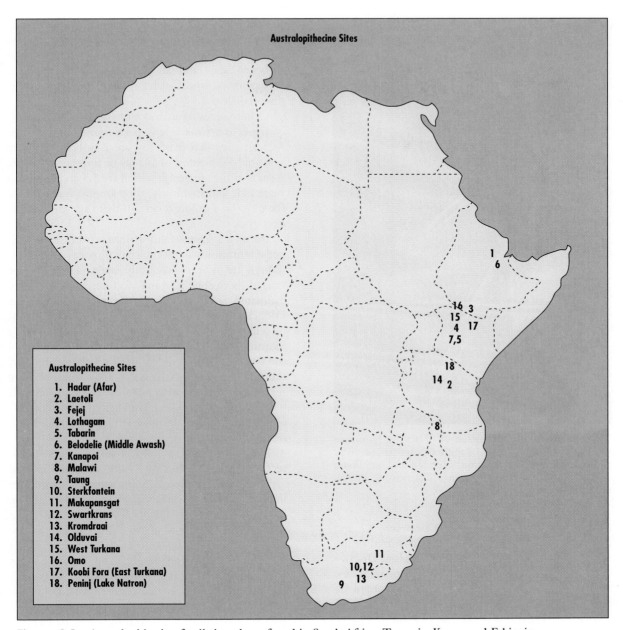

Australopithecine Sites

Australopithecine Sites

1. Hadar (Afar)
2. Laetoli
3. Fejej
4. Lothagam
5. Tabarin
6. Belodelie (Middle Awash)
7. Kanapoi
8. Malawi
9. Taung
10. Sterkfontein
11. Makapansgat
12. Swartkrans
13. Kromdraai
14. Olduvai
15. West Turkana
16. Omo
17. Koobi Fora (East Turkana)
18. Peninj (Lake Natron)

Figure 6.1 Australopithecine fossils have been found in South Africa, Tanzania, Kenya, and Ethiopia.

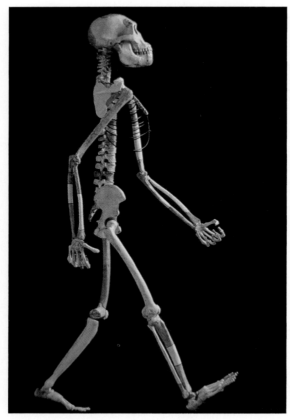

Sufficient parts of the skeleton of "Lucy," a hominine that lived between 2.6 and 3.3 million years ago, survived to permit this reconstruction. Her hip and leg bones reveal that she walked about in a distinctively human manner.

sixty-four individuals that lived between 3.2 and 2.9 million years ago; these were discovered in the 1970s in northern Ethiopia's Afar region. Discovered by Donald Johanson of the United States, these include the famous "Lucy," represented by bones from almost all parts of a single skeleton, and "the First Family," a collection of bones from 13 individuals of both sexes, ranging in age from infancy to adulthood, that died together as a result of some single calamity.

Similar material, close to 4 million years old, found by a team led by Mary Leakey at Laetoli, in Tanzania, is usually assigned to the same species as the Afar fossils. Although some have interpreted the wide variation exhibited by the *afarensis* specimens as indicative of the presence of two separate species, two recent studies support the single-species hypothesis,[1] and indicate that *afarensis* was sexually dimorphic, with the males about twice the size of females. In this respect, they were like the Miocene apes and all recent great apes except chimpanzees, whose males are only one third bigger than females.

Other pieces of australopithecines similar to *A. afarensis* or *africanus* have been found at other East African sites that generally are 2 million or more years old. The oldest of all may be fragments of jaws from two sites in Kenya which are 5.5 and 6 million years old. Unfortunately, they are too fragmentary for us to be absolutely certain that they are *Australopithecus*.

Both *A. afarensis* and *africanus* were erect, bipedal hominines about the size of modern pygmies, though far more powerfully built. Their stature ranged between 3.5 and 5 feet, and they are estimated to have weighed between 29 and 45 kilograms.[2] Their physical appearance was unusual by our standards: They may be described as looking like an ape from the waist up and like a human from the waist down. Their cranium was relatively low, the forehead sloped backward, and the brow ridge that helps give apes such massive-looking foreheads was also present. The lower half of the face was chinless and accented by jaws that were quite large, relative to the size of the skull.

Much has been written about *Australopithecus* teeth. Speaking generally, both *A. afarensis* and *africanus* possessed small incisors, short canines in line with adjacent teeth, and a rounded dental arch. The molars and premolars are larger in size but similar in form to modern human teeth (Figure 6.2). The molars are unevenly worn; the upper cheek teeth are worn from the inside, and the lower cheek teeth are worn from the outside. This indicates that both species chewed food in a hominine fashion, even though they were probably capable of two to four times the crushing force of modern human beings. There is usually no gap between the canines and the teeth next to them on the upper jaw,

[1] William R. Leonard and Michelle Hegman, "Evolution of P3 Morphology in *Australopithecus afarensis*," *American Journal of Physical Anthropology*, 73 (1987):60.

[2] Henry M. McHenry, "Body Size and Proportions in Early Hominids," *American Journal of Physical Anthropology*, 87 (1992):407.

This comparison of two skulls illustrates the degree of sexual dimorphism exhibited by australopithecines about 2 million years ago. The skull on the left is a female and the skull on the right is a male. Earlier australopithecines were equally dimorphic.

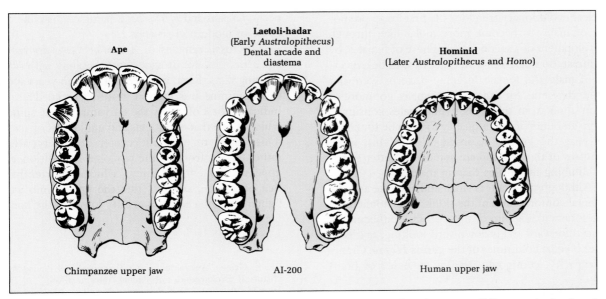

Ape

Laetoli-hadar
(Early *Australopithecus*)
Dental arcade and
diastema

Hominid
(Later *Australopithecus* and *Homo*)

Chimpanzee upper jaw   AI-200   Human upper jaw

Figure 6.2 The upper jaws of an ape, *Australopithecus,* and modern human show important differences in the dental arch and the spacing between the canines and adjoining teeth. Only in the earliest australopithecines can a diastema (a large gap between the teeth) be seen.

Homo erectus: Members of the genus *Homo*, which immediately precede *Homo sapiens*.

Genus *Homo*: Hominine genus characterized by expansion of brain and reduction of jaws; includes three species: *habilis*, *erectus*, and *sapiens*.

a trait common in apes. Further, the large mandible is very similar to that of the later hominine, ***Homo erectus.***

As one might expect, these features are most evident in the fossils of *A. africanus*, the more recent of the two species; the teeth of the earlier *afarensis*, from Ethiopia but especially from Laetoli, show numerous features reminiscent of the late Miocene sivapithecines which the later ones (of *africanus*) do not (see Figure 5.6). Generally, the incisors and canines are a bit larger in *afarensis*, the canines tend to project noticeably, the first lower premolars are less like molars and show more shearing wear, and the dental arch is less rounded. One jaw from Laetoli even shows a partial interlock of upper canines with lower canines and premolars. All of this strongly suggests a sivapithecine-like ancestor for *Australopithecus* back in Miocene times.

In addition to differences in the teeth between earlier *afarensis* and later *africanus*, there were also differences between the sexes. For example, there is a clear evolutionary trend for the first lower premolar of males to become more molar-like, through development of a second cusp. Those of females, by contrast, do not. Such differences are to be expected if male and female foraging patterns were not quite the same; for example, if females got more of their food from the trees, while males consumed large amounts of lower quality food to be found on or near the ground. Consistent with this, some features of the skeleton are somewhat better suited to climbing in females than in males.[3]

Although the brain is small and ape-like and the general conformation of the skull seems nonhuman, the foramen magnum of these australopithecines is placed forward and is downward-looking, as it is in later bipedal hominines of the **genus *Homo*.** Cranial capacity, commonly used as an index of brain

volume, varied from 310 to 485 cubic centimeters in *A. afarensis* and 428 to 510 cubic centimeters in *A. africanus*,[4] roughly the size of a large chimpanzee brain and about a third the size of a modern human brain. Intelligence, however, is not indicated by absolute brain size alone, but is roughly indicated by the ratio of brain to body size. Unfortunately, with such a wide range of adult weights it is not clear whether brain size was larger than an ape's relative to body size. Although some researchers think they see evidence for some expansion of the brain, others vigorously disagree. Moreover, the outside appearance of the brain, as revealed by natural casts of the inside of the skull, is more ape-like than human, suggesting that cerebral reorganization toward a human condition had not yet occurred.[5] Consistent with this is the fact that the system for drainage of the blood from the cranium of *A. afarensis* is significantly different from that of the genus *Homo*. At the moment, the weight of the evidence favors mental capabilities on the part of both *afarensis* and *africanus* as being comparable to those of modern great apes.

The fossil remains of *Australopithecus afarensis* and *africanus* have provided anthropology with two striking facts. First, as early as 4 million years ago, this hominine was bipedal, walking erect. This is indicated, first of all, by the curvature of the spine, which is like that of humans and unlike that of apes. This served to place the center of gravity over, rather than in front of, the hip joint. In addition, an upper arm bone from "Lucy," which is shorter than that of an ape, suggests that the upper limb was lighter and the center of gravity lower in the body

---

[3] Elwyn L. Simons, "Human Origins," *Science*, 245 (1989):1346.

[4] F. E. Grine, "Australopithecine Taxonomy and Phylogeny: Historical Background and Recent Interpretation," in *The Human Evolution Source Book*, eds. Russell L. Ciochon and John G. Fleagle (Englewood Cliffs, N.J.: Prentice-Hall, 1993), pp. 201–202.
[5] Dean Falk, "Ape-like Endocast of 'Ape-man' Taung," *American Journal of Physical Anthropology*, 80 (1989):339.

Figure 6.3 Examination of upper hip bones and lower limbs of *Homo sapiens, Australopithecus,* and an ape can be used to determine means of locomotion. The similarities of the human and australopithecine bones are striking and are indicative of bipedal locomotion. (The reconstruction of the australopithecine limb is based on the knee joint shown in the photograph.)

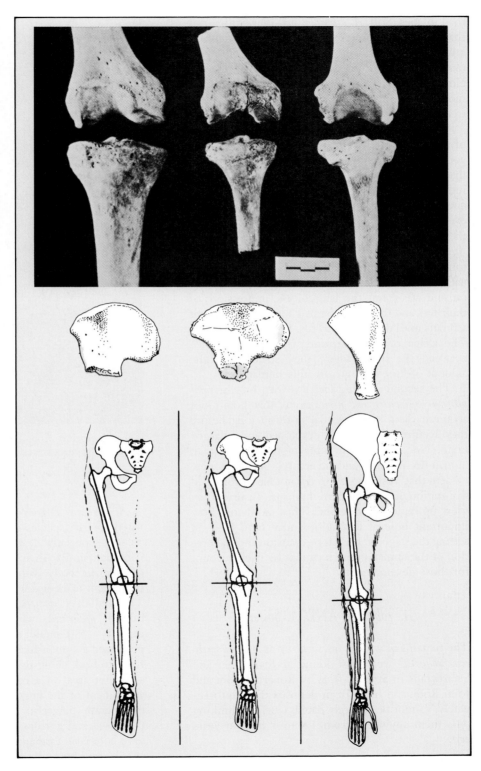

than in apes. Still, *A. afarensis* had longer forearms than *Homo*, the shoulder girdle was more adapted to arboreal performance, and fingers and toes show more curvature. Such traits indicate that the tree-climbing abilities of *A. afarensis* exceeded those of more recent hominines, and that they spent time in trees as well as on the ground.

Bipedal locomotion is also indicated by a number of leg and hip remains (Figure 6.3). There is general agreement that these are much more human than ape-like. In fact, a trait-by-trait comparison of individual bones shows that *Australopithecus* frequently falls within the range of modern *Homo*, even though the overall configuration is not exactly the same. But the most dramatic confirmation of *Australopithecus'* walking ability comes from Laetoli, where, nearly 4 million years ago, two individuals walked across newly fallen volcanic ash. Because it was damp, the ash took the impressions of their feet and these were sealed beneath subsequent ash falls until discovered by Dr. Paul Abell in 1978. The shape of the footprints, the linear distance between the heels where they struck, and the amount of "toe out" are all fully human.

The second striking fact provided by *Australopithecus afarensis* and *africanus* is that hominines acquired their erect bipedal position long before they acquired their highly developed and enlarged brain. Not only is the latter more ape-like than human in its size and structure, but it is now evident that *Australopithecus* did not have prolonged maturation as do modern humans; instead they grew up rapidly as do apes.[6] Thus, no matter how important bipedal locomotion may have been in setting the stage for the later expansion and elaboration of the human brain, it cannot by itself account for those developments.

A. robustus AND *A. boisei*

The remains of what is now known as *Australopithecus robustus* were first found at Kromdraai and Swartkrans in South Africa by Robert Broom and John Robinson in 1948 in deposits that, unfortunately, cannot be securely dated. Current thinking puts them anywhere from 1.8 to 1 million years ago.

[6] Simons, p. 1344.

These footprints from Laetoli, Tanzania, confirm that australopithecines were fully bipedal.

A. robustus shared practically all of the traits listed for the species of *Australopithecus*, just discussed, especially *A. africanus* from South Africa. Although similar in size to *A. africanus*, the bones of *robustus'* body were thick for their size, with prominent markings where their muscles attached. The skull of *A. robustus* was thicker and larger than that of *africanus*, with a slightly larger cranial capacity (530 cubic centimeters). Its skull also possessed a simian-like sagittal crest running from front to back along the top. This feature provides sufficient area on a relatively small braincase for attachment of the huge temporal muscles required to operate powerful jaws, such as *A. robustus* possessed and gorillas have today; hence what we have here is an example of convergent evolution in gorillas and hominines.

The first specimen of *Australopithecus boisei* to

LOUIS S. B. LEAKEY, MARY LEAKEY

(1903–1972), (1913–   )

Few figures in the history of paleoanthropology have discovered so many key fossils, received so much public acclaim, or stirred up as much controversy as Louis Leakey and his second wife, Mary. Born in Kenya of missionary parents, Louis received his early education from an English governess, and subsequently was sent to England for a university education. He returned to Kenya in the 1920s to begin his career there.

It was in 1931 that Louis and Mary began working in their spare time at Olduvai Gorge in Tanzania, searching patiently and persistently for remains of early hominids. It seemed a good place to look, for there were numerous animal fossils, as well as crude stone tools lying scattered about on the ground and eroding out of the walls of the gorge. Their patience and persistence were not rewarded until 1959, when Mary found the first

hominid fossil. A year later, another skull was found, and Olduvai was on its way to being recognized as one of the most important sources of hominine fossils in all of Africa. While Louis reconstructed, described, and interpreted the fossil material, Mary made the definitive study of the Oldowan tools.

The Leakeys' important discoveries were not limited to those at Olduvai. In the early 1930s, they found the first *Dryopithecus* fossils in Africa at Rusinga Island in Lake Victoria. Also in the 1930s, Louis found a number of skulls at Kanjera, Kenya, which show a mixture of modern and more primitive features. In 1961, at Fort Ternan, Kenya, the Leakeys found the first sivapithecine remains in Africa. Most recently, a member of an expedition led by Mary Leaky found the first footprints of *Australopithecus*, at Laetoli, Tanzania. In addition to all of

this, Louis Leakey promoted a good deal of important work on the part of others. He made it possible for Jane Goodall to begin her landmark field studies of chimpanzees; and later on, he was instrumental in getting similar studies started among gorillas and orangutans.

Louis Leakey had a flamboyant personality and a way of making interpretations of fossil materials that frequently did not stand up very well to careful scrutiny, but this did not stop him from publicly presenting his views as if they were the gospel. It was this aspect of the Leakeys' work that generated controversy. Nonethless, the Leakeys accomplished and promoted more work that resulted in the accumulation of knowledge about human origins than anyone before them. Anthropology clearly owes them a great deal.

be found in East Africa was discovered by Mary Leakey in the summer of 1959, the centennial year of the publication of Darwin's *On the Origin of Species*. She found it in Olduvai Gorge, a fossil-rich area near Ngorongoro Crater, on the Serengeti Plain of East Africa. Olduvai, sometimes called the Grand Canyon of East Africa, is a huge gash in the earth, about 25 miles long and 300 feet deep, which cuts through Pleistocene and recent geological strata revealing close to 2 million years of the earth's history.

Mary Leakey's discovery was reconstructed and

studied by her husband Louis, who gave it the name "*Zinjanthropus boisei.*" At first, he thought this hominine seemed more advanced than *Australopithecus* and extremely close to modern humans in evolutionary development. Further study, however, revealed that "*Zinjanthropus,*" the remains of which consisted of a skull and a few limb bones, was an East African representative of *Australopithecus*. Although similar in many ways to *A. robustus*, most commonly it is referred to as *Australopithecus boisei*. Potassium argon dating places this early hominine at about 1.75 million years old. Since the time of

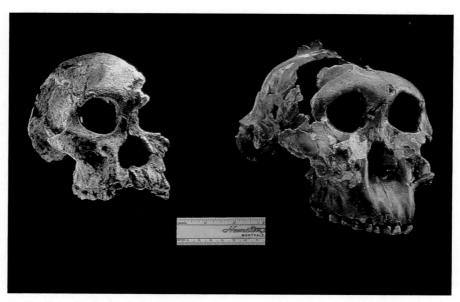

Skulls of *A. africanus* (left) and *A. boisei* (right) show significant differences. Both specimens are male.

Mary Leakey's original find, numerous other fossils of *A. boisei* have been found at Olduvai, as well as north and east of Lake Turkana in Ethiopia and Kenya. While one (often referred to as the "Black Skull") is known to be as much as 2.5 million years old, some date to as recently as 1.3 million years ago.

The size of the teeth and certain cranial features of *A. boisei* are reminiscent of *A. robustus*. Molars and premolars are enormous, as is the palate. The heavy skull, more massive even than its robust South African relative's, has a sagittal crest and prominent brow ridges; cranial capacity ranges from about 500 to 530 cubic centimeters. Body size too, is somewhat larger; whereas *robustus* is estimated to have weighed between 32 and 40 kilograms, *boisei* probably weighed from 34 to 49 kilograms.

Because the earliest skull (2.5 million years) in the *boisei* lineage, the so-called "Black Skull" from Kenya, retains a number of primitive features shared with *A. afarensis*, it is probable that *A. boisei* evolved from *afarensis* ancestors. Whether *A. robustus* represents a southern offshoot of the *boisei* lineage or convergent evolution from an *africanus* ancestor is so far not settled; arguments can be presented in favor of both interpretations. In either case, what happened was that the later australopith-

ecines developed molars and premolars that are both absolutely and relatively larger than those of earlier *afarensis* and *africanus*. Larger teeth require more bone to support them, hence the prominent jaws of *boisei* and *robustus*. Finally, the larger jaws and the chewing of more food require more in the way of jaw musculature which attaches to the skull. The marked crests seen on the skulls of the late australopithecines provide for the attachment of such a musculature on a skull that has increased very little in size. In effect, *boisei* and *robustus* had evolved into highly efficient "chewing machines." Clearly, their immense cheek teeth and powerful chewing muscles bespeak the kind of heavy chewing a diet restricted to uncooked plant foods requires. Many anthropologists believe that, by becoming a specialized consumer of plant foods, the late australopithecines avoided competing for the same niche with early *Homo*, with which they were contemporaries. In the course of evolution, the **law of competitive exclusion** dictates that, when two closely related species compete for the same niche, one will out compete the other, bringing about the "loser's" extinction. That early *Homo* and late *Australopithecus* did not compete for the same niche seems indicated by their coexistence for something like 1.5 million years.

ENVIRONMENT, DIET, AND AUSTRALOPITHECINE ORIGINS

Before discussing what we know about the earliest members of the genus *Homo* and the origins of this genus, we need to consider the evolutionary forces responsible for the appearance of *Australopithecus*. Since a major driving force in evolution is climatic change, in the late Miocene Epoch we must take into account the effects of such changes profound enough to cause the temporary drying up of the Mediterranean Sea. On the land, tropical forests underwent reduction or, more commonly, broke up into mosaics where patches of forest were interspersed with savanna or other types of open country. The forebears of the hominine line, probably to be found among the African sivapithecines, lived in places where there was access to both trees and open country. With the breaking up of forests, these early ancestors of ours found themselves spending more and more time on the ground and had to adapt to this new open environment.

The most obvious problem facing these hominine ancestors in their new situation, other than getting from one patch of trees to another, was food–getting. As the forest shrank, the traditional ape-type foods found in trees became less available to them. Therefore, it became more and more necessary to forage on the ground for foods such as seeds, grasses, and roots. Associated with this change in diet is a change in their dentition; male canines (used by other primates as defensive weapons) became as small as those of females (Figure 6.4), leaving both sexes relatively defenseless on the open plain and easy targets for numerous carnivorous predators. Many investigators have concluded that the hands of early hominines took over the weapon functions of the reduced canines, enabling them to threaten predators by using wooden objects as clubs and throwing stones at them. This set the stage for the much later manufacture of more efficient weapons from bone, wood, and stone.

Law of competitive exclusion: States that, when two closely related species compete for the same niche, one will out compete the other, bringing about its extinction.

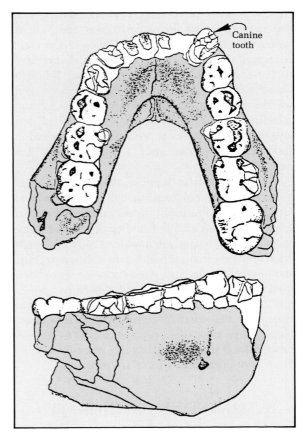

Figure 6.4 This lower jaw from Laetoli, Tanzania, is between 3.6 and 3.8 million years old and belonged to a hominine known as *Australopithecus*. Although its canine tooth projects a bit beyond the other teeth, it is a far cry from the projection seen in most other primates.

Although the hands of the later australopithecines were suitable for tool making, there is no evidence that any of them ever made stone tools. To illustrate the problem: Experiments with captive chimpanzees have shown that they are capable of making crude chipped stone tools, but they have never been known to do so under natural conditions. Thus, to have a potential is one thing, but whether it is realized is quite another. In fact, the earliest known stone tools are at least 1.5 million years younger than the oldest undoubted fossils of *Australopithecus*, nor has anyone been able to establish a clear association between stone tools and later *Australopithecus* (as opposed to *Homo*) fossils. Considering the number of sites and fossils known (several hundred), this appears to be significant. However,

Australopithecus certainly had no less intelligence and dexterity than do modern great apes, all of whom are capable of using tools when it is to their advantage to do so. The most adept and inventive tool user in captivity is the orangutan, although chimpanzees are the only apes that have been seen to use tools in the wild—throwing rocks and wielding clubs for defense as just described, but also for such purposes as procuring and processing food (termite probes and "nutting stones," for example).

It is reasonable to suppose, then, that australopithecines were tool users, though not tool makers. Unfortunately, few tools that they used are likely to have survived for a million and more years, and any that did would be unrecognizable as such. Although we cannot be certain about this, in addition to clubs and missiles for defense, stout sticks may have been used to dig up edible roots, and convenient stones may have been used to crack open nuts. We may also allow the possibility that, like chimpanzees, females may more often have used tools to get and process food than males, but the latter may more often have made use of tools as "weapons."[7]

HUMANS STAND ON THEIR OWN TWO FEET

From an ape-like carriage, the early hominines developed a fully erect posture; they became bipedal. Sivapithecines seem to have been primates who combined quadrupedal climbing with at least some brachiation and who, on the ground, were capable of assuming an upright stance, at least on occasion. Since no hominine fossils have been found dating from the period of two or more million years between the last known sivapithecines and the first known *Australopithecus*, we may assume that those hominine ancestors who did exist during the period were evolving into fully erect bipeds. *Australopithecus* is the first fully bipedal hominine of which we have a record.

Bipedalism, as a means of locomotion, has its drawbacks. For example, it makes an animal more visible to predators, exposes its "soft underbelly," or gut, and interferes with the ability to change direction instantly while running. Nor does it make for particularly fast running; quadrupedal chimpanzees and baboons, for example, are 30 to 34 percent faster than we bipeds. For 100-meter distances, our best athletes today may attain speeds of 34 to 37 kilometers per hour, but the larger African carnivores can attain speeds up to 60 to 70 kilometers per hour. Since all of these drawbacks would have placed our early hominine ancestors at risk from predators, what, we may ask, made bipedal locomotion worthwhile?

One suggestion that has received a great deal of attention is that it allowed males to gather food on the savanna and transport it back to females, who were restricted from doing so by the dependence of their offspring.[8] This is unlikely, however, in view of the fact that female apes, as well as women among food-foraging peoples, routinely combine infant care with foraging for food. Indeed, among food foragers, it is the women who normally supply the bulk of the food eaten by both sexes. Moreover, the pair-bonding (one male attached to one female) required by this model is not characteristic of terrestrial primates, nor of those displaying the degree of sexual dimorphism that was characteristic of *Australopithecus*. Nor is it really characteristic of *Homo sapiens*; in a substantial majority of recent human societies, including those in which people forage in nature for their food, some form of polygamy—marriage to two or more people at the same time—is not just permitted, but preferred. And even in the supposedly monogamous society of the United States, it is relatively common for one individual to marry two or more others (the only requirement is that one may not be married to them at the same time).

A more recent suggestion, that bipedal locomotion arose as an adaptation for nonterritorial scavenging of meat,[9] is also unlikely. While it is true that a biped is able to travel long distances without tiring, and that a daily supply of dead animal carcasses would have been available to hominines only if they were capable of ranging over vast areas, there is no evidence that hominines did much in the way of scavenging prior to about 2.5 million years

---

[7] Jane Goodall, *The Chimpanzees of Gombe: Patterns of Behavior* (Cambridge, Mass.: Belknap Press, 1986), pp. 552, 564.

[8] C. Owen Lovejoy, "The Origin of Man," *Science*, 211 (1981):341–350.

[9] Roger Lewin, "Four Legs Bad, Two Legs Good," *Science*, 235 (1987):969–971.

ago. Thus, it was likely an unforeseen byproduct of bipedal locomotion, rather than a cause of it.

The causes of bipedal locomotion are probably multiple. While we may reject the idea of male "breadwinners" provisioning "stay-at-home" females as culture bound, it is true that bipedal locomotion does make food transport possible. A fully erect biped out on the open savanna—whether male or female—has the ability to gather substantial quantities of food for transport back to a tree or other place of safety for consumption; the animal does not have to remain out in the open, exposed and vulnerable, to do all of its eating. But food may not have been the only thing transported. As we saw in Chapter 4, primate infants must be able to cling to their mother in order to be transported; since the mother is using her forelimbs in locomotion, to either walk or swing by, she can't very well carry her infant. Chimpanzee infants, for example, must cling for themselves to their mother, and even at the age of four, they make long journeys on their mothers' backs. Injuries caused by falling from the mother are a significant cause of infant mortality. Thus, mothers able to carry their infants would have made a significant contribution to the survivorship of their offspring, and the ancestors of *Australopithecus* would have been capable of doing just this.

Besides making food transport possible, bipedalism could have facilitated the food quest in other ways. With their hands free and body upright, the animals can reach otherwise unobtainable food on savanna thorn trees too flimsy to climb. Furthermore, with both hands free, they can gather food twice as fast. And in times of scarcity, their ability to travel far without tiring would help get them between widely distributed sources of food. Since the head is positioned higher than in a quadrupedal stance, sources of food and water may be spotted from afar, thereby facilitating their location.

Still other advantages of bipedalism would have enhanced survivability. With their heads well up above the ground, bipeds are able to spot predators before they get too close for safety. Finally, if they did get caught away from a safe place of refuge by a predator, manipulative and dexterous hands freed from locomotion provided hominines with a means of protecting themselves by brandishing and throwing objects at their attackers.

EARLY REPRESENTATIVES OF THE GENUS *HOMO*

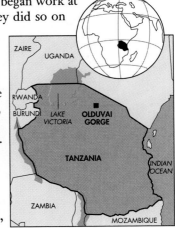

When the Leakeys began work at Olduvai Gorge, they did so on account of the presence of crude stone tools in deposits dating back to very early in the Pleistocene Epoch, which began about 2 million years ago. When they found the bones of *A. boisei* in 1959, in association with some of these tools, they thought they had found the remains of one of the toolmakers. They later changed their minds, however, and suggested that these tools were not produced by *A. boisei*, nor were the bones of the birds, reptiles, antelopes, and an extinct kind of pig found with the remains of *A. boisei*, the remains of the latter's dinner. Instead, *A. boisei* may have been a victim of a rather different contemporary who created the tools, ate the animals, and possibly had the unfortunate *A. boisei* for dessert. That contemporary was called by the Leakeys *Homo habilis* ("handy man").

The Leakeys discovered the remains of this second hominine in 1960, only a few months after their earlier discovery, just a few feet below it. The remains, which were those of more than one individual, consisted of a few cranial bones, a lower jaw, a clavicle, some finger bones (Figure 6.5), and the nearly complete left foot of an adult (Figure 6.6). These fossils date from about 1.8 million years ago and indicate a hominine with a cranial capacity in the 650 to 690 cubic centimeter range, a skull that lacks noticeable bony crests, and almost modern-looking hands and feet. Subsequent work at Olduvai has unearthed not only more skull fragments, but other parts of the skeleton of *Homo habilis* as well. These indicated that, in spite of their more modern-looking heads, hands and feet, the skeleton of this hominine from the neck down does not differ greatly from that of *Australopithecus afarensis* or *africanus*. Overall size was about the

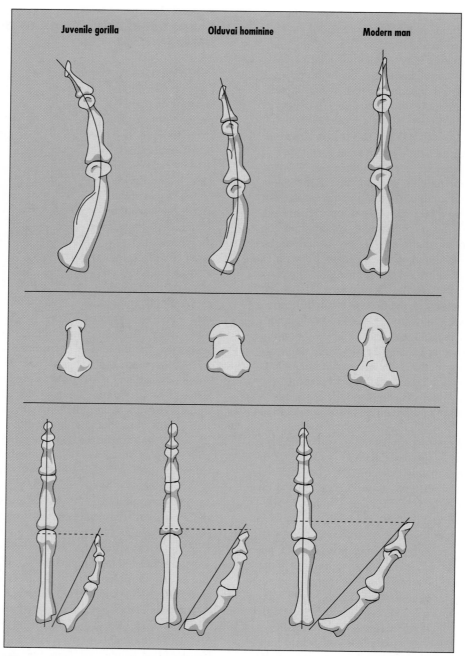

Figure 6.5   A comparison of hand bones of a juvenile gorilla, *Homo habilis* from Olduvai, and a modern human highlights important differences in the structure of the fingers and thumbs. In the top row are fingers and in the second row are terminal thumb bones. The bottom row compares thumb length and angle relative to the index finger.

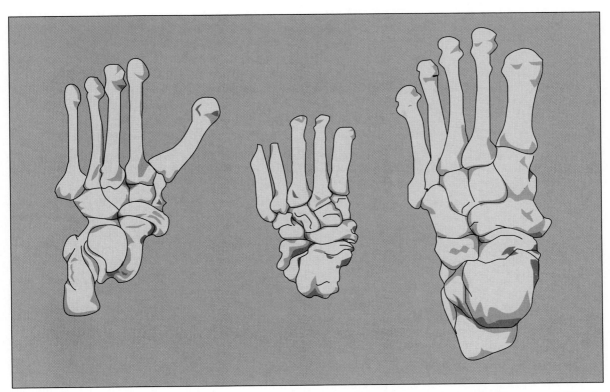

Figure 6.6   A partial foot skeleton of *Homo habilis* (center) is compared with the same bones of a chimpanzee (left) and a modern human (right).

same, males were twice the size of females, and they still climbed trees, although perhaps not quite so much as *Australopithecus*.[10] Moreover, dental evidence suggests that, as with *A. afarensis* and *africanus*, the period of infancy and childhood in *H. habilis* was not prolonged, as it is in modern humans, but was more in line with apes.[11]

Since the late 1960s, fossils of the genus *Homo* that are essentially contemporaneous with those from Olduvai have been recognized elsewhere in Africa; in South Africa, in Kenya near Lake Baringo, as well as east of Lake Turkana at Koobi Fora, and in Ethiopia just north of Lake Turkana. One of the best of these, known as KNM ER 1470, was discovered by the Leakeys' son Richard (the letters KNM stand for Kenya National Museum, the ER for East Rudolf, the former name for Lake Turk-

ana). The deposits in which it was found are about 1.9 million years old; these deposits, like those at Olduvai, also contain crude stone tools. The KNM ER 1470 skull is more modern in appearance than any *Australopithecus* skull and has a cranial capacity of 752 cubic centimeters. Furthermore, the inside of the skull shows a pattern in the left cerebral hemisphere that, in living people, is associated with a speech area.[12] This is in keeping with indications of brain asymmetry more like that of humans than apes, as well as evidence from wear patterns on tools evidently used by early *Homo* that reveal that these hominines were predominately right-handed. In humans, the speech organs and the right hand are controlled by adjacent areas in the left cerebral hemisphere. While this doesn't prove that early *Homo* had a spoken language, it does indicate that

[10] Roger Lewin, "The Earliest 'Humans' Were More Like Apes," *Science*, 236 (1987):106–163.
[11] Roger Lewin, "Debate Over Emergence of Human Tooth Pattern," *Science*, 235 (1987):749.

[12] Dean Falk, "Hominid Paleoneurology," in *The Human Evolution Source Book*, eds. Russell L. Ciochon and John G. Fleagle (Englewood Cliffs, N.J.: Prentice-Hall, 1993), p.62.

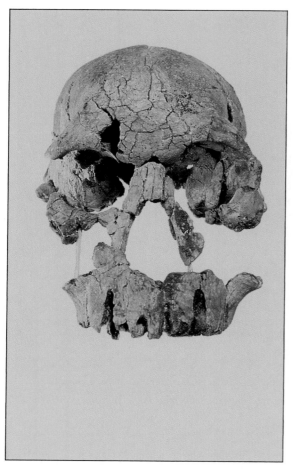

ER-1470, a skull of genus *Homo*, is close to 2 million years old.

its brain was not only larger than that of *Australopithecus*, but was reorganized along more human lines.

Although the 1470 skull and other early *Homo* fossils from localities other than Olduvai are frequently assigned to the same species, *H. habilis*, there are those who argue that two distinct species may be present. In favor of this is what appears to be an unusually wide degree of variation; on the other hand, those who suspect that two species are present cannot agree on how to apportion the fossils between them. Nor have they so far been able to demonstrate that they occupied different parts of the paleolandscape. Unless and until these difficulties are overcome, it seems best to regard all of this material as representative of a single species, **Homo habilis**.

RELATIONS BETWEEN *HOMO habilis* AND *AUSTRALOPITHECUS*

A consideration of brain size relative to body size clearly indicates that *Homo habilis* had undergone enlargement of the brain far in excess of values predicted on the basis of body size alone. This means that there was a marked advance in information-processing capacity over that of the australopithecines. Furthermore, although these hominines had teeth that are large by modern standards—or even those of a half million years ago—they are smaller in relation to the size of the skull than those of australopithecines. Since major brain-size increase and tooth-size reduction are important trends in the evolution of the genus *Homo*, but not of *Australopithecus*, it looks as if ER 1470 and similar hominines were evolving in a more human direction. Consistent with this are indications that the brain of KNM ER 1470 was less ape-like and more human in structure. It is probably no accident that the earliest fossils to exhibit these features appear by 2.4 million years ago (the age of the Baringo fossil), soon after the earliest evidence (to be discussed shortly) for stone toolmaking and increased consumption of meat.

As noted earlier, the australopithecine diet seems to have consisted for the most part of plant foods, although *A. afarensis* and *africanus* may have consumed limited amounts of animal protein as well. Later australopithecines (*A. boisei* and *robustus*) evolved into more specialized "grinding machines" as their jaws became markedly larger (Figure 6.7), while their brain size did not. Nor is there firm evidence that they made stone tools. Thus, in the period between 2.5 and 1 million years ago, two kinds of hominines were headed in very different evolutionary directions.

If neither *Australopithecus boisei* nor *robustus* belong in the direct line of human ancestry, what of earlier *Australopithecus*? From the standpoint of

Homo habilis: Earliest representative of the genus *Homo*; lived between 2.4 and 1.8 million years ago. Characterized by expansion and reorganization of the brain, compared to *Australopithecus*.

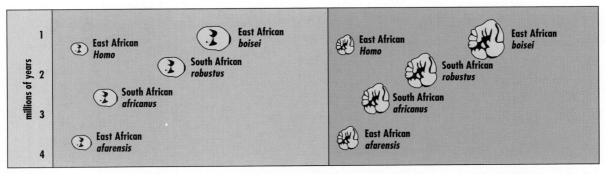

Figure 6.7   Premolars (left) and molars (right) of *Australopithecus* and *Homo habilis* show significant differences in size. The teeth of *Australopithecus* show a clear tendency to enlarge with time over those of *A. afarensis*, while the teeth of *H. habilis* differ little from those of *A. afarensis*.

anatomy alone, it has long been recognized that either *Australopithecus afarensis* or *africanus* constitutes a good ancestor for the genus *Homo*, and it now seems clear that the body of *Homo habilis* had changed little from that of either species. Precisely which of the two gave rise to *H. habilis* is vigorously debated. Most see *A. afarensis* as sufficiently generalized to have given rise to both the *Homo* and *boisei-robustus* patterns, noting that the earliest skull to show the latter, the so-called "Black Skull," nonetheless shows some holdovers from *A. afarensis*. This skull's age (2.5 million years), is too old for any but the very earliest *africanus* to have figured in its ancestry. Since the earliest *Homo habilis* skull is nearly as old, the same must be true for it. Evidently, a three-way split was under way by 2.5 million years ago, with the third line represented by *A. africanus* (Figure 6.8). This persisted until about 2 million years ago (or later, if *A. robustus* is a descendent of *africanus*, rather than an offshoot of *boisei*) by which time the other two lineages had become widespread in nonforested parts of Africa.

LOWER PALEOLITHIC TOOLS

The earliest tools known to have been made by hominines have been found in the vicinity of Lake Turkana in Kenya and southern Ethiopia, Olduvai Gorge in Tanzania, and Hadar in Ethiopia. Their appearance marks the beginning of the **Lower Paleolithic,** the first part of the Old Stone Age.

These early tools show striking similarities, indicating that they were the results of a cultural tradition of manufacturing tools according to a particular preconceived model or pattern. At Olduvai and Lake Turkana, these tools are close to 2 million years old. The Hadar tools have been found below a deposit dated by potassium argon to about 1.8 million years ago, but above another dated to about 2.8 million years; thus they are estimated to be about 2.5 million years old.

OLDUVAI GORGE

What is now Olduvai Gorge was once a lake. Almost two million years ago, its shores were inhabited not only by numerous wild animals but also by groups of hominines, including *Australopithecus boisei* and *Homo habilis* as well as the later *Homo erectus* (Chapter 7). The gorge, therefore, is a rich source of Paleolithic remains as well as a key site providing evidence of human evolutionary development. Among the finds are assemblages of stone tools that are about 2 million years old. These lie little disturbed from when they were left, together with the bones of now-extinct animals which were eaten. At one spot, in the lowest level of

Lower Paleolithic: The first part of the "Old Stone Age"; its beginning is marked by the appearance of Oldowan tools.

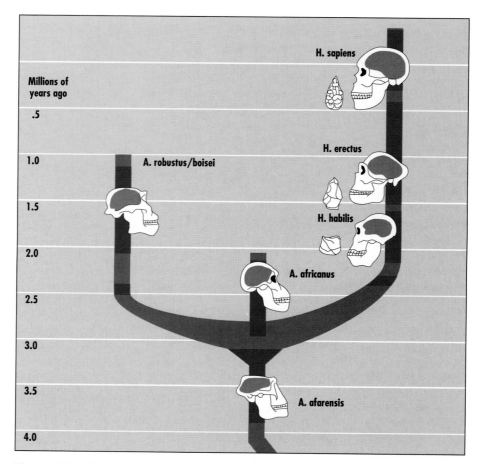

Figure 6.8   This diagram presents one plausible view of early human evolution.

the gorge, the bones of an elephant lay in close association with more than 200 stone tools. Apparently, the animal was butchered here; there are no indications of any other activity. At another spot, on a "living floor" 1.8 million years old, basalt stones were found grouped in small heaps so as to form a circle. The interior of the circle was practically empty, while numerous tools and food debris littered the ground outside, right up to the edge of the circle. Some interpret this as evidence for some sort of shelter, seeing the stone piles as supports for the framework of a protective fence of thorn branches, or perhaps a hut with a covering of animal skins or grass. Another possibility is that the stones were "stockpiled" ahead of time, to be made

into tools as needed, or to be hurled as missiles to hold off other scavengers while the hominines extracted meat, marrow, hide, and sinew from pieces of animal carcass.

OLDOWAN TOOLS

The oldest tools found at Olduvai Gorge belong to the **Oldowan tool tradition**, which is characterized by an all-purpose generalized chopping tool, produced by removing a few flakes from a stone (often a large water-worn pebble) either by using another stone as a hammer (hammerstone) or by striking the pebble against a large rock (anvil) to

Percussion method: A technique of stone tool manufacture by striking the raw material with a hammerstone or by striking raw material against a stone anvil to remove flakes.

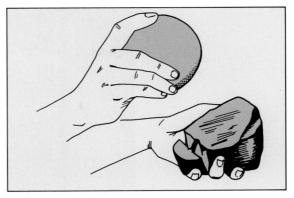

Figure 6.9 By 2.5 million years ago, hominines had invented the percussion method of stone tool manufacture. This technological breakthrough, which is associated with a significant increase in brain size, made possible the butchering of meat from scavenged carcasses.

remove the flakes. This system of manufacture is called the **percussion method** (Figure 6.9). The finished product had a jagged sharp edge, effective for cutting and chopping. The generalized form of the chopping tool suggests that it served many purposes, such as butchering meat, splitting bones for marrow, and perhaps also defending the owner. Also used were the flakes, which had sharp, useful edges (in fact, many so-called choppers may be no more than by-products of flake manufacture). Some flakes were used "as is," for cutting tools, while others were retouched for use as scrapers.

Crude as they were, Oldowan choppers and flakes mark an important technological advance for early hominines; previously, they depended on found objects requiring little or no modification, such as bones, sticks, or conveniently shaped stones. Oldowan tools made possible new additions to the diet, because, without such tools, hominines could eat few animals (only those that could be skinned by tooth or nail); therefore, their diet was limited in terms of animal proteins. The advent of Oldowan choppers and flakes meant more than just saving labor and time—they made possible the addition of meat to the diet on a regular, rather than occasional, basis. Much of a popular nature has been written about this, often with numerous colorful references to "killer apes." Such references are quite misleading, not only because hominines are not apes but also because killing has been greatly overemphasized. Meat can be obtained, after all, by scavenging, or by stealing it from other predators. What is significant is that a dentition

such as that possessed by *Australopithecus* and *Homo habilis* is poorly suited for meat eating. What is needed if substantial amounts of meat are to be eaten, in the absence of teeth like those possessed by carnivorous animals, are sharp tools for butchering.

The initial use of tools was probably the result of adaptation to an environment that we know was changing from forests to grasslands. The physical changes that adapted hominines to living in the new grassy terrain encouraged toolmaking. It has been observed that monkeys and apes, for example, often use objects, such as sticks and stones, in conjunction with threat displays. The change to a nearly upright bipedal posture, coupled with existing flexibility at the shoulder, arms, and hands, helped hominines to compete with, and survive in spite of, the large predatory carnivores that shared their environment.

What else do these assemblages of Oldowan tools and broken animal bones have to tell us about the life ways of early *Homo*?

First, they tell us that both *Homo habilis* and large carnivorous animals were active at these locations, for in addition to marks on the bones made by slicing, scraping, and chopping with stone tools, there are tooth marks from gnawing. Some of the gnawing marks overlie the butcher marks, indicating that enough flesh was left on the bones after the hominines were done with them to attract

Oldowan tool tradition: The earliest identifiable stone tools.

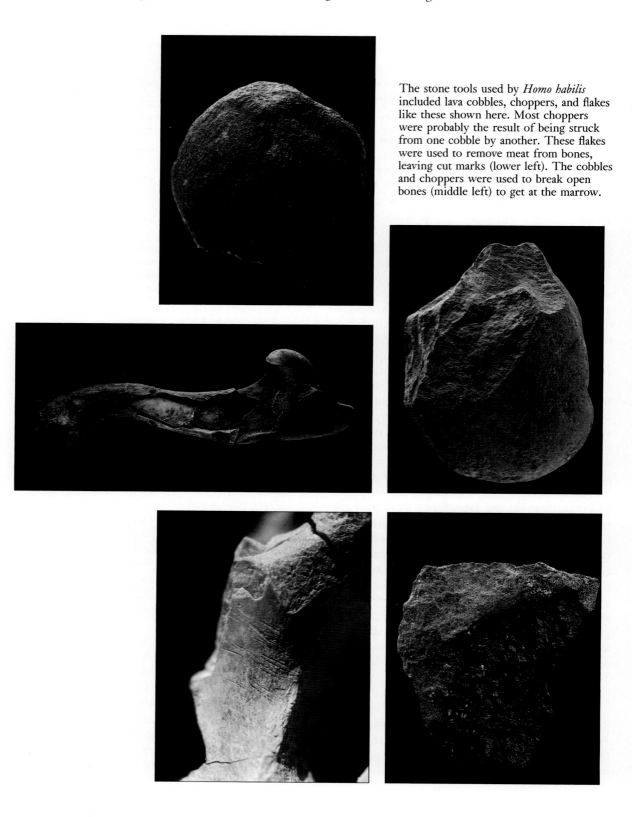

The stone tools used by *Homo habilis* included lava cobbles, choppers, and flakes like these shown here. Most choppers were probably the result of being struck from one cobble by another. These flakes were used to remove meat from bones, leaving cut marks (lower left). The cobbles and choppers were used to break open bones (middle left) to get at the marrow.

Like these modern jackals, *Homo habilis* gained access to meat through scavenging.

the other carnivores. In other cases, though, the butcher marks overlie the tooth marks of carnivores, indicating that the animals got there first. This is what we would expect if *H. habilis* were scavenging from the kills of other animals, rather than doing its own killing. Consistent with this is the fact that whole carcasses are not represented; evidently, only parts were transported away from the original location where they were obtained, again what we would expect if they were "stolen" from the kill of some other animal. The stone tools, too, were made of raw material procured at some distance from where they were used to process the parts of carcasses. Finally, the incredible density of bones at some of the sites and patterns of weathering indicate that, although *H. habilis* didn't linger longer than necessary at any one time (and for good reason—the carnivores attracted by the meat could have made short work of *habilis* as well), the sites were repeatedly used over periods of five to fifteen years.

All of this is quite unlike the behavior of historically known food-foraging peoples, who bring whole carcasses back to camp, where they are completely processed; neither meat nor marrow is left (as they were at Oldowan sites), and the bones themselves are broken up (as they were not at Oldowan sites) both to get at the marrow and to fabricate tools and other objects of bone. Nor do

historically known food foragers normally camp in the midst of so much garbage. The picture that emerges of our Oldowan forbears, then, is of scavengers, getting their meat from the lower Paleolithic equivalent of modern-day road kills, taking the spoils of their scavenging to particular places where tools, and the raw materials for making them, had previously been stockpiled for the purpose of butchering. At these sites, the remains were quickly processed, so that those doing the butchering could clear out before their lives were endangered by carnivores attracted by the meat. Thus, the Oldowan sites were not campsites or "home bases" at all. Quite likely, *H. habilis* continued to sleep in trees or rocky cliffs, as do other small-bodied terrestrial or semiterrestrial primates, in order to be safe from predators. However, the advanced preparation for meat processing implied by the caching of stone tools, and the raw materials for making tools, attests to considerable foresight and ability to plan ahead.

TOOLS, MEAT, AND BRAINS

As we have seen, by 1.5 million years or so after early hominines became fully bipedal, the size and structure of the brain were beginning to change. Up until about 2.5 million years ago, early hominines lived on foods that were around to be picked or gathered: plants, fruits, invertebrate animals such as ants and termites, and perhaps even an occasional piece of meat scavenged from kills made by other animals. After 2.5 million years ago, meat became more important in their diet, and they began to scavenge for it on a more regular basis.

Since early hominines lacked size and strength to drive off predators, or to compete directly with other scavengers attracted to kills, they must have had to rely on their wit and cunning for success. One may imagine them lurking in the vicinity of a kill, sizing up the situation as the predator ate its fill, while hyenas and other scavengers gathered, and devising strategies to outwit them all so as to seize a piece of the carcass. A hominine depending on stereotyped instinctual behavior in such a situation would have been at a competitive disadvantage. One that could anticipate problems, devise distractions, bluff competitors into temporary retreat, and recognize, the instant it came, its opportunity to rush in and grab what it could of the carcass, stood a much better chance of surviving, reproducing, and proliferating.

One means by which early hominines gained access to a reasonably steady supply of carcasses while at the same time minimizing the risks involved is suggested by recent field studies of leopards. How this could have worked and the arguments in favor of it are discussed in the following Original Study. (Note that its author uses the term *hominid* in its old sense, rather than *hominine*, to refer to human ancestors.)

ORIGINAL STUDY

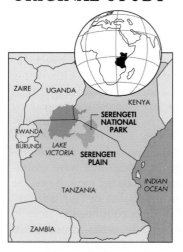

CAT IN THE HUMAN CRADLE[13]

Recent evidence, such as marks on some of the Olduvai bones, indicates that animals the size of wildebeests or larger were killed, eaten, and abandoned by large predators such as lions, hyenas, and saber-toothed cats; hominids may have merely scavenged the leftovers. Several specialists now agree that early hominids obtained at least marrow mainly in this way. The picture with regard to the remains of smaller animals, such as gazelle-sized antelopes, is less certain. Paleoanthropologists Henry Bunn and Ellen Kroll believe that the cut-marked upper limb bones of small, medium-sized, and large animals found at Olduvai Gorge demonstrate that hominids were butchering the meaty limbs with cutting tools. Since modern-day lions and hyenas rapidly and completely consume small prey, leaving little or nothing for potential scavengers, Bunn and Kroll conclude that hominids must have acquired the smaller animals by hunting. But another scholar, Kay Behrensmeyer, suggests that a small group of hominids could have obtained these bones, not by hunting, but by driving off timid predators, such as cheetahs or jackals, from their kills.

Since carnivores play a key role in all these scenarios, three years ago I began thinking about studying their behavior and ecology. About the same time, a colleague directed me to a paper on the tree-climbing abilities of early hominids. The authors (anatomists Randall L. Susman, Jack T. Stern, and William L. Jungers) analyzed the limb bones of *Homo habilis* specimens from Olduvai Gorge, as well as those of the early hominid *Australopithecus afarensis* (better known as Lucy). They concluded that early hominids were probably not as efficient as we are at walking on two feet, but they were better than we are at climbing trees and suspending themselves from branches. At the very least, given their apparent lack of fire, early hominids must have used trees as refuges from large predators and as sleeping sites.

One evening, as I watched a documentary film by Hugh Miles about a female leopard and her cubs in Kenya's Masai Mara Reserve, carnivore behavior and early hominid tree climbing suddenly connected for me. In the film, a pack of hyenas attempt to scavenge an antelope that the mother leopard has killed. At the sight of the hyenas, the leopard grabs the prey in her jaws and carries it up a small tree. This striking behavior sparked my curiosity and sent me to the library the next morning to find out more about leopards.

I learned that the leopard differs from other large African carnivores in a variety of ways. Although it occasionally kills large animals, such as adult wildebeests and topi or young giraffes, the leopard preys primarily on smaller antelopes, such as Thomson's gazelles, impala, and Grant's gazelles, and on the young of both large and small species. Unable to defend its kills on the ground from scavenging by lions and spotted hyenas, both of which often forage in groups, the usually solitary leopard stores each kill in a tree, returning to feed but otherwise frequently abandoning it for varying lengths of time.

Although the leopard may not consume its entire prey immediately, the tree-stored kills are relatively safe from theft. (Even lions, which can climb trees, usually take little notice of this resource.) As a result, a kill can persist in a tree for several days. Also, leopard kills appear to be more predictably located than those of lions and hyenas because leopards tend to maintain a small territorial range for several years and occasionally reuse feeding trees. Finally, leopard kills are usually found in the woodlands near lakes and rivers, the habitat apparently preferred by early hominids. Such circumstances, I reasoned, might have once provided an ideal feeding opportunity for tree-climbing hominids, particularly *Homo habilis*. By scavenging from the leopard's temporarily abandoned larder, early hominids could have obtained the fleshy and marrow-rich bones of small- to medium-sized prey animals in relative safety.

Fossil evidence shows that ancestors of present-day leopards were contemporaneous with early hominids and shared the same habitats. The antiquity of tree-caching behavior is harder to prove, but it is supported by paleoanthropologist C.K. Brain's excavations of ancient caves in southern Africa's Sterkfontein Valley. In the vertical, shaftlike caves, Brain found the fossil remains of hominids, baboons, and antelopes, and of leopards and other large carnivores. The size of the prey animals and the selection of body parts, as well as puncture marks on some of the cranial bones of hominids and baboons, suggested that many of these fossils were the remains of leopard meals. Brain guessed that they had fallen into the caves from leopard feeding trees growing out of the mouths of the caves.

Given its similarities to the ancient environments represented at the early archeological sites—extensive grasslands with wooded lakes, rivers and streams— the Serengeti National Park in northern Tanzania seemed an ideal living laboratory in which to test my hypothesis. I traveled there in July 1987, accompanied by Robert J. Blumenschine, who had conducted an earlier study there on scavenging opportunities provided by lions and hyenas. Along the Wandamu River, a tributary of the Seronera, we were fortunate to find an adult female leopard and her

This leopard has carried part of a Thomson's gazelle up into a tree, to prevent other scavengers from consuming what is left. Such tree-stored carcasses may have been the principle source of meat for *Homo habilis*.

thirteen-month-old (nearly full grown) male cub that tolerated our Land-Rover. We spent a total of about fifty hours, during the day and at night, observing these leopards at three fresh, tree-stored kills of Thomson's gazelles. The leopards frequently left the carcasses unguarded between feedings. On one occasion, a complete young Thomson's gazelle, killed the previous evening, was abandoned for nine daylight hours (we found the leopards resting approximately two miles away). Without directly confronting these predators, therefore, a creature able to climb trees could have easily carried off the same amount of flesh and marrow as it could obtain from hunting.

While Brain's work in South Africa implicates leopards as predators of early hominids, including the genus *Homo*, some hominids may have also benefitted from living near these carnivores. Tree-stored leopard kills could have provided an important resource to early scavenging hominids and the sharp, broken limb bones from the partly eaten prey could been used to peel back the hide, expose the flesh of the carcasses, and remove large muscle bundles. This activity may even have given early hominids the initial impetus to make and use tools in the extraction of animal nutrients.

Some paleoanthropologists have argued that scavenging was an unlikely subsistence strategy for early hominids, since large predators require expansive home ranges and kills by these carnivores are rare in any particular area. They also contend that very little is left over from such kills after the predator is finished and that hominid competition with large carnivores for these leftovers would be a dangerous activity. My 1988 observations suggest something quite different. During approximately two months in the dry season, I documented sixteen kills of small and medium antelopes made by my adult male and female leopards within an approximately four-by-eight-mile area. The majority of these kills, still retaining abundant flesh and marrow, were temporarily abandoned by the leopard for three to eight and a half hours during a single day.

The tree-stored leopard kills consisted mainly of adult and juvenile Thomson's gazelles. Compared with kills of similar-sized prey made on the ground by Serengeti lions and hyenas, as recorded by Blumenschine, the tree-stored leopard kills lasted longer, offering large quantities of flesh and marrow for two or more days. In part this was because they were not subject to many scavengers. The leopard kills were also more predictably located on the landscape than those of lions in the same area. In modern leopard populations, a male maintains a relatively large territory that overlaps with the usually smaller territories of several females. This pattern often means that several tree-stored kills are available simultaneously during a given period of time within a relatively small area.

An obvious question is how leopards would have responded to repeated theft of their tree-stored kills by early hominids. Would they, perhaps, have abandoned portions of their ranges if such thefts occurred with sufficient regularity? Although I haven't yet tested this, I don't think they would have. According to my observations and those of other researchers, leopards are usually more successful at hunting larger prey, such as gazelles and impala, at night. This gives them the opportunity to consume part of such kills before the arrival of any daytime scavengers. They thus should be able to obtain enough nourishment to warrant remaining in a territory, despite some such losses.

Like modern baboons and chimpanzees, early hominids may have killed some small animals, such as newborn antelopes. But they could have acquired all sizes of animal carcasses without hunting if the prey killed by leopards is taken into account. The wide assortment of animal bones at sites like Olduvai Gorge, which have been attributed to ground-based hunting and scavenging, could instead be attributed to scavenging only, both in trees and on the ground. Leopard kills would then have provided much of the flesh consumed by early hominids, while carcasses abandoned on the ground by other large predators would have yielded primarily bone marrow. Additional flesh may have come from the remains of large kills made by saber-toothed cats or from the carcasses of animals that drowned when herds migrated across ancient lakes.

While we can't observe the behavior of our early ancestors, the present-day interactions between leopards and some other primate species can be instructive. Baboons, for example, often fall victim to leopards while they sleep at night in trees or caves. During the day, however, baboons regularly attack, displace, and according to one account, even kill leopards. In western Tanzania, a park ranger reported that during the day, a group of baboons saw a leopard in a tree with the carcass of an impala. Barking out alarm calls, the adult and adolescent male baboons chased the leopard for about three-tenths of a mile. The females and young baboons stayed with the carcass and began to eat, until the males returned and took possession of the kill.

Similarly, although chimpanzees in western Tanzania are the occasional prey of leopards, there is a report that one day some chimpanzees scavenged what was apparently a tree-stored leopard kill. On a more dramatic occasion, also during the day, a group of chimpanzees was observed noisily surrounding a leopard lair from which an adult leopard was heard growling (see "Leopard Killers of Mahale," *Natural History*, March 1988). A male chimpanzee entered the lair and emerged with a leopard cub, which it and the others killed without reprisal from the adult leopard. This type of shifting day-night, predatory-parasitic relationship may once have existed between leopards and our early hominid ancestors.

[13] John A. Cavallo, "Cat in the Human Cradle," *Natural History*, 2/90 (1990):54–56, 58–60.

Several lines of evidence suggest it was probably the early hominine males, rather than females, who did most of the scavenging. What set them up for this may have been the foraging habits of the earlier australopithecines. As already noted, dental and skeletal differences between males and females suggest that males may have fed on the ground and lower levels of trees more heavily than females, who had a higher proportion of fruit in their diet.[14] Something like this pattern is seen today among orangutans, where it is a response to highly dispersed resources. As a consequence, males consume larger amounts of low-quality food such as bark than do females. A major difference, of course, is that orangutan males still forage in the forest, whereas male *Australopithecus* did not. In such a situation, the latter may have been tempted to try out supplementary sources of food on the ground, especially if existing sources became scarcer, as they likely did; a markedly cold, dry episode has been identified in the crucial period between 2.6 and 2.3 million years ago.[15] Already bipedal, australopithecines were capable of covering, in an energetically efficient way, the considerable distances (on the order of 32 square miles, based on the Original Study) necessary to ensure a steady supply of meat.

Another consideration is that, without contraceptive devices and formulas that could be bottle fed to infants, females in their prime, when not pregnant, must have had infants to nurse. While this would not have restricted their local mobility, any more than it does a female ape or monkey, or women among historically known food-foraging peoples, it would have been less easy for them than for males to range over the vast distances required to search out carcasses. Another necessity for the successful scavenger would have been the ability to mobilize rapidly high bursts of energy, in order to elude the many carnivores active on the savanna. Although anatomical and physiological differences between the sexes in humans today are relatively insignificant compared to *H. habilis*, as a general rule, men can still run faster than women (even though some women can certainly run faster than some men). Finally, even for the smartest and swiftest individuals, scavenging would still have been a risky business. To place early *Homo* females at risk would have been to place their offspring, actual and potential, at risk as well. Males, on the other hand, would have been relatively expendable, for, to put the matter bluntly, a very few males are capable of impregnating a large number of females. In evolutionary terms, the population that places its males at risk is less likely to jeopardize its chances for reproductive success than is the one that places its females at risk.

In order to gain access to some of the meat scavenged by males, early hominine females, too,

[14] Leonard and Hegman, p. 61.
[15] Randall R. Skelton, Henry M. McHenry, and Gerrell M. Drawhorn, "Phylogenetic Analysis of Early Hominids," *Current Anthropology*, 27 (1986):31.

ADRIENNE ZIHLMAN

(1940–   )

Up until the 1970s, the study of human evolution, from its very beginnings, was permeated by a deep seated bias reflecting the privileged status enjoyed by men in western society. Beyond the obvious labeling of fossils as particular types of "men," irrespective of sex of the individual represented, it took the form of portraying males as the active sex in human evolution. Thus, it was males who were seen as providers and innovators, using their wits to become ever more effective providers of food and protection for passive females. The latter were seen as spending their time getting pregnant and caring for offspring, while the men were "getting ahead" by becoming ever smarter. Central to such thinking was the idea of "man the hunter," constantly honing his wits through the pursuit and killing of animals. Thus, hunting by men was seen as the pivotal humanizing activity in evolution.

We now know, of course, that such ideas are culture bound, reflecting the hopes and expectations of late nineteenth and early twentieth century European and European-American culture. Recognition of this fact came in the 1970s, and was a direct consequence of the entry of a number of highly capable women into the profession of paleoanthropology. Up until the 1960s, there were few women in any field of physical anthropology, but with the expansion of graduate programs and changing attitudes towards the role of women in society, increasing numbers of them went on to earn the Ph.D. One of these was Adrienne Zihlman, who earned her doctorate at the University of California at Berkeley in 1967. Subsequently, she authored a number of important papers critical of "man the hunter" scenarios. She was not the first to do so; as early as 1971, Sally Linton had published a preliminary paper on "Woman the Gatherer," but it was Zihlman from 1976 on who especially elaborated on the importance of woman's activities for human evolution. Others have joined in the effort, including Zihlman's companion in graduate school and later colleague, Nancy Tanner, who collaborated with Zihlman on some of her papers and has produced important works of her own.

The work of Zihlman and her coworkers was crucial in forcing a reexamination of existing "man the hunter" scenarios, out of which came recognition of the importance of scavenging in early human evolution as well as the importance of female gathering and other activities. While there is still plenty to learn about human evolution, thanks to these women we now know that it wasn't a case of women being "uplifted" as a consequence of their association with progressively evolving men. Rather, the two sexes evolved together with each making its own important contribution to the process.

had to "sharpen their wits." For the most part, they continued to gather the same kinds of foods that their ancestors had been eating all along. But instead of consuming all this food themselves as they gathered it (as other primates do), they provided some to the males who, in turn, provided the females with meat. To do this, they had to plan ahead so as to know where food would be found in sufficient quantities, devise means by which it could be transported to some agreed upon location for division at the proper time, while at the same time preventing its loss through spoilage, or to such animals as rats and mice. Thus, female gathering played no less important a role in the development of better brains than did male scavenging.

The new interest in meat on the part of evolving hominines is a point of major importance. Out on the savanna, it is hard for a primate with a digestive system like that of humans to satisfy its amino-acid requirements from available plant resources. Moreover, failure to do so has serious consequences: growth depression, malnutrition, and ultimately death. The most readily accessible plant sources would have been the proteins available in leaves and legumes (nitrogen-fixing plants, familiar modern examples being beans and peas), but these are hard for primates like us to handle digestively, unless they are cooked. The problem is that leaves and legumes contain substances that cause the proteins to pass right through the gut without being absorbed.[16]

Chimpanzees have a similar problem when out on the savanna. In such a setting, they spend about 37 percent of their time going after insects like ants and termites on a year-round basis, while at the same time increasing their predation on eggs and vertebrate animals. Such animal foods not only are easily digestible, but they provide high-quality proteins that contain all the essential amino acids, in just the right percentages. No one plant food does this by itself; only if the right combination is consumed can plants provide what meat does by itself in the way of amino acids. Moreover, there is abundant meat to be had on the savanna. All things considered, then, we should not be surprised if our own ancestors solved their "protein problem" in somewhat the same way that chimps on the savanna do today.

Increased meat consumption on the part of early hominines did more than merely ensure an adequate intake of essential amino acids, important though this was. Animals that live on plant foods must eat large quantities of vegetation, and obtaining such foods consumes much of their time. Meat eaters, by contrast, have no need to eat so much, or so often. Consequently, meat-eating hominines may have had more leisure time available to explore and manipulate their environment; like lions and leopards, they would have time to spend lying around and playing. Such activity, coupled with the other factors already mentioned, probably was a stimulus to hominine brain development.

The importance of meat eating for early hominine brain development is suggested by the size of their brains: The cranial capacity of the largely plant-eating *Australopithecus* ranged from 310 to 530 cubic centimeters; that of the most primitive known meat eater, *Homo habilis* from East Africa, ranged from 580 to 752 cubic centimeters; whereas *Homo erectus*, who hunted as well as scavenged for meat, possessed a cranial capacity of 775 to 1225 cubic centimeters.

THE EARLIEST SIGNS OF CULTURE: TOOLS

The use of specially made tools of stone appears to have arisen as a result of the need for implements to butcher and prepare meat, because hominine teeth were inadequate for the task. Even chimpanzees, whose canine teeth are far larger and sharper, frequently have trouble tearing through the skin of other animals.[17] Besides overcoming this problem, the manufacturing of stone tools must have played a role in the evolution of the human brain, first by putting a premium on manual dexterity and fine manipulation, as opposed to hand use emphasizing power rather than precision. This in turn put a premium on improved organization of the nervous system. Second, the transformation of a lump of stone into a "chopper," "knife," or "scraper" is a far cry from what a chimpanzee does when it transforms a stick into a termite probe. While the probe is not unlike the stick, the stone tool is unlike the lump of stone. Thus, the toolmaker must have in mind an abstract idea of the tool to be made, as well as a specific set of steps that will accomplish the transformation. Furthermore, only certain kinds of stone have the flaking properties that will allow the transformation to take place, and the toolmaker must know about these.

COOPERATION AND SHARING

With an ape-like brain and a diet like that of monkeys and apes when out on the savanna, *Australopithecus* probably behaved much like other hominoids. Like apes, adults probably foraged for their own food, which was rarely shared with other adults. Among modern apes, however, there is one notable exception to this behavior: Although adult

[16] Ann Brower Stahl, "Hominid Dietary Selection Before Fire," *Current Anthropology*, 25 (1984):151–168.

[17] Goodall, p. 372.

A power grip (left) utilizes more of the hand while the precision grip (right) relies on the fingers for control.

chimpanzees rarely share plant food with one another, males almost always share meat, frequently with females.[18] Thus, increased consumption of meat on the part of *Homo habilis* may have promoted even more sharing among adults. Moreover, a regular supply of meat would have required that substantial amounts of time and energy be devoted to the search for carcasses, and food gathered by females and shared with males could have provided the latter with both.

Sharing and cooperation between the sexes need not necessarily have been between mated males and females, but may just as well have been between brothers and sisters and mothers and sons. On the other hand, the ability to engage in sexual activity at any time she deems appropriate on the part of females may have promoted that between a male and one or more sex partners, for among most catarrhine primates, males attempt to monopolize females when the latter are at the height of sexual receptivity. As discussed in Chapter 17, the ability to engage in sex at any time that is characteristic of the human female alone among the primates probably was an incidental by-product of bipedal locomotion; hence, it should have been characteristic of the earliest hominines.

Although chimpanzees can and do hunt alone, they frequently cooperate in the task. In the case of *Homo habilis*, cooperation would seem to have been even more crucial to success in scavenging. It is hard to imagine a creature lacking the formidable canines of a chimpanzee competing on an individual basis with carnivores far more powerful than itself.

In summary, then, it seems reasonable to assume that *Homo habilis* engaged in more sharing and cooperative behavior than one sees among present-day chimpanzees. How much more is certainly not known, and probably fell far short of what has been observed among any historically known food-foraging peoples. After all, *Homo habilis* was not just a different sort of hominine from *Australopithecus*; it was different from *Homo sapiens*, as well.

---

[18] Ibid.

Chapter Summary

The course of hominine evolution, we know from fossil finds, has not been a simple, steady "advance" in the direction of modern humans. One early hominine, that appeared by at least 4 million years ago, was *Australopithecus*, a genus that anthropologists divide into four species. *Australopithecus afarensis* and *africanus* walked erect; they were about the size of a modern human pygmy; they chewed food like humans; and their general appearance was that of an ape-like human. The size and outward appearance of their brain suggest a degree of intelligence probably not greatly different from that of a modern chimpanzee or gorilla. Like chimpanzees, *afarensis* and *africanus* may have made some use of objects as tools.

Australopithecus boisei and *robustus* shared practically all of the traits listed for *afarensis* and *africanus*, but were more highly specialized for the consumption of plant foods.

During the late Miocene and Pliocene, the climate became markedly cooler and drier; many areas that had once been heavily forested became woodland and open savanna. The ancestors of hominines found themselves spending more and more time on the ground; they had to adapt to this altered, open environment, and food-getting became a problem. As their diet changed, so did their dentition. On the whole, teeth became smaller, and many of the defensive functions once performed by the teeth seem to have been taken over by the hands.

Sivapithecines are believed to have been part-time brachiators who may at times have walked erect. *Australopithecus* is the first full biped hominine with erect posture whom we know about. Some disadvantages of bipedalism as a means of locomotion are that it makes an animal more visible to predators, exposes its "soft underbelly," is relatively slow, and interferes with the ability to change direction instantly while running. Its advantages are that it provides hominines with a means of protecting themselves and of holding objects while running, the ability to travel long distances without tiring, and the ability to see further.

Since 1960 a number of fossils have been found in East Africa at Olduvai Gorge, Lake Baringo and east of Lake Turkana, and in South Africa at Sterkfontein, which have been attributed to *Homo habilis*, the earliest representative of this genus. Among them is the well-known KNM ER 1470 skull, which is more modern in appearance than any *Australopithecus* skull. From the neck on down, however, the skeleton of *Homo habilis* differs little from that of *Australopithecus*. Because they do show a significant increase in brain size, and some reorganization of its structure, their mental abilities must have exceeded those of *Australopithecus*. By 2.4 million years ago, the evolution of *Homo* was proceeding in a direction different from that of *Australopithecus*.

The same geological strata that have produced *Homo habilis* have also produced the earliest known stone tools. These lower Paleolithic artifacts from Olduvai Gorge, Lake Turkana and Hadar, Ethiopia, are remarkably similar, suggesting that they were the products of a cultural tradition in which tools were manufactured according to a model.

Finds made at Olduvai Gorge have provided important evidence of human evolutionary development. The oldest Lower Paleolithic tools found at Olduvai are in the Oldowan tool tradition, which is characterized by all-purpose generalized chopping tools, and flakes. Lower Paleolithic people used the percussion method to manufacture tools. The crude Oldowan choppers and flakes made possible the addition of meat to the diet on a regular basis because people could now butcher meat, skin any animal, and split bones for marrow. Many Oldowan archaeological sites appear to be where meat was processed, rather than campsites.

Some changes in the brain structure of *Homo habilis* seem to have been the result of the changed diet. Increased consumption of meat, beginning about 2.5 million years ago, made new demands on their coordination and behavior. Successful procurement of meat through scavenging depended on *H. habilis'* ability to out-think far more powerful predators and scavengers. Obtaining animal food presented problems that very often had to be solved on the spot; a small scavenger depending on stereotyped instinctual behavior alone would have been at a competitive disadvantage in such a situation. Moreover, eaters of high-protein foods, such as meats, do not have to eat as often as vegetarians do. Consequently, meat-eating hominines may have had more leisure time available to explore and experiment with their environment.

Toolmaking and use also favored the development of a more efficient brain. To make stone tools, one must have in mind at the beginning a clear vision of the tool to be made, one must know the precise set of steps necessary to transform the raw material into the tool, and one must be able to recognize the kind of stone that can be successfully worked. Advanced eye-hand coordination is also required.

A prime factor in the success of early hominines was the development of some cooperation in the procurement of foods. While the males probably supplied much of the meat, the females continued to gather the sorts of food eaten by other primates; however, instead of consuming what they gathered as they gathered it, they shared a portion with the males in exchange for meat. This required foresight and planning on the part of females, which played as important a role as male scavenging in favoring the development of better brains. Food sharing with a sexual division of labor is characteristic of modern food foragers, and some hint of it can be seen among chimpanzees, among whom meat is frequently shared.

Suggested Readings

Campbell, Bernard G. *Humankind Emerging*, 6th ed. New York: HarperCollins, 1992.
Several physical anthropology texts have good coverage of the earliest hominines; this one is distinguished by its accessible writing style and lavish illustrations from the Time-Life *Emergence of Man* and *Life Nature Library* series.

Ciochon, Russell L., and John G. Fleagle, eds. *The Human Evolution Source Book*. Englewood Cliffs, N.J.; Prentice-Hall, 1993.
In the first four parts of this book, the editors have assembled articles to present data and survey different theories on the evolution and diversification of the earliest hominines. A short editors' introduction to each section places the various articles in context.

Johanson, Donald, and Maitland Edey. *Lucy: The Beginnings of Humankind*. New York: Simon & Schuster, 1981.

This book tells the story of the discovery of "Lucy" and the other fossils of *Australopithecus afarensis*, and why they have enhanced our understanding of the early stages of human evolution. It reads like a first-rate detective story, at the same time giving one of the best descriptions of australopithecines, and one of the best accounts of how paleoanthropologists analyze their fossils, to be found in literature.

Johanson, Donald, and James Shreeve. *Lucy's Child: The Discovery of a Human Ancestor*. New York: Avon, 1989.
This sequel to *Lucy* is written in the same engaging style. Although it covers some of the same ground with respect to *Australopithecus*, its focus is on *Homo habilis*. Besides giving a good description of this earliest member of the genus *Homo*, it presents one of the best discussions of the issue involved in the arguments over when (and why) *Homo* appeared.

7

HOMO erectus AND THE EMERGENCE OF HUNTING AND GATHERING

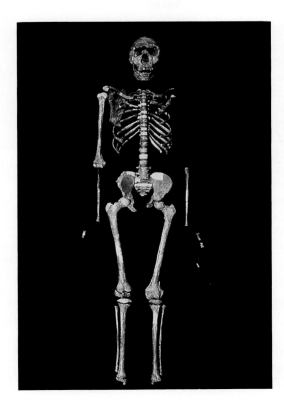

More "human" than Homo habilis, *though less so than* H. sapiens, Homo erectus *emerged in Africa by 1.6 million years ago and had spread to other parts of the Old World by 1 million years ago. Shown here is the oldest and most complete* H. erectus *fossil ever found, the so-called "Strapping Youth" from Lake Turkana. The remains are those of a robust boy who died in his early teens.*

WHO WAS *HOMO erectus*?

Homo erectus was the direct descendant of earliest members of the genus *Homo*, as have been found in East Africa. Populations of *Homo erectus* were widespread between about 1.6 million and 400,000 years ago, living in Africa, China, Europe, and Southeast Asia.

WHAT WERE THE CULTURAL CAPABILITIES OF *HOMO erectus*?

Having larger brains than its ancestors, *Homo erectus* became better able to adapt to different situations through the medium of culture. This is reflected by better-made tools, a greater variety of tool types, regional diversification of tool kits, use of fire, and improved organizational skills.

WHAT WERE THE CONSEQUENCES OF *HOMO erectus*' IMPROVED ABILITIES TO ADAPT THROUGH CULTURE?

As culture became more important as the vehicle through which this species secured its survival, life became somewhat easier than it had been. As a result selective pressures, other than those favoring increased capacity for culture, were reduced, reproduction became easier and more offspring survived than before. This allowed populations to grow, causing "spillover" into previously uninhabited regions. This in turn contributed to the further evolution of culture, as populations of *Homo erectus* had to find solutions to new problems of existence in newly inhabited regions.

In 1891, the Dutch army surgeon Eugene Dubois, intent on finding the fossils of a "missing link" between humans and apes, set out for Java, which he considered to have provided a suitable environment for such a creature. At Trinil, Java, Dubois found what he was searching for: the fossil remains of a primitive kind of hominine, consisting of a skull cap, a few teeth, and a thigh bone. Its features seemed to Dubois part ape, part human. Indeed Dubois at first thought the remains did not even belong to the same individual. The flat skull, for example, with its enormous brow ridges and small size, appeared to be like that of an ape, but it possessed a cranial capacity much larger than an ape's. The femur, or thigh bone, was clearly human in shape and proportions and indicated the creature was a biped. Although Dubois called his find *Pithecanthropus erectus*, or "erect ape man," it has since been assigned to the species *Homo erectus*.

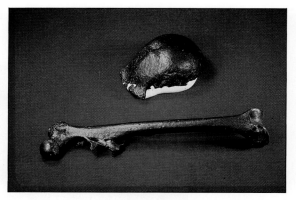

These casts of the skull cap and thigh bone of *Homo erectus* were made from the original bones found by Eugene Dubois at Trinil, Java.

HOMO *erectus* FOSSILS

Evidently, *Homo erectus* was the first hominine to extend its range outside of eastern and southern Africa. Fossils of this species are now known from a number of localities not just in Africa, but in China, Europe and India, as well as Java (Figure 7.1). In spite of the fact that remains of this species have been found in so many different places on three continents, the remains show very little significant physical variation. Evidence suggests, however, that populations of *H. erectus* in different parts of the world do show some differences from one another on a subspecific level.

HOMO *erectus* FROM JAVA

For a long time, the scientific community was reluctant to accept Dubois' claim that his Javanese fossils were of human lineage. It was not until the 1930s, particularly when other fossils of *H. erectus* were discovered by G.H.R. von Koenigswald at Sangiran, Java, in the Early Pleistocene Djetis beds, that scientists almost without exception agreed both discoveries were the remains of an entirely new kind of early hominine. Von Koenigswald found a small skull that fluorine analysis and (later)

potassium-argon dating indicated to be older than Dubois' approximately 500,000- to 700,000-year-old Trinil specimen. Since 1960, additional fossils have been found in Java. A long continuity of *H. erectus* populations in Southeast Asia is indicated, from perhaps as much as 1.3 million years to about 500,000 years ago, at least.

HOMO *erectus* FROM CHINA

A second population of *H. erectus* was found in the mid-1920s by Davidson Black, a Canadian anatomist then teaching at Peking Union Medical College. After purchasing in a Peking drugstore a few teeth sold to local inhabitants for their supposed medicinal properties, Black set out for the nearby countryside to discover the owner of the teeth and perhaps the species of early hominine. At a place called Dragon Bone Hill in Zhoukoudian, 30 miles from Beijing, he found one molar tooth on the day before closing camp at the end of his first year of excavation. Subsequently, a skull encased in limestone was found by W. C. Pei, and between 1929 and 1934, the year of his death, Black labored along with Pei in the fossil-rich deposits of Zhoukoudian, uncovering fragment after fragment of the hominine Black had named, on the basis of that first molar tooth, *Sinanthropus pekinesis*, or "Chinese man of Peking"—now recognized as an East Asian representative of *H. erectus*.

After his death, Black's work was continued by Franz Weidenreich, a Jewish refugee from Nazi

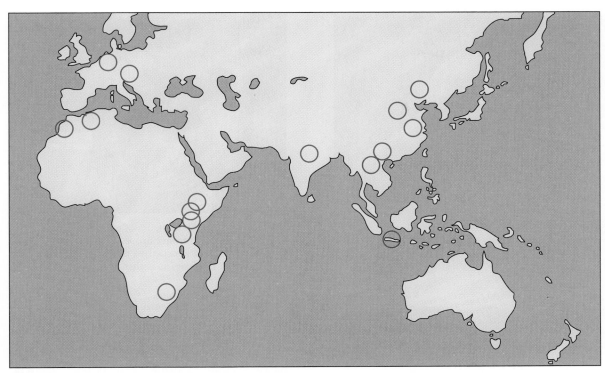

Figure 7.1 Remains of *Homo erectus* have been found from Africa and Europe to Asia.

Germany. By 1938, the remains of more than forty individuals, consisting of teeth, jawbones, and incomplete skulls, had been dug out of the limestone. World War II brought a halt to the digging, and the original Zhoukoudian specimens were lost during the Japanese invasion of China. Fortunately, Weidenreich had made superb casts of most of the fossils and sent them to the United States. After the war, other specimens of *H. erectus* were discovered in China, at Zhoukoudian and at a number of other localities. The oldest is a skull about 700,000 to 800,000 years old from Lantian in Shensi Province. The original Zhoukoudian remains appear, by contrast, to be no more than about 500,000 years old.

Although the two populations overlap in time, the Chinese fossils are, on the whole, not quite so old as those from Java. Not surprisingly, Chinese *H. erectus* is a bit less "primitive" looking. Its average cranial capacity is about 1000 cubic centimeters, compared to 900 cc for Javanese *H. erectus*. The smaller teeth, short jaw, and lack of diastema in the lower dentition—a gap in the teeth to accommodate a large upper canine when the jaws are closed—of the Chinese are further evidence of their more modern status.

HOMO erectus FROM AFRICA

Although our best samples of *H. erectus* remain those from Asia, a number of important specimens are now known from Africa. Fossils now assigned to this species were discovered there as long ago as 1933, but the better-known finds have been made since 1960, at Olduvai and at Lake Turkana. Among them is the oldest—at 1.6 million years—and most complete *H. erectus* skeleton ever found, that of a boy who died at about the age of 12. Another partial skeleton, that of an adult, had diseased bones, possibly the result of a massive overdose of vitamin A. This could have come from eating the livers of carnivorous animals, for they accumulate this vitamin in their livers at levels that are poisonous to human beings.

Generally speaking, African *H. erectus* skulls are quite similar to those from Asia; one difference is that their bones aren't quite as thick. It may be, too,

In Asia, Chinese drugstores are good places to look for fossils—including those of *Homo erectus*—among "dragon" bones and teeth. Actually fossils from many species of animals, these are ground up to make various medicines. This typical assortment of "dragon" teeth, including some from a hominine (top row), is accompanied by the formula for converting them into medicine.

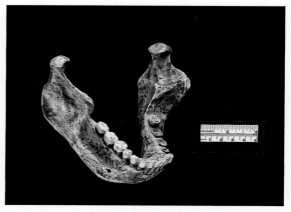

This massive mandible—from Mauer, Germany—is one of the oldest known from Europe. The great space across the back, where it attached to the cranium, bespeaks a skull broad at the base, as is that of *H. erectus.*

that individuals living in China were shorter and stockier, on the whole, than those living in Africa. Overall, however, the Africans reveal no more significant physical variations from their Asian counterparts than are seen if modern human populations from East and West are compared. As in Asia, the most recent fossils are less "primitive" in appearance, and the oldest fossils display features reminiscent of the earlier *Homo habilis*. Indeed, one of the problems in Africa is distinguishing early *H. erectus* from late *H. habilis*, precisely what one would expect if the one evolved from the other.

HOMO erectus FROM EUROPE

Although Europe seems to have been inhabited by at least 700,000 years ago, few fossils attributable to *H. erectus* have so far been found there. A large lower jaw from Mauer, Germany, that may be

almost a half-million years old certainly came from a skull wide at the base, as is that of *H. erectus.* Other European fossils are not as old, and display a mosaic of features characteristic of both *H. erectus* and subsequent archaic *H. sapiens.* Here, as in Africa and Asia, a distinction between late *erectus* and early *sapiens* is difficult to make. Until sufficiently old fossils are found, knowledge of *H. erectus* in Europe must remain limited.

PHYSICAL CHARACTERISTICS OF *HOMO erectus*

Apart from its skull, the skeleton of *H. erectus* differs only subtly from that of modern humans. Although its bodily proportions are like ours, it was more heavily muscled, its rib cage was conical rather than barrel-shaped, and its hips were narrower. With a small birth canal, gestation must have been short, with infants born in a relatively immature state. Stature seems to have been in the modern range, as the youth from Lake Turkana was about 5 feet, 4 inches tall. Compared to *Homo habilis*, *H. erectus* was significantly larger, but displayed significantly less sexual dimorphism.

Cranial capacity in *H. erectus* ranged from 780 to 1225 cubic centimeters (average about 1000 cc), which compares with 752 cc for the nearly 2 million-year-old ER 1470 skull from East Africa,

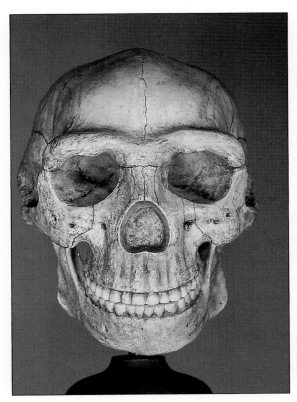

This photo is of a late *H. erectus* skull from Zhoukoudian, China. It may be compared with the earlier African *erectus* skull in the next photo.

This photo is of an early *H. erectus* skull from East Africa. It may be compared with the later *erectus* skull in the preceding photo.

and 1000 to 2000 cc (average 1300 cc) for modern human skulls (Figure 7.2). The cranium itself had a low vault, and the head was long and narrow. When viewed from behind, its width was greater than its height, with its greatest width at the base. The skulls of modern humans, when similarly viewed, are higher than they are wide, with the widest dimension in the region above the ears. Moreover, the shape of the inside of *H. erectus'* brain case showed near-modern development of the brain, especially in the speech area. Although some anthropologists argue that the vocal apparatus was not adequate for speech, others argue that asymmetries of the brain suggest the same pattern of right-handedness with left cerebral dominance that, in modern peoples, is correlated with the capacity for language.[1]

Massive ridges over the eyes gave this early hominine a somewhat simian, "beetle-browed" appearance. *H. erectus* also possessed a sloping forehead and a receding "chin." Powerful jaws with large teeth, protruding mouth, and huge neck muscles added to the generally rugged appearance. Nevertheless, the face, teeth, and jaws of this hominine are smaller than those of *Homo habilis*.

RELATIONSHIP BETWEEN *HOMO erectus* AND *HOMO habilis*

The smaller teeth and larger brains of *H. erectus* seem to mark continuation of a trend first seen in *Homo habilis*. What is new is the increased body size, reduced sexual dimorphism, and more "human" body form of *erectus*. Nonetheless, there is some resemblance to *habilis*; for example, in the conical shape of the rib cage, the long neck and low neck angle of the thigh bone, and smaller brain size

[1] Ralph L. Holloway, "The Indonesian *Homo erectus* Brain Endocasts Revisited," *American Journal Of Physical Anthropology*, 55 (1981):521.

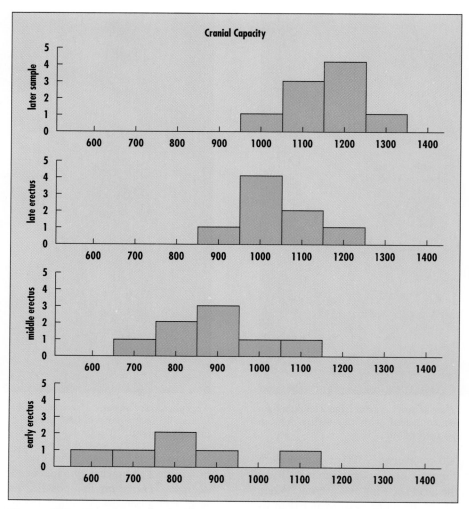

Figure 7.2 Cranial capacity in *Homo erectus* increased over time, as illustrated by the above bar graphs shown in cubic centimeters. The top graph depicts cranial capacity in skulls transitional from *erectus* to *sapiens*.

in the earliest *erectus* fossils. Indeed, as already noted, it is very difficult to distinguish between the earliest *erectus* and the latest *habilis* fossils. Presumably the one form evolved from the other, evidently fairly abruptly, in the period between 1.8 and 1.6 million years ago.[2]

[2] Roger Lewin, "The Earliest 'Humans' Were More Like Apes," *Science*, 236 (1987):1061.

THE CULTURE OF *HOMO erectus*

As one might expect given its larger brain, *H.erectus* outstripped its predecessors in cultural development. In Africa, Europe, and Southwest Asia, there was refinement of the stone toolmaking technology begun by the makers of earlier flake and chopper tools. At some point, fire began to be used for protection, warmth, and cooking, though precisely when this occurred is still a matter for debate.

Finally, there is indirect evidence that the organizational abilities of *H. erectus*, or at least the later ones, were improved over those of their predecessors.

THE ACHEULEAN TOOL TRADITION

Associated with the remains of *Homo erectus* in Africa, Europe, and Southwest Asia are tools of the **Acheulean tradition.** Characteristic of this tradition are hand axes, pear-shaped tools pointed at one end with a sharp cutting edge all around. In East Africa, the earliest hand axes are about 1.4 million years old; those found in Europe and Southwest Asia are no older than about 750,000 years. In East Asia, chopping tool traditions reminiscent of the Oldowan, rather than Acheulean and derived traditions, continued through much of the **Paleolithic.**

That the Acheulean grew out of the Oldowan tradition is indicated by an examination of the evidence discovered at Olduvai. In Bed I, the lowest level, chopper tools were found along with remains of *Homo habilis*. In lower Bed II, the first crude hand axes were found intermingled with chopper tools. Acheulean hand axes having a more "finished" look about them appear in middle Bed II, together with *H. erectus* remains.

Early Acheulean tools represent a definite step

Homo erectus made a variety of Acheulean hand axes.

beyond the generalized cutting, chopping, and scraping tools of the Oldowan tradition. Like chopper tools, the hand axes were probably general-purpose implements for food procurement, processing, and defense. However, they were more standardized in form, having been shaped by regular blows rather than by random strikes. In this way, sharper points and more regular cutting edges were produced, and more cutting edge was available from the same amount of stone.

During this period, tool cultures began to diversify (Figure 7.3). Besides hand axes, *H. erectus* used tools that functioned as cleavers (these were hand axes with a straight edge where the point would otherwise be), and flake tools (generally smaller tools made by hitting a flint core with a hammerstone, thus knocking off flakes with sharp edges). Many flake tools were byproducts of hand axe and cleaver manufacture. Their sharp edges made them useful as is, but many were retouched to make points, scrapers, borers, and other sorts of tools. Diversification of tool kits is also indicated by the smaller numbers of hand axes in northern and eastern Europe, where people relied more on simply flaked choppers, a wide variety of unstandardized flakes, and supplementary tools of bone, antler, and wood. Evidently, these people expended less effort in their toolmaking than did their contemporaries living to the south and west. In eastern Asia, by contrast, many tools may have been made of bamboo and other local woods, from which excellent knives, scrapers, and the like comparable to those of stone can be made.

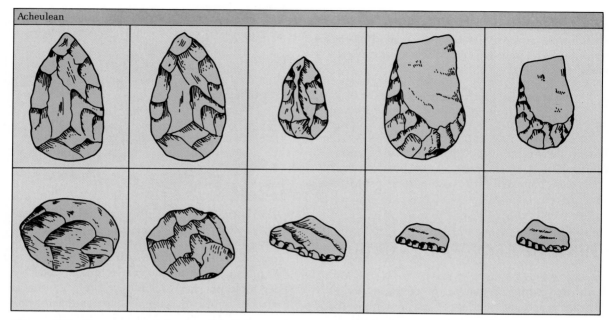

Figure 7.3   Ten percent of the shaped tools in a typical Acheulean assemblage are of the forms drawn here.

ORIGINAL STUDY

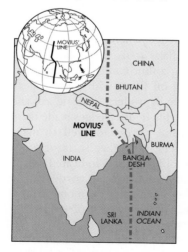

HOMO erectus AND THE USE OF BAMBOO[3]

Bamboo provides, I believe, the solution to a puzzle first raised in 1943, when the late archeologist Hallam Movius of Harvard began to publish his observations on paleolithic (Old Stone Age) cultures of the Far East. In 1937 and 1938 Movius had investigated a number of archeological localities in India, Southeast Asia, and China. Although most of the archeological "cultures" that he recognized are no longer accepted by modern workers, he made another, more lasting contribution. This was the identification of the "Movius line" (which his colleague Carleton Coon named in his honor): a geographical boundary, extending through northern India, that separates two long-lasting Paleolithic cultures. West of the line are found collections of tools with a high percentage of symmetrical and consistently proportioned hand axes (these are called Acheulean tools, after the French site of Saint Acheul). More or less similar tool kits also occur in Mongolia and Siberia, but with few exceptions (which are generally relatively late in time), not in eastern China or Southeast Asia, where more crudely made tools known as choppers and chopping tools prevail [Figure 7.4].

My own research on the Movius line and related questions evolved almost by accident. During the course of my work in Southeast Asia, I excavated many sites, studied a variety of fossil faunal collections, and

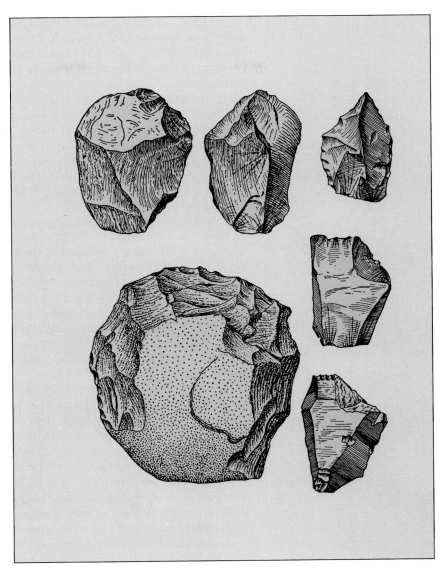

Figure 7.4 Choppers and flakes such as these were used by *Homo erectus* at Zhoukoudian, China.

reviewed the scientific literature dealing with Asia. As part of this research I compared fossil mammals from Asia with those recovered from other parts of the world. In the beginning, my purpose was biostratigraphic—to use the animals to estimate the most likely dates of various sites used by early hominids [in more recent terminology, hominines]. On the basis of the associated fauna, for example, I estimate that Kao Pah Nam may be as old as 700,000 years.

After years of looking at fossil collections and faunal lists, I realized that something was very strange about the collections from Southeast

Asia: There were no fossil horses of Pleistocene age or for a considerable time before that. The only exceptions were a few horse fossils from one place in southern China, the Yuanmou Basin, which was and is a special small grassland habitat in a low, dry valley within the Shan-Yunnan Massif.

To mammalian biostratigraphers this is unusual, since members of the horse family are so common in both the Old and New World that they are a primary means of dating various fossil localities. Fossil horses have been reported from western Burma, but the last one probably lived there some 20 million years ago. Not a single fossil horse turns up later than that in Southeast Asia, although they are known from India to the west and China to the north and every other part of Europe and Asia.

I then began to wonder what other normally common animals might be missing. The answer soon became apparent: camels—even though they too were once widespread throughout the world—and members and relatives of the giraffe family. Pleistocene Southeast Asia was shaping up as a kind of "black hole" for certain fossil mammals! These animals—horses, camels, and giraffids—all dwell in open country. Their absence on the Southeast Asian mainland and islands (all once connected, along with the now inundated Sunda Shelf) is indicative of a forested environment. The mammals that are present—orangutans, tapirs, and gibbons—confirm this conclusion.

The significance of this is that most reconstructions of our evolutionary past have emphasized the influence of savanna grassland habitats, so important in Africa, the cradle of hominid evolution. Many anthropologists theorize that shrinking forests and spreading grasslands encouraged our primarily tree-dwelling ancestors to adapt to ground-dwelling conditions, giving rise to the unique bipedal gait that is the hallmark of hominids [that is, hominines]. Bipedalism, in turn, freed the hands for tool use and ultimately led to the evolution of a large-brained, cultural animal. Tropical Asia, instead, apparently was where early hominids had to readapt to tropical forest.

In studying the record, I noticed that the forested zone—the zone that lacked open-dwelling mammals—coincided generally with the distribution of the chopper-chopping tools. The latter appeared to be the products of a forest adaptation that, for one reason or another, deemphasized the utilization of standardized stone tools. At least this held for Southeast Asia; what at first I could not explain was the existence of similar tools in northern China, where fossil horses, camels, and giraffids were present. Finally, I came upon the arresting fact that the distribution of naturally occurring bamboo coincided almost directly with the distribution of chopper-chopping tools. The only exceptions that may possibly be of real antiquity—certain hand ax collections from Kehe and Dingcun, in China, and Chonggok-Ni, in Korea—fall on the northernmost periphery of the distribution of bamboo and probably can be attributed to fluctuation of the boundary.

Today there are, by various estimates, some 1000 to 1200 species of bamboo. This giant grass is distributed worldwide, but more than 60 percent of the species are from Asia. Only 16 percent occur in Africa, and those on the Indian subcontinent—to an unknown extent the product of human importation and cultivation—are discontinuous in distribution and low in diversity. By far, the greatest diversity occurs in East and Southeast Asia.

Based on these observations, I hypothesized that the early Asians relied on bamboo for much of their technology. At first I envisioned bamboo simply as a kind of icon representing all nonlithic technology. I now think bamboo specifically must have been an extremely important resource. This was not, in my opinion, because appropriate rock was scarce but because bamboo tools would have been efficient, durable, and highly portable.

There are few useful tools that cannot be constructed from bamboo. Cooking and storage containers, knives, spears, heavy and light projectile points, elaborate traps, rope, fasteners, clothing, and even entire villages can be manufactured from bamboo. In addition to the stalks, which are a source of raw material for the manufacture of a variety of artifacts, the seeds and shoots of many species can be eaten. In historical times, bamboo has been to Asian civilization what the olive tree was to the Greeks. In the great cities of the Far East, bamboo is still the preferred choice for the scaffolding used in the construction of skyscrapers. This incomparable resource is also highly renewable. One can actually hear some varieties growing, at more than one foot per day.

Some may question how bamboo tools would have been sufficient for killing and processing large and medium-size animals. Lethal projectile and stabbing implements can in fact be fashioned from bamboo, but their importance may be exaggerated. Large game accounts for a relatively small proportion of the diet of many modern hunters and gatherers. Furthermore, animals are frequently trapped, collected, killed, and then thrown on a fire and cooked whole prior to using bare hands to dismember the roasted carcass. There are many ethnographic examples among forest peoples of this practice.

The only implements that cannot be manufactured from bamboo are axes or choppers suitable for the working of hard woods. More than a few archaeologists have suggested that the stone choppers and resultant "waste" flakes of Asia were created with the objective of using them to manufacture and maintain nonlithic tools. Bamboo can be easily worked with stone flakes resulting from the manufacture of choppers (many choppers may have been a throwaway component in the manufacture of flakes).

[3] Adapted from "Bamboo and Human Evolution," by Geoffrey G. Pope, *Natural History* 10/89, pp. 50–54.

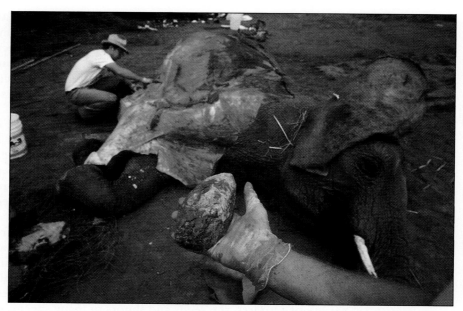

Experimentation on an elephant that died of natural causes demonstrates the effectiveness of Acheulean tools. Simple flint flakes easily slice through the thick hide, while hand axes sever large muscles. With such tools, two men can butcher 100 pounds of meat each in an hour.

The greater variety of tools found in the Acheulean and contemporary traditions is indicative of *H. erectus'* increased ability to deal with the environment. The greater the range of tools used, the greater the range of natural resources capable of being exploited in less time, with less effort, and with a higher degree of efficiency. For example, hand axes may have been used to kill game and dig up roots; cleavers to butcher; scrapers to process hides for bedding and clothes; and flake tools to cut meat and shape wooden objects. As argued in the Original Study, the differences between tool kits for the Far East and West are likely indicative of adaptation to specific regions. The same may be indicated by the differences between the tool kits of northern and eastern Europe on the one hand, and southern and western Europe on the other. One suggested explanation for this is that resources were scarcer in the latter region, which was more heavily forested than the former, and that this

scarcity was a spur to increasing the efficiency of technology.[4]

The improved technological efficiency of *H. erectus* is also evident in the selection of raw materials. While Oldowan toolmakers frequently used coarse-grained stone such as basalt, their Acheulean counterparts generally used such stone only for their heavier implements, preferring flint or other stones with a high silica content for the smaller ones. During later Acheulean times, two techniques were developed which produced thinner, more sophisticated axes with straighter, sharper cutting edges. The **baton method** of percussion manufacture involved using a bone or antler punch to hit the edge of the flint core. This method

---

[4] Clive Gamble, *The Paleolithic Settlement of Europe* (Cambridge, England: Cambridge University Press, 1986), p. 310.

Archaeologists excavate a hearth at a rock shelter in Kao Poh Nam, Thailand. This hearth testifies to human use of fire 700,000 years ago.

produced shallow flake scars, rather than the crushed edge that the hammerstone method produced on the earlier Acheulean hand axes. In later Acheulean times, the striking platform method was also used to create sharper, thinner axes; the toolmakers would often strike off flakes to create a flat surface near the edge. These flat surfaces, or striking platforms, were set up along the edge of the tool perpendicular to its sides, so that the

Baton method: The technique of stone tool manufacture by striking the raw material with a bone or antler "baton" to remove flakes.

toolmaker could remove long thin flakes stretching from the edge across each side of the tool.

THE USE OF FIRE

Another sign of *H. erectus'* developing technology is evidence of fires and cooking. Although use of fire may be indicated by burned layers in the cave at Zhoukoudian, this is problematical. Most of the bones and tools in the cave were probably carried there by carnivorous animals and/or water, and the burned layers appear to have resulted from combustion of extensive guano deposits.[5] This could have

[5] Lewis R. Binford and Chuan Kun Ho, "Taphonomy at a Distance: Zhonkoudian, The Cave Home of Beijing Man?" *Current Anthropology,* 26 (1985):428–429.

occurred naturally; yet, *H. erectus* did enter the cave, at least occasionally, and could have been responsible for the fires that ignited the guano. Better evidence comes from the 700,000-year-old Kao Poh Nam rock shelter in Thailand, where a roughly circular arrangement of fire-cracked basalt cobbles has been found in association with artifacts and animal bones. Since such rocks are not native to the rock shelter, and are quite heavy, they probably had to have been carried in by hominines. The reason more readily available limestone rocks were not used for hearths is that when burned, they produce a quicklime, which causes itchy and burning skin rashes.[6] The bones associated with the hearth (which was located near the rock shelter entrance, away from the deeper recesses favored by denning animals) show clear evidence of cut marks from butchering, as well as burning.

Although we do not know precisely when *H. erectus* learned to use fire, once they did so, it enabled them to do more than just keep warm. In places like Europe and China, food would have been hard to come by in the long, cold winters, as edible plants were unavailable and the large herds of animals, whose mobility exceeded the potential of humans to maintain contact, dispersed and migrated. One solution would have been to search out the frozen carcasses of animals that had died naturally in the late fall and winter, using long wooden probes to locate them beneath the snow, wooden scoops to dig them out, and fire to thaw them so that they could be butchered and eaten.[7] Furthermore, such fire-assisted scavenging would have made available meat and hides of wooly mammoths, wooly rhinoceroses, and bison, which were probably beyond the ability of *H. erectus* to kill, at least until late in the species' career.

Perhaps it was the use of fire to thaw carcasses that led to the idea of cooking food, thereby altering the forces of natural selection, which previously favored individuals with heavy jaws and large, sharp teeth (food is tougher and needs more chewing when it is uncooked), thus promoting

further reduction in tooth size as well as supportive facial architecture. So we find that, between early and late *H. erectus*, chewing-related structures undergo reduction at a rate markedly above the fossil vertebrate average.[8] Cooking did more than soften food, though; because it detoxifies a number of otherwise poisonous plants, alters digestion-inhibiting substances so that important vitamins, minerals, and proteins can be absorbed while in the gut, rather than just passing through it unused, and makes complex carbohydrates like starch—high-energy foods—digestible, the basic resources available to humans were substantially increased and made more secure.

Like tools, then, fire gave people more control over their environment. Possibly, *H. erectus* in Southeast Asia used fire, as have more recent populations living there, to keep areas in the forest clear for foot traffic. Certainly, the resistance to burning characteristic of many hardwood trees in this forest today indicates that fire has for a long time been important in their evolution. Fire may also have been used at least occasionally by *H. erectus*, as it was by subsequent hominines, to frighten away cave-dwelling predators so that they might live in the caves themselves, and it could then be used to provide warmth and light in these cold and dark habitations. Even more, it modified the natural succession of day and night, perhaps encouraging *H. erectus* to stay up after dark to review the day's events, and plan the next day's activities. That *H. erectus* was capable of at least some planning is implied by the existence of populations in temperate climates, where the ability to anticipate the needs of the winter season by preparing in advance to protect against the cold would have been crucial to survival.[9]

---

[6] Geoffrey G. Pope, "Bamboo and Human Evolution," *Natural History* 10/89, p. 56.

[7] Gamble, p. 387.

[8] M.H. Wolpoff, "Evolution in *Homo erectus*: The Question of Stasis," in *The Human Evolution Source Book*, eds. Russell L. Ciochon and John G. Fleagle (Englewood Cliffs, N.J.: Prentice-Hall, 1993), p. 396.

[9] Ward H. Goodenough, "Evolution of the Human Capacity for Beliefs," *American Anthropologist*, 92 (1990):601.

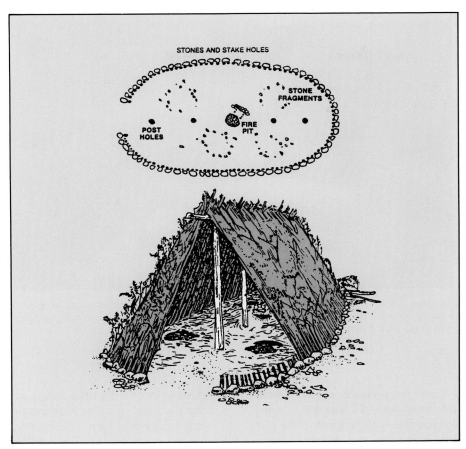

Figure 7.5   An artist proposed this reconstruction of a *H. erectus* hut based on remains found at Terra Amata.

OTHER ASPECTS OF *HOMO erectus'* CULTURE

There is no evidence that populations of *H. erectus* lived anywhere outside the Old World tropics prior to a million years ago. Presumably, control of fire was a key element in permitting them to move into cooler regions like Europe and China. In cold winters, however, a fire is of little use without adequate shelter, and *H. erectus'* increased sophistication in the construction of shelters is indicated by the remains of what may be several huts at Terra Amata (Figure 7.5). Here several huts appear to have been built, probably of saplings. They seem to have been seasonally reoccupied over a number of

years, and each apparently had a hearth in the center of its floor.

Keeping warm by the hearth is one thing, but keeping warm away from the hearth when procuring food or other necessities is another. Studies of modern humans indicate that they can remain reasonably comfortable down to 50°F with a minimum of clothing so long as they are active; below that temperature, the extremities cool to the point of pain;[10] thus the dispersal of early humans into

---

[10] John W. M. Whiting, John A. Sodergem, and Stephen M. Stigler, "Winter Temperature as a Constraint to the Migration of Preindustrial Peoples," *American Anthropologist*, 84 (1982):289.

At some point, *H. erectus* ceased relying on scavenging as a source of meat, in favor of hunting live animals. One of those animals was the elephant hunted at Ambrona, Spain, where the tusk remains.

regions where winter temperatures regularly went below 50°, as they must have in China and Europe, was probably not possible without more in the way of clothing than hominines had hitherto worn. Unfortunately, we have no direct evidence as to the kind of clothing worn by *H. erectus*; we only know that it must have been more sophisticated than before.

That *H. erectus* was able to organize in order to hunt live animals is suggested by remains such as those from the 400,000-year-old sites of Ambrona and Torralba, in Spain. At the latter site, in what was an ancient swamp, were found the remains of several elephants, horses, red deer, wild oxen, and rhinoceroses. Since their skeletons were dismembered, rather than in proper anatomical order, a fact that cannot be explained as a result of any natural geological process, it is clear that these animals did not accidently get mired in a swamp where they simply died and decayed.[11] In fact, the bones are

closely associated with a variety of stone tools—a few thousand of them. Furthermore, there is very little evidence of carnivore activity, and none at all for the really big carnivores. Clearly, hominines were involved, not just in butchering the animals, but evidently in killing them as well. In fact, it is likely that the animals were actually driven into the swamp so that they could be easily dispatched. The remains of charcoal and carbon, widely but thinly scattered in the vicinity, raises the possibility that grass fires were used to drive the animals into the swamp. In any event, what we have here is evidence for more than opportunistic scavenging; not only was *H. erectus* able to hunt, but considerable organizational and communicative skills are implied as well.

There is no evidence to indicate that *H. erectus* became an accomplished hunter all at once. Presumably, the most ancient members of this species, like *Homo habilis* before them, got the bulk of their meat through scavenging. As their cultural capabilities increased, however, they could have devised ways of doing their own killing, rather than waiting for animals to die or be killed by other predators. As they became more proficient predators over

[11] Leslie G. Freeman, "Ambrona and Torralba: New Evidence and Interpretation." Paper presented at the 91st Annual Meeting of the American Anthropological Association, December 1992.

At Terra Amata in France, a hearth was found that consists of a depression surrounded by stones.

time, they would have been able to count on a more reliable supply of meat.

Evidence for a developing symbolic life comes from a site in France, where an engraved ox rib was found in an Acheulean context. This could be the earliest of a number of Paleolithic artifacts which have no obvious utility or model in the natural world. Such apparently symbolic artifacts became more common in later phases of the Paleolithic, as more modern forms of the genus *Homo* appeared on the scene. Alexander Marshack argues that the use of such symbolic images requires some sort of spoken language, not only to assign meaning to the images but to maintain the tradition.[12] That a tradition was maintained is suggested by similar motifs on later Paleolithic artifacts. It is also in a late Acheulean context that we have our earliest evidence for the use of red ochre, a pigment that

more modern forms of *Homo* employed to color symbolic as well as utilitarian artifacts, the bodies of the dead, to paint the bodies of the living and (ultimately) to make notations and paint pictures.

With *H. erectus*, then, we find a clearer manifestation of the interplay among cultural, physical, and environmental factors than ever before. However slowly, social organization, technology, and communication developed along with an increase in brain size and complexity. In fact, the cranial capacity of late *H. erectus* is 31 percent greater than the mean for early *erectus*, a rate of increase more rapid than the average fossil vertebrate rate.[13] As a consequence of these developments, *H. erectus'* resource base was enlarged significantly; the supply of meat could be increased by hunting as well as by scavenging, and the supply of plant foods was increased as cooking allowed the consumption of previously toxic or indigestible vegetables. This, along with an increased ability to modify the environment in advantageous ways—for example, by using fire to provide warmth—undoubtedly contributed to a population increase and territorial expansion. In humans, as in other mammals, any kind of adaptation that makes life significantly easier than it had been reduces selective pressures, reproduction becomes easier, more offspring survive than before, and so populations grow. This causes fringe populations to "spill over" into neighboring regions previously uninhabited by the species.

Thus, *Homo erectus* was able to move into areas that had never been inhabited by hominines before; first into the warm, southern regions of Asia, and ultimately into the cooler regions of China and Europe.

[12] Alexander Marshack, "Some Implications of the Paleolithic Symbolic Evidence for the Origin of Language," *Current Anthropology*, 17(2) (1976):280.

[13] Wolpoff, pp. 392, 396.

Chapter Summary

The remains of *Homo erectus* have been found at several sites in Africa, Europe, China, and Java. The earliest is 1.6 million years old, and the species endured until about 400,000 years ago, by which time fossils exhibit a mosaic of features characteristic of both *erectus* and *H. sapiens*. It appears to have evolved, rather abruptly, from *Homo habilis*. From the neck on down, the body of *H. erectus* was essentially modern in appearance. The brain, although small by modern standards, was larger than that of *Homo habilis*. The skull was generally low, with maximum breadth near its base, and massive brow ridges. Powerful teeth and jaws added to a generally rugged appearance.

With *H. erectus* we find a greater interaction among cultural, physical, and environmental factors than ever before. Social organization and improved technology developed along with an increase in brain size. The Oldowan chopper evolved into the Acheulean hand axe. These tools, the earliest of which are about 1.4 million years old, are pear-shaped, with pointed ends and sharp cutting edges. Like the chopper, they served a general purpose. During Acheulean times, tool cultures began to diversify. Along with hand axes, tool kits included cleavers, scrapers, and flakes. Further signs of *H. erectus'* developing technology was the selection of different stone for different tools and the use of fires for protection, warmth, light, thawing frozen carcasses, and cooking. Cooking is a significant cultural adaptation because it took the place of certain physical adaptations such as large heavy jaws and teeth, since cooked food is easier to chew. Since it detoxifies various substances in plants, cooking also increased the food resources available. During later Acheulean times, *H. erectus* used the baton and striking platform methods to make thinner axes with straighter, sharper cutting edges. From France comes evidence of the building of huts and the making of nonutilitarian artifacts; from Spain comes evidence of cooperative efforts to kill large amounts of game.

H. erectus' improved organizational, technological, and communicative abilities led to more effective hunting and a greater ability to modify the environment in advantageous ways. As a result, the populations of these early hominines increased and they expanded into new geographic areas.

Suggested Readings

Campbell, Bernard G. *Humankind Emerging*, 6th ed. New York: HarperCollins, 1992.
This book, incorporating material from the Time-Life *Emergence of Man* series, has good, up-to-date coverage of *Homo erectus* and their way of life.

Ciochon, Russell L., and John G. Fleagle, eds. *The Human Evolution Source Book*. Englewood Cliffs, N.J.: Prentice-Hall, 1993.
Part V of this book reproduces eight articles that deal with a variety of topics on the history of recovery, diversity, tempo and mode of evolution and culture of *H. erectus*. An introduction by the editors puts the articles in context.

Gamble, Clive. *The Paleolithic Settlement of Europe*. Cambridge, England: Cambridge University Press, 1986.
Although it does not deal exclusively with *Homo erectus*, it does discuss material from Europe associated with this species. In doing so, it takes a critical stance to conventional interpretations and offers new explanations of *H. erectus*' behavior based on a better understanding of the process of archeological site formation.

Rightmire, G. Philip. *The Evolution of Homo erectus: Comparative Anatomical Studies of an Extinct Human Species*. Cambridge, England: Cambridge University Press, 1990.
This is the standard work on our current understanding of *Homo erectus*.

White, Edmond, Dale Brown, and the editors of Time-Life. *The First Men*. New York: Time-Life, 1973.
This magnificently illustrated volume in the Time-Life *Emergence of Man* series deals with *Homo erectus*. Its one drawback is that it portrays early *H. erectus* as too much of a "big game hunter"; nonetheless, it remains a good introduction to the fossils, sites, and tools associated with this hominine.

CHAPTER

8

HOMO sapiens

AND THE LATER

PALEOLITHIC

The intellectual capabilities of Upper Paleolithic peoples, whose skeletons differ in no significant way from our own, are reflected in the efficiency with which some of them hunted game far larger and more powerful than themselves, as well as by the sophistication of their art. The painting of animals such as the one shown here attests not only to the artist's technical skill, but also his or her knowledge of the animal's anatomy.

WHO WAS "ARCHAIC" *HOMO sapiens*?

"Archaic" *Homo sapiens* is the name used for members of this species who lived prior to about 35,000 years ago. Included are the Neandertals, descendants of *Homo erectus*, who lived in Europe and western Asia between about 100,000 and 35,000 years ago, and other populations somewhat like them who lived in Africa, China, and Southeast Asia. All had essentially modern-sized brains in skulls which still retained a number of primitive features.

WHEN DID MORE MODERN FORMS OF *HOMO sapiens* APPEAR?

Although some fossils as much as 100,000 years old from Africa and Southwest Asia have been interpreted as essentially modern in appearance, there is now reason to question this. Fossils of *Homo sapiens* that are unequivocally modern in their anatomy were present certainly by 45,000 years ago.

WHAT HAPPENED TO CULTURE AFTER HUMANS ACHIEVED MODERN-SIZED BRAINS?

By 100,000 years ago, human culture had become rich and varied. People not only made a wide variety of stone tools for special purposes, but they also made objects for purely symbolic purposes, engaged in ceremonial activities, and cared for the old and disabled. Although the human brain has not become larger since then, culture has continued to evolve and change to the present time. In the latter part of the Paleolithic, cultural diversity increased as people adapted ever more specifically to the diverse regions in which they already lived, and into which expanding human populations were moving. In the Mesolithic, or Middle Stone Age, the process of regional adaptation continued, as environments throughout the world changed in the immediate post-glacial era.

The anthropologist attempting to piece together the innumerable parts of the puzzle of human evolution must be as good a detective as a scholar, for the available evidence is often scant, enigmatic, or full of misleading clues. The quest for the origin of modern humans from more ancient representatives of the genus *Homo* has some of the elements of a detective story, for it contains a number of mysteries concerning the emergence of humanity, none of which has been completely solved to this day. The mysteries involve the appearance of the first fully sapient humans, the identity of the Neandertals, and the relationship of both to more modern forms.

THE APPEARANCE OF *HOMO* sapiens

At various sites in Europe and Africa, a number of hominine fossils have been found which seem to date, roughly, between 400,000 and 200,000 years ago. These include skulls and skull fragments from Casablanca and Salé in Morocco, Arago in France, Steinheim and Bilzingsleben in Germany, Swanscombe in England, Vertessöllös in Hungary, Petralona in Greece, and Bodo in Ethiopia; and jaws and jaw fragments from Casablanca (two sites), Rabat, and Temara in Morocco as well as Arago and Montmaurin in France. Some of these—most commonly the African fossils, but also the Arago skull—have been called *H. erectus*; others—most commonly those from Steinheim and Swanscombe —have been called *H. sapiens* . In fact, what they all have in common is a mixture of characteristics of both forms, which is what one would expect of remains transitional between the two. For example, the skulls from Bodo, Steinheim, and Swanscombe had rather large brains for *H. erectus*. The overall appearance of the skulls, however, is different from ours. They are large and robust with their maximum breadth lower on the skull, and they had more prominent brow ridges, larger faces, and bigger teeth. Conversely, the Salé skull, which had a rather small brain for *H. sapiens* (about 930 to 960 cc), looks surprisingly modern from the back. Finally, the various jaws from Morocco and France seem to combine features of *H. erectus* with those of the European Neandertals.

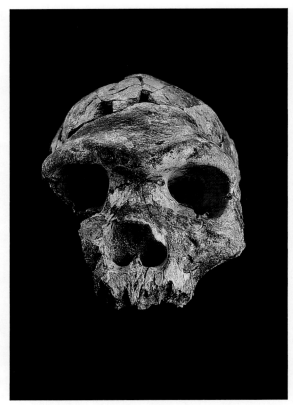

This skull, from Ethiopia, is one of several from Africa indicative of a transition from *Homo erectus* to *Homo sapiens*.

A similar situation exists in East Asia, where skulls from Ngandong in Java as well as several fossils from sites in China exhibit the same sort of mix of *erectus* and *sapiens* characteristics. Whether one chooses to call any of these early humans "primitive" *H. sapiens* or "advanced" *H. erectus* seems to be a matter of taste; whichever one calls them does not alter their apparently transitional status. Despite their retention of a number of features of *H. erectus*, their brain size shows a clear increase over that of even late representatives of that species (see Figure 7.2).

THE LEVALLOISIAN TECHNIQUE

The culture of the hominines transitional between *H. erectus* and *H. sapiens* seems little changed from

Levalloisian technique: Toolmaking technique developed about 200,000 years ago by which three or four long triangular flakes were detached from a specially prepared core.

---

that of their predecessors. Primitive *sapiens* (or advanced *H. erectus*, if that is what one wishes to call them), for example, employed the kinds of heavy-duty tools such as hand axes and smaller flake tools used by *H. erectus* for thousands of years; however, by 200,000 years ago, the **Levalloisian technique** of tool manufacture had come into use. Levalloisian flake tools have been found widely in Africa, Europe, the Middle East, and even China, where practically no hand axes have been uncovered. It is likely that this is a case of independent invention, since eastern Asia is quite distinct culturally from the West. In the Levalloisian technique, the core was shaped by removal of flakes over its surface, following which a striking platform was made by a crosswise blow at one end of the core of stone (Figure 8.1). Then the platform was struck, removing three or four long flakes, leaving a nodule that looked like a tortoise shell. This method produced a longer edge for the same amount of flint than the previous ones. The edges were sharper and could be produced in less time.

ARCHAIC *HOMO* sapiens

The scarcity of *H. sapiens* fossils predating 100,000 years ago is in marked contrast to the situation after that date, by which time the Neandertals were becoming widespread in Europe and western Asia, while other representatives of archaic *H. sapiens* are known from East Asia and Africa.

In 1856, three years before publication of Darwin's *On the Origin of Species*, the skeletal remains of an early man were discovered in the Neander Valley—Neandertal in German—near Dusseldorf, Germany. Although the discovery was of considerable interest, the experts were generally at a loss as to what to make of it. Examination of the fossil skull, a few ribs, and some limb bones revealed that the individual was a human being, showing primi-

tive and modern characteristics. The cranial capacity had reached modern size, but the skull was still primitive looking. Some people believed the bones were those of a sickly and deformed contemporary. Others thought the skeleton belonged to a soldier who had succumbed to "water on the brain" during the Napoleonic Wars. A prominent anatomist thought the remains were those of an idiot suffering from malnutrition, whose violent temper had gotten him into many scrapes, flattening his forehead and making his brow ridges bumpy.

The idea that **Neandertals** were somehow deformed or aberrant was given impetus by an analysis of a Neandertal skeleton found in 1908 near La Chapelle-Aux-Saints in France. The analysis mistakenly concluded that the specimen's brain was ape-like and that it walked like an ape. Although a team of North American investigators subsequently proved that this French Neandertal specimen was that of an elderly *H. sapiens* who had suffered from malnutrition, arthritis of the spine, and other deformities, the ape-like image has persisted. To many nonanthropologists, Neandertal has become the quintessential "caveman," portrayed by imaginative cartoonists as a slant-headed, stooped, dim-witted individual, clad in animal skins and carrying a big club as he plods across the prehistoric landscape, perhaps dragging behind him an unwilling female or a dead leopard. In the best-selling novel, *Clan of the Cave Bear*, Neandertals are depicted as bow-legged and barrel-chested with extra long arms, more like those of apes than humans and incapable of the full range of human arm movements, muzzle-like jaws, and a body covering of coarse brown hair; not quite a pelt but not far from it. This brutish image is completed by portraying them as incapable of spoken language, abstract thought, thinking in new ways, or even thinking ahead.

Neandertals: Representatives of "archaic" *Homo sapiens* in Europe and western Asia, living from about 100,000 years ago to about 35,000 years ago.

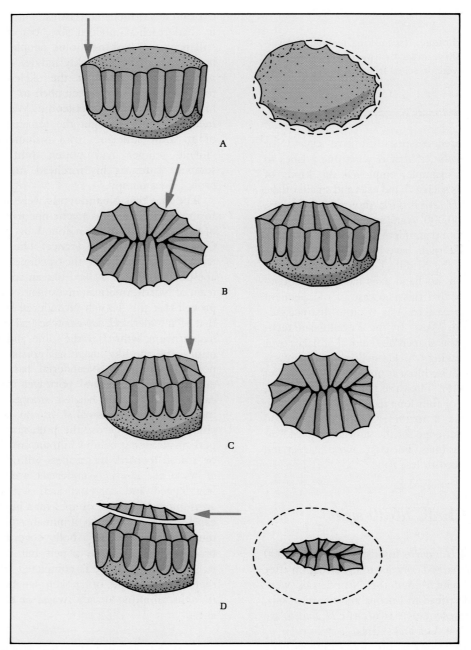

Figure 8.1   These drawings show top and side views of the steps in the Levalloisian technique. Drawing A shows the trimming of the edge of the stone nucleus; B, the trimming of the top surface; C, the striking platform; and D, the final step.

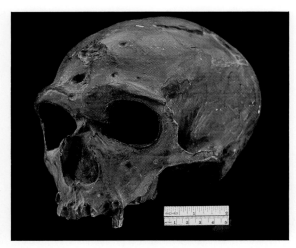

This "classic" Neandertal skull is from La Chapelle Aux Saints, France.

With the discovery that Neandertals were nowhere near as brutish and ape-like as originally portrayed, some scholars began to see them as no more than "less finished" versions of the anatomically modern populations that held exclusive sway in Europe and the Middle East after 30,000 years ago. For example, Ashley Montagu argued that some faint ancestral Neandertal characteristics may still be seen even in today's Middle Eastern and European populations, with their relatively prominent brow ridges, deep eye sockets, and receding foreheads and chins.[1] Nevertheless, recent work has shown that significant differences do exist between Neandertals and anatomically modern populations. Although they had modern-sized brains (average cranial capacity 1400 ccs, versus 1300 for modern *H. sapiens*), Neandertal skulls are distinctive in the mid-facial projection of their noses and teeth, which form a kind of prow. This is due at least in part to the large size of their front teeth, which were heavily used for tasks other than chewing. In many individuals, they were worn down to the stubs of their roots by 35 to 40 years of age. The eye sockets were also positioned well forward, with prominent brow ridges above them.

At the back of the skull, a bony mass provided for attachment of powerful neck muscles.

Both sexes were extraordinarily muscular, with extremely robust and dense limb bones. Details of the shoulder blades indicate the importance of overarm and downward thrusting movements; their arms were exceptionally powerful, and pronounced attachments on their hand bones attest to a remarkably strong grip. Their massive foot and leg bones (their shin bones, for example, were twice as strong as those of any recent human population) suggest a high level of endurance; evidently, Neandertals spent long hours walking and scrambling about. Since brain size is related to overall body mass as well as intelligence, the large average size of the Neandertal brain (compared to that of modern humans) is accounted for by their heavy robust bodies.

The Neandertal pelvis, too, shows differences from that of anatomically modern humans, but these do not support suggestions that obstetric requirements were different for Neandertals than they are for modern humans. Although the pelvic outlet is small by modern standards, it is still within the present-day range of variation, and the size of the pelvic inlet is virtually the same.[2] Differences in pelvic shape are easily accounted for as a consequence of posture-related biomechanics and deviation in modern humans from a shape characteristic of earlier hominines. Once born, however, Neandertal infants did mature more rapidly than do our own, as the characteristic Neandertal robustness can be discerned in the bones of children who died even before the age of five. Furthermore, their teeth erupted earlier, and their brains grew more rapidly after birth than do our own.

AFRICAN, CHINESE, AND JAVANESE POPULATIONS

Because Neandertal fossils are so numerous, have been known for so long, and are relatively well

[1] Ashley Montagu, *Man: His First Two Million Years* (New York: Columbia University Press, 1969).

[2] Robert G. Tague, "Sexual Dimorphism in the Human Bony Pelvis, with a Consideration of the Neanderthal Pelvis from Kebara Cave, Israel," *American Journal of Physical Anthropology*, 88 (1992):1–21.

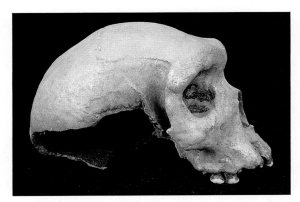

This skull of archaic *Homo sapiens* is from Broken Hill, Zambia.

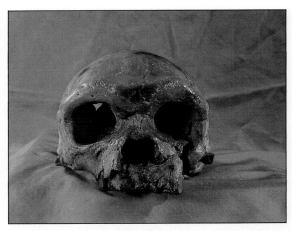

This skull from Dali, China, is representative of archaic *H. sapiens* in East Asia.

dated, they have received much more attention than have other populations of archaic *H. sapiens*. Nevertheless, outside of Europe and western Asia, a number of skulls have been found in Africa, China, and Java, which are roughly contemporary with the Neandertals, or at least the earliest ones. They differ from the Neandertals primarily in their lack of midfacial projection and the absence of such massive muscle attachments on the back of their skulls. Thus, the Neandertals represent an extreme form of archaic *sapiens*. Elsewhere, the archaics look like robust versions of the early modern populations that lived in the same regions or, if one looks backward, somewhat less primitive versions of the *H. erectus* populations that preceded them. All had fully modern-sized brains.

THE CULTURE OF ARCHAIC *HOMO sapiens*

As the first hominines to possess brains of modern size, it is not surprising to find that the cultural capabilities of archaic *H. sapiens* were significantly improved over those of earlier hominines. Such a brain made possible an advanced technology as well as conceptual thought of considerable sophistication, and communication was almost surely by speech. In short, Neandertals and others like them were a fully sapient species of human being, rela-

tively successful in surviving and thriving even in environments that would seem to us impossibly cold and hostile.

MIDDLE PALEOLITHIC

The improved toolmaking capabilities of archaic *H. sapiens* are represented by various **Middle Paleolithic** traditions, of which the best known are the Mousterian and Mousterian-like traditions of Europe, western Asia, and North Africa, which date between about 166,000 to 40,000 years ago; they represent a technological advance over Acheulean and Levalloisian tools. The 16 inches of working edge that an Acheulean flint worker could get from a two-pound core compares with the six feet the Mousterian could get from the same core.

Middle Paleolithic: That part of the Paleolithic characterized by the emergence of archaic *H. sapiens* and the development of the Mousterian tradition of toolmaking.

Mousterian tradition: Toolmaking tradition of the Neandertals and their contemporaries of Europe, western Asia, and northern Africa, featuring flake tools lighter and smaller than Levalloisian flake tools.

Tools such as these are characteristic of the Mousterian tradition.

THE MOUSTERIAN TRADITION

The **Mousterian tradition** is named after the Neandertal site of Le Moustier, France. The presence of Acheulean hand axes at Mousterian sites is one indication that this culture was ultimately rooted in the older Acheulean tradition. Neandertals and their contemporaries improved upon Levalloisian techniques; Mousterian flake tools are lighter and smaller than those of the Levalloisian. Whereas Levalloisian toolmakers obtained only two or three flakes from one core, Mousterian toolmakers obtained many more smaller flakes, which were then skillfully retouched and sharpened.

The Mousterian tool kits contained a much greater variety of tool types than the previous traditions: hand axes, flakes, scrapers, borers, gravers, notched flakes for sawing and shredding wood, and many types of points that could be attached to wooden shafts to form thrusting spears. This variety of tool types indicates that the Mousterian tool kit intensified human utilization of food resources and increased the availability and quality of clothing and shelter. For the first time, people could cope with truly arctic conditions, which became prevalent in Europe beginning about 70,000 years ago.

People likely came to live in cold climates as a result of a slow but steady population increase during the Paleolithic era. As this caused populations to "spill over" into previously uninhabited colder regions, humans developed a series of cold-climate adaptations that increased their cultural variability. Under arctic conditions vegetable foods are only rarely or seasonally available, and meat is the staff of life. In particular animal fats, rather than carbohydrates, become the chief source of energy on account of their slower rate of metabolism. Abundant animal fat in the diets of cold-climate meat-eaters provides them with the extra energy needed for full-time hunting, as well as needed body heat. Insufficient fat in the diet produces lower resistance to disease, lassitude, and a loss of the will to work. That meat was important to the makers of Mousterian tools is indicated by the following Original Study.

ORIGINAL STUDY

SUBSISTENCE PRACTICES OF MOUSTERIAN PEOPLES[3]

Most of the recent discussions of changes in subsistence strategies across the archaic/modern human transition have focused on a series of generalizations formulated in the recent publications of Binford. In essence, these can be reduced to three basic propositions:

1. **Prior to the emergence of anatomically modern populations, the exploitation of animal resources was focused primarily on the**

scavenging of meat and bone marrow from carnivore kills and included only a relatively minor and secondary component of deliberate hunting of game.

2. Where some hunting was practiced by these archaic populations, it was focused almost entirely on the smaller species of game, especially various species of cervids [deer family] and some of the smaller species of bovids [cattle family].

3. Any deliberate hunting or killing of game by archaic populations was undertaken essentially on an opportunistic or encounter basis and involved little if any deliberate planning, forethought, or "logistical organization" on the part of the human groups.

Binford's interpretations are original and provocative and have undoubtedly served to stimulate more sharply focused research on the problems of Lower and Middle Paleolithic subsistence. Recently, however, they have been challenged from a number of perspectives. In particular, Chase and others have drawn attention to at least three aspects of the current data which would appear to run directly counter to Binford's hypotheses:

1. The faunal assemblages recovered from several Middle Paleolithic sites in Europe reveal a heavy bias in favor of one particular species, which would seem difficult if not impossible to account for by any hypothesis of essentially random or opportunistic exploitation. Examples of these heavily single-species-dominated faunas have been recorded at Staroselje in the Crimea, Ilskaya, Teshik-Tash, and Volgograd in southern Russia, and Ehringsdorf in Germany, as well as at several recently excavated sites in France. One of the most striking illustrations of this single-species orientation has been documented in the recent excavations at Mauran in the French Pyrenees, where (according to preliminary reports) well over 90 percent of the faunal assemblage (representing at least 108 animals) consists of the remains of large bovids (*Bos/Bison*). As Chase points out, it is difficult to visualize these heavily specialized faunas as the result of either opportunistic scavenging or unstructured encounter hunting on the part of Neanderthal groups. Both of the latter sample the whole range of animal species within the immediate catchment areas of the sites, roughly in proportion to their relative frequencies in the local faunal communities. The fact that the faunal assemblage from Mauran (as well as other sites) consisted almost entirely of very large game (large bovids, with individual carcass weights up of to 900 kg) runs counter to Binford's hypothesis that hunting was focused exclusively on the smaller species of game.

2. The detailed studies carried out by Chase, Levine, and others of the faunal assemblages from the long Mousterian succession at Combe Grenal (southwestern France) have produced results which conflict in several respects with those reported by Binford from his earlier studies at this site. Thus, Chase has demonstrated that the remains of both horses and large bovids at Combe Grenal (which Binford has maintained were exclusively *scavenged*) are represented more frequently by

the major meat-bearing bones from the *upper* parts of the limbs than by the meat-poor bones from the lower limbs and that these bones frequently bear clear cut marks (presumably through fresh flesh) as opposed to indications of heavy chopping through the remains of partially desiccated carcasses. Both these observations are much more consistent with the notion of deliberate hunting of large game than with that of scavenging of remains from natural-death carcasses or abandoned carnivore kills. Similarly, Levine has shown that the age profiles of the horse remains from three separate levels at Combe Grenal appear to indicate an essentially "catastrophic" pattern closely similar to that to be expected in a living herd. This pattern again bears little resemblance to what one would anticipate from the scavenging of carnivore kills, which would be likely to reflect a primary emphasis on the oldest and youngest age-classes, the most vulnerable elements in the animal herds. As Levine points out, these age profiles would conform best to some form of unselective, mass hunting strategies on the part of the Mousterian groups.

3. Finally, the specific character and location of several Middle Paleolithic sites in Europe may well provide some direct insight into the methods by which large game was hunted by Mousterian groups. At the site of La Quina in western France, for example, a dense accumulation of bones of bovids, horses, and reindeer (many with clear indications of butchery marks) occurs immediately at the base of a steep cliff, the only topographic feature of this kind within several kilometres of the site. As Jelinek, Debenath, and Dibble and Chase have pointed out, there would seem to be a strong implication in this case that the site represents a typical jump or cliff-fall hunting site, in which the animals were deliberately driven over the cliff as part of a systematic hunting strategy. A similar situation has been documented in the recent excavations at Mauran, where an accumulation of several thousands of bones of large bovids again occurs immediately at the foot of a steep riverside escarpment. And in a slightly different context, Scott has recently argued that the highly localized and dense accumulations of mammoth and woolly rhinoceros bones at the site of La Cotte de Saint-Brelade (Channel Islands) can only be plausibly explained in terms of some similar strategy of cliff-fall hunting—in this case into a deep coastal ravine. In none of these cases is there any convincing way of explaining the bone accumulations as accidental death assemblages. The strong implication, in other words, is that Middle Paleolithic populations in Europe were practicing some form of organized, systematic cliff-fall hunting in many ways reminiscent of that reflected in the Paleo-Indian bison-jump kill sites of North America [see p. 211]. As a further indication of the deliberate killing of game in Middle and Lower Paleolithic contexts, one could refer to the well-documented discoveries of wooden spears at the sites of Clacton (England) and Lehringen (Germany) and the recent confirmation from microwear studies that at least certain forms of Mousterian and Levallois points would seem

to have functioned as the hafted tips of either thrusting or throwing spears.

The combination of the preceding data leaves little doubt that the Neanderthal populations of Europe *were* practicing a good deal of deliberate hunting of very large game, and in a way that can hardly be described as totally unstructured or opportunistic.

[3] Paul Mellars, "Major Issues in the Emergence of Modern Humans," *Current Anthropology*, 30 (1989):356–357.

The importance of hunting to Mousterian peoples may also be reflected in their hunting implements, which are more standardized with respect to size and shape than are their domestic and maintenance implements. The complexity of the tool kit needed for survival in a cold climate may have played a role in lessening the mobility of the "owners" of all of these possessions. That they were less mobile is suggested by the greater depth of deposits at Mousterian sites compared with those from the earlier Paleolithic. Similarly, evidence for long sequences of production, resharpening and discard of tools, large-scale butchery and cooking of game, and evidence of efforts to improve accommodations in some caves and rock shelters through pebble paving, construction of simple walls, the presence of postholes and artificial pits all suggest that Mousterian sites were more than mere stopovers in peoples' constant quest for food. The large number of Mousterian sites uncovered in Europe and western Asia, as well as clear differences between them are closely related to Neandertal's improved hunting techniques, based on superior technology in weapon and toolmaking and more efficient social organization than before. These, in turn, were closely related to Neandertal's increased brain size.

Neandertal society had developed even to the point of being able to care for handicapped members of the group, as we have evidence that the disabled were cared for by their companions. The remains of a blind amputee discovered in Shanidar Cave in Iraq and a man crippled by arthritis unearthed at La Chapelle attest to this fact. Whether or not this indicates true "compassion" on the part of these early people is not known; what is certain is that culture had become more than barely adequate to ensure survival.

Although earlier reports of evidence for some sort of "cave bear cult" have turned out to be far-fetched, indications of some sort of symbolic life do exist. At several sites, there is clear evidence for deliberate burial of the dead. For example, at Kebara Cave, in Israel, sometime between 64,000 and 59,000 years ago, a Neandertal male aged between 25 and 35 years old was placed in a pit, on his back, with his arms folded over his chest and abdomen. Some time later, after complete decay of attaching ligaments, the grave was reopened and the skull removed (a practice which, interestingly, is sometimes seen in burials in the same region roughly 50,000 years later). To cite but one other example, at Shanidar Cave, evidence was found of a burial accompanied by funeral ceremonies. In the back of the cave a Neandertal was buried in a pit. Pollen analysis of the soil around the skeleton indicated that flowers had been placed below the body and in a wreath about the head. Moreover, the flowers consist solely of varieties valued in historic times for their medicinal properties.

Other evidence for symbolic behavior in Mousterian culture comes from the use of two different pigments: manganese dioxide and red ochre. These show clear evidence of scraping to produce powder, as well as crayon-like facets. Thus, Mousterian peoples were clearly using these for applying color to things. One example is the carved and shaped section of a mammoth tooth illustrated on page 195 that was worked by Mousterian peoples about 50,000 years ago. One of a number of carved and engraved objects that may have been made for purely symbolic purposes, it is similar to a number of plaques of bone and ivory made by later Paleo-

This carved symbolic plaque or "churinga" made from a section of a mammoth molar was excavated at the Mousterian site of Tata, Hungary. The edge is rounded and polished from long handling. The plaque has been symbolically smeared with red ocher. The reverse face of the plaque (right) shows the beveling and shaping of the tooth.

lithic peoples, and it is also similar to the "churingas" made of wood by Australian aborigines for ritual purposes. The Mousterian object, which was once smeared with red ocher, has a highly polished face as if from long handling. Microscopic examination reveals that it was never provided with a working edge for any utilitarian purpose. As Alexander Marshack observes: "A number of researchers have indicated that the Neandertals did in fact have conceptual models and maps as well as problem-solving capacities comparable to, if not equal to, those found among anatomically modern humans."[4]

NEANDERTALS AND SPOKEN LANGUAGE

Among modern humans, the sharing of thoughts and ideas, as well as the transmission of culture from one generation to the next, is dependent upon

[4] Alexander Marshack, "Evolution of the Human Capacity: The Symbolic Evidence," *Yearbook of Physical Anthropology*, 32 (1989):22.

a spoken language. Since the Neandertals had modern-sized brains and a tool kit comparable to that being used in historic times by Australian aborigines, it might be supposed that they had some form of spoken language. In spite of this, the argument has been made that the Neandertals lacked the physical features necessary for spoken language. It has been shown, however, that the reconstruction of the Neandertal larynx, on which this argument is partially based, is faulty. In fact, the position in the skeleton from the Kebara Cave burial of the hyoid bone (the "wish bone," associated with the larynx) shows that the vocal tract was quite adequate for speech. Moreover, the brain (as reflected by endocranial casts) suggests that Neandertals had the neural development necessary for language. Finally, modern adults with as much flattening of the skull base and facial protrusion as some Neandertals have no trouble talking. Talking Neandertals make a good deal of sense in view of the evidence, sparse though it may be, for the manufacture of objects of apparently symbolic significance. Objects such as the mammoth tooth "churinga" already described would seem to have required some form of linguistic explanation. On the other hand, any language

FRANZ WEIDENREICH

(1873—1948)

Franz Weidenreich was born and educated in Germany, where he went on to hold professorships in anatomy, first at Strassburg and then at Heidelberg. Although his early work was primarily in hematology (the study of blood), his scientific work shifted to the study of bones and related tissues, and in 1926 he published his first study of a human fossil, an archaic *Homo sapiens* cranium from Ehringsdorf. Two years later, he was appointed professor of anthropology at the University of Frankfurt.

In 1935, he was sent by the Rockefeller Foundation to take up the study of fossils of *Homo erectus* from Zhoukoutien, China, following the death of their discoverer, Davidson Black. When the Japanese invasion of China forced Weidenreich to leave, he took with him to the United States several painstakingly prepared casts, as well as detailed notes on the actual fossils. From these he was able to prepare a major monograph which set new standards for a paleoanthropological report. For this alone, anthropology owes him a great debt, for the fossils themselves were among the casualties of World War II.

Unlike many physical anthropologists of his time or ours, Weidenreich had an extensive first hand knowledge of extant human fossils from several parts of the Old World: Europe (where he had worked before going to China), China, and Southeast Asia (he collaborated in the 1930s study of *Homo erectus* and later fossils from Java). What struck him about the fossils in each of these regions was the evident continuity to be seen, going from the earliest to the latest specimens. Out of this observation developed his polycentric theory of human evolution, which received its first clear statement in a 1943 publication. In it, he argued the thesis that human populations of common ancestry thereafter evolved in the same direction in four different geographical regions. (Africa, was the fourth.) Although he failed to come up with an adequate explanation for such a phenomenon, others have since taken up the challenge, and Weidenreich's ideas live on in the modern multiregional theory of human evolution.

spoken by Neandertals need not have been as complex as those used by their later Paleolithic successors.

ARCHAIC *HOMO sapiens* AND MODERN HUMAN ORIGINS

One of the hot debates in paleoanthropology today is over the question: Did populations of archaic *H. sapiens* in most, if not all, parts of the Old World evolve simultaneously into anatomically modern humans (the "multiregional hypothesis"), or was there a single, geographic place of origin, from which anatomically modern *H. sapiens* spread to replace existing populations of the archaic species everywhere else (The "Eve" or "Out of Africa" hypothesis)? Based on the fossil evidence from Africa and some parts of Asia, a good case can be made for the former, as opposed to the latter, hypothesis. As several anthropologists have noted, African, Chinese, and Southeast Asian fossils of archaic *H. sapiens* imply local population continuity across the *Homo erectus* to modern transition,[5]

[5] M. H. Wolpoff, "Multiregional Evolution: The Fossil Alternative to Eden," in *The Human Evolution Source Book*, eds. Russell L. Ciochon and John G. Fleagle (Englewood Cliffs, N.J.: Prentice-Hall, 1993), pp. 476–497.

Aurignacian tradition: Toolmaking tradition of anatomically modern *H. sapiens* in Europe and western Asia at the beginning of the Upper Paleolithic.

lending strong support to the interpretation that there was genetic continuity in these regions. Instead of evolving extremely pointed faces and massive neck musculature, as did the Neandertals, these other populations experienced a reduction in total facial protrusion as facial robusticity decreased, while the backs of their skulls took on a more modern form.

One evident exception to this scenario consists of the Neandertals of Europe. About 35,000 to 40,000 years ago, a new technology, known as the **Aurignacian tradition,** spread into Europe from Southwest Asia, where its appearance marks the start of the **Upper Paleolithic** period. In both regions, human skeletons associated with Aurignacian tools are invariably modern in their features. Nevertheless, Neandertals are known to have survived in western Europe until 33,000 to 35,000 years ago, so coexistence between the modern and archaic forms of *sapiens* is indicated. Given the striking anatomical differences between the two, some form of population replacement, rather than simple evolution from one to the other, must have occurred.

How or why this replacement took place remains a mystery. There seems to have been nothing in the physical or mental makeup of Neandertals to prevent them from leading a "typical" Upper Paleolithic way of life, as in fact the final Neandertals of

western, central, and eastern Europe did.[6] Borrowing many ideas and techniques from the Aurignacians, they created their own Upper Paleolithic cultures (see Figure 8.2).

A number of scholars have argued for coexistence of the two forms in Southwest Asia as well. While Neandertal skeletons are clearly present at sites such as Kebara and Shanidar caves, skeletons from some older sites have been described as anatomically modern. At Qafzeh, in Israel, for example, 90,000-year-old skeletons are said to show none of the Neandertal hallmarks; although their faces and bodies are large and heavily built by today's standards, they are nonetheless said to be within the range of living peoples. By contrast, a recent statistical study comparing a number of measurements between Qafzeh, Upper Paleolithic and Neandertal skulls shows those from Qafzeh to fall in between, though slightly closer to the Neandertals.[7] Furthermore, an individual from the nearby site of Skuhl, whose skeleton was similar to those from Qafzeh, was part of a population whose continuous range of variation included individuals with markedly Neandertal characteristics. Nor does the idea of two distinctly different but coexisting populations receive any support from cultural remains, inasmuch as people such as those living at Skuhl and Qafzeh were making and using the same Mousterian tools as those at Kebara and Shanidar. Thus, there are no indications of groups with different cultural traditions coexisting in the same region. For that matter, the actual behaviors represented by Middle Paleolithic and early Upper Paleolithic cultures were not all that different. In Kebara Cave, for example, the Upper Paleolithic people who used the cave continued to live in exactly the same way as their Neandertal predecessors: They procured the same foods, processed them in the same way, used similar hearths, and disposed of their trash in the same way. The only evident difference is that the Neandertals did not bank their fires for warmth with small

Upper Paleolithic: The last part of the Paleolithic, characterized by the emergence of anatomically modern hominines and an emphasis on the blade technique of toolmaking.

[6] Mellars, p. 378.

[7] Robert S. Corruccini, "Metrical Reconsideration of the Skhul IV and IX and Border Cave I Crania in the Context of Modern Human Origins," *American Journal of Physical Anthropology,* 87 (1992):433–445.

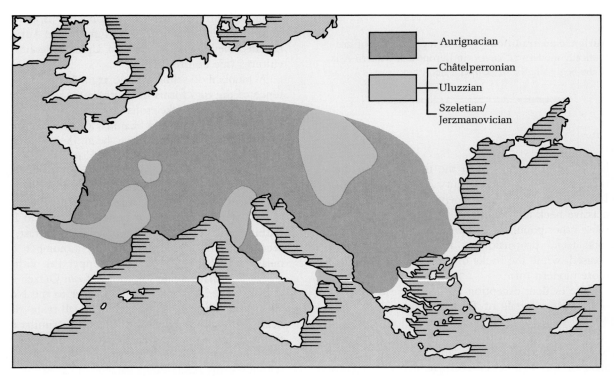

Figure 8.2 About 30,000 to 40,000 years ago the Mousterian-derived Upper Paleolithic industries of the last Neandertal populations in Europe coexisted with the Aurignacian industry, associated with anatomically modern *Homo sapiens*.

stones or cobbles as did their Upper Paleolithic successors.[8]

THE "EVE" OR "OUT OF AFRICA" HYPOTHESIS

This alternative to the multiregional hypothesis states that anatomically modern humans are descended from one specific population of *H. sapiens*, replacing not just the Neandertals, but other populations of archaic *H. sapiens* as our ancestors spread out of their original homeland. Evidence for this hypothesis came not from fossils, but from a

---

[8] O. Bar-Yosef, B. Vandermeesch, B. Arensburg, A. Belfer-Cohen, P. Goldberg, H. Laville, L. Meignen, Y. Rak, J.D. Speth, E. Tchernov, A-M. Tillier, and S. Weiner, "The Excavations in Kebara Cave, Mt. Carmel." *Current Anthropology*, 33 (1992):534.

relatively new technique that uses mitochondrial DNA to reconstruct family trees. Unlike the DNA that determines physical traits, mitochondrial DNA is located outside the cell nucleus, in compartments that produce energy needed to keep cells alive. Since the male sperm is not large enough to carry mitochondrial DNA, it is inherited only from one's mother and is not "rescrambled" with each succeeding generation. Therefore, it should be altered only by mutation. By comparing the mitochondrial DNA of living individuals from diverse geographical populations, anthropologists and molecular biologists seek to determine when and where modern *H. sapiens* originated. As widely reported in the popular press (including a cover story in *Newsweek*), preliminary results suggested that the mitochondrial DNA of all living humans could be traced back to a "Mitochondrial Eve" who lived in Africa (though some argued for Asia) some 200,000 years ago. If so, all other populations of archaic *H. sapiens*, as well as early *H. erectus*, would have to be ruled out of the ancestry of modern humans.

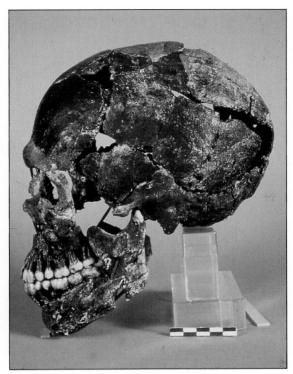

Showing a strikingly modern appearance, this *H. sapiens* skull from Qafzeh, Israel, is 90,000 years old. Measurements taken on the skull, however, fall slightly closer to those of the Neandertals than they do those of anatomically modern Upper Paleolithic people.

Although a number of scholars have interpreted fossils from Africa as exhibiting the transition from *H. erectus* to *sapiens* on that continent, this by itself offers no confirmation of the "Out of Africa" hypothesis. After all, proponents of the multiregional model also argue that the transition took place here, as in other parts of the Old World. If, however, anatomically modern fossils could be shown to be significantly older in Africa than elsewhere, this would bolster the argument for an African homeland for modern humanity. To date, the strongest candidates for such fossils consist of a skull from Border Cave and fragments of jaws of at least ten people from a cave at the Klasies River mouth. Both sites are in South Africa. Unfortunately, the Border Cave skull is not adequately dated, nor is it as similar to modern African skulls as is often claimed.[9] The Klasies River material is well

dated to between 120,000 and 90,000 years ago, but is too fragmentary (they were cut and burned anciently, suggesting cannibalism) to permit categorical statements as to its modernity. Although one mandible displays a well-developed chin, this feature occasionally shows up in fossils of archaic *sapiens* (for example, a Neandertal mandible from La Ferrassie, France). Certainly, the remains are not inconsistent with the sort of wide variation just discussed for Southwest Asia.

It is true that the people of Klasies River were culturally precocious. For one thing, they are the first people we know of to augment resources of the land with those from the sea; their collection of shellfish led to the buildup of middens comparable to those left by later Upper Paleolithic peoples. Their Middle Stone Age technology was also advanced in the common production of blades; long parallel-sided flakes of a sort not made in Europe until some 40,000 years ago. By 70,000 years ago, the people at Klasies River were blunting the backs of blades, much as later Europeans did, for hafting in composite tools. To some, these signs of cultural "advancement" would seem to be indicative of anatomically modern status. The fallacy of such argument, however, should be indicated by the evidence from Europe and Southwest Asia indicative of cognitive abilities on the part of archaic *H. sapiens* comparable to those of modern *sapiens*.

The fossil evidence presents other problems for the "Out of Africa" hypothesis, as well. For one thing, we would expect an early replacement of archaic *sapiens* in Southwest Asia as more anatomically modern humans moved up out of Africa but, as we have already seen, we have no clear evidence for such a replacement. Nor is such evidence available for East Asia, where evidence for continuity from regional *H. erectus*, through arachic to anatomical *H. sapiens* populations is, if anything, better than the evidence for such continuity in Africa. Consistent with this, the archaeological record of East Asia, though distinctly different from Europe, Africa, and western Asia, shows the same kind of continuity as do the fossils.[10] There is no sign of invasion by people possessing a superior, or even different, technology.

[9] Corruccini, p. 436.

[10] Geoffrey G. Pope, "Craniofacial Evidence for the Origin of Modern Humans in China," *Yearbook of Physical Anthropology*, 35 (1992):291.

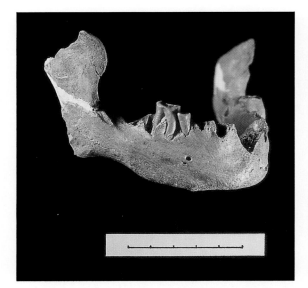
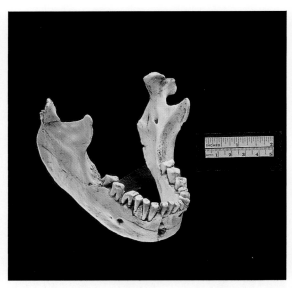

A mandible from the Klasies River in South Africa (left) is compared with a Neandertal mandible from La Ferrassie in France (right). Because of its chin, the South African fossil has been called "modern," yet the La Ferrassie jaw shows that even Neandertals sometimes had chins.

Finally, there are methodological problems as well; for example, the rate of change calculated for mitochondrial DNA, if applied to the time of splitting between the human and chimpanzee lines of evolution, would result in a wholly improbable estimate of 2.1 million years for divergence. Using a different calculation, based on the accepted date of five to eight million years ago for the chimp-human split would suggest that humans emerged from Africa roughly 1 million years ago,[11] close enough to the time that the fossils tell us that *Homo erectus* emerged from its original homeland. There are other problems as well, a major one being the discovery in 1992 that the computer program used to interpret the analysis of mitochondrial DNA had been misapplied.

In short, with the possible exception of the European Neandertals, it is definitely premature to read out of the modern human ancestry all populations of archaic *sapiens* save those of Africa. At the moment, the evidence seems to favor a multiregional emergence of anatomically modern humans, but the debate is by no means resolved.

[11] Elwyn L. Simons, "Human Origins," *Science*, 245 (1989):1349.

UPPER PALEOLITHIC PEOPLES: THE FIRST MODERN HUMANS

Although populations of archaic and anatomically modern *Homo sapiens* managed to coexist for a time in Europe, by 30,000 years ago, anatomically modern peoples with Upper Paleolithic cultures had the world to themselves. The remains of these ancient peoples who looked so much like us were first discovered in 1868 at Les Eyzies in France in a rock shelter called Cro-Magnon, and so European remains from the Upper Paleolithic are often referred to as **Cro-Magnons**. Between 1872 and 1902, the fossils of 13 other specimens were unearthed in the caves of the Cote d'Azur near the Italian Riviera. Since then, various other Cro-Magnon skeletons have been unearthed in various parts of Europe.

The Cro-Magnons have suffered their share of idealization on the part of physical anthropologists;

Cro-Magnons: The first fully modern Europeans, of Upper Paleolithic times.

The original Cro-Magnon skull differs very little from modern European skulls.

at one time they were made to look like Greek gods, in contrast to the Neandertals, who supposedly stood just a step ahead of the ape. The idea lives on in *The Clan of the Cave Bear*, in which the heroine is portrayed as a tall, slender, blonde-haired blue-eyed beauty. As more Upper Paleolithic remains have been found, in Africa and Asia as well as Europe, more physical variability has been shown, as is to be expected from any human population. Therefore, it is hardly surprising to find specimens that exhibit distinct features. In some ways, such as in the size of the brain, in the narrow nasal openings, and in the high, broad forehead, the European Cro-Magnons resembled modern Europeans. But their faces, for example, were shorter and broader than those of modern Europeans, and their brow ridges were a bit more prominent.

Generally speaking, Upper Paleolithic people in all parts of the world evolved a modern-looking face; the full-sized brain had already been achieved by archaic *H. sapiens*, no doubt as a consequence of increased reliance on cultural adaptation. Ultimately, this emphasis on cultural adaptation led to the development of more complex tool kits. The modernization of the face of Upper Paleolithic peoples is the result of a reduction in the size of the teeth, and eventually the jaw, as specialized tools increasingly took over the cutting, softening, and clamping functions once performed by the front teeth. The cooking of food (which began with *H. erectus*) had already favored a reduction in size of the teeth and muscles involved in chewing; consequently, the jaws reduced in size, accompanied by loss of robust sites for muscle attachment and features

like brow ridges that buttress the skull from the stresses and strains imposed by massive jaw muscles.

Technological improvements also reduced the intensity of selective pressures favoring especially massive, robust bodies. With more emphasis on elongate tools with greater mechanical advantages, more effective techniques of hafting, and a switch from thrusting to throwing spears, there was a marked reduction in overall muscularity. Moreover, the skeletons of Upper Paleolithic peoples show far less evidence of trauma than do those of archaic *H. sapiens*, whose bones almost always show evidence of injury.

Upper Paleolithic peoples also tended to live longer than their archaic predecessors. Furthermore, the prolonged period of development characteristic of the human species today, which allows people to learn so much before they are responsible for themselves as adults, was associated with the appearance of anatomically modern peoples. Perhaps both have something to do with the burst of creativity that was a part of Upper Paleolithic culture. Being too old for most day-to-day subsistence activities, but able to recall events beyond the experience of younger adults, elders could have spent more time, passing on a greater store of wisdom, to youngsters who were capable of absorbing it all.

UPPER PALEOLITHIC TOOLS

The typical Upper Paleolithic tool was the blade, a flint flake at least twice as long as it is wide. Although Middle Paleolithic toolmakers, especially in Africa, also made blades, they did not do so to the extent that their Upper Paleolithic successors did. What made this possible were new techniques of core preparation which allowed more intensive production of highly standardized blades. To make these, the toolmaker formed a cylindrical core, struck the blade off near the edge of the core, and repeated this procedure, going around the core in one direction until finishing near its center (Figure 8.3). The procedure is analogous to peeling long leaves off an artichoke. With this **blade technique**, an Upper Paleolithic flint knapper could get 75 feet of working edge from a two-pound core; his Mousterian

ANTHROPOLOGY APPLIED

STONE TOOLS FOR MODERN SURGEONS

In 1975, Don Crabtree, then at the Idaho State University Museum, underwent heart surgery; in 1980, an unnamed patient in Boulder, Colorado, underwent eye surgery; and in 1986, David Pokotylo, of the Museum of Anthropology at the University of British Columbia, underwent reconstructive surgery on his hand. What these operations had in common was that the scalpels used were not of surgical steel. Instead, they were made of obsidian (a naturally occurring volcanic "glass") by the same technique used by Upper Paleolithic people to make blades. In all three cases, the scalpels were hand made by archaeologists who specialized in the study of ancient stone tool technology: Crabtree himself, Payson Sheets at the University of Colorado, and Pokotylo with his colleague Len McFarlane (who hafted the blades) of the Museum of Anthropology.

The reason for the use of scalpels modeled on ancient stone tools, rather than modern steel, or even diamond scalpels, is because the obsidian is superior in almost every way: 210 to 1050 times sharper than surgical steel, 100 to 500 times sharper than a razor blade, and three times sharper than a diamond blade (which costs many times more and cannot be made with more than 3mm of cutting edge), obsidian blades are easier to cut with, and do less damage in the process (under a microscope, incisions made with the sharpest steel blades show torn ragged edges and are littered with bits of displaced flesh).* As a consequence, the surgeon has better control over what she or he is doing, the incisions heal faster with less scarring, and with less pain.

In order to develop and market obsidian scalpels, Sheets has formed a corporation in partnership with Boulder, Colorado, eye surgeon Dr. Firmon Hardenbergh. So far, they have developed a means of producing cores of uniform size from molten glass, as well as a machine to detach blades from the cores. Once this equipment is tested and refined, they hope, someday, to go into production for the surgical supply trade.

*Payson D. Sheets, "Dawn of a New Stone Age in Eye Surgery," in Robert J. Sharer and Wendy Ashmore, *Archaeology: Discovering Our Past* (Palo Alto, Calif.: Mayfield, 1987), p. 231.

counterpart could get only six feet from the same-sized core.

Other efficient techniques of tool manufacture also came into common use at this time. One such method was **pressure-flaking,** in which a bone, antler, or wooden tool was used to press rather than strike off small flakes as the final step in stone tool

Blade technique: A technique of stone tool manufacture by which long, parallel-sided flakes are struck off the edges of a specially prepared core.

Pressure-flaking; A technique of stone tool manufacture in which a bone, antler, or wooden tool is used to press, rather than strike off, small flakes from a piece of flint or similar stone.

manufacture (Figure 8.4). The advantage of this technique was that the toolmaker had greater control over the final shape of the tool than is possible with percussion-flaking. The Solutrean laurel leaf blades found in Spain and France are examples of this technique. The longest of these blades is thirteen inches and only about a quarter of an inch thick. Pressure-flaking also provided great precision in retouching cutting edges for extra sharpness.

Another Upper Paleolithic development was the **burin,** a stone tool with chisel-like edges. Although invented in the Middle Paleolithic, burins became

Burins: Stone tools of the Upper Paleolithic with a chisel-like edge used for working bone and antler.

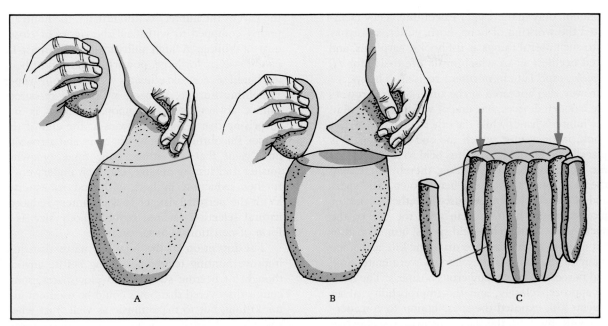

Figure 8.3 During the Upper Paleolithic, a new technique was used to manufacture blades. The stone is broken to create a striking platform, then vertical pieces are flaked off the side of the flint, forming sharp-edged tools.

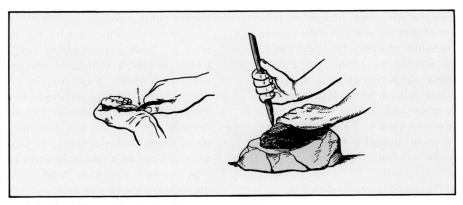

Figure 8.4 Two methods used for pressure flaking.

common only in the Upper Paleolithic. They facilitated the working of bone, horn, antler, and ivory into such useful things as fishhooks, harpoons, and eyed needles, all of which made life easier for *H. sapiens*, especially in northern regions. The spear-thrower also appeared at the time. Spear-throwers are wooden devices, one end of which is gripped in the hunter's hand, while the other end has a hole or hook, in or against which the end of the spear is placed (see Figure 8.5, c). It is held so as to increase the length of the hunter's arm, thereby increasing the velocity of the spear when thrown. The spear and spear–thrower, when used together, make for more efficient hunting than does the use of the spear alone. With hand-held spears, hunters had to get close to their quarry to make the kill, and since many of the animals they hunted were quite large and fierce, this was a dangerous business. The need to approach closely, and the improbability of an instant kill, exposed the spear hunter to considerable risk. But with the spear–thrower, the effective killing distance was increased; experiments indicate that the effective killing distance of a spear when used with a spear–thrower is between 18 and 27 meters.[12]

A further improvement of hunting techniques came with the invention of the bow and arrow, which appeared first in North Africa, but not until the end of the Upper Paleolithic in Europe. The greatest advantage of the bow is that it increases the distance between hunter and prey; beyond 18 to 27 meters, the accuracy and penetration of a spear thrown with a spear–thrower is quite poor, whereas even a poor bow will shoot an arrow farther, with greater accuracy and penetrating power. A good bow is effective even at 91 meters. Thus, hunters were able to maintain a safe distance between themselves and dangerous prey, dramatically decreasing their chances of being seriously injured by an animal fighting for its life.

These changes in hunting weaponry had important consequences for human biology. Spear hunting, particularly where large, fierce animals are the prey as they were in Upper Paleolithic Europe, demands strength, power, and overall robusticity on the part of the hunter. Without them, the hunter is poorly equipped to withstand the rigors of close-quarter killing. A high nutritional price must be paid however, for large, powerful, and robust bodies, but in severe cold climates such as that of Upper Paleolithic Europe, adequate nutritional resources cannot always be relied upon. Thus it is not surprising that when Europeans at the end of the Upper Paleolithic began to use bows and arrows to hunt game that was at the same time somewhat smaller and less aggressive, the men underwent a further reduction in body size and robusticity. With the personal danger to the hunters reduced, natural selection favored reduced body size as a form of nutritional conservation.[13]

The invention of the bow did more than just improve hunting techniques. Long before anyone thought of beating swords into plowshares, some genius discovered that bows could be used not just for killing, but to make music as well. Just when and where this discovery was made we don't know, but we do know that there was music in the lives of Upper Paleolithic peoples, for bone flutes and whistles as much as 30,000 years old have been found. We also know that the musical bow is the oldest of all the stringed instruments, and its invention ultimately made possible the development of all of the stringed instruments with which we are familiar today.

Upper Paleolithic peoples not only had better tools but also a greater diversity of types than earlier peoples. The highly developed Upper Paleolithic kit included tools for use during different seasons, and regional variation in tool kits was greater than ever before (see Figure 8.5 for some examples of Upper Paleolithic tools). Thus, it is really impossible to speak of an Upper Paleolithic culture, even in a relatively small region like Europe; instead, one must make note of the many different traditions that made it possible for people to adapt ever more specifically to the various environments in which they were living. Just how proficient (and even wasteful) people had become at securing a livelihood is indicated by boneyards containing thousands of skeletons. At Solutré in France, for example, Upper Paleolithic hunters killed 10,000 horses; at Predmost

[12] David W. Frayer, "Body Size, Weapon Use, and Natural Selection in the European Upper Paleolithic and Mesolithic," *American Anthropologist*, 83 (1981):58.

[13] Ibid.

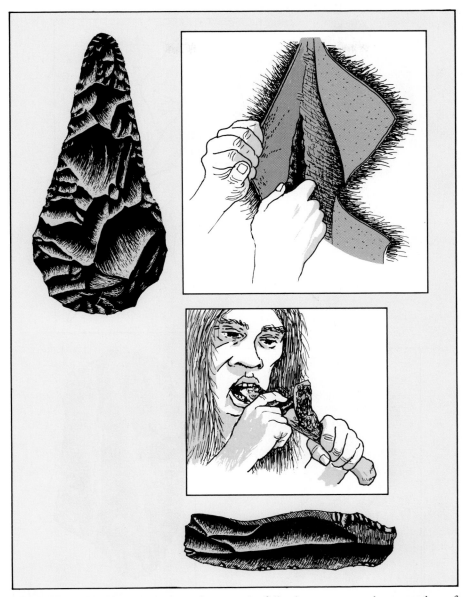

Figure 8.5   This figure, which continues on the following two pages, shows a variety of tools commonly found in Upper Paleolithic tool kits, along with an artist's reconstruction of the way they were used.

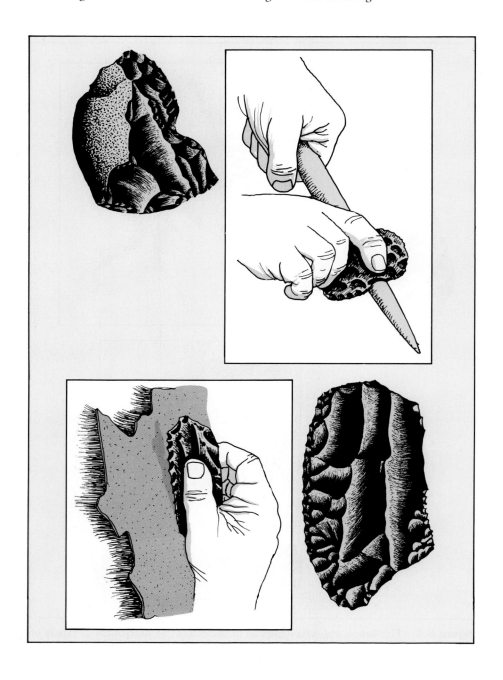

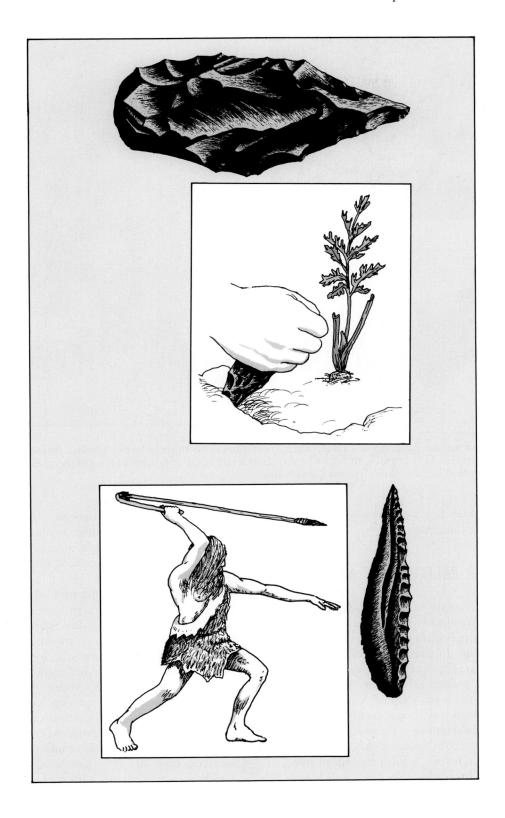

Upper Paleolithic art was quite varied: a carved antler spear-thrower ornamented by two headless ibexes (from Enlene Cave, France); a female Venus figurine of yellow steatite (from a cave at Liguria, Italy); and one of the sandstone lamps by which artists worked in caves (from Lascaux Cave, France).

in Czechoslovakia, they were responsible for the deaths of 1000 mammoths.

UPPER PALEOLITHIC ART

Although the creativity of Upper Paleolithic peoples is evident in the tools and weapons they made, it is nowhere more evident than in their outburst of artistic expression. In Europe, the earliest of this art took the form of sculpture and engravings often portraying such animals as reindeer, horses, bears, and ibexes, but there are also numerous portrayals of voluptuous women with exaggerated sexual and reproductive characteristics. These so-called "Venus" figures have been found at sites from southwestern France as far east as Siberia. Made of stone, ivory, antler, or baked clay, they differ little in style from place to place, testifying to the sharing

of ideas over vast distances. Although some have interpreted the Venuses as objects associated with a fertility cult, others suggest that they may have been exchanged to cement alliances between groups.

Most spectacular are the paintings on the walls of 200 or so caves in southern France and northern Spain, the oldest of which date from about 15,000 years ago. Most common are visually accurate portrayals of ice-age mammals, including bison, bulls, horses, mammoths, and stags, often painted one on top of another. Rarely portrayed are humans, nor are scenes or depictions of events at all common. Instead, the animals are usually abstracted from nature and rendered two-dimensionally without regard to the confirmations of the surfaces they are on—no small achievement for these early "artists." Often, the paintings are in hard-to-get-at places, while suitable surfaces in more accessible places remain untouched. In some caves, the lamps by which the artists worked have been found; these are spoon-shaped objects of sandstone in which animal fat was burned. Experimentation has shown that such lamps would have provided adequate illumination over several hours.

Hypotheses to account for this early art are difficult because they must depend on conjectural and subjective interpretations. Some have argued that it is art for art's sake, but if that is so, why were animals so often painted over one another, and why were they so often placed in inaccessible places? The latter might suggest that they were for ceremonial purposes and that the caves served as religious sanctuaries. One suggestion is that the animals were drawn to ensure success in the hunt, another that their depiction was seen as a way to promote fertility and increase the size of the herds on which humans depended. Some support for this comes from a major reassessment of the art of Altimira Cave in northern Spain. Here, the ceiling of the great hall does seem to be a true composition, representing a herd of bison in the rutting season. Elsewhere in the cave, too, the art shows a pervasive concern for the sexual reproduction of the bison.[14] In other caves, though, the species depicted are not always those most frequently hunted; there are few depictions of animals being hunted or killed, nor are there depictions of animals copulating or with exaggerated sexual parts as there are in the Venus figures. Another suggestion is that rites by which youngsters were initiated into adulthood took place in the painted galleries. In support of this idea, footprints, most of which are small, have been found in the clay floors of several caves, and in one, they even circle a modeled clay bison. The animals painted may have had to do with knowledge being transmitted from the elders to the youths. Whether or not that was so, the transmission of information is suggested by countless so-called signs, apparently abstract designs that accompany much Upper Paleolithic art. Some have interpreted these as tallies of animals killed, and/or a reckoning of time according to a lunar calendar. Perhaps all Upper Paleolithic art reflects an increased need to communicate information, and if so, it may have paralleled an increase in the complexity of spoken language. But when all is said and done, according to Henri Delaporte of France's Musé des Antiquités Nationales, "There were probably many different reasons why people produced art of different kinds, and we shouldn't just think of single explanations."[15]

Although the Upper Paleolithic art of Europe is particularly famous, equally sophisticated art that is just as old, and in some cases older, is known from other parts of the world. In southern Africa, for example, engravings and paintings are known from rock shelters and outcrops; shown are scenes in which humans and animals appear, sometimes accompanied by geometric and other abstract motifs. Because this rock art tradition continued down into historic times among the !Kung and related peoples, it has been possible to discover what this art is all about. There is a close connection between the art and shamanism, and many scenes depict visions seen in a state of trance. Distortions in the art represent sensations felt by individuals in a state of trance, abstract designs depict illusions that originate in the central nervous system in altered states of consciousness (sufferers of migraines experience similar hallucinations), and some of the animals are mythical beasts such as the "rain eland," important in rain making and other rituals.

Artistic expression, whatever its purpose may have been, was not confined to cave walls and portable objects alone. Upper Paleolithic peoples also ornamented their bodies, with necklaces of perforated animal teeth, shells, beads of bone, stone, and ivory; rings; bracelets; and anklets. Clothing, too, was adorned with beads. This should alert us to the probability that quite a lot of art was executed in perishable materials—wood carving, paintings on bark or animal skins, and the like. Thus, the rarity or absence of Upper Paleolithic art in some parts of the inhabited world may be more apparent than real, as people elsewhere worked with materials unlikely to survive so long in the archeological record.

[14] John Halverson, "Review of *Altimira Revisited and Other Essays on Early Art*," *American Antiquity*, 54 (1989):883.

[15] Roger Lewin, "Myths and Methods in Ice Age Art," *Science*, 234 (1986):938.

In South Africa, rock art, like these engravings and paintings from Namibia, depict things seen by dancers while in states of trance. The beginnings of this art predate the famous cave paintings of Europe.

OTHER ASPECTS OF UPPER PALEOLITHIC CULTURE

Upper Paleolithic peoples lived not only in caves and rock shelters, but also in structures built out in the open. In the Ukraine, for example, the remains have been found of sizeable settlements, in which huts were built on frameworks of intricately stacked mammoth bones. Where the ground was frozen, cobblestones were heated and placed in the earth to sink in, thereby providing sturdy, dry floors. Their hearths, no longer shallow depressions or flat surfaces that radiated back little heat, were instead stone-lined pits that conserved heat for extended periods and made for more efficient cooking. For the outdoors, they had the same sort of tailored clothing worn in historical times by the natives of Siberia, Alaska, and Canada. And they engaged in long-distance trade, as indicated, for example, by the presence of seashells and Baltic amber at sites several hundred kilometers from the sources of these materials. Although Middle Paleolithic peoples made use of rare and distant materials, they did not do so with the regularity seen in the Upper Paleolithic.

THE SPREAD OF UPPER PALEOLITHIC PEOPLES

Such was the effectiveness of their cultures that Upper Paleolithic peoples were able to expand into regions previously uninhabited by their archaic forebears. Colonization of Siberia can be clearly documented by 30,000 to 35,000 years ago, but even before that—perhaps as early as 40,000 to

45,000 years ago—people had gotten to Australia and New Guinea. To get there, they used some kind of watercraft to make the difficult crossing of at least 90 kilometers of water that separated Australia and New Guinea (then a single land mass) from the Asian continent throughout Paleolithic times. Once in Australia, these people created some of the world's first sophisticated rock art some 5000 to 10,000 years earlier than the more famous European cave paintings. Other evidence for sophisticated ritual activity in early Australia is provided by 26,000-year-old cremation burials associated with red ochre. It may be that this pigment had more than symbolic value; for example, its iron salts have antiseptic and deodorizing properties, and there are recorded instances in which red ochre is associated with prolonging life, and is used medicinally to treat particular conditions or infections. One historically known native Australian society is reported to use ochre to heal wounds, scars and burns, and a person with internal pain is covered with the substance and placed in the sun to promote sweating. What is especially interesting in view of the impressive accomplishments of native Australians is that the tools used by these people are remarkably similar to those of the Eurasian Middle Paleolithic. Clearly, simplicity of tool kits does not bespeak absence of sophisticated intellectual capabilities.

To get to the Americas, voyages of the sort undertaken by the first Australians were not necessary. With much of the world's water supply taken up by the great continental glaciers, there was a worldwide lowering of sea levels, causing an emergence of land joining Siberia to Alaska. With expanding populations in Asia, brought about by increasingly effective cultural adaptations, it was only a matter of time before human populations began to drift gradually eastward over this dry land. The precise timing of their first arrival is still debated, but securely dated remains from Meadowcroft Rockshelter in southwestern Pennsylvania indicate that populations had spread as far as the eastern United States by 15,000 years ago, if not earlier. Moreover, people seem to have gotten as far south as central Chile, where remains of huts have been found at Monte Verde and reliably dated to about 13,000 years ago.

Technologies roughly comparable to the old East Asian chopper tool industries gave rise in North

Paleoindians, like their Upper Paleolithic contemporaries in Eurasia, were such accomplished hunters that they, too, could kill more animals than could possibly be used at one time. These bones are the remains of some 200 bison that Paleoindian hunters stampeded over a cliff 8500 years ago.

America, about 12,000 years ago, to the distinctive fluted spear points of **Paleoindian** hunters of big game, such as mammoths, caribou, and now-extinct forms of bison. Fluted points are finely made, with large channel flakes removed from one or both surfaces. They are found from the Atlantic seaboard to the Pacific coast, and from Alaska down into Panama. So efficient were the hunters who made these points that they may have hastened the extinction of the mammoth and other large Pleistocene mammals. By driving large numbers of animals over cliffs, they killed many more than they could possibly use, thus wasting huge amounts of meat.

Paleoindian: Inhabitants of North America around 12,000 years ago, who hunted big game such as mammoths, with spears tipped with distinctive fluted points.

Fluted points, such as these, tipped the spears of Paleoindian hunters.

WHERE DID UPPER PALEOLITHIC PEOPLE COME FROM?

As noted earlier in this chapter, we cannot be sure whether the transition from archaic to anatomically modern *H. sapiens* took place in one specific population or was the result of in situ evolution on the part of populations living in Africa and Asia between 100,000 and 40,000 years ago. At the moment, though, the odds seem to favor the latter hypothesis. In all of these regions, since the time of *H. erectus*, more and more emphasis was placed on cultural, as opposed to biological, adaptation. To handle environmental stress, reliance was placed more and more on the development of appropriate tools, clothes, shelter, use of fire, and so forth, as opposed to alteration of the human organism itself. This was true whether human populations lived in hot or cold, wet or dry, forest or grassland areas. Since culture is learned and not carried by genes, it is ultimately based on what might loosely be called "brain power" or, more formally, **cognitive capacity**. While this includes intelligence, in the IQ sense, it is broader than that, for it also includes such skills as educability, con-

cept formation, self-awareness, self-evaluation, reliability of performance under stress, attention span, sensitivity in discrimination, and creativity.

The major thrust in the evolution of the genus *Homo*, then, has been toward improved cognitive capacity through the evolution of the brain regardless of the environmental and climatic differences between the regions in which populations of the genus lived. Hence, there has been a certain similarity of selective pressures in all regions. In addition, this evolution of all populations of the genus *Homo* would have been helped along by a certain amount of gene flow between populations. In an evolving species, genes having survival value anywhere tend to spread from one population to

Cognitive capacity: A broad concept including intelligence, educability, concept formation, self-awareness, self-evaluation, attention span, sensitivity in discrimination, and creativity.

another. In the case of the human species, these would be whatever genes happen to relate to cognitive capacity.

It is impossible to know just how much gene flow took place between ancient human populations, but that some took place is consistent with the sudden appearance of novel traits in one region later than their appearance elsewhere. For example, Upper Paleolithic remains from North Africa exhibit the kind of midfacial flatness previously seen only in East Asian fossils; similarly, various Cro-Magnon fossils from Europe show the short upper jaws, horizontally oriented cheek bones and rectangular eye orbits previously seen in East Asians. Conversely, the round orbits, large frontal sinuses and thin cranial bones seen in some archaic *sapiens* skulls from China represent the first appearance there of traits that have greater antiquity in the West.[16] What appears to be happening, then, is that genes from the East are being introduced into western gene pools and vice versa. Not only is such gene flow consistent with the remarkable tendency that historically known humans have to "swap genes" between populations, even in the face of cultural barriers to gene flow, it is also consistent with the tendency of other primates to produce hybrids when two subspecies (and sometimes even species) come into contact.[17] Moreover, without such gene flow, multiregional evolution inevitably would have resulted in the appearance of multiple species of modern humans, something that clearly has **not** happened.

THE MESOLITHIC ERA

By 12,000 years ago, glacial conditions in the world were moderating, causing changes in human habitats. Throughout the world, sea levels were on the rise, ultimately flooding many areas that had been above sea level during periods of glaciation, such as the Bering Straits, parts of the North Sea, and an extensive area that had joined Indonesia to Southeast Asia. In northern regions, milder climates

brought about marked changes as tundras were ultimately replaced by hardwood forests. In the process, the herd animals upon which northern Paleolithic peoples had depended for food, clothing, and shelter disappeared from many areas. Some, like the reindeer and musk ox, moved to colder climates; others, like the mammoths, died out completely. Thus, the northerners especially were forced to adapt to new conditions. In the new forests, animals were more solitary in their habits and so not as easy to hunt as they had been, and large, cooperative hunts were no longer very productive. However, plant food was more abundant than before, and there were new and abundant sources of fish and other food around lake shores, bays, and rivers. Hence, human populations developed new and ingenious ways to catch and kill animals, while at the same time they devoted more energy to fishing and the collection of wild plant foods. This new way of life marks the end of the Paleolithic and the start of the **Mesolithic**, or **Middle Stone Age**. In a sense, it marks a return to more typical hominine subsistence patterns.

MESOLITHIC TOOLS AND WEAPONS

New technologies were developed for the changed postglacial environment (Figure 8.6). Ground stone tools, shaped and sharpened by grinding the tool against sandstone (often using sand as an additional abrasive), made effective axes and adzes. Such implements, though they do take longer to make, are less prone to breakage, given heavy-duty usage, than are those made of chipped stone. Thus, they were helpful in clearing forest areas and in the woodwork needed for the creation of dugout canoes and skin-covered boats. Although some kind of watercraft had been developed early enough to get humans to Australia by about 40,000

Mesolithic, or Middle Stone Age: Began about 12,000 years ago.

---

[16] Pope, pp. 287–288.
[17] Simons, p. 1349.

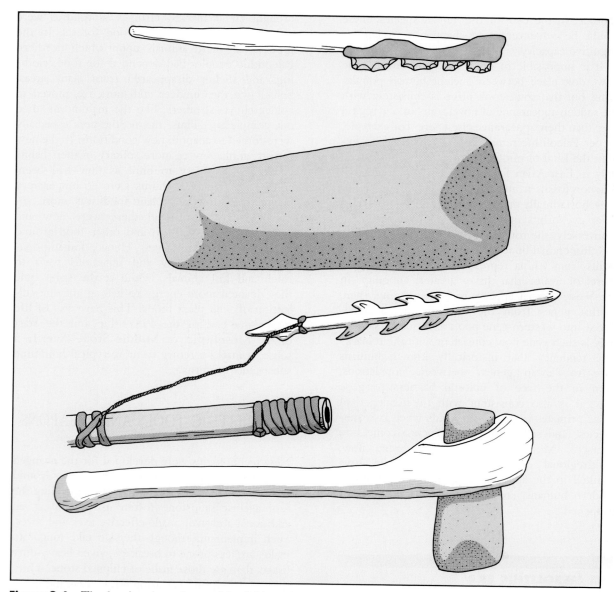

Figure 8.6   The drawing above shows a Mesolithic tool consisting of a wooden or bone handle with microliths set into it. Below is a bone tool of a somewhat earlier date, fitted out for service as a harpoon. The ground stone ax at the bottom has a smooth stone blade set in a wooden handle that gives increased leverage.

Microlith: A small flint blade characteristic of the Mesolithic, several of which were hafted together in wooden handles to make tools.

Natufian culture: A Mesolithic culture of Israel, Lebanon, and western Syria, between about 12,500 and 10,200 years ago.

years ago, boats become prominent only in Mesolithic sites, indicating that human foraging for food frequently took place on the water as well as the land. Thus, it was possible to make use of deep-water resources as well as those of coastal areas.

The characteristic Mesolithic tool was the **microlith,** a small but hard, sharp blade. Microliths could be mass-produced because they were small, easy to make, and could be of materials other than flint. Also, they could be attached to arrow shafts by using melted resin as a binder. Thus, the bow and arrow with the microlith arrowhead became the deadliest and most common weapon of the Mesolithic.

The development by Mesolithic peoples of microliths provided them with an important advantage over their Upper Paleolithic forbearers: The small size of the microlith enabled them to devise a wider array of composite tools made out of stone and wood or bone (see Figure 8.6, top). Thus, they could make sickles, harpoons, arrows, and daggers by fitting microliths into grooves in wood or bone handles. Later experimentation with these forms led to more sophisticated tools and weapons.

It is possible that the Mesolithic was a more sedentary period for humans than earlier eras. Dwellings from this period seem more substantial, an indication of permanency. Indeed, this is a logical development: Most hunting cultures and cultures depending on herd animals are nomadic. To be successful, one must follow the game. This is not necessary for peoples subsisting on a diet of seafood and plants, as the location of shore and vegetation remains relatively constant.

CULTURAL DIVERSITY IN THE MESOLITHIC

In the warmer parts of the world, the collection of wild plant foods had been more of an equal partner in subsistence activities in the Upper Paleolithic than had been the case in the colder north. Hence, in areas like the Middle East, the Mesolithic represents less of a changed way of life than was true in Europe. Here, the important **Natufian culture** flourished.

The Natufians were a people who lived between 12,500 and 10,200 years ago at the eastern end of the Mediterranean Sea in caves, rock shelters, and small villages with stone- and mud-walled houses. Nearby, their dead were buried in communal cemeteries, usually in shallow pits without grave goods or decorations. A small shrine is known from one of their villages, a 10,500-year-old settlement at Jericho. Basin-shaped depressions in the rocks found outside homes at Natufian sites are thought to have been storage pits. Plastered storage pits beneath the floors of the houses were also found, indicating that the Natufians were the earliest known Mesolithic people to have stored crops. Certain tools found in the Natufian remains bear evidence that they were used to cut grain. These Mesolithic sickles, for that is what they were, consisted of small stone blades set in straight handles of wood or bone.

In the Americas, cultures comparable to Mesolithic cultures of the Old World developed, but here they are referred to as **Archaic cultures.** Outside of the Arctic, microlithic tools are not prominent in them, as they are in parts of the Old World, but ground stone tools such as axes, adzes, gouges, plummets, and spear-thrower weights are

Archaic cultures: Term used to refer to Mesolithic cultures in the Americas.

At Nuliak, Labrador, maritime archaic peoples lived in large, long houses with stone foundations. Once such foundation is shown here before excavation.

common. Archaic cultures were widespread in the Americas; one of the more dramatic was the **Maritime archaic**, which developed about 7000 years ago around the Gulf of St. Lawrence. These people developed an elaborate assortment of bone and ground slate tools with which they hunted a wide variety of sea mammals, including whales; fish, including swordfish; and sea birds. To get some of these, they regularly paddled their dugout canoes far off shore. They also developed the first elaborate burial cult in North America, involving the use of red ochre ("red paint") and the placement of finely made grave goods with the deceased.

Maritime archaic culture: An archaic culture of northeastern North America, centered on the Gulf of St. Lawrence, which emphasized the utilization of marine resources.

MAJOR PALEOLITHIC AND MESOLITHIC TRENDS

Certain trends stand out from the information anthropologists have gathered about the Old and Middle Stone ages. These are general progressions that occurred from one culture to the next in most parts of the world.

One trend was toward increasingly more sophisticated, varied, and specialized tool kits. Tools became progressively lighter and smaller, resulting in the conservation of raw materials and a better ratio between length of cutting edge and weight of stone. Tools became specialized according to region and function. Instead of crude all-purpose tools, more effective particularized devices were made to deal more efficiently with the differing conditions of savanna, forest, and shore.

This more efficient tool technology enabled human populations to increase and spill over into more diverse environments; it also was responsible for the loss of heavy physical features, favoring instead decreased size and weight of face and teeth, the development of larger and more complex brains, and ultimately a reduction in body size and robusticity. This dependence on intelligence rather than bulk provided the key for peoples' increased reliance on cultural rather than physical adaptation. As the brain became modernized, conceptual thought developed, as evidenced by symbolic artifacts and signs of magico-religious ceremonies.

By the Upper Paleolithic, the amount of sexual dimorphism, too, was greatly reduced, as size differences between men and women were relatively slight compared to what they were in *Australopithecus*, *Homo habilis*, or even *Homo erectus*. This has important implications for gender relations. As noted in earlier chapters, among primates, marked sexual dimorphism is associated with male dominance over females. Lack of sexual dimorphism, by contrast, correlates with a lack of such dominance. In evolving humans, it appears that a loss of male dominance went hand in hand with the ever increasing importance of cooperative relationships.

Through Paleolithic times, at least in the colder parts of the world, there appeared a trend toward the importance of, and proficiency in, hunting. People's intelligence enabled them to develop tools that exceeded other animals' physical equipment, as well as the improved social organization and cooperation so important for survival and population growth. This trend was reversed during the Mesolithic, when hunting lost its preeminence and the gathering of wild plants and seafood became increasingly important.

As human populations grew and spread, regionalism also became more marked. Tool assemblages developed in different ways at different times in different areas. General differences appeared between north and south, east and west. Although there are some indications of cultural contact and intercommunication, such as the development of long-distance trade in the Upper Paleolithic, regionalism was a dominant characteristic of the Paleolithic and Mesolithic eras. The persistence of regionalism is probably due in large part to the need to adapt to differing environments. Paleolithic peoples eventually spread over all the continents of the world, including Australia and America, and as they did so, changes in climate and environment called for new kinds of adaptations. Thus Paleolithic and Mesolithic tool kits had to be altered to meet the requirements of many varying locations. In forest environments, people needed strong axes for working wood; on the open savanna and plains, they used the bow and arrow to hunt the game they could not stalk closely; the people in settlements that grew up around lakes and along rivers and coasts developed harpoons and hooks; in the subarctic regions they needed tools to work the heavy skins of seals and caribou; in the grasslands they needed tools for harvesting grain and separating the usable part from the chaff. The fact that culture is first and foremost an adaptive mechanism meant that it was of necessity a regional thing.

Chapter Summary

At various sites in Europe, Africa, and East Asia, a number of fossils have been found which date between about 200,000 and 400,000 years ago, and which show a mixture of traits characteristic of both *H. erectus* and *H. sapiens*. They are indicative of evolution from the older into the younger species. Their culture was much like that of *H. erectus*, until about 200,000 years ago, when they developed a new technique of tool manufacture known as the Levalloisian.

By 100,000 years ago, populations of archaic *H. sapiens* lived in all parts of the inhabited world. Although some populations of this species, most notably the Neandertals of Europe and western Asia, survived until at least 35,000 years ago, others evolved into anatomically modern humans.

The brains of archaic *H. sapiens* had reached modern size, although their skulls retained some primitive characteristics. With a larger brain, they were able to utilize culture as a means of environmental adaptation to a far greater extent than any of their predecessors; they were capable of an advanced technology and sophisticated conceptual thought.

The cultures of archaic *H. sapiens* are known as Middle Paleolithic, and the best known is the Mousterian of Europe, northern Africa, and western Asia. Mousterian tools included hand axes, flakes, scrapers, borers, wood shavers, and spears. Flake tools were lighter and smaller than those of the Levalloisian. Mousterian tools increased the availability and quality of food, shelter, and clothing. Archaeological evidence indicates that Mousterian peoples buried their dead, cared for the disabled, and made a number of objects for purely symbolic purposes.

All populations of archaic *H. sapiens* are easily derivable from earlier populations of *H. erectus* from the same regions. With the exception of the Neandertals, all populations of archaic *H. sapiens* could be ancestral to more modern populations in the same regions. An alternative hypothesis is that the transition from archaic to anatomically modern *H. sapiens* took place in one specific population, probably in Africa. From here, people spread to other regions, replacing older populations as they did so.

The Cro-Magnons and the other anatomically modern peoples that held exclusive sway in the world after 30,000 years ago, in addition to a full-sized brain, possessed a physical appearance somewhat similar to our own. The modernization of the face of Upper Paleolithic peoples is a result of a reduction in the size of the teeth and the muscles involved in chewing as a consequence of the fact that teeth were no longer being used as tools. Similarly, bodies became somewhat less massive and robust as improved technology reduced the need for brute strength.

The emphasis in evolution of the genus *Homo* in all parts of the world has been toward increasing cognitive capacity through development of the brain. This progression took place regardless of environmental or climatic conditions under which the genus lived. In addition, evolution of the genus *Homo* undoubtedly was aided by gene flow between populations.

Upper Paleolithic cultures evolved out of the Middle Paleolithic cultures of Africa and Asia. The typical Upper Paleolithic tool was the blade. The

blade technique of toolmaking saved much more flint than Middle Paleolithic methods. Other efficient Upper Paleolithic toolmaking techniques were pressure-flaking, and using chisel-like stones called burins to fashion bone, antler horn, and ivory into tools. The cultural adaptation of Upper Paleolithic people became specific; they developed different tools for different seasons. There is no one Upper Paleolithic culture, as different environments produced different cultures. Northern Upper Paleolithic cultures supported themselves by the hunting of large herd animals. Upper Paleolithic cultures contain the earliest remains of pictorial art.

The ending of the glacial period caused great physical changes in human habitats. Sea levels raised, vegetation changed, and herd animals disappeared from many areas. The European Mesolithic period marked a return to more typical hominine ways of subsistence, as big game hunters returned to more of a balance between hunting and gathering. Increased reliance on seafood and plants made the Mesolithic a more sedentary period for people. Groundstone tools, including axes and adzes, answered postglacial needs for new technologies. The characteristic Mesolithic tool in the Old World was made with microliths, small, hard, sharp flint blades which could be mass-produced and hafted with others to produce implements like sickles. Reliance on the bow and arrow to hunt generally smaller, less aggressive animals resulted in a reduction of the size and robusticity of men, at least in Europe.

Three trends emerged from the Paleolithic and Mesolithic periods. First was a trend toward more sophisticated, varied, and specialized tool kits. This trend enabled people to increase their population and spread to new environments. It also was adaptive, leading to decreased size and weight of face and teeth, the development of larger, more complex brains, and ultimately a reduction in body size, mass and degree of sexual dimorphism. Second was a trend toward the importance of and proficiency in hunting. The importance of hunting was somewhat reversed during the Mesolithic period, as the hunting of large game became less important than smaller game and the gathering of plants and seafood. Third was a trend toward regionalism, as people's technology and life habits increasingly reflected their association with a particular environment.

Suggested Readings

Campbell, Bernard G. *Humankind Emerging*, 6th ed. New York: HarperCollins, 1992.

Adapted in part from Time-Life's *Emergence of Man* and *Life Nature Library*, this is a richly illustrated, up-to-date account of the Paleolithic. In it, Campbell integrates paleontological and archaeological data with ethnographic data on modern food foragers to present a rich picture of evolving Paleolithic ways of life.

Ciochon, Russell L. and John G. Fleagle, eds. *The Human Evolution Source Book*. Englewood Cliffs, N.J.: Prentice Hall, 1993.

Two parts of this book contain articles on the evolution of *Homo sapiens* and the Neandertal problem and modern human origins. The debate between proponents of the "Out of Africa" and multiregional hypotheses are well covered, and the editors' introduction to the two sections places the articles in context.

Gamble, Clive. *The Paleolithic Settlement Of Europe*. Cambridge, England: Cambridge University Press, 1986.

Although not the easiest book to read, it is important for the way it looks at old data in new ways. Instead of presenting yet another descriptive synthesis of archaeologically recovered things, it tries to explain what happened in the past in light of a better understanding of how archeological sites are formed.

Pfeiffer, John E. *The Creative Explosion*. Ithaca, N.Y.: Cornell University Press, 1985.

A fascinating and readable discussion of the origins of art and religion.

Prideaux, Tom, and the editors of Time-Life. *Cro-Magnon Man*. New York: Time-Life, 1973.

This beautifully illustrated volume in the *Time-Life Emergence of Man* series covers the period between 10,000 and 40,000 years ago. A whole chapter is devoted to "The Subtle Mind of Cro-Magnon."

STATUE,
SRI
LANKA

PART III

HUMAN BIOLOGICAL AND CULTURAL EVOLUTION SINCE THE END OF THE OLD STONE AGE

INTRODUCTION

N THE UPPER PALEOLITH-
IC, BY 30,000 YEARS AGO, ANATOMICALLY MODERN VARIETIES OF
HUMANS, WITH CULTURES COMPARABLE TO THOSE KNOWN FOR
RECENT FOOD-FORAGING PEOPLES, HAD SOLE POSSESSION OF THE
INHABITED PARTS OF THE WORLD. THE

story of human evolution in the Paleolithic is one of a close interrelation between developing culture and developing humanity. The critical importance of culture as the human adaptive mechanism seems to have imposed selective pressures favoring a better brain, and a better brain, in turn, made possible improved cultural adaptation. Indeed, it seems fair to say that modern humans look the way they do today because cultural adaptation came to play such an important role in the survival of our ancient ancestors. Because cultural adaptation worked so well, human populations were able to grow, probably rather slowly, with a consequent expansion into previously uninhabited parts of the world. And this, too, affected cultural adaptation, as adjustments were made to meet new conditions.

Although food foraging served humans well for hundreds of thousands of years in the

Paleolithic, far-reaching changes began to take place in some parts of the world as much as 11,000 years ago. This second major cultural revolution consisted of the emergence of food production, the subject of Chapter 9. Eventually, most of the world's people became food producers, even though food foraging remained a satisfactory way of life for some. At the present time, no more than a quarter of a million people—less than 0.0005 percent of a world population of more than 5 billion—remain food foragers. Just as the emergence of food foraging was followed by modifications and improvements leading to regional variants of this pattern, so the advent of food production opened the way for new cultural variants based upon it. Chapter 10 discusses the result: further cultural diversity, out of which developed civilization, the basis of modern life.

In spite of the increasing effectiveness of

culture as the primary mechanism by which humans adapt to diverse environments, our species has continued to evolve biologically. In the course of their movement into other parts of the world, humans had already developed considerable biological variation from one population to another. On top of this, populations of food producers were exposed to selective pressures of a different sort than those affecting food foragers, thereby inducing further changes in human gene pools. Such changes continue to affect the human species today, even though it remains the same species now as it was at the end of the Paleolithic. Chapter 11 discusses how the variation to be seen in *Homo sapiens* today came into existence as the result of forces acting to alter the frequencies of genes in human gene pools, and why such variation probably has nothing to do with intelligence. The chapter concludes with a look at forces apparently active today to produce further changes in those same gene pools.

9

CULTIVATION

AND

DOMESTICATION

Beginning about 11,000 years ago, some of the world's people embarked on a new way of life based on food production. This included new attitudes toward the earth and forces of nature, reflected in monumental construction. One of these structures is Stonehenge, the famous ceremonial and astronomical center in England, which dates back to about 2500 B.C.

WHEN AND WHERE DID THE CHANGE FROM FOOD FORAGING TO FOOD PRODUCTION BEGIN?

Centers of early plant and animal domestication exist in Africa, China, Mesoamerica, North and South America, as well as Southwest and Southeast Asia. From these places, food production spread to most other parts of the world. It began at different times in these different places; for example, it began about 10,300 years ago in Southwest Asia, but sometime between 8800 and 5000 years ago in Southeast Asia.

WHY DID THE CHANGE TAKE PLACE?

Since food production by and large requires more work than hunting and gathering, is not necessarily a more secure means of subsistence, and requires people to eat more of the foods that food foragers eat only when they have no other choice, it can be assumed that people probably did not become food producers through choice. Of various theories that have been proposed, the most likely is that food production came about as a consequence of a chance convergence of separate natural events and cultural developments.

WHAT WERE THE CONSEQUENCES OF THE CHANGE TO FOOD PRODUCTION?

Although food production generally provides less leisure time than food foraging, it does permit some reallocation of the work load. Some people can produce enough food to allow others to spend more time at other tasks, and so a number of technological developments, such as weaving and pottery making, generally accompany food production. In addition, it makes possible a more sedentary way of life in villages, with more substantial housing. Finally, the new modes of work and resource allocation require new ways of organizing people, generally into lineages, clans, and common-interest associations.

Throughout the Paleolithic, people depended exclusively on wild sources of food for their survival. In cold northern regions, they came to rely primarily on the hunting of herds of mammoth, bison, and reindeer. Elsewhere, they hunted, fished, or gathered whatever nature was kind enough to provide. There is no evidence in Paleolithic remains to indicate that livestock was kept or plants cultivated. Paleolithic people followed wild herds and gathered wild plant foods, relying on their wits and muscles to acquire what nature provided. Whenever favored sources of food became scarce, as sometimes happened, people adjusted by increasing the variety of food eaten, and incorporating less-favored food into their diet.

About 12,000 years ago, the subsistence practices of some people began to change in ways that were to transform radically their way of life, although no one involved had any way of knowing it at the time. Not until these changes were well advanced could people become aware that their mode of subsistence differed from that of other cultures—that they had become farmers, rather than food foragers.[1] This change in the means of obtaining food had important implications for human development, for it meant that by taking matters into their own hands, people could become more sedentary. Moreover, by reorganizing the work load, some of them could be freed from the food quest to devote their energies to other sorts of tasks. With good reason, the **Neolithic period**, when this change took place, has been called a revolutionary time in human history. This period, and the changes that took place within it, are the subjects of this chapter.

THE MESOLITHIC ROOTS OF FARMING AND PASTORALISM

The Mesolithic may be viewed either as the final stage of the Paleolithic (sometimes called the Epipaleolithic) or as the beginning of the Neolithic. Fixed as having begun around 12,000 years ago,

[1] David Rindos, *The Origins of Agriculture: An Evolutionary Perspective* (Orlando, Fla.: Academic Press, 1984), p. 99.

Neolithic period: The New Stone Age, which began about 11,000 years ago in Southwest Asia.

people during this period turned increasingly toward abundant food supplies available in the rivers, lakes, and oceans. These waterways were teeming with aquatic life because of the rising seas brought about by warmer temperatures and melting glaciers. In addition, people gathered a broad spectrum of plant foods on land, and hunted a variety of birds and smaller mammals. Generally, this new way of life offered more secure supplies of food and therefore an increased margin of survival. In some parts of the world, people started living in larger and more sedentary groups, now cooperating with others outside the sphere of family or hunting bands. They became settled village–dwellers, and some of these settlements were shortly to expand into the first farming villages, towns, and ultimately cities.

THE NEOLITHIC REVOLUTION

The Neolithic, or New Stone Age, was characterized by the transition from foraging for food to dependence upon domesticated plants and animals. It was by no means a smooth or rapid transition; in fact, it spread over many centuries and was a direct outgrowth of the preceding Mesolithic. Where to draw the line between the two is not always clear.

The term "New Stone Age" is derived from the polished stone tools that are characteristic of this period. But more important than the presence of these tools is the transition from a hunting, gathering, and fishing to a food-producing economy, representing a major change in the subsistence practices of early peoples. One of the first regions to undergo this transition, and certainly the most intensively studied, was Southwest Asia. The remains of domesticated plants and animals are known from parts of Israel, Jordan, Syria, Turkey, Iraq, and Iran, all before 8000 years ago.

V. GORDON CHILDE

(1892–1957)

This distinguished Australian, once the private secretary to the premier of New South Wales, went on to become one of the most eminent of British archaeologists. His knowledge of the archaeological sequences of Europe and the Middle East was unsurpassed, and led to his writing of two of the most popular and influential descriptions of prehistory ever wirtten: *Man Makes Himself* in 1936, and *What Happened in History* in 1942. In these, he described two great "revolutions" which added measurably to the capacity of humans to survive: the Neolithic and urban revolutions. The first of these transformed food foragers into farmers and brought with it a drastic reordering of society; populations increased, a cooperative group spirit arose, trade began on a large scale, and new religions arose to ensure the success of crops. This set the stage for the urban revolution, which transformed society from one of egalitarianism with a simple age-sex division of labor into one of social classes and organized political bodies. The result of these ideas was to generate a whole new interest in the evolution of human culture in general.

DOMESTICATION: WHAT IS IT?

Domestication is an evolutionary process whereby humans modify, either intentionally or unintentionally, the genetic makeup of a population of plants or animals, sometimes to the extent that members of the population are unable to survive and/or reproduce without human assistance. As such, it constitutes a special case of a kind of relationship between different species frequently seen in the natural world, as in the case of one species that has come to depend for its protection and reproductive success on some other that feeds upon it. In the case of plants, for instance, there are numerous species that rely on some type of animal —in some cases birds, in others mammals, and in yet others, insects—for protection and dispersal of their seeds. The important thing is that both parties benefit from the arrangement; reliance on animals for seed dispersal ensures that the latter will be carried further afield than would otherwise be possible, thereby cutting down on competition for sun and nutrients between young and old plants and reducing the likelihood that any diseases or parasites harbored by one will be transmitted to the others. Added vigor is apt to come to plants that are freed from the need to provide themselves with built-in defensive mechanisms such as thorns, toxins, or chemical compounds that make them taste bad. This enhanced vigor may be translated into larger and more tasty edible parts to attract the animals that feed upon them, thereby cementing the relationship between the protected and protector.

Domestication: An evolutionary process whereby humans modify, either intentionally or unintentionally, the genetic makeup of a population of plants or animals, sometimes to the extent that members of the population are unable to survive and/or reproduce without human assistance.

Wild wheat kernels from a site in Syria (top) are compared with those of a domestic variety grown in Greece 2000 or 3000 years later (bottom). Increased size of edible parts is a common feature of domestication.

EVIDENCE OF EARLY PLANT DOMESTICATION

The characteristics of plants under human domestication that set them apart from their wild ancestors, and have made them attractive to those who eat them, include increased size, at least of edible parts; reduction or loss of natural means of seed dispersal; reduction or loss of protective devices such as husks or distasteful chemical compounds; and loss of delayed seed germination (important to wild plants for survival in times of drought or other adverse conditions of temporary duration), along with simultaneous ripening of the seed or fruit.

Unconscious selection: The preservation of valued representatives of a plant or animal species and the destruction of less-valued ones, with no thought as to the long-range consequences.

Many of these characteristics can be seen in plant remains from archaeological sites; thus, paleobotanists can often tell the fossil of a wild plant species from a domesticated one; for example, by studying the seed of cereal grasses, such as barley, wheat, and maize (corn). Wild cereals have a very fragile stem, whereas domesticated ones have a tough stem. Under natural conditions, plants with fragile stems scatter their seed for themselves, while those with tough stems do not. The structural change from a soft to a tough stem in early domesticated plants involves a genetic change, undoubtedly the result of what Darwin referred to as **unconscious selection**: the preservation of valued individuals and the destruction of less-valued ones, with no thought as to long-range consequences.[2] When the grain stalks were harvested, their soft stem would shatter at the touch of sickle or flail, and many of their seeds would be lost. Inevitably, most of the seeds that people harvested would have been taken from the tough plants. Early domesticators probably also tended to select seed from plants having few husks or none at all—eventually breeding them out— because husking prior to pounding the grains into meal or flour was much too time-consuming. Size of plants is another good indicator of the presence of domestication. For example, the large ear of corn we know today is a far cry from the tiny ears (about an inch long) characteristic of early corn. In fact, the ear of corn may have arisen when a simple gene mutation transformed male tassel spikes of the wild grass, Teosinte, into small and primitive versions of the female corn ear.[3] Small and primitive though these were, however, they were radically different in structure from the ears of Teosinte.

[2] Ibid., p. 86.

[3] Stephen Jay Gould, *The Flamingo's Smile, Reflections in Natural History* (New York: Norton, 1985), p. 368.

EVIDENCE OF EARLY ANIMAL DOMESTICATION

Domestication also produced changes in the skeletal structure of some animals. For example, the horns of wild goats and sheep differ from those of their domesticated counterparts (domesticated female sheep have none). Another structural change that occurred in domestication involves the size of the animal or its parts. For example, certain teeth of domesticated pigs are smaller than those of wild ones.

A study of age and sex ratios of butchered animals at a site may indicate whether or not animal domestication was practiced. Investigators have assumed that if the age and/or sex ratios at the site differ from those in wild herds, the imbalances are due to conscious selection. For example, at the site of Zawi Chemi Shanidar, in northern Iraq, about 50 percent of the sheep killed were under one year of age. Evidently, the occupants of Zawi Chemi Shanidar were slaughtering the young males for food and saving the females for breeding. Although this does not prove that the sheep were fully domesticated, such herd management does suggest a first step in the domestication process.

In Peru, the prominence of bones of newborn llamas at archaeological sites (up to 72 percent at some), dating to around 6300 years ago, is probably indicative of at least incipient domestication. Such high mortality rates for newborn animals are uncommon in wild herds, but are common where animals are penned up. Under confined conditions, a buildup of mud and filth harbors bacteria that cause diarrhea and enterotoxemia, both of which are fatal to newborn animals.

THE BEGINNINGS OF DOMESTICATION

Over the past 30 years, a good deal of information has accumulated about the beginnings of domestication, primarily in Southwest Asia as well as Central and South America. We still do not have all the answers about how and why it took place. Nonetheless, some observations of general validity can be made which help us to understand how the switch to food production may have taken place.

The first of these observations is that the switch to food production was not the result of such discoveries that seeds, if planted, grow into plants. Food foragers are far from ignorant about the forces of nature and are perfectly aware of the role of seeds in plant growth, that plants grow better under certain conditions than others, and so forth. In fact, they frequently put their knowledge to work so as to manage actively the resources on which they depend. For example, Indians living in the northern part of Canada's Alberta province put to use a sophisticated knowledge of the effects of fire to create local environments of their own design. Similarly, Indians in California used fire to perpetuate oak woodland savanna, to promote hunting and the collection of acorns. And in northern Australia, runoff channels of creeks were deliberately altered so as to flood extensive tracts of land, converting them into fields of wild grain. Food foragers do not remain as such through ignorance, but through choice.

A second observation is that a switch from food foraging to food production does not free people from hard work. The available ethnographic data indicate just the opposite—that farmers, by and large, work far longer hours than do most food foragers. Furthermore, it is clear that early farming required people not only to work longer hours but also to eat more "third choice" food. Typically, food foragers divide potentially edible food resources into first, second, and third choice categories; third choice foods are eaten only by necessity, when there is no other option. And in Southwest Asia and Mexico, at least, the plants that were brought under domestication were clearly third choice plants.

A final observation is that food production is not necessarily a more secure means of subsistence than food foraging. Seed crops in particular, of the sort domesticated in Southwest Asia, Mexico, and Peru, are highly productive but very unstable on account of low species diversity. Without constant human attention, their productivity suffers.

From all of this, it is little wonder that food foragers do not necessarily regard farming and animal husbandry as superior to hunting, gathering, and fishing. Thus, there are some people in the world who have remained food foragers down into the 1990s, although it has become increasingly difficult for them, as food-producing peoples have deprived them of more and more of the land base necessary for their way of life. But as long as existing practices worked well, there was no felt need to abandon them. After all, their traditional way of life gave them all the food they needed and an eminently satisfactory way of living in small, intimate groups. Free from tedious routine, their lives were often more exciting than those of farmers. Food could be hunted, gathered, or fished for as needed, but in most environments they could relax when they had enough to eat. Why raise crops by backbreaking work, when the whole family could camp under a tree bearing tasty and nutritious nuts? Farming brings with it a whole new system of human relationships that offers no easily understood advantages, and disturbs an age-old balance between humans and nature as well as the people who live together (for more on the food foraging way of life, see Chapter 15).

WHY HUMANS BECAME FOOD PRODUCERS

In view of what has been said so far, we may well ask: Why did any human group abandon food foraging in favor of food production?

Several theories have been proposed to account for this change in human subsistence practices. One older theory, stated by V. Gordon Childe, is the "desiccation," or "oasis," theory based on climatic determinism. Its proponents advanced the idea that the glacial cover over Europe and Asia caused a southern shift in rain patterns from Europe to northern Africa and Southwest Asia. When the glaciers retreated northward, so did the rain patterns. As a result, northern Africa and Southwest Asia became dryer, and people were forced to congregate at oases for water. Because of the scarcity of wild animals in such an environment, people were driven by necessity to collect the wild grasses and seeds growing around the oases. Eventually they had to cultivate the grasses to provide enough food for the community. According to this theory, animal domestication began because the oases attracted hungry animals, such as wild goats, sheep, and also cattle, which came to graze on the stubble of the grain fields. People, finding these animals too thin to kill for food, began to fatten them up.

In spite of its initial popularity, evidence in support of the oasis theory was not immediately forthcoming. Moreover, as systematic fieldwork into the origins of domestication began in the late 1940s, other theories gained favor. One of the pioneers in this work was Robert Braidwood of the University of Chicago, who proposed what is sometimes called the "hilly flanks" theory. Contrary to Childe, Braidwood argued that plants and animals were domesticated by people living in the hill country surrounding the fertile crescent (Figure 9.1). They had reached the point in their evolutionary development where they were beginning to "settle in"—that is, become more sedentary—a consequence of which was that they could become intimately familiar with the plants and animals around their settlements. Given the human capacity and enthusiasm for experimentation, it was inevitable that they would have experimented with grasses and animals, bringing them under domestication. Problems with this theory include the ethnocentric notion that non-sedentary food foragers are not intimately familiar with the plants and animals on which they rely for survival, and its projection onto all human cultures of the great value Western culture places on experimentation and innovation for its own sake. In short, the theory was culture bound, strongly reflecting the notions of progress in which people in the Western world had such faith in the period following World War II.

Yet another theory, that became popular in the 1960s, is one in which population growth played a key role. In Southwest Asia, so this theory goes, people adapted to the cool dry conditions of the last glacial period by developing a mixed pattern of resource utilization: They hunted such animals as were available, harvested wild cereal grasses, collected nuts, and collected a wide variety of birds, turtles, snails, crabs, and mussels. They did so well that their populations grew, requiring the development of new ways of providing sufficient food. The result, especially in marginal situations where wild foods were least abundant, was to improve productivity through the domestication of plants and animals.

Just as there are problems with Braidwood's theory, so are there problems with this one. The most serious is that it requires an intentional decision on the part of the people involved to

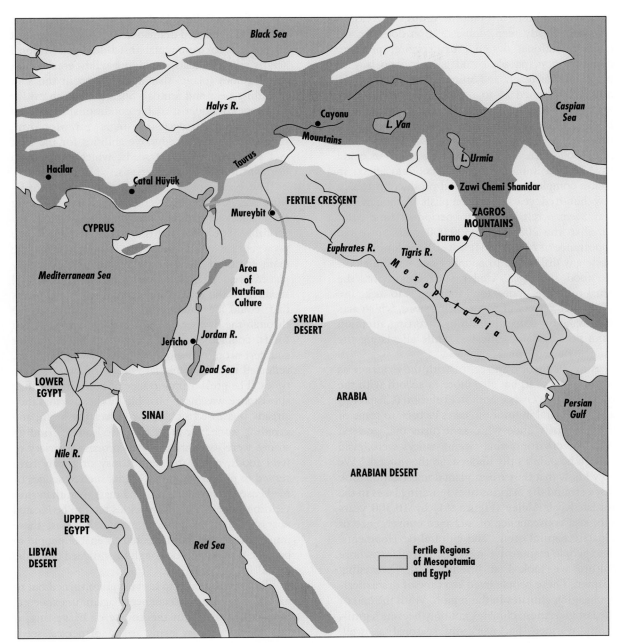

Figure 9.1   In Southwest Asia, early domestication of plants began in the Jordan River Valley and spread from there. Early animal domestication began in the Zagros Mountains and the hills of northern Iraq, spreading to other regions from there.

become producers of domestic crops, whereas, as we have already seen, domestication does not require intentional design. Furthermore, prior to domestication, people could have had no way of knowing that plants and animals could be so radically transformed as to permit a food-producing way of life (even today, the long-term outcome of plant breeding cannot be predicted). Finally, even if people had wanted to become producers of their own food, there is no way such a decision could have had an immediate and perceptible effect; in fact, a complete switch to food production took a few hundred years to accomplish. Although this may seem a relatively short period of time compared to the 200,000 or 300,000 years since the appearance of *H. sapiens*, it was still too long to have made any difference to people faced with immediate food shortages. Under such conditions, the usual response among food foragers is to make use of a wider variety of foods than before, which acts as a brake on domestication by diverting attention from potential domesticates, while alleviating the immediate problem.

Another theory, in accord with the evidence as we now know it, but also more in accord with the role played by chance both in evolution (Chapter 3) and in cultural innovation, takes us back to some of the ideas of Childe who, as it turns out, guessed what the environmental circumstances were, even though he didn't fully understand the process.[4] We now know that the earliest plant domestication took place around the margins of evaporating lakes in the Jordan River Valley (Figure 9.1) by 10,300 years ago, as a consequence of a chance convergence of separate natural events and cultural developments. The people responsible were the Natufians, whose culture we looked at briefly in the preceding chapter. These people lived at a time of dramatically changing climates in the region. With the end of the last glaciation, climates not only became significantly warmer, but markedly seasonal as well. Between 12,000 and 6000 years ago, the lands east of the Mediterranean experienced the most extreme seasonality in their history, with summer aridity significantly longer and more pronounced than today. As a consequence of increased evaporation, many shallow lakes dried up, leaving just three

in the Jordan Valley. At the same time, the region's plant cover changed dramatically. Those plants best adapted to environmental instability and seasonal aridity were annuals, including wild cereal grains and legumes (plants that fix nitrogen in the soil, including peas and lentils). Such plants can evolve very quickly under unstable conditions, since they complete their life cycle in a single year. Moreover, they store their reproductive abilities for the next wet season in abundant seeds, which can remain dormant for prolonged periods.

The Natufians, who lived where these conditions were especially severe, adapted by modifying their subsistence practices in two ways: They probably regularly fired the landscape to promote browsing for red deer and grazing for gazelles, the main focus of their hunting activities, and they placed greater emphasis on the collection of wild seeds from the increasingly abundant annual plants that could be effectively stored to see people through the dry season. The importance of stored foods, coupled with the scarcity of reliable water sources, promoted more sedentary living patterns, reflected in the substantial villages of late Natufian times. The greater importance of seeds in Natufian subsistence was made possible by the fact that they already possessed sickles for harvesting grain, and grinding stones for processing seeds. The grinding stones were used originally to process a variety of wild foods, while the sickles may originally have served to procure nonfood plants such as sedges or reeds used to make baskets and mats (Natufian sites yielding large numbers of sickles tend to be located near coastal marshes and swamps).[5] Thus, these implements were not invented to enable people to become farmers, even though they turned out to be useful for that purpose.

The use of sickles to harvest grain turned out to have important consequences, again unexpected, for the Natufians. In the course of harvesting, it was inevitable that many easily dispersed seeds would be "lost" at the harvest site, whereas those from plants that did not readily scatter their seeds would mostly be carried back to where people processed and stored them.[6] Genetic mutations

[4] Joy McCorriston and Frank Hole, "The Ecology of Seasonal Stress and the Origins of Agriculture in the Near East," *American Anthropologist*, 93 (1991):46–69.

[5] Deborah I. Olszewki, "Comment," *Current Anthropology*, 32 (1991):43.
[6] Mark A. Blumer and Roger Byrne, "The Ecological Genetics and Domestication and the Origins of Agriculture," *Current Anthropology*, 32 (1991):30.

against easy dispersal would inevitably arise in the wild stocks, but would be at a competitive disadvantage compared to variants that could readily disperse their seeds. Moreover, the rate of this and other mutations potentially useful to human consumers might have been unknowingly increased by the periodic firing carried out to promote the deer and gazelle herds, for heat is known to be an effective mutagenic agent, and fire can drastically and quickly change gene frequencies. In any event, with seeds for non-dispersing variants being carried back to settlements, it was inevitable that some lost seeds would germinate and grow there on dump heaps and other disturbed sites (latrines, areas cleared of trees, or burned over). As it turns out, many of the plants that became domesticated were colonizers, that do particularly well in disturbed habitats. Moreover, with people becoming increasingly sedentary, disturbed habitats became more extensive as resources in proximity to settlements were depleted over time, thus variants of plants particularly susceptible to human manipulation had more and more opportunity to flourish where people were living, and where they would inevitably attract attention. Under such circumstances, it was inevitable that people sooner or later would begin to actively promote their growth, even by deliberately sowing them, especially as people otherwise had to travel further afield to procure the resources that were depleted near their villages. An inevitable consequence of increased human manipulation would be the appearance of other mutant strains of particular benefit. For example, barley, which in its wild state can be tremendously productive but difficult to harvest and process, had developed the tougher stems that make it easier to harvest by 9000 years ago; by 8000 years ago "naked" barley, which is easier to process, was common, and by 7500 years ago six-row barley, which is more productive than the original two-row, was widespread. Sooner or later, people realized that they could play a more active role in the process by deliberately trying to breed more useful strains. With this, domestication may be said to have shifted from a process that was unintentional, to one that was intentional.

The development of animal domestication in Southwest Asia seems to have proceeded along somewhat similar lines but in the hilly country of northern Iraq and the Zagros Mountains of Iran

---

Transhumance: Among pastoralists, the grazing of sheep and goats in the low steppelands in the winter, moving to high pastures on the plateaus in the summer.

(Figure 9.1). Here were to be found large herds of wild sheep and goats, as well as much in the way environmental diversity. From the low, alluvial plains of the valley of the Tigris and Euphrates rivers, for example, travel to the north or east takes one into the high country through three other zones: first steppeland, then oak and pistachio woodlands, and, finally, high plateau country with grass, scrub, or desert vegetation. Valleys that run at right angles to the mountain ranges afford relatively easy access between these zones. Today, a number of pastoral peoples in the region practice a pattern of **transhumance,** in which they graze their herds of sheep and goats on the low steppelands in the winter, moving to high pastures on the plateaus in the summer.

Moving 12,000 years backward in time to the Mesolithic, we find that the region was inhabited by peoples whose subsistence pattern, like that of the Natufians, was one of food foraging. Different plants were found in different ecological zones and, because of the difference in altitude, plant foods matured at different times in different zones. The animals hunted for meat and hides by these people included several species, among them bear, fox, boar, and wolf. Most notable, though, were the hoofed animals: deer, gazelles, wild goats, and wild sheep. Their bones are far more common in human refuse piles than those of other animals. This is significant, for most of these animals are naturally transhumant in the region, moving back and forth from low winter pastures to high summer pastures. People followed these animals in their seasonal migrations, making use along the way of other wild foods in the zones through which they passed: dates in the lowlands; acorns, almonds, and pistachios higher up; apples and pears higher still; wild grains maturing at different times in different zones; woodland animals in the forested zone between summer and winter grazing land. All in all, it was a rich, varied fare.

There was in hunting, then, a concentration on hoofed animals, including wild sheep and goats, which provided meat and hides. At first, animals of all ages and sexes were hunted. But, beginning about 11,000 years ago, the percentage of immature sheep eaten, for example, increased to about 50 percent of the total. At the same time, the percentage frequency of female animals decreased. Apparently, people were learning that they could increase yields by sparing the females for breeding, while feasting on ram lambs. This marks the beginning of human management of sheep. As this management of flocks became more and more efficient, sheep were increasingly shielded from the effects of natural selection. Eventually, they were introduced into areas outside their natural habitat. For example, sheep and goats were kept by farmers at ancient Jericho, in the Jordan River Valley, 8000 years ago (by which time farming, too, had spread from its original homeland far to the north into Turkey and far to the east into the Zagros Mountains). As a consequence of this human intervention, variants that usually were not successful in the wild were able to survive and reproduce. Although variants that were perceived as being of immediate advantage would have attracted peoples' attention, they did not arise out of need, but independent of it at random, as mutations do. In such a way did those features characteristic of domestic sheep, such as greater fat and meat production, excess wool (Figure 9.2), and so on, begin to develop. By 9000 years ago, the bones of domestic sheep had become distinguishable from those of wild sheep.

In sum, the domesticators of plants and animals sought only to increase to the maximum extent the food sources available to them. They were not aware of the revolutionary consequences their actions were to have. But as the process continued, the productivity of the domestic species increased, relative to wild species. Thus they became increasingly more important to subsistence, resulting in further intensification of interest in, and management of, the domesticates. Inevitably, the result would be further increases in productivity.

OTHER CENTERS OF DOMESTICATION

In addition to Southwest Asia, the domestication of plants and, in some cases, animals took place independently in Southeast Asia, parts of the Americas (southern Mexico, Peru, the Amazon Basin of South America, and eastern North America) and possibly northern China and Africa (Figure 9.3). In Southeast Asia, domestication took place sometime between 8800 and 5000 years ago. Plant remains, none of them showing any detectable differences from wild strains, have been found in Spirit Cave in northern Thailand in levels dating back as far as 10,000 years. The oldest domestic plant so far identified is rice, in pottery dated to sometime before 5000 years ago. In addition to rice, Southeast Asians domesticated root crops, most notably yams and taro. Root crop farming, or **vegeculture**,

Although sheep and goats were first valued for their meat, hides, and sinew, the changes wrought by domestication made them useful for other purposes as well. This impression, from a 4500-year-old seal, shows a goat being milked.

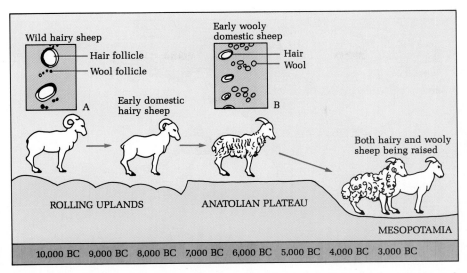

Figure 9.2   The domestication of sheep resulted in evolutionary changes that created more wool. Drawing A shows a section, as seen through a microscope, of skin of wild sheep, showing the arrangement of primary (hair) and secondary (wool) follicles. Drawing B shows a section of similarly enlarged of skin of domestic sheep, showing the changed relationship and the change in the size of follicles that accompanied the development of wool.

typically involves the growing of many different species together in a single field. Because this approximates the complexity of the natural vegetation, vegeculture tends to be more stable than seed crop cultivation.

In Mexico, the domestication of plants took place in the period between 9000 and 3500 years ago. Archaeological evidence from the Tehuacan Valley in the Mexican state of Puebla shows that crops such as maize, beans, and squash very gradually came to make up a greater percentage of the food eaten (see Figure 9.4). Like the hill country of Southwest Asia, the Tehuacan Valley is environmentally diverse, and the people living there had a cyclical pattern of hunting and gathering which made use of the resources of different environmental zones. In the course of their seasonal movements, people carried the wild precursors of future

domesticates out of their native habitat, exposing them to different selective pressures. Under such circumstances, potentially useful (to humans) variants that did not do well in the native habitat would, by chance, do well in novel settings, again (as in Southwest Asia) attracting human attention.

The change to food production also took place in South America, earliest in the highlands of Peru, again an environmentally diverse region. While a number of crops first grown in Mexico eventually came to be grown here, there was more of an emphasis on root crops, such as potatoes, sweet potatoes, and manioc. South Americans domesticated guinea pigs, llamas, alpacas, and ducks, whereas the Mexicans never did much with domestic livestock. They limited themselves to dogs, turkeys, and bees.

THE SPREAD OF FOOD PRODUCTION

Although population growth and the need to feed more people cannot explain the origin of the food-producing way of life, it does seem to have a lot to do with its subsequent spread. As already noted, domestication inevitably leads to higher

Vegeculture: The cultivation of domesticated root crops, such as yams and taro.

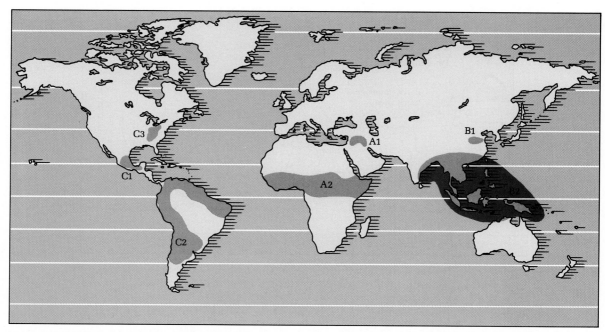

Figure 9.3   Early plant and animal domestication occurred in such widely scattered areas as Southwest Asia (A1), Central Africa (A2), China (B1), Southeast Asia (B2), Mesoamerica (C1), South America (C2), and North America (C3).

yields, and higher yields make it possible to feed more people. In addition, farmers have available a variety of foods that are soft enough to be fed to infants, which food foragers usually do not. Hence, farmers do not need to nurse their children so intensively, nor for so many years. In humans, prolonged nursing, so long as it involves frequent stimulation of the nipple by the infant, has a dampening effect on ovulation. As a result, women in food-foraging societies are less likely to become fertile as soon after childbirth as they are in food-producing societies. Coupled with this, too many children to care for at once interferes with the foraging activities of women in hunting, gathering, and fishing societies. Among farmers, however, numerous children are frequently seen as assets, to help out with the many household chores. Small wonder, then, that a sharp upsurge in the birthrate commonly follows a switch from food foraging to farming.

Paradoxically, while domestication increases productivity, so does it increase instability. This is so because those varieties with the highest yields become the focus of human attention, while other varieties are less valued and ultimately ignored. As a result, farmers become dependent on a rather narrow range of resources, compared to the wide range utilized by food foragers. Modern agriculturists, for example, rely on about 20 crops, versus the more than 100 species regarded as edible by the !Kung of Africa's Kalahari Desert. This dependence upon fewer varieties means that when a crop fails, for whatever reason, farmers have less to fall back on than do food foragers. Furthermore, the likelihood of failure is increased by the common farming practice of planting crops together in one locality, so that a disease contracted by one plant can easily spread to others. Moreover, by relying on seeds from the most productive plants of a species to establish next year's crop, farmers favor genetic uniformity over diversity. The result is that if some virus, bacterium, or fungus is able to destroy one plant, it will likely destroy them all. This is what happened in the famous Irish potato famine of 1845 to 1846, which sent waves of Irish immigrants to the United States.

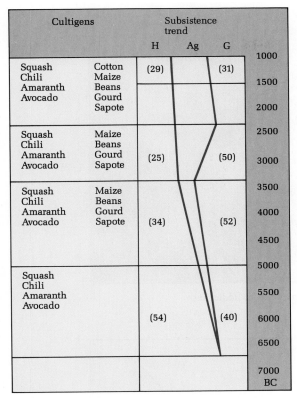

Cultigens		Subsistence trend			
		H	Ag	G	
Squash Chili Amaranth Avocado	Cotton Maize Beans Gourd Sapote	(29)		(31)	1000 · 1500 · 2000
Squash Chili Amaranth Avocado	Maize Beans Gourd Sapote	(25)		(50)	2500 · 3000
Squash Chili Amaranth Avocado	Maize Beans Gourd Sapote	(34)		(52)	3500 · 4000 · 4500
Squash Chili Amaranth Avocado		(54)		(40)	5000 · 5500 · 6000 · 6500
					7000 BC

Figure 9.4 Tehuacan Valley subsistence trends show that dependence on horticulture came about gradually, over a prolonged period of time. H = % hunting; AG = % horticulture; G = % wild plant use.

The Irish potato famine illustrates how the combination of increased productivity and vulnerability may contribute to the geographical spread of farming. Time and time again in the past, population growth followed by crop failures has triggered movements of people from one place to another, where they have reestablished the subsistence practices with which they were familiar. Thus, once farming came into existence, it was more or less guaranteed that it would spread to neighboring regions (see Figure 9.5). From Southwest Asia, for instance, it spread to southeastern Europe by 8000 years ago, reaching central Europe and the Netherlands by 4000 years ago, and England between 4000 and 3000 years ago.

In some instances, farming appears to have been adopted by food foragers from food-producing neighbors. By way of illustration, a crisis developed

on the coast of Peru some 4500 years ago as continental uplift caused lowering of the water table and destruction of marine habitats at a time of growing population; the result was an increasing shortage of the wild food resources on which people depended. Their response was to begin growing along the edges of rivers many of the domestic plants that their highland neighbors to the east had begun to cultivate a few thousand years earlier. Here, then, farming appears to have been a subsistence practice of last resort, which a food-foraging people took up only because they had no real choice.

CULTURE OF NEOLITHIC SETTLEMENTS

A number of Neolithic settlements have been excavated, particularly in Southwest Asia. The structures, artifacts, and food debris found at these sites have revealed much about the daily activities of their former inhabitants as they pursued the business of making a living.

EARLIEST FULL-FLEDGED FARMING SETTLEMENTS

Dated to between 10,000 and 9000 years ago, the earliest known sites containing domesticated plants and animals are found in Southwest Asia. These sites occur in a region extending from the Jordan Valley northward across the Taurus Mountains into Turkey, and eastward across the flanks of the Taurus Mountains into northeastern Iran, and southward into Iraq and Iran along the hilly flanks of the Zagros Mountains. The sites contain evidence of domesticated barley, wheat, goats, sheep, dogs, and pigs.

These sites are generally the remains of small village farming communities—small clusters of houses built of mud, each with its own storage pit and clay oven. Their occupants continued to use stone tools of Mesolithic type, plus a few new types of use in farming. Probably the people born into these communities spent their lives in them in a common effort to make their crops grow and their animals prosper. At the same time, they participated in long-distance trade networks. Obsidian found at

Stands of wild wheat are still to be found in parts of the Middle East.

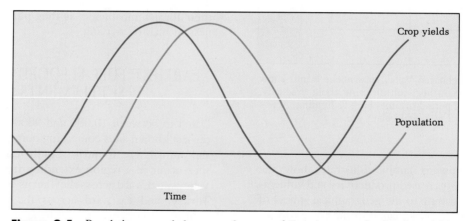

Figure 9.5 Population growth has a tendency to follow increases in farming yields. Inevitably, this results in too large a population to be fed when crops fail, as they periodically do. The result is an outward migration of people to other regions.

Jarmo, Iraq, for instance, was imported from 300 miles away.

JERICHO: AN EARLY FARMING COMMUNITY

At the Neolithic settlement which later grew to become the biblical city of Jericho, excavation has revealed the remains of a sizable farming community occupied as early as 10,350 years ago. Located in the Jordan River Valley, what

made the site attractive was the presence of a bounteous spring and the rich soils of an ice age lake that had dried up about 3000 years earlier. Here, crops could be grown almost continuously, since the fertility of the soil was regularly renewed by flood-borne deposits originating in the Judean Highlands, to the west. To protect their settlement against these floods and associated mudflows, the people of Jericho built massive walls of stone around it.[7] Within these walls, an estimated 400 to 900 people lived in houses of mud brick with plastered floors arranged around courtyards. In addition to these houses, a stone tower that would have taken 100 people as many days to build was located inside one corner of the wall, near the spring. A staircase inside it probably led to a mud brick building on top. Nearby were mud brick storage facilities as well as peculiar structures of possible ceremonial significance. A village cemetery also reflects the sedentary life of these early people; nomadic groups, with few exceptions, rarely buried their dead in a single central location.

[7] O. Bar-Yosef, "The Walls of Jericho: An Alternative Interpretation," *Current Anthropology*, 27 (1986):160.

Evidence of domestic plants and animals is scant at Jericho. However, indirect evidence in the form of harvesting tools and milling equipment has been uncovered at the site, and wheat, barley, and other domestic plants are known from sites of similar age in the region. We do know that the people of Jericho were keeping sheep and goats by 8000 years ago, although some hunting still went on. Some of the meat from wild animals may have been supplied by food-foraging peoples whose campsites have been found everywhere in the desert of the Arabian peninsula. Close contacts between these people and the farmers of Jericho and other villages are indicated by common features in art, ritual, use of prestige goods, and burial practices. Other evidence of trade consists of obsidian and turquoise from Sinai as well as marine shells from the coast, all discovered inside the walls of Jericho.

NEOLITHIC TECHNOLOGY

Early harvesting tools were made of wood or bone with serrated flints inserted. Later tools continued to be made by chipping and flaking stone, but during the Neolithic period, stone that was too hard to chip was ground and polished for tools (Figure 9.6). People developed scythes, forks, hoes, and plows to replace their simple digging sticks. Pestles and mortars were used for preparation of grain. Plows were later redesigned when domesticated cattle became available for use as draft animals, after 8000 years ago.

POTTERY

In addition to the domestication of plants and animals, one of the characteristics of the Neolithic period is the extensive manufacture and use of pottery. In food-foraging societies, most people are involved in the food quest. In food-producing societies, even though people have to work as long—if not longer—at subsistence activities than food foragers, this need not be the case. Hard work on the part of those producing the food may free other members of the society to devote their energies to other craft specialties. One such craft is pottery making, and different forms of pottery were created for transporting and storing food,

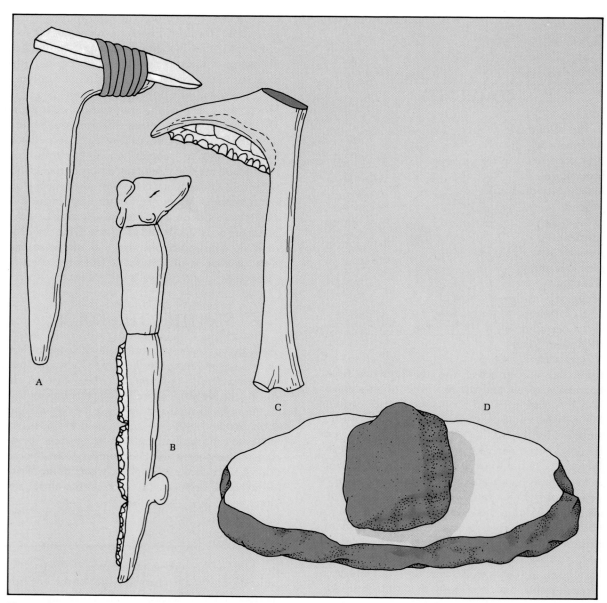

Figure 9.6   In Southwest Asia, many tools fabricated by Neolithic peoples made use of flint microliths in bone or wood handles, as had been done in the Mesolithic, but some tools were made of ground and polished stone.

artifacts, and other material possessions. Because pottery vessels are impervious to damage by insects, rodents, and dampness, they could be used for storing small grain, seeds, and other materials. Moreover, food can be boiled in pottery vessels directly over the fire rather than by such ancient techniques as dropping stones heated directly in the fire into the food being cooked. Pottery is also used for pipes, ladles, lamps, and other objects, and some cultures used large vessels for burial of the dead.

In the Middle East, the first domestic animals (aside from dogs) were sheep and goats. Pigs, however, followed not long afterward. This pottery vessel in the shape of a pig, found at a site in Turkey, was made about 5600 B.C.

Significantly, pottery containers remain important for much of humanity today.

The invention of pottery, which is manufactured from clay and fired, probably resulted from the accidental firing of clay used to make ovens and to line basins located near cooking areas. Its widespread use is a good, though not foolproof, indication of a sedentary community, and it is found in abundance in all but a few of the earliest Neolithic settlements. At ancient Jericho, for example, the earliest Neolithic people lacked pottery. Its fragility and weight make it impractical for use by nomads and hunters, who use baskets and containers made of hide. Nevertheless, there are some modern nomads who make and use pottery, just as there are farmers who lack it. In fact, food foragers in Japan were making pottery by 13,000 years ago, long before it was being made in Southwest Asia.

The manufacture of pottery is a difficult art and requires a high degree of technological sophistication. To make a useful pot requires a knowledge of clay and the techniques of firing or baking. Neolithic pots, for example, are often coarse and ill-made because of improper clay mixture or faulty firing technique.

Pottery is decorated in various ways. For example, designs can be engraved on the vessel before firing, or special rims, legs, bases, and other details may be made separately and fastened to the finished pot. Painting is the most common form of pottery decoration, and there are literally thousands of painted designs found among the pottery remains of ancient cultures.

HOUSING

Food production and the new sedentary life-style engendered another technological development—house building. Permanent housing is of limited interest to food foragers who usually have to move from time to time. Cave shelters, pits dug in the earth, and simple lean-tos made of hides and tree limbs serve their purpose of keeping the weather out. In the Neolithic, however, dwellings became more complex in design and more diverse in type. Some, like Swiss Lake Dwellings, were constructed of wood, housed several families per building, had doors, and contained beds, tables, and other furniture. More elaborate shelters were made of stone, sun-dried brick, or branches plastered together with mud or clay.

Although permanent housing frequently goes along with food production, there is archaeological evidence that one can have substantial houses without food production. For example, at Mureybit, in Southwest Asia, storage pits and year-round occupation of stone houses indicate that its occupants had definitely settled down between 10,200 and 9500 years ago. Yet the remains and artifacts indicate that the occupants were food foragers, not farmers.

CLOTHING

During the Neolithic, for the first time in human history, clothing was made of woven textiles. The raw materials and technology necessary for the production of clothing came from three sources: flax and cotton from farming, wool from domesticated sheep, and the spindle for spinning and the loom for weaving from the inventive human mind.

SOCIAL STRUCTURE

Evidence of all the economic and technological developments listed thus far has enabled archaeologists to draw certain inferences concerning the

Neolithic farming communities, such as Jericho in the Jordan River Valley, were made possible by the result of the domestication of plants and animals. Jericho was surrounded by a stone wall as protection against floods. The wall included a tower (left). People lived in substantial houses (right).

organization of Neolithic society. The general absence of elaborate buildings in all but a few settlements may suggest that neither religion nor government was yet a formally established institution able to wield real social power. Although there is evidence of ceremonial activity, little evidence of a centrally organized and directed religious life has been found. Burials, for example, show a marked absence of patterning; variation seems to have been the order of the day. Since early Neolithic graves were rarely constructed of, or covered by stone slabs, and rarely included grave goods, it is believed that no person had attained the superior social status that would have required an elaborate funeral. The smallness of most villages suggests that the inhabitants knew each other very well, so that most of their relationships were probably highly personal ones, charged with emotional significance.

The general picture that emerges is one of an egalitarian society with little division of labor and probably little development of new and more specialized social roles. Villages seem to have been made up of several households, each providing for its own needs. The organizational needs of society beyond the household level were probably met by kinship groups and common-interest associations.

NEOLITHIC CULTURE IN THE NEW WORLD

Outside of Mesoamerica (southern Mexico and northern Central America) and Peru, hunting, fishing, and the gathering of wild plant foods remained important elements in the economy of Neolithic peoples in the New World. Apparently, most American Indians never experienced a complete change from a food-foraging to a food-producing mode of life, even though maize and other domestic crops were cultivated just about everywhere that climate permitted. Farming developed independently of Europe and Asia, and the crops differed because of different natural conditions and cultural traits.

Textiles like this one, produced in Peru sometime between 500 and 200 B.C., remain unsurpassed anywhere in the world, even though weaving began later in the Americas then in some parts of the Old World.

The Neolithic developed later in the New World than in the Old. For example, Neolithic agricultural villages were common in Southwest Asia between 9000 to 8000 years ago, but similar villages did not appear in the New World until about 4500 years ago, in Mesoamerica and Peru. Moreover, pottery, which arose in the Old World shortly after plant and animal domestication, did not develop in the New World until about 4500 years ago. Neither the potter's wheel nor the loom and spindle were used by early Neolithic people in the New World. Both pottery and textiles were manufactured by manual means, and evidence of the loom and spindle does not appear in the New World until 3000 years ago. None of these indicate any "backwardness" on the part of New World peoples; rather, older practices continued to be satisfactory for relatively long periods of time.

THE NEOLITHIC AND HUMAN BIOLOGY

Although we tend to think of the invention of food production in terms of its cultural impact, it obviously had a biological impact as well. From studies of human skeletons from Neolithic burials, physical anthropologists have found evidence for a somewhat lessened mechanical stress on peoples' bodies and teeth. Although there are exceptions, the teeth of Neolithic peoples show less wear, their bones are less robust, and osteoarthritis (the result of stressed joint surfaces) is not as marked as in the skeletons of Paleolithic and Mesolithic peoples. They have also found clear evidence for a marked deterioration in health and mortality. Anthropologist Anna Roosevelt sums up our knowledge of this in the following Original Study.

ORIGINAL STUDY

HISTORY OF MORTALITY AND PHYSIOLOGICAL STRESS[8]

Although there is a relative lack of evidence for the Paleolithic stage, enough skeletons have been studied that it seems clear that seasonal and periodic physiological stress regularly affected most prehistoric hunting-gathering populations, as evidenced by the presence of enamel hypoplasias [horizontal linear defects in tooth enamel] and Harris lines [horizontal lines near the ends of long bones]. What also seems

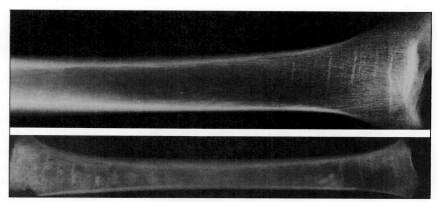

Harris lines near the ends of these youthful thigh bones, found in a prehistoric farming community in Arizona, are indicative of recovery after growth arrest, caused by famine or severe disease.

Enamel hypoplasias such as those shown on these teeth are indicative of arrested growth caused by severe disease or famine. The teeth are from an adult who lived in an ancient farming community in Arizona.

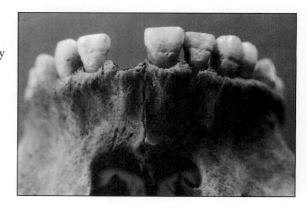

clear is that severe and chronic stress, with high frequency of hypoplasias, infectious disease lesions, pathologies related to iron-deficiency anemia, and high mortality rates, is not characteristic of these early populations. There is no evidence of frequent, severe malnutrition, and so the diet must have been adequate in calories and other nutrients most of the time. During the Mesolithic, the proportion of starch in the diet rose, to judge from the increased occurrence of certain dental diseases, but not enough to create an impoverished diet. At this time, diets seem to have been made up of a rather large number of foods, so that the failure of one food source would not be catastrophic. There is a possible slight tendency for Paleolithic people to be healthier and taller than Mesolithic people, but there is no apparent trend toward increasing physiological stress during the Mesolithic. Thus, it seems that both hunter-gatherers and incipient agriculturalists regularly underwent population pressure, but only to a moderate degree.

During the periods when effective agriculture first comes into use there seems to be a temporary upturn in health and survival rates in a few regions: Europe, North America, and the eastern Mediterranean. At this stage, wild foods are still consumed periodically and a variety of plants are cultivated, suggesting the availability of adequate amounts of different nutrients. Based on the increasing frequency of tooth disease related to high carbohydrate consumption, it seems that cultivated plants probably increased the storable calorie supply, removing for a time any seasonal or periodic problems in food supply. In most regions, however, the development of agriculture seems not to have had this effect, and there seems to have been a slight increase in physiological stress.

Stress, however, does not seem to have become *common* and widespread until after the development of high degrees of sedentism, population density, and reliance on intensive agriculture. At this stage in all regions the incidence of physiological stress increases greatly, and average mortality rates increase appreciably. Most of these agricultural populations have high frequencies of porotic hyperostosis and cribra orbitalia [bone deformities indicative of chronic iron-deficiency anemia], and there is a substantial increase in the number and severity of enamel hypoplasias and pathologies associated with infectious disease. Stature in many populations appears to have been considerably lower than would be expected if genetically determined height maxima had been reached, which suggests that the growth arrests documented by pathologies were causing stunting. Accompanying these indicators of poor health and nourishment, there is a universal drop in the occurrence of Harris lines, suggesting a poor rate of full recovery from the stress. Incidence of carbohydrate-related tooth disease increases, apparently because subsistence by this time is characterized by a heavy emphasis on a few starchy food crops. Populations seem to have grown beyond the point at which wild food resources could be a meaningful dietary supplement, and even domestic animal resources were commonly reserved for farm labor and transport rather than for diet supplementation.

It seems that a large proportion of most sedentary prehistoric populations under intensive agriculture underwent chronic and life-threatening malnutrition and disease, especially during infancy and childhood. The causes of the nutritional stress are likely to have been the poverty of the staple crops in most nutrients except calories, periodic famines caused by the instability of the agricultural system, and chronic lack of food due to both population growth and economic expropriation by elites. The increases in infectious disease probably reflect both a poorer diet and increased interpersonal contact in crowded settlements, and it is, in turn, likely to have aggravated nutritional problems.

[8] Anna Curtenius Roosevelt, "Population, Health, and the Evolution of Subsistence: Conclusions from the Conference," in *Paleopathology and the Origins of Agriculture*, eds. Mark N. Cohen and George J. Armelagos (Orlando, Fla.: Academic Press, 1984), pp.572–574.

For the most part, the crops on which Neolithic peoples came to depend were selected for their higher productivity and storability, rather than their nutritional value. Moreover, their nutritional shortcomings would have been exacerbated by their susceptibility to periodic failure, as already noted, particularly as populations grew in size. Thus, the worsened health and mortality of Neolithic peoples is not surprising. Some have gone so far as to assert that the switch from food foraging to food production was the worst mistake that humans ever made!

Another key contributor to the increased incidence of disease and mortality was probably the new mode of life in Neolithic communities. Sedentary life in fixed villages brings with it sanitation problems that do not exist for small groups of people who move about from one campsite to another. Moreover, airborne diseases are more easily transmitted in such villages. Another factor, too, may have been close association between humans and their domestic animals, a situation conducive to the transmission of some animal diseases to humans. Smallpox, chicken pox, and in fact all of the infectious diseases of childhood that were not overcome by medical science until the latter half of the present century seem to have been transmitted to humans through their close association with domestic animals.

Another example of the biological impact of food production on human biology is that of the abnormal hemoglobin responsible for sickle-cell anemia, discussed in Chapter 3. Other abnormal hemoglobins are associated with the spread of farming from Southwest Asia westward around the Mediterranean, and also with the spread of farming in Southeast Asia. In all these regions, changes in human gene pools took place as a biological response to malaria, which had become a problem as a result of farming practices.

Higher mortality rates in Neolithic villages seem to have been offset by increased fertility, for population growth accelerated dramatically at precisely the moment that health and mortality worsened. The factors responsible for this increased natality have already been discussed earlier in this chapter.

The chicken pox from which this infant suffers is a direct consequence of the domestication of animals thousands of years earlier. Close and continuing contact with domestic stock allowed for the transfer of many animal diseases to humans.

THE NEOLITHIC AND THE IDEA OF PROGRESS

One of the more deeply held biases of Western culture is that human history is basically a record of steady progress over time. The transition from food foraging to food production is generally viewed as a great step upward on a supposed "ladder of progress." To be sure, farming allowed people to increase the size of their population, to live together in substantial sedentary communities, and to reorganize the work load in ways that permitted craft specialization. If one chooses to regard this as "progress," that is fine—progress is, after all, whatever it is defined as, and different cultures hold different views of this.

Whatever the benefits of food production, however, a substantial price was paid. As anthropologists Mark Cohen and George Armelagos put it:

Taken as a whole, indicators fairly clearly suggest an overall decline in the quality—and probably in the length—of human life associated with the adoption of agriculture. This decline was offset in some regions, but not in others, by a decline in physical demands on the body. The studies support recent ethnographic statements and theoretical arguments about the relatively good health and nutrition of hunter–gatherers. They also suggest that hunter–gatherers were relatively well buffered against episodic stress. These data call in question simplistic popular ideas about human progress. They also call in question models of human population growth that are based on assumed progressive increases in life expectancy. The data suggest that the well documented expansion of early farming populations was accomplished in spite of general diminution of both child and adult life expectancy rather than being fueled by increased survivorship.[9]

Rather than imposing ethnocentric notions of progress on the archaeological record, it is best to view the advent of food production as but one more factor contributing to the diversification of cultures, something that had begun in the Paleolithic. While some societies continued to practice hunting, gathering, and fishing, others became **horticultural**—small communities of gardeners working with simple hand tools and using neither irrigation nor the plow. Horticulturists typically cultivate different varieties of crops in small gardens they have cleared by hand. Some horticultural societies, however, became **agricultural**. Technologically more complex than the horticulturalists, agriculturalists often employ irrigation, fertilizers, and the wooden or metal plow pulled by two harnessed draft animals, such as oxen or water buffalo, to produce food on larger plots of land. The

[9] Mark N. Cohen and George J. Armelagos, "Paleopathology and the Origins of Agriculture: Editors' Summation," in Cohen and Armelagos, p. 594.

Horticulture: Cultivation of crops carried out with hand tools such as digging sticks or hoes.

Agriculture: Intensive farming of large plots of land, employing fertilizers, plows, and/or extensive irrigation.

Pastoralists: People who rely on herds of domestic animals for their subsistence.

distinction between horticulturalist and agriculturalist is not always an easy one to make. For example, the Hopi Indians of the North American Southwest traditionally employed irrigation in their farming, while at the same time using simple hand tools.

Some societies became specialized **pastoralists** in environments that were too dry or too grassy for effective horticulture or agriculture. For example, the Russian steppes, with their heavy grass cover, were not suitable to farming without a plow, but they were ideal for herding. Thus, a number of peoples living in the arid grasslands and deserts that stretch from North Africa into Central Asia kept large herds of domestic animals, relying on their neighbors for plant foods. Finally, some societies went on to develop civilizations—the subject of the next chapter.

Chapter Summary

Throughout the Paleolithic, people were strictly food foragers moving from place to place as the food supply became exhausted. The change to food production, which (in Southwest Asia) began about 10,300 years ago, meant that people could become more sedentary and reorganize the work load, freeing some people from the food quest to pursue other tasks. From the end of the Mesolithic, human groups became larger and more permanent as people turned to animal breeding and crop growing.

A domesticated plant or animal is one which has become genetically modified as an intended or unintended consequence of human manipulation. Analysis of plant and animal remains at a site will usually indicate whether or not its occupants were food producers. Wild cereal grasses, for example, usually have fragile stems, whereas cultivated ones have tough stems. Domesticated plants can also be identified because they are usually larger than their wild counterparts. Domestication produces skeletal changes in some animals. The horns of wild goats and sheep, for example, differ from those of domesticated ones. Age and sex imbalances in herd animals may also indicate manipulation by human domesticators.

Several theories have been proposed to account for the changes in the subsistence patterns of early humans. One theory, the "oasis" or "desiccation" theory, is based on climatic determination. Domestication began because the oasis attracted hungry animals, which were domesticated instead of killed by early humans. Although once popular, it fell out of favor as systematic studies of the origins of domestication began in the late 1940s. One alternative idea was that domestication began in the hilly flanks of the fertile crescent because culture was ready for it. This somewhat culture-bound idea was replaced by theories, popular in the 1960s, that saw domestication as a response to population growth. However, this would require a deliberate decision on the part of people who could have had no knowledge of the long-range consequences of domestication. The most probable theory is that domestication came about as a consequence of a chance convergence of separate natural events and cultural developments. This happened independently and at somewhat different times in Southwest and Southeast Asia, highland Mexico and Peru, South America's Amazon forest, eastern North America, China, and Africa.

Two major consequences of domestication are that crops become more productive but also more vulnerable. This combination periodically causes population to outstrip food supplies, whereupon people are apt to move into new regions. In this way, farming has often spread from one region to another, as into Europe from Southwest Asia. Sometimes, food foragers will adopt the cultivation of crops from neighboring peoples, in response to the shortage of wild foods, as happened in ancient Peru.

Among the earliest known sites containing domesticated plants and animals, about 10,000 to 9000 years old, are those of Southwest Asia. These sites were mostly small villages of mud huts with individual storage pits and clay ovens. There is evidence not only of cultivation and domestication but also of trade. At ancient Jericho, remains of tools, houses, and clothing indicate the oasis was occupied by Neolithic people as early as 10,350 years ago. At its height, Neolithic Jericho had a population of 400 to 900 people. Similar villages developed independently in Mexico and Peru by about 4500 years ago.

During the Neolithic, stone that was too hard to be chipped was ground and polished for tools. People developed scythes, forks, hoes, and plows to replace simple digging sticks. The Neolithic was also characterized by the extensive manufacture and use of pottery. The widespread use of pottery is a good indicator of a sedentary community; it is found in all but a few of the earliest Neolithic settlements. The manufacture of pottery requires a knowledge of clay and the techniques of firing or baking. Neolithic pottery is often coarse. Other technological developments that accompanied food production and the sedentary life were the building of permanent houses and the weaving of textiles.

Archaeologists have been able to draw some inferences concerning the social structure of Neolithic society. No evidence has been found indicating that religion or government was yet a centrally organized institution. Society was probably egalitarian, with little division of labor and little development of specialized social roles.

The development of food production had biological, as well as cultural, consequences. New diets, living arrangements, and farming practices led to increased incidence of disease and higher mortality rates. Increased fertility of women seems to have more than offset mortality.

Suggested Readings

Childe, V. Gordon. *Man Makes Himself.* New York: New American Library, 1951.
In this old classic, originally published in 1936, Childe presented his concept of the "Neolithic Revolution." He places special emphasis on the technological inventions that helped transform humans from food gatherers to food producers.

Rindos, David. *The Origins of Agriculture: An Evolutionary Perspective.* Orlando, Fla.: Academic Press, 1984.
This is the most important book on agricultural origins to appear in recent times. After identifying the weaknesses of existing theories, Rindos presents his own evolutionary theory of agricultural origins.

Smith, Philip E. L. *Food Production and its Consequences*, 2nd ed. Menlo Park, Calif.: Cummings, 1976.
This book is the author's personal interpretation of the ways in which food production influenced and transformed the more important aspects of humans and society, through its effects on demography, settlements, technology, social and political organization, religion, and so on.

Struever, Stuart, ed. *Prehistoric Agriculture.* Garden City, N.Y.: Natural History Press, 1970.
This book presents a worldwide survey of the when, where, and how of the rise of agriculture and the development of agrarian societies. The emphasis is upon the adaptation of a society to a particular environment. There are studies of agrarian societies of Europe, the Near East, and North and South America.

Wernick, Robert, and the editors of Time-Life Books. *The Monument Builders.* New York: Time-Life, 1973.
This volume of the *Time-Life Emergence of Man* series deals with the spread of the Neolithic to Europe and the emergence of distinctive patterns there of this way of life. Like all volumes in this series, it is richly illustrated and contains a useful bibliography.

10

THE RISE OF CITIES

AND

CIVILIZATION

One of the largest cities of the ancient world was Teotihuacan in Central Mexico. At its height, just before its violent end in the eighth century A.D., a population of 125,000 people may have lived there. This photo, taken from one of the two main pyramids, looks south down the city's principal avenue.

WHEN AND WHERE DID THE WORLD'S FIRST CITIES FIRST DEVELOP?

Cities—urban settlements with well-defined nuclei, populations that are large, dense, and diversified both economically and socially—are characteristic of civilizations which developed initially in China, the Indus and Nile Valleys, Mesopotamia, Mesoamerica, and Peru. The world's oldest cities were those of Mesopotamia, but one of the world's largest was located in Mesoamerica.

WHAT CHANGES IN CULTURE ACCOMPANIED THE RISE OF CITIES?

Four basic culture changes mark the transition from Neolithic village life to that in civilized urban centers. These are agricultural innovation, as new farming methods were developed; diversification of labor, as more people were freed from food production to pursue a variety of full-time craft specialties; the emergence of centralized governments to deal with the new problems of urban life; and the emergence of social classes as people were ranked according to the work they did, or the position of the families into which they were born.

WHY DID CIVILIZATIONS DEVELOP IN THE FIRST PLACE?

A number of theories have been proposed to explain why civilizations develop. Most of them emphasize the interrelation of people and what they do on the one hand, and their environment on the other. For example, some civilizations may have developed as populations grew, causing competition for space and scarce resources, which necessitated the development of centralized authority to control resources and organize warfare. Some civilizations, though, appear to have developed as a result of certain beliefs and values which brought people together into large, heavily populated centers, again necessitating centralized authority to manage the problems—of which there are many—of living in such a way. Thus, it may be that civilizations arose in different places for somewhat different reasons.

A walk down a street of a busy North American city brings us in contact with numerous activities that are essential to the well-being of North American society. The sidewalks are crowded with people going to and from offices and stores. The traffic of cars, taxis, and trucks is heavy, sometimes almost at a standstill. In a brief two-block stretch, there may be a department store, shops selling clothing, appliances, or books, a restaurant, a newsstand, a gasoline station, and a movie theater. Perhaps there will also be a museum, a police station, a school, a hospital, or a church. That is quite a number of services and specialized skills to find in such a small area.

Each of these services or places of business is dependent on others. A butcher shop, for instance, depends on slaughterhouses and beef ranches. A clothing store depends on designers, farmers who produce cotton and wool, and workers who manufacture synthetic fibers. Restaurants depend on refrigerated trucking and vegetable and dairy farmers. Hospitals depend on a great variety of other institutions to meet their more complex needs. All

institutions, finally, depend on the public utilities—the telephone, gas, and electric companies. Although interdependence is not immediately apparent to the passerby, it is an important aspect of modern cities.

The interdependence of goods and services in a big city is what makes so many products readily available to people. For example, refrigerated air transport makes it possible to buy fresh California artichokes on the East Coast. This same interdependence, however, has undesirable effects if one service stops functioning, for example, because of strikes or bad weather. Thus, every so often, major North American cities have had to do without services as vital as newspapers, subways, schools, and trash removal. The question is not so much "Why does this happen?" but rather "Why doesn't it happen more often, and why does the city continue to function as well as it does when one of its services stops?" The answer is that services are not only interdependent, but they are also adaptable. When one breaks down, others take over its functions. During a long newspaper strike in New

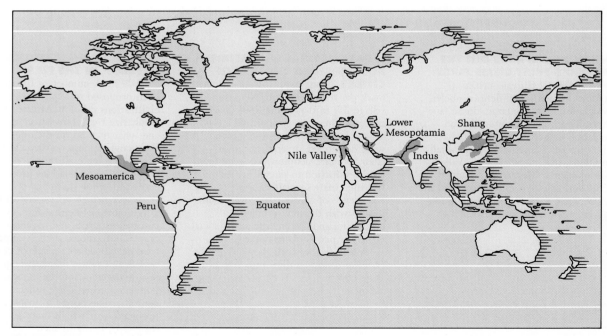

Figure 10.1   The major early civilizations sprang from Neolithic villages in various parts of the world. Those of North and South America developed wholly independently of those in Africa and Asia; Chinese civilization may well have developed independently of Southwest Asian (including the Nile and Indus) civilizations.

York City in the 1960s, for example, several new magazines were launched, and television expanded its coverage of news and events.

On the surface, city life seems so orderly that we take it for granted, but a moment's pause reminds us that the intricate fabric of city life did not always exist, and the goods which are so accessible to us were once simply not available.

WHAT CIVILIZATION MEANS

This complicated system of goods and services available in such a small space is a mark of civilization itself. The history of civilization is intimately bound up with the history of cities. This does not mean that civilization is to be equated with modern industrial cities or with present-day North American society. People as diverse as the ancient preindustrial Aztecs and the industrial North Americans of today are included in the term "civilization," but each represents a very different kind. It was with the development of the earliest preindustrial cities, however, that civilization first developed (Figure 10.1). In fact, the word comes from the Latin *civis*, which refers to one who is an inhabitant of a city, and *civitas*, which refers to the community in which one dwells. The word "civilization" contains the idea of "citification," or "the coming-to-be of cities."

THE EMERGENCE OF CIVILIZATION

The world's first cities sprang up in some parts of the world as Neolithic villages grew into towns, some of which in turn grew into cities. This happened first in Mesopotamia (in modern-day Iraq), then in Egypt and the Indus Valley, between 6000 and 4500 years ago. The inhabitants of Sumer, in southern Mesopotamia, developed the world's first civilization about 5000 years ago. In China, civilization was under way by 4100 years ago. Independent of these developments in the Old World, the first cities appeared in Mesoamerica and Peru 2000 and 3000 years ago.

What characterized these first cities? Why are they called the birthplaces of civilization? The first characteristic of cities—and of civilization—is

their large size and population. But the first cities were far more than expanded Neolithic villages. The changes that took place in the transition from village to city were so great that the emergence of urban living is considered by some to be one of the great "revolutions" in human culture. The following case study gives us a glimpse of one of the world's ancient cities, how it was studied by archaeologists, and how it may have grown from a smaller farming community.

TIKAL: A CASE STUDY

The ancient city of Tikal, one of the largest lowland Maya centers in existence, is situated about 200 miles by air from Guatemala City. Tikal was built on a broad limestone terrace in a rainforest setting. Here the Maya settled in the last millennium B.C., and their civilization flourished until about A.D. 869.

At its height, Tikal covered about 120.5 square kilometers, and its nucleus, or "epicenter," was the Great Plaza, a large, paved area surrounded by about 300 major structures and thousands of houses. Starting from a small, dispersed population, the population of Tikal swelled to large proportions. By A.D. 600, the density of Tikal was on the order of 600 to 700 persons per square kilometer, six times that of the surrounding regions.

From 1956 through the 1960s, Tikal and the surrounding region were intensively explored under the joint auspices of the University Museum of the University of Pennsylvania and the Guatemalan government. Until 1959, the Tikal Project had investigated only the major temple and palace structures found in the vicinity of the Great Plaza, at the site's epicenter. It became evident, however, that in order to gain a balanced view of Tikal's develop-

The buildings shown here make up the civic and ceremonial heart of Tikal. In the foreground are the palaces where the city's rulers lived and carried out their administrative tasks. Beyond are the temples erected over the tombs of past kings.

ment and composition, considerable attention would have to be devoted to hundreds of small mounds, thought to be the remains of dwellings, which surround the larger buildings. Just as one cannot get a realistic view of Washington, D.C., by looking at its monumental public buildings alone, so one cannot obtain a realistic view of Tikal without examining the full range of ruins in the area.

It became evident that a long-range program of excavation of small structures, most of which were probably houses, was necessary at Tikal. Such a program would provide some basis for an estimate of the city's population size and density; this information is critical to test the traditional assumption that the Maya could not have sustained large concentrations of population because their subsistence patterns were not adequate. Extensive excavation would also provide a sound basis for a reconstruction of the everyday life of the Maya, previously known almost entirely through a study of ceremonial remains. Moreover, the excavation might shed light on the social organization of the Maya. For example, differences in house construction and in the quality and quantity of associated remains might suggest social class differences, or features of house distribution might indicate the

existence of extended families or other types of kin groups. The excavation of both large and small structures could reveal the variations in architecture and associated artifacts and burials; such variations might reflect the social structure of the total population of Tikal.

SURVEYING THE SITE

Six square kilometers surrounding the Great Plaza had already been extensively surveyed by mapping crews by the time the first excavations of small structures were undertaken. For this mapping, aerial photography was worthless because the tree canopy in this area is often 100 feet above the ground and obscures all but the tallest temples; many of the small ruins are practically invisible even to the observer on the ground. The only way to explore the region is on foot. Once a ruin is found, it is not easy to mark its exact location. After four years of careful mapping, the limits of the site still had not been revealed. Ancient Tikal was far larger than the six square kilometers so far surveyed. More time and money were required to continue surveying the area in order to define the city's boundaries. To simplify this problem, straight survey trails oriented toward the four cardinal directions, with the Great Plaza as the center point, were cut through the forest, measured, and staked by government surveyors. The distribution of ruins was plotted, using the trails as reference points, and the overall size of Tikal was estimated.

The area selected for the first small structure excavation was surveyed in 1957 while it was still covered by forest. A map was drawn, and two years later the first excavations were undertaken. Six structures, two plazas, and a platform were investigated. The original plan was to strip each of the structures to bedrock, in order to obtain every bit of information possible. Three obstacles prevented this, however. First was the discovery of new structures not visible before excavation; second, the structures turned out to be much more complex architecturally than anyone had expected; and, finally, the enormous quantity of artifacts found then had to be washed and cataloged, a time-consuming process. Consequently, not every structure was completely excavated, and some remained uninvestigated.

EVIDENCE FROM THE EXCAVATION

Following this initial work, more than 100 additional small structures were excavated in different parts of the site, in order to ensure that a representative sample was investigated. Numerous test pits were sunk in various other small structure groups to supplement the information gained from more extensive excavations.

Excavation at Tikal revealed evidence of trade in nonperishable items. Granite, quartzite, hematite, pyrite, jade, slate, and obsidian were all imported, either as raw materials or finished products. Marine materials came from Atlantic and Pacific coastal areas. Tikal itself is located on a source of abundant flint, which may have been exported in the form of raw material and finished objects. The site also happens to be located between two river systems to the east and west, and so may have been on a major overland trade route between the two. There is indirect evidence that trade went on in perishable goods such as textiles, feathers, salt, and cacao. We can safely conclude that there were full-time traders among the Tikal Maya.

In the realm of technology, specialized wood-

Carved monuments like this were commissioned by Tikal's rulers to commemorate important events in their reigns. Portrayed on this one is a king who ruled between A.D. 768 and A.D. 790 or a bit later. Such skilled stone carving could only have been accomplished by a specialist. (For a translation of the inscription, see Figure 10.3.)

working, pottery, obsidian, and shell workshops have been found. The skillful stone carving displayed by carved monuments suggests that this was done by occupational specialists. The complex Maya calendar required astronomers, and in order to control the large population, estimated to have been at least 50,000 people, there must have been some form of bureaucratic organization. We do know that the government was headed by a hereditary ruling dynasty. Although we do not have direct evidence, there are clues to the existence of textile workers, dental workers, makers of bark cloth "paper," and other occupational specialists.

The religion of the Tikal Maya probably developed as a means to cope with the uncertainties of agriculture. When people are faced with problems unsolvable by technological or organizational means, they resort to manipulation of magic and the supernatural. Soils at Tikal are thin, and there is no water except that which can be collected in ponds. Rain is abundant in season, but its onset tends to be unreliable. Once the wet season arrives, there may be dry spells of varying duration which can seriously affect crop productivity. Or there may be too much rain, so that crops rot in the fields. Other risks include storm damage, locust plagues, and incursions of wild animals. To this day, the native inhabitants of the region display great concern about these very real risks involved in agriculture over which they have no direct control.

The Maya priesthood devoted much of its time to calendrical matters; the priests tried not only to placate the deities in times of drought but also to propitiate them in times of plenty. They determined the most auspicious time to plant crops and were concerned with other agricultural matters. The dependence of the population in and around Tikal upon their priesthood to manipulate supernatural beings and forces in their behalf, in order that their crops would not fail, tended to keep them in or near the city, in spite of the fact that a slash-and-burn method of agriculture, which was probably the prevailing method early in Tikal's history, required the constant shifting of plots and consequently tended to disperse the population over large areas.

As the population increased, land for agriculture became scarcer, and the Maya were forced to find new methods of food production that could sustain the dense population concentrated at Tikal. From slash-and-burn agriculture as their main form of subsistence, they turned to collecting the very nutritious fruit of the breadnut tree for food. It may be that breadnut trees were abundant and the fruit could be easily picked. Along with increased reliance on breadnuts for subsistence went the construction of artificially raised fields in areas that were flooded each rainy season. In these fields, crops could be intensively cultivated year after year, so long as they were carefully maintained. As these changes were taking place, a class of artisans, craftspeople, and other occupational specialists emerged to serve the needs first of religion, then of an elite consisting of the priesthood and a ruling dynasty. The arts flourished, and numerous temples, public buildings, and houses were built.

For several hundred years, Tikal was able to

This clay tablet map of farmland outside of the Mesopotamian city of Nippur dates to 1300 B.C. Shown are irrigation canals separating the various fields, each of which is identified with the name of the owner.

sustain its ever-growing population. Then the pressure for food and land reached a critical point, and population growth was halted. This event is marked archaeologically by a pullback from prime land, by the advent of nutritional problems as evidenced by the bones from burials, and by the construction of a system of ditches and embankments that probably served in the defense of the city and as a means of regulating commerce by limiting its accessibility. In other words, a period of readjustment set in, which must have been directed by an already strong central authority. Activities then continued as before, but without further population growth for another 250 years or so.

CITIES AND CULTURAL CHANGE

If someone who grew up in a small village of Maine, Wyoming, or Mississippi were to move to Chicago, Detroit, or Los Angeles, that person

One technique of agricultural intensification used by the Maya reclaimed swamp land by excavating canals between plots of land to drain excess water. The system shown here served until ca. A.D. 200, by which time rising water levels made further use impossible.

would experience a number of marked changes in his or her way of life. Some of the same changes in daily life would have been felt 5000 years ago by a Neolithic village dweller upon moving into one of the world's first cities in Mesopotamia. Of course, the differences would be less extreme today. In the twentieth century, every North American village, however small, is part of civilization; back when cities first developed, they were civilization, and the villages for the most part represented a continuation of Neolithic life.

Four basic culture changes mark the transition from Neolithic village life to life in the first urban centers.

AGRICULTURAL INNOVATION

The first culture change characteristic of life in cities—hence, of civilization itself—was change in farming methods. The ancient Sumerians, for example, built an extensive system of dikes, canals, and reservoirs to irrigate their farmlands. With such a system, they could control water resources at will; water could be held and then run off into the

fields as necessary. Irrigation was an important factor affecting an increase of crop yields. Because farming could now be carried on independently of the seasons, more crops could be harvested in one year. On the other hand, this intensification of agriculture did not necessarily mean that people ate better than before. Under centralized governments, intensification was generally carried out with less regard for human health than when such governments did not exist.[1]

The ancient Maya who lived at Tikal developed systems of tree cultivation and constructed raised fields in seasonally flooded swamplands to supplement their earlier slash-and-burn farming. The resultant increase in crop yields provided for a higher population density. Increased crop yields, resulting from agricultural innovations such as those of the ancient Maya and Sumerians, were probably a factor contributing to the high population densities of all civilized societies.

---

[1] Anna C. Roosevelt, "Population, Health, and the Evolution of Subsistence: Conclusions from the Conference," in *Paleopathology and the Origins of Agriculture*, eds. Mark N. Cohen and George J. Armelagos (Orlando, Fla.: Academic Press, 1984), p. 568.

ANTHROPOLOGY APPLIED

ECONOMIC DEVELOPMENT AND TROPICAL FORESTS

Prime targets for development in the world today, in the eyes of governments and private corporations alike, are vast tracts of tropical forests. On a global basis, forests are being rapidly cleared for lumber and fuel, as well as to make way for farms, ranches, mines, and other forms of economic development. The world's largest uninterrupted tracts are the forests of the Amazon and Orinoco watersheds of South America, which are being destroyed at about the rate of 4 percent a year. Just what the rate is for the world as a whole no one is quite sure, but it is clearly accelerating. And already there are signs of trouble, as extensive tracts of once-lush growth have been converted to semi-desert. What happens is that essential nutrients are lost, either through erosion (which increases by several orders of magnitude under deforestation), or by leaching too deeply, as soils are exposed to the direct force of the heavy tropical rains.

The problem is that developers, until recently, have lacked reliable models by which the long-term impact of their actions might be assessed. Such a model now exists, thanks to the efforts of archaeologists unraveling the mystery of how the ancient Maya, in a tropical rain-forest setting, carried out large-scale urban construction and sustained huge numbers of people successfully for two millennia. The key to the Maya success was their implementation of sophisticated practices to reduce re-gion-wide processes of nutrient loss, deterioration of soil structure, destabilization of water flows, soil erosion, and loss of productive components of their environment.* These included construction of terraces, canals, and raised fields, the fertility of which was maintained through mulching with water plants and the addition of organic wastes. Coupled with all this, crops were planted in such a way as to produce complex patterns of foliage distribution, canopy heights, and nutrient demands. Far different from "modern" monocrop agriculture, this reduced the impact on the soils of intensive farming, while making maximum use of nutrients and enhancing their cycling in the system.

In Mexico, where population growth has threatened the country's ability to provide sufficient food for its people, archaeologists and agriculturalists are already cooperating to apply our knowledge of ancient Maya techniques to the problems of modern food production in the tropics. Application of these techniques in other tropical forested countries, like Brazil, could do much to alleviate food shortages.

* Don S. Rice and Prudence M. Rice, "Lessons from the Maya" *Latin American Research Review*, 19(3) (1984):24–28.

DIVERSIFICATION OF LABOR

The second culture change characteristic of civilization is diversification of labor. In a Neolithic village that possessed neither irrigation nor plow farming, the members of every family were primarily concerned with the raising of crops. The high crop yields made possible by new farming methods and the increased population freed more and more people from farming. For the first time, a sizable number of people were available to pursue nonagricultural activities on a full-time basis. In the early cities, some people still farmed, but a large number of the inhabitants were skilled workers or craftspeople.

Ancient public records indicate there was a considerable variety of such skilled workers. For example, an early Mesopotamian document from the city of Lagash lists the artisans, craftspeople, and others paid from crop surpluses stored in the temple granaries. Among them were coppersmiths, silversmiths, sculptors, merchants, potters, tanners, engravers, butchers, carpenters, spinners, barbers, cabinetmakers, bakers, clerks, and brewers. At the ancient Maya city of Tikal we have evidence for traders, potters, woodworkers, obsidian workers, sculptors, and perhaps textile workers, dental workers, shell workers, and paper makers.

With specialization came the expertise that led to the invention of new and novel ways of making

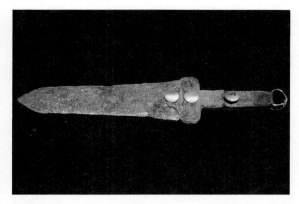 

Bronze tools and weapons were more durable than their stone counterparts, which were more easily broken. The bronze sword (left) comes from Mycenae, Greece, dating to about 1200 B.C. The ear pendant from Greece of about the same age is a fine example of the artistry that became possible with the introduction of bronze.

Aztec spears tipped and edged with obsidian blades are shown in this sixteenth-century drawing of battle with their Spanish conquerors. Though superior to steel for piercing, cutting, and slashing, the brittleness of obsidian placed the Aztecs at a disadvantage when faced with Spanish swords.

and doing things. In the Old World, civilization ushered in what archaeologists often refer to as the **Bronze Age**, a period marked by the production of tools and ornaments of this metal. Metals were in great demand for the manufacture of farmers' and artisans' tools, as well as for weapons. Copper, tin (the raw materials from which bronze is made), and eventually iron were separated from their ores, then smelted, purified, and cast to make plows, swords, axes, and shields. In wars over border disputes or to extend a state's territory, stone knives, spears, and slings could not stand up against bronze spears, arrowheads, swords, or armor.

The native civilizations of the Americas also made use of metals—in South America, for tools as well as ceremonial and ornamental objects, but in Mesoamerica, for ceremonial and ornamental objects alone. Why people like the Aztecs and Maya continued to rely on stone for their everyday tools has puzzled those who assume that metal is inherently superior. The answer, however, is simple: The availability of obsidian (a glass formed by volcanic activity), its extreme sharpness (many

Bronze Age: In the Old World, the period marked by the production of tools and ornaments of bronze; began about 3000 B.C., in Southwest Asia.

times sharper than the finest steel) and the ease with which it could be worked made it perfectly suited to their needs.

In order to procure the raw materials needed for their technologies, extensive trade systems were developed by the early civilizations. Extensive trade agreements were maintained with distant peoples, not only to secure basic raw materials but to provide luxury items as well.

Boats gave greater access to trade centers; they could easily carry back to cities large loads of imports at less cost than if they had been brought back overland. A one-way trip from Egypt to the northern city of Byblos in Phoenicia took only four to eight days by rowboat. With a sailboat, it took even less.

Egyptian pharaohs sent expeditions to the Sinai Peninsula for copper, to Nubia for gold, to Arabia for spices and perfumes, to Asia for lapis lazuli (a blue semiprecious stone) and other jewels, to Lebanon for cedar, wine, and funerary oils, and to central Africa for ivory, ebony, ostrich feathers, leopard skins, cattle, and slaves.

With technological innovation, along with increased contact with foreign peoples through trade, came new knowledge. It was within the early civilizations that sciences such as geometry and astronomy were first developed. Geometry was used by the Egyptians for such purposes as measuring the area of a field or staking off an accurate right angle at the corner of a building.

Astronomy grew out of the need to know when to plant and harvest crops or to hold religious observances and to find exact bearings on voyages. Astronomy and mathematics were used to devise calendars. The Maya calculated that the solar year was 365 days (actually, it is 365 1/4 days), accurately predicted the appearances of the planet Venus as the morning and evening "star," and were able to predict eclipses. The Babylonians were able to calculate the exact date of the new moon.

CENTRAL GOVERNMENT

The third culture change characteristic of civilization is the emergence of a governing elite, a strong central authority required to deal with the many problems arising within the new cities, owing to their size and complexity. The new governing elite saw to it that different interest groups, such as

Among the occupational specialists in ancient civilizations were astronomers. This structure, at the ancient Maya city of Chichen Itza in Mexico, was built as an observatory.

farmers, craftsmen, or moneylenders, provided the services that were expected of them and did not infringe on each other's rights. It ensured that the city was safe from its enemies by constructing walls and raising an army. It levied taxes and appointed tax collectors so that construction workers, the army, and other public expenses could be paid. It saw to it that merchants, carpenters, or farmers who made legal claims received justice. It guaranteed safety for the lives and property of ordinary people and assured that any harm done one person by another would be justly dealt with. In addition, surplus food had to be stored for times of scarcity, and public works such as extensive irrigation systems had to be supervised by competent, detached individuals. The mechanisms of government served all these functions.

EVIDENCE OF CENTRALIZED AUTHORITY

Evidence of a centralized authority in ancient civilizations comes from such sources as law codes, temple records, and royal chronicles. Excavation of

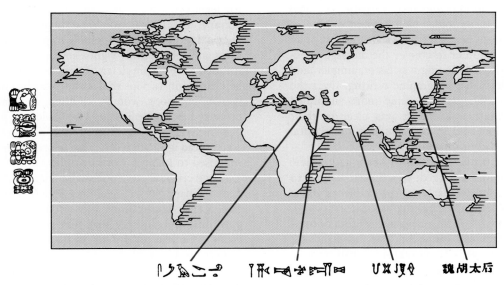

Figure 10.2 The impermanence of spoken words contrasts with the relative permanence of written records. In all of human history, writing has been independently invented no more than five times.

the city structures themselves provides further evidence. For example, archaeologists believe that the cities of Mohenjodaro and Harappa in the Indus Valley were governed by a centralized authority because they show definite signs of city planning. They are both over three miles long; their main streets are laid out in a rectangular grid pattern, and both contain citywide drainage systems.

Monumental buildings and temples, palaces, and large sculptures are usually found in civilizations. The Maya city of Tikal contained more than 300 major structures, including temples, ball courts, and "palaces" (residences of the aristocracy). The Pyramid of the Sun in the pre-Aztec city of Teotihuacan is 700 feet long and over 200 feet high. Its interior is filled by more than one million cubic yards of sun-dried bricks. The tomb of the Egyptian pharaoh Cheops, known as the Great Pyramid, is 755 feet long and 481 feet high. It contains about 2,300,000 stone blocks, each with an average weight of 2.5 tons. The Greek historian Herodotus reports that it took 100,000 men 20 years to build this tomb. Such gigantic structures could be built only because the considerable manpower, engineering skills, and raw materials necessary for their

construction could be harnessed by a powerful central authority.

Another indicator of the existence of centralized authority is writing (Figure 10.2). In the Old World, early governments found it useful to keep records of state affairs, such as accounts of their food surplus, tribute records, and other business receipts. The earliest documents appear to be just such records—lists of vegetables and animals bought and sold, tax lists, and storehouse inventories. Writing was an extremely important invention, because governments could keep records of their assets instead of simply relying upon the memory of administrators.

Prior to 5000 years ago, "writing" consisted of pictures drawn or carved on stone, bone, or shell to commemorate a notable event, such as a hunt, a military victory, or the deed of some king. The earliest picture–writing—called pictographs—functioned much like historical paintings or newspaper photos.

The figures in such pictures gradually became simplified and generalized and stood for ideas of things, rather than for the things themselves. Thus, a royal palace could be represented by a simple stick drawing of a house with a crown placed above it.

This representation of the idea of a palace is called an ideogram. In the older pictographic writing, it would have been necessary to draw a likeness of an actual palace in order to convey the message effectively. Ideographic writing was faster, simpler, and more flexible than pictographic writing. Over the centuries the ideograms became more simplified and, although their meaning was clear to their users, they looked less and less like the natural objects they had originally depicted.

In Mesopotamia, about 6000 years ago, a new writing technique emerged, which used a stylus to make wedge-shaped markings on a tablet of damp clay. Originally, each marking stood for a word. Since most words in this language were monosyllabic, the markings came, in time, to stand for syllables. There were about 600 signs, half of them ideograms, the others functioning either as ideograms or as syllables.

In the New World, systems of writing came into use among various Mesoamerican peoples, but the most sophisticated was that of the Maya. Their hieroglyphic system had less to do with keeping track of state belongings than with "dynastic bombast." Maya lords glorified themselves by recording their dynastic genealogies, important conquests, and royal marriages, by using grandiose titles to refer to themselves, and by associating their actions with important astrological events (Figure 10.3). Often, the latter involved complicated mathematical calculations.

THE EARLIEST GOVERNMENTS

The government organization of the earliest cities was typically headed by a king and his special advisers. In addition, there were sometimes councils of lesser advisers. Formal laws were enacted and courts sat in judgment over the claims of rival litigants or the criminal charges brought by the government against an individual.

Of the many ancient kings known, one stands out as truly remarkable for the efficient government organization and highly developed legal system that characterized his reign. This is Hammurabi, the Babylonian king who lived sometime between 1950 and 1700 B.C. He promulgated a set of laws for his kingdom, known as the Code of Hammurabi, which is important because of its thorough detail and standardization. It prescribes the correct form

for legal procedures and determines penalties for perjury, false accusation, and injustice done by judges. It contains laws applying to property rights, loans and debts, family rights, and damages paid for malpractice by a physician. There are fixed rates to be charged in various trades and branches of commerce. The poor, women, children, and slaves are protected against injustice. The Code was publicly displayed on huge stone slabs so that no one accused could plead ignorance. Even the poorest citizen was supposed to know his or her rights.

Some civilizations flourished under a ruler with extraordinary governing abilities, such as Hammurabi. Other civilizations possessed a widespread governing bureaucracy that was very efficient at every level. The government of the Inca civilization is a case in point.

The Inca empire of Peru reached its zenith in the sixteenth century A.D., just before the arrival of the Spanish. In the mid-1400s, the Inca kingdom probably did not extend more than 20 miles beyond the modern-day city of Cuzco, which was then its center. Within a 30-year period, in the late 1400s, the Inca kingdom enlarged a thousand times its original size. By A.D. 1525, it stretched 2500 miles from north to south and 500 miles from east to west, making it at the time the greatest empire on the face of the earth. Its population numbered in the millions, composed of people of various ethnic groups. In the achievements of its governmental and political system, Inca civilization surpassed every other civilization of the New World and most of those of the Old World. At the head of the government was the emperor, regarded as semidivine, followed by the royal family, the aristocracy, imperial administrators, the lower nobility, and the masses of artisans, craftsmen, and farmers.

The empire was divided into four administrative regions, further subdivided into provinces, and so on down to villages and families. Planting, irrigation, and harvesting were closely supervised by government agricultural experts and tax officials. Teams of professional relay runners could carry messages up to 250 miles in a single day over a network of roads and bridges that remains impressive even today. The Inca are unusual in that they had no writing that we know about; public records and historical chronicles were kept in the form of an ingenious system of colored beads, knots, and ropes.

Figure 10.3 Translation of the text on the monument shown on page 255 gives some indication of the importance of dynastic genealogy to Mayan rulers. The "scattering" mentioned may refer to bloodletting as part of the ceremonies associated with the end of one 20-year period, or *Katun*, and the beginning of the next.

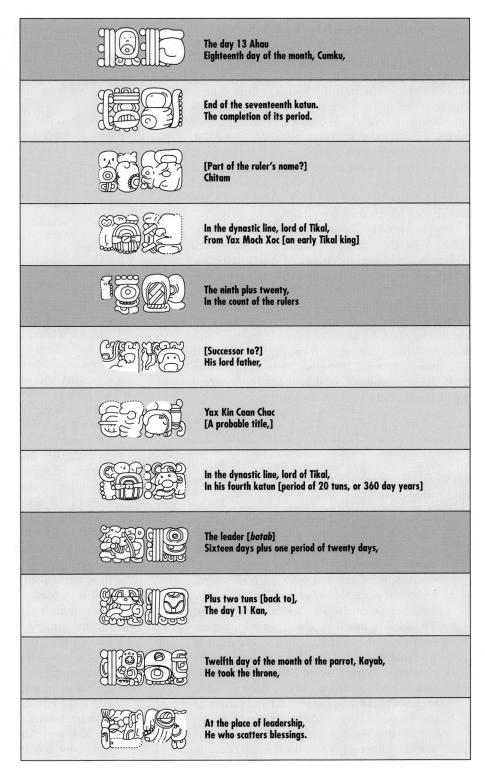

The day 13 Ahau
Eighteenth day of the month, Cumku,

End of the seventeenth katun.
The completion of its period.

[Part of the ruler's name?]
Chitam

In the dynastic line, lord of Tikal,
From Yax Moch Xoc [an early Tikal king]

The ninth plus twenty,
In the count of the rulers

[Successor to?]
His lord father,

Yax Kin Caan Chac
[A probable title,]

In the dynastic line, lord of Tikal,
In his fourth katun [period of 20 tuns, or 360 day years]

The leader [*batab*]
Sixteen days plus one period of twenty days,

Plus two tuns [back to],
The day 11 Kan,

Twelfth day of the month of the parrot, Kayab,
He took the throne,

At the place of leadership,
He who scatters blessings.

SOCIAL STRATIFICATION

The rise of large, economically diversified populations presided over by centralized governing authorities brought with it the fourth culture change characteristic of civilization: social stratification, or the emergence of social classes. The nature of social stratification is discussed in Chapter 20. Here we may note that symbols of special status and privilege appeared for the first time in the ancient cities of Mesopotamia, and people were ranked according to the kind of work they did or the family into which they were born.

People who stood at or near the head of government were the earliest holders of high status. Although economic specialists of one sort or another—metalworkers, tanners, traders, or the like—generally outranked farmers, such specialization did not necessarily bring with it high status. Rather, people engaged in economic activity were either of the lower class or outcasts.[2] The exception was those merchants who were in a position to buy their way into some kind of higher class status. With time, the possession of wealth, and the influence it could buy, became in itself a requisite for status.

EVIDENCE OF SOCIAL STRATIFICATION

How do archaeologists know that there were different social classes in ancient civilizations? There are four main ways:

1. *Burial customs.* Graves excavated at early Neolithic sites are mostly simple pits dug in the ground, containing few, if any, grave goods. Grave goods consist of things such as utensils, figurines, and personal possessions, which are placed in the grave in order that the dead person might use them in the afterlife. The lack of much variation between burials in terms of the wealth implied by grave goods in Neolithic sites indicates an essentially classless society. Graves excavated in civilizations, by contrast, vary widely in size, mode of burial, and the number and variety of grave goods. This indicates a stratified society—one divided into social classes. The graves of important persons contain not only

This "palace," which housed members of Tikal's ruling dynasty, may be compared with the lower class house in the next photo.

a great variety of artifacts made from precious materials, but sometimes, as in some early Egyptian burials, even the remains of servants evidently killed to serve their master in his afterlife. The skeletons from the burials may also give evidence of stratification. At Tikal, skeletons from elaborate tombs indicate that the subjects of these tombs had longer life expectancy, ate better food, and enjoyed better health than the bulk of that city's population. In stratified societies, the elite usually live longer, eat better, and enjoy an easier life than other members of society.

2. *The size of dwellings.* In early Neolithic sites, dwellings tended to be uniformly small in size. In the oldest excavated cities, however, some dwellings were notably larger than others, well spaced, and located together in one district, whereas dwellings in other parts of the city were much smaller, sometimes little more than hovels. In the city of Eshnunna in Mesopotamia, archaeologists excavated houses that occupied an area of 200 meters situated on main thoroughfares, and huts of but 50 meters located along narrow back alleys. The rooms in the larger houses often contained impressive artwork, such as friezes or murals. At Tikal, and other Maya cities, the elite lived in large masonry, multi-roomed houses, mostly in the city's center, while lower-class people lived in small, peripherally scattered houses of one or two rooms, built partly or wholly of pole and thatch materials.

3. *Written documents.* Preserved records of

[2] Gideon Sjoberg, *The Preindustrial City* (New York: Free Press, 1960), p. 325.

Lower-class residents of Tikal lived in the same sort of houses in which most Maya live today.

business transactions, royal chronicles, or law codes of a civilization reveal much about the social status of its inhabitants. Babylonian and Assyrian texts reveal three main social classes—aristocrats, commoners, and slaves. The members of each class had different rights and privileges. This stratification was clearly reflected by the law. If an aristocrat put out another's eye, then that person's eye was to be put out too. Hence, the saying "an eye for an eye . . ." If the aristocrat broke another's bone, then the first aristocrat's bone was broken in return. If the aristocrat put out the eye or broke the bone of a commoner, however, the punishment was to pay a mina of silver.[3]

4. *Correspondence*. European documents describing the aboriginal cultures of the New World as seen by visitors and explorers also offer evidence of social stratification. Letters written by the Spanish Conquistadors about the Aztec empire indicate that they found a social order divided into three main classes: nobles, commoners, and serfs. The nobles operated outside the lineage system on the basis of land and serfs allotted them by the

ruler from conquered peoples. The commoners were divided into lineages, on which they were dependent for land. Within each of these, individual status depended on the degree of descent from the founder; those more closely related to the lineage founder had higher status than those whose kinship was more distant. The third class in Aztec society consisted of serfs bound to the land and porters employed as carriers by merchants. Lowest of this class were the slaves. Some had voluntarily sold themselves into bondage; others were captives taken in war.

Informative though written records may be, they are not without their problems. For example, European explorers did not always understand what they saw; moreover, they had their own interests (or those of their sponsors) to look out for, and were not above falsifying information to further those interests. These points are of major importance, given the tendency of Western peoples, with their long tradition of literacy, to assume that written documents are reliable. In fact, they are not always reliable, and must be checked for accuracy against other sources of information. The same is true of ancient documents written by other people about themselves, for they, too, had their particular agendas. A case in point is provided by the following Original Study.

[3] Sabatino Moscati, *The Face of the Ancient Orient* (New York: Doubleday, 1962), p. 90.

ORIGINAL STUDY

STAR WARS AT TIKAL, OR DID CARACOL DO WHAT THE GLYPHS SAY THEY DID?[4]

In 1986, discovery of a ballcourt marker at the Maya city of Caracol, bearing a text in which is recorded a "Star War" event at Tikal, created something of a sensation. Apparently recording a military defeat of Tikal by Caracol, it has become commonplace to use the word "conquest" in referring to this event. Unfortunately, this word has a certain ambiguity to it. While it clearly means "the gaining of victory," it may or may not at the same time have the meaning: "to get possession of," or "to acquire." Often, the word is used in this latter sense, to connote an actual political takeover. To cite but one example, Schele and Freidel in their book *Forest of Kings*, imply such a takeover by likening Tikal's defeat to an earlier victory over Uaxactun by Tikal, at which time they assert that the victors wiped out Uaxactun's dynasty and took political control. As they put it: "Caracol had mastered the same Tlaloc-Venus war that had defeated Uaxactun two centuries earlier" (p. 173), and "Tikal had been undone by the very same Tlaloc-Venus war that the brothers Great Jaguar Paw and Smoking Frog had waged against Uaxactun 180 years earlier." (p. 179). Elsewhere, we are told that "Lord Water's war had indeed broken the back of Tikal's pride, *independence* [italics mine], and prosperity" (p. 173), and that "Double Bird [Tikal's losing King] had no doubt been captured and killed, his dynasty ended, and his remaining ahauob [nobles] cut off from the vast trade routes that provided their wealth" (p. 174, see also p. 179).

Reasonable though this scenario may seem in the abstract, we need to ask, is it really justified in terms of what we actually know? Assuming that Caracol did in fact achieve a military victory over Tikal, does this necessarily mean that they took political control of Tikal, or even that they actually killed its king? In order to deal with these questions we must look to the archaeological record for assistance.

Evidentially the King of Tikal at the time of the "Star War" event was Double Bird, who is listed on Stela 17 as the 21st successor of Yax Moch Xoc, surely not Tikal's first king, but the one from whom rulers of the Classic period counted their reigns. Stela 17 also tells us that Double Bird took office on 9.5.3.9.15, in A.D. 537, a katun [a 20-year period in the Maya calendar] earlier than the last certain date on the monument (9.6.3.9.15, or A.D. 557). A mere five years after this latter date is when Caracol achieved its victory.

On the basis of this information, Double Bird's reign is placed within Time Span 6 of Tikal's Group 5D-2, which archaeologist William Coe estimates to have run from about 9.2.0.0.0 (A.D. 475) to ca. 9.8.0.0.0 (A.D. 593). A major piece of construction undertaken during this period was Structure (Str.) 5D-22–1st which, until the much later construction of Str. 5D-33–1st (probably no earlier than A.D. 682, when Ruler A came to power) was the tallest temple ever built at Tikal, and clearly the North Acropolis' paramount edifice. Coe's best estimate for the time of its construction is midway through Time Span 6, which places it right about the time of Double Bird's accession.

At the center of Caracol in Belize is this massive acropolis.

Thus, it seems probable, though not provable, either that Double Bird was responsible for its construction as one of his first acts upon taking power, or that it was commissioned specifically to coincide with his inauguration.

After a period of use during which, from time to time, cached offerings were placed beneath the structure's floors, a tomb (Burial 200) was intruded into the fill of 22–1st. Unfortunately, in Terminal Classic times, this tomb was looted by the Maya themselves in a quest for jade and other items of value, so we do not know the identity of the individual whose corpse was originally placed here, nor can the interment be precisely dated. We do know that Ik pottery [a type in use between ca. A.D. 550 and 700] was placed in the chamber, and that it probably predates Burial 195, which itself dates around 9.8.0.0.0 (A.D. 593). In fact, Coe states that "It cannot be ruled out . . . that . . . Burial 200 . . . belonged to the very same personage who commissioned 22–1st"(*Tikal Report No. 14*, p. 839). Furthermore, considering its placement on the important central axis of the North Acropolis, within Tikal's paramount building, it is hard to imagine Burial 200 being that of anyone other than a king. As were other royal tombs, this one was overlain by masses of flint flakes and obsidian debris; within were placed at least nine pottery vessels, numerous flint and obsidian eccentrics, jade and shell mosaic items, a broad range of marine items, and two teenage sacrificial victims (the standard number for royal tombs at Tikal from the time of Stormy Sky's Burial 48 until Burial 195 established the practice of excluding such victims). The presence of other jade jewelry as well as spondylous shells is implied by the subsequent looting by people known to have been looking for precisely such items. In fact at least one, but possibly three, jade beads found in or near the ransacked tomb seem to represent pieces of jewelry dropped or overlooked by the looters as they went about their work.

If Burial 200 was in fact a king's tomb—and to me no other conclusion seems reasonable—then it is unlikely to be that of anyone but Double Bird. Later than his inauguration, placed within the building associated with his reign, and earlier than Burial 195 in which was placed the body of his successor (of which more in a moment), no other possibility seems likely. It is even possible that the entombment dates from about the time of the Caracol victory, by which time Ik pottery may recently have come into production. If Double Bird did die in battle, or was killed soon afterward by the victors, this does not appear to have interfered with his burial in full regal splendor. Indeed, in view of such treatment, we may wonder if he might not have survived Caracol's victory to die a natural death at some later time. In support of this is what appears to be a distance number on Stela 17 leading to a date five years *after* the "Star War" event.

Whether or not Double Bird met his end at the hands of Lord Water, it is evident that his death did not mark the demise of Tikal's dynasty, or even the end of the city's prosperity. In Burial 195, which probably dates not long after 9.8.0.0.0 (A.D. 593) lies the body of a ruler who epigrapher Christopher Jones calls Animal Skull. Not much is known about him, since we have no carved monuments associated with his reign, but a plate included in his grave bears not only his name glyph, but a notation that he was the 22nd successor of Yax Moch Xoc. During his reign, he was responsible for a very rich offering made in Structure 5D-22-1st, his predecessor's temple and last resting place. This is Cache 185 which, in addition to lots of shells and other marine items, eccentric flints and obsidians, incised obsidians and lancets, included numerous items of jade: five carved and incised objects, five spherical or hemispherical objects, three beads, 165 jade bits, and pieces of some other polished object. Present also was a worked sheet of calcite crystal and a mosaic of shell and pyrite. In no way does this suggest a dynasty fallen on hard times.

Although he was not much of a builder in life, Animal Skull's death was associated with one of the most massive remodellings of Tikal's epicenter ever carried out. Although it cannot be proven, some of this construction may have been planned in advance by this king; at least, he may have planned the new temple (5D-32-1st) to be built over his grave, as Ruler A later seems to have planned the one that was subsequently put up over his. Coe has commented on the unusually thick walls of 32-1st, which may have been necessary to support an unusually massive roof comb. For all we know, this could have been faced with a larger than life portrayal of the ruler entombed beneath, as was common practice later on. In any event, we cannot assert (as do Schele and Freidel, p. 174) that there was no public portrayal of Animal Skull; maybe there was, and maybe there wasn't.

Other construction associated with the entombment of Animal Skull was the laying of new floors over the Great Plaza and North Acropolis, construction of new stairs on the east side of the Acropolis, new floors over the terraces south and east of the Acropolis, a new stairway (the final one) from the Great Plaza to the North Terrace, with new facings at either end, and new stairs to the terrace and plaza west and north of the Acropolis. On top of the Acropolis itself, Strs. 5D-25–1st and 27–1st replaced their prototypes on the southeast and southwest corners, while between them, Str. 5D-26–1st underwent major alterations and additions to become -1st A. Construction of Strs. 5D-20–2nd and 21–2nd on the northeast and northwest corners completed the eight temple arrangement that was retained throughout all the rest of Tikal's history. Elsewhere in Group 5D-2, a new wall was built connecting the Great and East Plazas, and on the latter a new ballcourt was built over the remains of a twin pyramid group. Off the south end of the playing alley was placed a small "shrine." Both shrine and ballcourt were built in a distinctively foreign style. The significance of this is not known, but it is noteworthy that the outside influences involved seem to emanate from the north, rather than the southeast where Caracol is located.

In fact, influences from the southeast are not strong at Tikal until around the time of Ruler A's accession, which took place on 9.12.9.17.16 (A.D. 682). Beneath Str. 5D-33–1st, built early in the reign of Ruler A, lies Burial 23, which in several ways is reminiscent of Caracol burials. Moreover, ten years after assuming power, Ruler A put up a twin pyramid group in which he placed a carved stela and altar, showing himself standing over a "giant ahau" altar [so called on account of the huge glyph for the day *ahau* on its surface] of the sort commonly commissioned by the rulers of Caracol up until this same date, 9.13.0.0.0 (A.D. 692). Perhaps around the same time, Ruler A placed a slate monument either in front of, or on the stair block of Temple II. Unusual in the material used, as well as in design and the figure's costume, Coe suggests that the stela may have been imported already carved. One possible place of origin is Caracol, one of the few places where shale was a frequently used stone for monuments.

What we seem to have, then, is an *absence* of evident Caracol influence at Tikal precisely when Lord Water is supposed to have "conquered" the city. Not until at least 100 years later, by which time Tikal had entered its final era of greatness in the reign of Ruler A, is influence from Caracol apparent in its art and burials.

So where does this leave us? What do we really know about Lord Water's victory over Tikal in A.D. 562? Very little, save that it apparently took place. We certainly cannot say that Caracol took control of Tikal, or that it brought about the demise of Double Bird's dynasty. We can't even be sure that Double Bird himself was killed either during or immediately after the war. Nor can we say that Tikal's prosperity suffered, or that it was cut off from its trade routes. Not until the death of Animal Skull do ritual deposits in Tikal's epicenter appear significantly less impressive than before; instead of finely made objects like eccentrics of high quality flint or obsidian, incised obsidian and jade items, structure caches consist of unfired clay heads and marine materials wrapped in leaves sometimes with pigments present. If I were to pick a time when Tikal's political fortunes did take a turn for the worse, when its dynasty did perhaps lose power, it would be following the death of Animal Skull when these changes in offertory practices take place, when Tikal's old Great Plaza ballcourt and East Plaza twin pyramid group were abolished, and when foreign influences, though not from Caracol, *do* show up in the city's architecture. But that, as they say, is another story that waits to be told. Meanwhile, although we should welcome the important contributions that the glyphs have to make to our knowledge of the Maya, we need to be careful about how we interpret what they tell us. Not even the glyphs "speak for themselves" and we need to check out what they say against the archaeological record.

[4] William A. Haviland, "Star Wars at Tikal, or Did Caracol Do What the Glyphs Say They Did?" Paper presented at the 90th Annual Meeting of the American Anthropological Association, 1991.

THE MAKING OF CIVILIZATION

From Mesopotamia to China to the South American Andes, we witness the enduring achievements of the human intellect: magnificent palaces built high above ground; sculptures so perfect as to be unrivaled by those of contemporary artists; engineering projects so vast and daring as to awaken in us a sense of wonder. Looking back to the beginnings of history, we can see a point at which humans transform themselves into "civilized" beings; they begin to live in cities and to expand the scope of their achievements at a rapid pace. How is it, then, that humans at a certain moment in history became consummate builders, harnessing mighty rivers so that they could irrigate crops, developing a system whereby their thoughts could be preserved in writing? The fascinating subject of the development of civilization has occupied the minds of philosophers and anthropologists alike for a long time. We do not yet have the answers, but a number of theories have been proposed.

THEORIES OF CIVILIZATION'S EMERGENCE

Each of the theories sees the appearance of centralized government as the point at which there is no longer any question whether or not a civilization exists. So, the question they pose is: What brought about the appearance of a centralized government? Or, stated another way: What caused the transition from a small, egalitarian farming village to a large urban center in which population density and diversity of labor required a centralized government?

IRRIGATION SYSTEMS

One popular theory concerning the emergence of civilization was given its most forceful statement by Karl Wittfogel[5], and variants of this theory are still held by some anthropologists. Simply put, the irrigation, or **hydraulic theory** holds that Neolithic farmers in ancient Mesopotamia and Egypt, and later in the Americas, noticed that the river valleys

Hydraulic theory: The theory that sees civilization's emergence as the result of the construction of elaborate irrigation systems, the functioning of which required full-time managers whose control blossomed into the first governing body and elite social class.

[5] Karl A. Wittfogel, *Oriental Despotism, A Comparative Study of Total Power* (New Haven, Conn.: Yale University Press, 1957).

that were periodically flooded contained better soils than those that were not, but they also noted that violent floods destroyed their planted fields and turned them into swamps. So the farmers built dikes and reservoirs to collect the floodwater and save it until it was needed. Then they released it into canals and ran it over the fields. At first, these dikes and canals, built by small groups of neighboring farmers, were very simple. The success of this measure led to larger, more complex irrigation systems, which eventually necessitated the emergence of a group of "specialists"—people whose sole responsibility was managing the irrigation system. The centralized effort to control the irrigation process blossomed into the first governing body and elite social class, and civilization was born.

There are several objections to this theory. One of them is that some of the earliest large-scale irrigation systems we know about anywhere in the world developed in highland New Guinea, where strong centralized governments never emerged. Conversely, actual field studies of ancient Mesopotamian irrigation systems reveal that by the year 2000 B.C., by which time many cities had already flourished, irrigation was still carried out on a small scale, consisting of small canals and diversions of natural waterways. If there were state-managed irrigation, it is argued, such a system would have been far more extensive than excavations show it really was. Moreover, documents indicate that in about 2000 B.C. irrigation was regulated by officials of local temples and not by centralized government. Irrigation systems among the American Indian civilizations of Central and South America began on a very small scale, suggesting they were built and run by families, or, at most, by small groups of local farmers. It can just as well be argued that more extensive irrigation works were a consequence of civilization's development, rather than a cause.

TRADE NETWORKS

Some anthropologists argue that trade was a decisive factor in the development of civilizations. In regions of ecological diversity, so the argument goes, trade mechanisms are necessary to procure scarce resources. In Mexico, for example, maize was grown just about everywhere, but chilies were grown in the highlands; cotton and beans were planted at intermediate elevations; certain animals were found only in the river valleys; and salt was found along the coasts.

This theory holds that some form of centralized authority was necessary in order to organize trade for the procurement of these and other commodities. Once procured, some system was necessary in order to redistribute commodities throughout the population. Redistribution, like procurement, must have required a centralized authority, promoting the growth of a centralized government.

While trade may have played an important role in the development of some civilizations, it did not invariably do so. For example, the native peoples of northeastern North America traded widely with each other for at least 6000 years without developing civilizations comparable to those of Mexico or Peru. In the course of this trade, copper from deposits around Lake Superior wound up in such faraway places as New England, as did chert from Labrador and marine shells from the seacoasts of the Gulf of Mexico. Wampum, made on the shores of Long Island Sound, was carried westward, and obsidian from the Yellowstone region has been found in mounds in Ohio.[6]

ENVIRONMENTAL AND SOCIAL CIRCUMSCRIPTION

In a series of papers, Robert Carneiro[7] has advanced the theory that civilization develops where populations are hemmed in by such things as mountains, seas, or other human populations. As such populations grow, they have no space in which to expand, and so they begin to compete for increasingly scarce resources. Internally, this results in the development of social stratification, in which an elite controls important resources to which lower classes have limited access. Externally, this leads to warfare and conquest, which, to be successful, require elaborate organization under a centralized authority.

---

[6] William A. Haviland and Marjory W. Power, *The Original Vermonters*, 2nd. ed. (Hanover, N.H.: University Press of New England, 1994).
[7] Robert L. Carneiro, "A Theory of the Origin of the State," *Science*, 169 (1970):733–738.

RELIGION

The three theories just summarized exemplify ecological approaches to explaining the development of civilization. Such theories emphasize the interrelation between people and what they do on the one hand and their environment on the other. Most recent theories of the emergence of civilization take some such approach. While few anthropologists would deny the importance of the human-environment interrelationship, a growing number of them are dissatisfied with theories that do not take into account the beliefs and values which regulate the interaction between people and their environment.[8]

An example of a theory that does take into account the role of beliefs is one which seeks to explain the emergence of Maya civilization in Mesoamerica.[9] This theory holds that Maya civilization was the result of a process of urbanization which occured at places like Tikal. In the case study on Tikal earlier in this chapter, it is suggested that Maya religion probably developed as a means of coping with the uncertainties of agriculture. In the last millennium B.C., Tikal seems to have been an important religious center. Because of its religious importance, people sought to settle there, with the result that its population grew in size and density. Because this was incompatible with the prevailing slash-and-burn agriculture, which tends to promote dispersed settlement, new subsistence techniques were developed. By chance, these were sufficiently productive to permit further population growth and, by A.D. 600, Tikal had become an urban settlement of at least 50,000 people. Craft specialization also developed, at first in the service of religion but soon in the service of an emerging social elite as well. This social elite was concerned at first with calendrical ritual, but it soon developed into the centralized governing elite needed to control a population growing larger and more diversified in its interests.

This mosaic death mask of greenstone, pyrite, and shell was worn by a king of the Maya city of Tikal who died ca. A.D. 527. Obviously the product of skilled craft work, such specialization developed first to serve the needs of religion, but soon served the needs of the emerging elite as well.

Developing craft specialization served as another factor to pull people into Tikal, where their crafts were in demand. It also required further development of trade networks, if only to provide exotic raw materials. More long-distance trade contacts, of course, brought more contact with outside ideas. In other words, what we seem to have is a complex system with several factors acting upon each other, with religion playing a central role in getting the system started in the first place.

In their search for explanations for civilization's emergence, anthropologists have generally sought to find one theory to explain all cases. Yet, we may have here the cultural equivalent of what biologists call convergent evolution, where somewhat similar forms come about in quite different ways. Thus, a theory that accounts for the rise of civilization in one place may not account for its rise in another.

---

[8] Kent V. Flannery and Joyce Marcus, "Formative Oaxaca and the Zapotec Cosmos," *American Scientist*, 64 (1976):374, 375.
[9] William A. Haviland, "The Ancient Maya and the Evolution of Urban Society," *University of Colorado Museum of Anthropology, Miscellaneous Series*, (1975) No. 37.

CIVILIZATION AND STRESS

Living in the context of civilization ourselves, we are inclined to view its development as a great step upward on some sort of ladder of progress. Whatever benefits civilization has brought, though, the cultural changes it represents seem to have produced new sorts of problems. Among them is the problem of waste disposal. Actually, waste disposal probably began to be a problem in settled, farming communities even before the emergence of civilization. But as villages grew into towns and towns grew into cities, the problem became far more serious, as the buildup of waste created optimum environments for such diseases as bubonic plague.

Quite apart from sanitation problems, the rise of towns and cities brought with it a problem of acute, infectious diseases. In a small population such diseases, which include influenza, measles, mumps, polio, rubella, and smallpox, will kill or immunize so high a proportion of the population that the virus cannot continue to propagate. Hence, such diseases, when introduced into small populations, spread immediately to the whole population and then die out. Their continued existence depends upon the presence of large population aggregates, such as towns and cities provide.

In essence, early cities tended to be disease-ridden places, with relatively high death rates. Not until relatively recent times did public health measures reduce the risk of living in cities, and had it not been for a constant influx of rural peoples, they would have been hard pressed to maintain their population size, let alone increase it. One might wonder, then, what would have led people to go live in such unhealthy places? The answer is, they were attracted by the same sorts of things that lure people to cities today; they are vibrant, exciting places that also provide people with opportunities not available in rural communities. Of course, their experience in the cities did not always live up to advance expectations, anymore than is true today.

Early cities faced social problems strikingly similar to those found in modern North America. Dense population, class systems, and a strong centralized government created internal stress. The slaves and the poor saw that the wealthy had all the things that they themselves lacked. It was not just a question of luxury items; the poor did not have

Signs of warfare are common in ancient civilizations. China's first emperor wanted his army to remain with him—in the form of 7000 life-sized terra cotta figures of warriors.

enough space in which to live with comfort and dignity.

Evidence of warfare in early civilizations is common. Cities were fortified; documents list many battles, raids, and wars between groups; cylinder seals, paintings, and friezes depict battle scenes, victorious kings, and captured prisoners of war. Increasing population and the accompanying scarcity of good farming land often led to boundary disputes and quarrels over land between civilized states or between tribal peoples and a state. Open warfare often developed. People tended to crowd into walled cities for protection and to be near irrigation systems.

The class system also caused internal stress. As time went on, the rich became richer and the poor poorer. In early civilizations one's place in society was relatively fixed. Wealth was based on free slave labor. For this reason there was little or no impetus for social reform. Records from the Mesopotamian city of Lagash indicate that social unrest due to exploitation of the poor by the rich grew during this period. Members of the upper class received tracts of farmland some twenty times larger than those granted the lower class. An upper-class reformer, Urukaginal saw the danger and introduced changes to protect the poor from exploitation by the wealthy, thus preserving the stability of the city.

Given the problems associated with civilization, it is perhaps not surprising that a recurring phenomenon is their collapse. Nonetheless, the rise of cities and civilization laid the basis for modern life. It is sobering to note that many of the problems associated with the first civilizations are still with us. Waste disposal, health problems associated with pollution, crowding, social inequities, and warfare continue to be serious problems. Through the study of past civilizations, we now stand a chance of understanding why such problems persist. Such an understanding will be required if the problems are ever to be overcome. It would be nice if the next cultural revolution saw the human species transcending these problems. If this comes about, anthropology, through its comparative study of civilizations, will have played a key role.

Chapter Summary

The world's first cities grew out of Neolithic villages between 6000 and 4500 years ago, first in Mesopotamia, then in Egypt and the Indus Valley. Four basic culture changes mark the transition from Neolithic village life to life in civilized urban centers. The first culture change is agricultural innovation as new farming methods were developed. For example, the ancient Sumerians built an irrigation system that enabled them to control their water resources and thus increase crop yields.

The second culture change is diversification of labor. With the growth of large populations in cities, some people were freed from agricultural activities to develop skills as artisans and craftspeople. With specialization came the development of new technologies, leading to the beginnings of extensive trade systems. An outgrowth of technological innovation and increased contact with foreign people through trade was new knowledge; within the early civilizations sciences such as geometry and astronomy were first developed.

The third culture change that characterized urban life is the emergence of central government with authority to deal with the complex problems associated with cities. Evidence of a central governing authority comes from such sources as law codes, temple records, and royal chronicles. With the invention of writing, governments could keep records of their transactions and/or boast of their own glory. Further evidence of centralized government comes from archeological excavations of city structures.

Typically, the first cities were headed by a king and his special advisers. The reign of the Babylonian King Hammurabi, sometime between 1950 and 1700 B.C., is well known for its efficient government organization and the standardization of its legal system. In the New World, in Peru, the Inca empire reached its culmination in the sixteenth century A.D. With a population of several million people, the Inca state, headed by an emperor, possessed a widespread governing bureaucracy that functioned with great efficiency at every level.

The fourth culture change characteristic of civilization is social stratification, or the emergence of social classes. In the early cities of Mesopotamia, symbols of status and privilege appeared for the first time, and individuals were ranked according to the work roles they filled or the position of their families. Archaeologists have been able to verify that social classes existed in ancient civilizations in four ways: by studying burial customs, as well as skeletons, through grave excavations; by noting the size of dwellings in excavated cities; by examining preserved written documents; and by studying the correspondence of Europeans who described the great civilizations that they destroyed in the New World.

A number of theories have been proposed to explain why civilizations developed. The irrigation, or hydraulic, theory holds that the effort to build and control an irrigation system required a degree of social organization that eventually led to the formation of a civilization. There are several objections to this theory, however; one might argue that sophisticated irrigation systems were a result of the development of civilization rather than a cause. Another theory suggests that in the multicrop economies of both the Old and the New Worlds, some kind of system was needed to distribute the various food products throughout the population. Such a procedure would have required a centralized authority, leading to the emergence of a centralized government. A third theory holds that civilization develops where populations are circumscribed by environmental barriers or other societies. As such populations grow, competition for space and scarce resources leads to the development of centralized authority to control resources and organize warfare.

These theories all emphasize the interrelation of people and what they do on the one hand and their environment on the other. A theory that lays greater stress on the beliefs and values which regulate the interaction between people and their environment seeks to explain the emergence of Maya civilization in terms of the role religion may have played in keeping the Maya in and about cities like Tikal.

Sanitation problems in early cities, coupled with large numbers of people living in close proximity, created environments in which infectious diseases were rampant. Early urban centers also faced problems strikingly similar to our own. Dense population, class systems, and a strong centralized government created internal stress. Warfare was a common occurrence; cities were fortified and armies served to protect the state. Nevertheless, a recurrent phenomenon in all civilizations has been their ultimate collapse.

Suggested Readings

Hamblin, Dora Jane, and the editors of Time-Life Books. *The First Cities*. Boston: Little, Brown, 1973.
This well-illustrated volume in the *Time-Life Emergence of Man* series deals with the earliest cities in the Middle East and the Indus River Valley. Written for a popular audience, it is a good survey of the data and theories relating to these early civilizations.

Melter, David, Don Fowler, and Jeremy Sabloff, eds. *American Archaeology: Past and Future*. Washington, D.C.: Smithsonian Institution Press, 1986.
This collection of articles contains one by Henry Wright, "The Evolution of Civilization," an excellent, up-to-date comparative consideration of the subject.

Pfeiffer, John E. *The Emergence of Society*. New York: McGraw-Hill, 1977.
This is a comprehensive survey of the origins of food production and the world's first cities. In order to write the book, the author traveled to archaeological sites throughout the world and consulted with numerous investigators. The book is notable for its inclusion of much data as yet unpublished elsewhere, as well as its readability.

Redman, Charles E. *The Rise of Civilization: From Early Farmers to Urban Society in the Ancient Near East*. San Francisco: Freeman, 1978.

One of the best-documented examples of the rise of urban societies is that of Greater Mesopotamia in the Middle East. This clearly written textbook focuses on that development, presenting the data, discussing interpretations of those data, as well as problems.

Sabloff, Jeremy A. *The Cities of Ancient Mexico*. New York: Thames and Hudson, 1989.
This well-written and lavishly illustrated book describes the major cities of the Olmecs, Zapotecs, Maya, Teotihuacanos, Toltecs, and Aztecs. Following the descriptions, Sabloff discusses the question of origins, the problems of archaeological reconstruction, and the basis on which he provides vignettes of life in the ancient cities. The book concludes with a gazetteer of fifty sites in Mesoamerica.

Sabloff, J. A., and C. C. Lamberg-Karlovsky, eds. *The Rise and Fall of Civilizations, Modern Archaeological Approaches to Ancient Cultures*. Menlo Park, Calif.: Cummings, 1974.
The emphasis in this collection of articles is theoretical or methodological rather than purely descriptive. Special emphasis is on Mesopotamia and Mesoamerica, but papers are included on Peru, Egypt, the Indus Valley, China, and Europe.

One of the notable characteristics of the human species today is its great variability. Human diversity has long fascinated people, but unfortunately, it also has led to discrimination and even bloodshed.

WHAT ARE THE CAUSES OF PHYSICAL VARIABILITY IN MODERN ANIMALS?

In the gene pool of a species like *Homo sapiens,* there are various alleles for any given physical characteristic. When such a species is divided into geographically dispersed populations, as is the human species, forces such as drift and natural selection operate in slightly different ways, causing the store of genetic variability to be unevenly expressed. Thus, for example, genes for dark skin pigmentation are found in high frequency in human populations native to regions of heavy ultraviolet radiation, while genes for light skin pigmentation have a high incidence in populations native to regions of reduced ultraviolet radiation.

IS THE CONCEPT OF RACE USEFUL FOR STUDYING HUMAN PHYSICAL VARIATION?

No. Because races are arbitrarily defined, it is difficult to agree on any specific classification. The problem is compounded by the tendency for "racial" characteristics to occur in gradations from one population to another, without sharp breaks. Furthermore, while one characteristic may be distributed in a north-south gradient, another may occur in an east-west gradient. For these and other reasons, most anthropologists have found it most productive to study the distribution and significance of specific characteristics.

ARE THERE DIFFERENCES IN INTELLIGENCE FROM ONE POPULATION TO ANOTHER?

Probably not, in spite of the fact that some populations receive lower average scores on IQ tests than others. Even so, many individuals in "low-scoring" populations score higher than some in the "higher-scoring" populations. Part of the problem is that there is no agreement on what intelligence really is, except that it is made up of several different talents and abilities. Certainly, there are genes affecting these, but they may be independently assorted, and their expression is known to be affected significantly by environmental factors.

"**W**hat a piece of work is man," said Hamlet. "How noble in reason, how infinite in faculties, in form and moving how express and admirable, in action how like an angel, in apprehension how like a god: the beauty of the world, the paragon of animals! And yet to me what is this quintessence of dust?"

What people are to each other is the province of anthropology: Physical anthropology reveals what we are; cultural anthropology reveals what we think we are. Our dreams of ourselves are as varied as our languages and our physical bodies. We are the same, but we differ. We speak English or French, our hair is curly or straight, our skin is lightly to heavily pigmented, and in height we range from short to tall. Human genetic variation generally is distributed in such a continuous range, with varying clusters of frequency. The significance we give our variations, the way we perceive them—in fact, whether or not we perceive them at all—is determined by our culture. For example, in many Polynesian countries, where skin color is not a determinant of social status, people really do not notice this physical characteristic; in South Africa, it is the first thing people do notice.

VARIATION AND EVOLUTION

Many behavioral traits—reading, for instance—are learned or acquired by living in a society; other characteristics, such as blue eyes, are passed on physically by heredity. Environment affects both. A person growing up surrounded by books learns to read. If the culture insists that brown-eyed people watch TV and blue-eyed people read, the brown-eyed people may end up making videotapes while the blue-eyed people are writing books. These skills or tastes are acquired characteristics. Changes in such things within one population but not another are capable of making the two distinct in learned behavioral characteristics within relatively few generations.

PHYSICAL VARIABILITY

The physical characteristics of both populations and individuals, as we saw in Chapter 3, are a

Polymorphic: A species in the gene pool of which there are alternative forms (alleles) for particular genes.

product of the interaction between genes and environments. Thus, one's genes predispose one to a particular skin color, for example, but the skin color one actually has is strongly affected by environmental factors such as the amount of solar radiation. In this case, phenotypic expression is strongly influenced by environment; in some others, such as one's A–B–O blood type, phenotypic expression closely reflects genotype.

For most characteristics there are within the gene pool of *Homo sapiens* various alternative genes, or alleles. In the color of an eye, the shape of a hand, the texture of skin, many variations can occur. This kind of variability, found in many animal species, signifies a rich potential for new combinations of characteristics in future generations. Such a species is called **polymorphic.** Our blood types, determined by the alleles for A, B, O blood, are an example of a polymorphic trait, which in this case may appear in any of four distinct phenotypic forms. A polymorphic species faced with changing environmental conditions has within its gene pool the possibility of producing individuals with traits appropriate to its altered life. Many may not achieve reproductive success, but those whose physical characteristics enable them to do well in the new environment will usually reproduce, so that their genes will show up more frequently in subsequent generations. Thus, humankind, being polymorphic, has been able to occupy a variety of environments.

A major expansion into new environments began with *Homo erectus* (Chapter 7), populations of which were living in Africa, Southeast Asia, Europe, and China. Each of these places constitutes a different **faunal region,** which is to say that each

Faunal region: A geographic region with its own distinctive assemblage of animal life, not precisely like that of other regions.

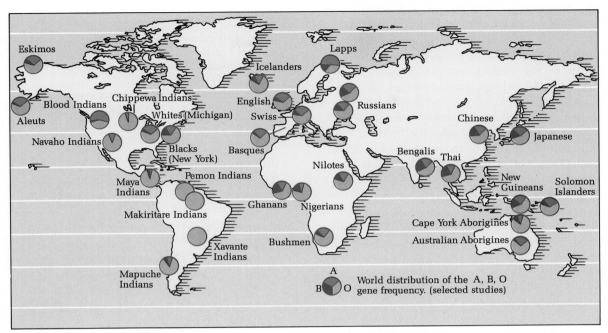

Figure 11.1   Frequencies of the three alleles for the A, B, and O blood groups for selected populations around the world demonstrate the polytypic nature of *H. sapiens*.

possesses its own distinctive assemblage of animal life, not precisely like that of other regions. This differentiation of animal life is the result of selective pressures that, through the Pleistocene, differed from one region to another. For example, the conditions of life were quite different in China, which lies in the temperate zone, than they were in tropical Southeast Asia. Coupled with differing selective pressures were geographical features that restricted or prevented gene flow between populations of different faunal regions.

When a polymorphic species is divided into geographically dispersed populations, it usually is **polytypic**; that is, the store of genetic variability is unevenly expressed. Genetic variants will be expressed in different frequencies in different popula-

---

Polytypic: The expression of genetic variants in different frequencies in different populations of a species.

---

tions. For example, in the Old World, populations of *H. sapiens* living in the tropics have a higher frequency of genes for dark skin color than do those living in more northerly regions. In blood type, *H. sapiens* is polymorphic, with four distinct groups (A, B, O, or AB). In the distribution of these types, the polytypic nature of the species is again revealed. The frequency of the O allele is highest in American Indians, especially among some populations native to South America; the highest frequencies of the allele for type A blood tend to be found among certain European populations (although the highest frequency of all is found among the Blackfoot and Blood Indians of North America); the highest frequencies of the B allele are found in some Asian populations (see Figure 11.1). We would expect the earlier species, *H. erectus*, with populations in the four faunal regions of the Old World, to have been polytypic. This appears to have been the case, for the fossils from each of the four regions show some differences from those in the others. It seems, then, that the human species has been polytypic since at least the time of *H. erectus*.

THE MEANING OF RACE

Early anthropologists tried to explore the polytypic nature of the human species by systematically classifying *H. sapiens* into subspecies, or **races**, based on geographic location and phenotypic (physical) features such as skin color, body size, head shape, and hair texture. Such classifications were continually challenged by the presence of individuals who did not fit the categories, such as light-skinned Africans or dark-skinned "Caucasoids." To get around the problem, it was assumed that these individuals were hybrids or racial mixtures. Lack of concordance between traits—for example, the fact that long prominent noses are not only common among Europeans, but are common in various East African populations as well—was usually explained away in a similar manner. The fact is, generalized references to human types such as "Asiatic" or "Mongoloid," "European" or "Caucasoid," and "African" or "Negroid" were at best mere statistical abstractions about populations in which certain physical features appeared in higher frequencies than in other populations; no example of "pure" racial types could be found. These categories turned out to be neither definitive nor particularly helpful. The visible traits were found to occur not in abrupt shifts from population to population, but in a continuum that changed gradually, with few sharp breaks. To compound the problem, one trait might change gradually over a north-south gradient, while another might show a similar change from east to west. Human skin color, for instance, becomes progressively darker as one moves from northern Europe to central Africa, while blood type B becomes progressively more common as one moves from western to eastern Europe. Finally, there were many variations within each group, and those within groups were often greater than those between groups. In Africa, the skin color of someone from the Kalahari Desert might more closely resemble that of a person of East Indian extraction than the darkly pigmented Nilotic Sudanese who was supposed to be of the same race.

The Negroid was characterized as having dark skin, thick lips, a broad nose, and tightly curled hair; the Mongoloid, straight hair, a flat face, a flat nose, and spread nostrils; and the Caucasoid, pale

Race: A population of a species that differs in the frequency of the variants of some gene or genes from other populations of the same species.

skin, a narrow nose, and varied eye color and hair form. The classification then expanded to take in American Indians, Australians, and Polynesians, but even the expanded system failed to account for dramatic differences in appearance among individuals, or even populations, in each racial category; for example, Europeans, Arabs, and East Indians were all lumped together as Caucasoids.

In an attempt to encompass such variations, schemes of racial classification multiplied. In 1926, J. Deniker classified 29 races according to texture of hair, presumably improving upon Roland B. Dixon's 1923 classification based on three indexes of body measures. Hair texture and body build were the characteristics used for another set of racial categories proposed in 1930. By 1947, Earnest Hooton had proposed three new composite races resulting from the interbreeding of "primary" races. Despite these classificatory attempts on the part of Western anthropologists, no definitive grouping of distinct, discontinuous biological groups was found for modern humanity.

A turning point is represented by the publication in 1950 of a book called *Races* by Carleton Coon, Stanley Garn, and Joseph Birdsell. Like their predecessors, they too tried to classify modern humans into a number of racial groups—thirty in this case—but they rejected a trait-list approach. Instead, they recognized races as populations that owed certain common characteristics to environmental, primarily climatic, adaptation, which continued to change in response to evolutionary forces such as gene flow and altered selective pressures. While this book certainly had its weaknesses, it represented a significant departure from previous attempts at racial classification and was influential in paving the way for our more recent understanding of human variation.

These pictures of people from different parts of Africa show the wide range of variation that can be seen within a supposedly single racial category.

The "openness" of races to gene flow is illustrated by this picture of an Asian and African American couple with their children.

RACE AS A BIOLOGICAL CONCEPT

To understand why the racial approach to human variation has been so unproductive, we must first understand the race concept in strictly biological terms. Briefly, a race may be defined as a population of a species that differs in the frequency of different states of some gene or genes from other populations of the same species. Simple and straightforward though such a definition may seem, there are three very important things to note about it. First, it is arbitrary; there is no agreement on how many genetic differences it takes to make a race. For some who are interested in the topic, different frequencies in the variants of one gene are sufficient; for others, differences in frequencies involving several genes were necessary. The number of genes and precisely which ones are the more important for defining races are still open to debate.

The second thing to note about the biological definition of race is that it does not mean that any one race has exclusive possession of any particular variant of any gene or genes. In human terms, the frequency of the allele for blood group O may be high in one population and low in another, but it is present in both. Races are genetically "open," meaning that gene flow takes place between them. Because they are genetically "open," they are apt to be impermanent and subject to reamalgamation. Thus, one can easily see the fallacy of any attempt to identify "pure" races; if gene flow cannot take place between two populations, either directly or indirectly through intermediate populations, then they are not races, but are separate species.

The third thing to note about the biological definition of race is that individuals of one race will not necessarily be distinguishable from those of another. In fact, as we have just noted with respect to humans, the differences between individuals within a population may be greater than the differences among populations. This follows from the genetic "open-ness" of races; no one race has an exclusive claim to any particular gene or allele.

THE CONCEPT OF HUMAN RACES

As a device for understanding polytypic variation in humans, the biological race concept has serious drawbacks. One is that the category is arbitrary to begin with, which makes agreement on any given classification difficult. For example, if one researcher emphasizes skin color, while another emphasizes blood group differences, it is unlikely that they will classify people in the same way. Perhaps if the human species were divided into a number of relatively discrete breeding populations, this wouldn't be such a problem, but even this is open to debate. What has happened, though, is that human populations have grown in the course of human evolution, and with this growth have come increased opportunities for contact and gene flow among populations. Since the advent of food production, the process has accelerated as higher birthrates and periodic food shortages have prompted the movement of farmers from their homelands to other places (see Chapter 9). Thus, differences between human populations today are probably less clear-cut than back in the days of *H. erectus*, or even archaic *H. sapiens*.

If this isn't enough of a problem, things are complicated even more because humans are so complicated genetically. Thus, the genetic underpinnings of the phenotypic traits upon which traditional racial classifications are usually based are poorly understood. To compound the problem, "race" exists as a cultural, as well as a biological, category. In various different ways, cultures define religious, linguistic, and ethnic groups as races, thereby confusing linguistic and behavioral traits with physical traits. For example, in many Central and South American countries, people are commonly classified as "Indian," "Mestizo" (mixed), or "Latino" (of Spanish descent). But in spite of the biological connotations of these terms, the criteria used for assigning individuals to these categories consist of such things as whether they wear shoes, sandals, or go barefoot; speak Spanish or some Indian language; live in a thatched hut or a European-style house; and so forth. Thus, an Indian, by speaking Spanish, wearing Western-style clothes, and living in a house in a non-Indian neighborhood, ceases to be an Indian, no matter how many "Indian genes" he or she may possess.

This sort of confusion of nonbiological characteristics with what are spoken of as biological categories is by no means limited to Central and South American societies. To one degree or another, such confusion is found in most Western societies, including those of Europe and North America. What makes it worse is that it is frequently combined with attitudes that are then taken as excuses to exclude whole categories of people from certain roles or positions in society. In the United States, for example, it has frequently been asserted that "blacks are born with rhythm," which somehow is thought to give them a "natural affinity" for jazz, "soul music," and similar forms of musical expression. The corollary of this is that African Americans are unsuited "by nature" for symphonic music. Hence, until recently, one did not find an African American at the head of any major symphony orchestra in the United States, even though African-American conductors such as James de Priest, Paul Freeman, and Dean Dixon have had distinguished careers in Canada and Europe.

One of the prime examples of the evil consequences of misconstruction of race occurred in Germany in the 1930s and 1940s when the Nazis declared the superiority of the "Aryan race" (which is really a linguistic grouping and not a race at all), and the inferiority of the Gypsy and Jewish "races" (really ethnic/religious categories), and then used this distinction as an excuse to exclude Gypsies and Jews from life altogether. Tragically, such programs of extermination of one group by another continue to occur in many parts of the world today, including parts of South America, Africa, Europe, and Asia. "Holocausts" are by no means things of the past, nor are Gypsies and Jews their only victims. The well-meant vow "never again" contrasts with the reality of "frequently again."

Considering all the problems, confusion, and evil consequences, it is small wonder that there has been a lot of debate not just about how many human races there may be, but about what "race" is and is not. Often forgotten is the fact that a race, even if it can be defined, is the result of the operation of evolutionary processes. Because it is these processes rather than racial categories themselves in which we are really interested, most anthropologists have abandoned the race concept as being of no particular utility. Instead, they prefer to study the distribution and significance of specific, genetically based

Attempts by one group of people to exterminate another did not end with the Holocaust of World War II, as this picture of Serbian commandos kicking the bodies of Bosnian Muslims they already have killed illustrates. Unfortunately, Yugoslavia is but one of several cases of genocide to be seen in the world today.

characteristics, or else the characteristics of small breeding populations that are, after all, the smallest units in which evolutionary change occurs.

SOME PHYSICAL VARIABLES

In spite of all the debate about the reality of human races, human biological variation is a fact of life, and physical anthropologists have learned a great deal about it. Much of it seems related to climatic adaptation. For example, a correlation has been noted between body build and climate. Generally, people native to regions with cold climates tend to have greater body bulk (not to be equated with fat) relative to their extremities (arms and legs) than do people native to regions with hot climates, who tend to be long and slender. Anthropologists generally argue that such differences of body build represent a climatic adaptation; certain body builds are better suited to particular living conditions than others. A person with larger body bulk and shorter extremities may suffer more from summer heat than someone whose extremities are long and whose body is slender. But they will conserve needed body

heat under cold conditions. The reason is that a bulky body tends to conserve more heat than a less bulky one, since it has less surface relative to volume. People living in hot, open country, by contrast, benefit from a body build that can get rid of excess heat quickly so as to keep from overheating; for this, long extremities and a slender body, which increase surface area relative to volume, are advantageous.

Studies of body build and climatic adaptation are complicated by the intervening effects on physique of diet, since dietary differences will cause variation in body build. Another complicating factor is clothing. For example, Inuit peoples (the proper name for "Eskimos") live in a region where it is cold much of the year. To cope with this, they long ago developed efficient clothing to keep the body warm. Because of this, the Inuit are provided with what amount to artificial tropical environments inside their clothing. In spite of such considerations, it remains true that in northerly regions of the world, bulky body builds predominate, whereas the reverse is true in the tropics.

Anthropologists have also studied such body features as nose, eye shape, and hair textures in

The epicanthic eye fold is common among peoples native to eastern Asia.

Epicanthic eye fold: A fold of skin at the inner corner of the eye that covers the true corner of the eye; common in Asiatic populations.

Melanin: The chemical responsible for dark skin pigmentation which helps protect against damage from ultraviolet radiation.

relation to climate. A wide flaring nose, for example, is common in populations living in tropical forests; here the air is warm and damp, and so the warming and humidifying functions of the nose are secondary. Longer, more prominent noses, common among cold dwellers, are helpful in humidifying and warming cold air before it reaches the lungs. They are also useful in cleaning and humidifying dry, dusty air in hot climates as well, which is why long prominent noses are not restricted to places like Europe. Coon, Garn, and Birdsell once proposed that the "Mongoloid face," common in populations native to East and Central Asia, as well as arctic North America, exhibits features adapted to life in very cold environments. The **epicanthic eye fold**, which reduces eye exposure to the cold to a minimum, a flat facial profile, and extensive fatty deposits may help to protect the face against frostbite. Although experimental studies have failed to

sustain the frostbite hypothesis, it is true that a flat facial profile generally goes with a round head. A significant percentage of body heat may be lost from the head; however, a round head, having less surface area relative to volume, loses less heat than a longer, more elliptical head. As one would predict from this, long-headed populations are generally found in hotter climates; round-headed ones are more common in cold climate areas.

SKIN COLOR: A CASE STUDY IN ADAPTATION

In the United States, race is most commonly associated with skin color. Perhaps this is inevitable, since it is such an obvious physical trait. Skin color is subject to great variation, and there are at least four main factors associated with it: transparency or thickness of the skin, a copper-colored pigment called carotene, reflected color from the blood vessels, and the amount of **melanin** found in a given area of skin. Exposure to sunlight increases the amount of melanin and, hence, the skin darkens. Melanin is known to protect skin against damaging ultraviolet solar radiation;[1] consequently, darkly pigmented peoples are less susceptible to skin cancers and sunburning than are those whose skin lacks much in the way of melanin. They may also be less susceptible to photo-destruction of certain vitamins. Since the highest concentration of dark-skinned people tends to be found in the tropical regions of the world, it appears that natural selection has favored heavily pigmented skin as a protection against the strong solar radiation of equatorial

[1] Robert M. Neer, "The Evolutionary Significance of Vitamin D, Skin Pigment, and Ultraviolet Light," *American Journal of Physical Anthropology*, 43 (1975):409–416.

latitudes, where ultraviolet radiation is most intense. Because skin cancers generally do not develop until later in life, they are unlikely to have interfered with the reproductive success of lightly pigmented individuals in the tropics, and so are unlikely to have been the agent of selection. On the other hand, severe sunburn, which is especially dangerous to infants, causes the body to overheat and interferes with its ability to sweat, by which it might rid itself of excess heat. Furthermore, it makes one susceptible to other kinds of infection. In addition to all this, decomposition of folate, a vitamin sensitive to heavy doses of ultraviolet radiation, can cause anemia, spontaneous abortion, and infertility.[2]

[2] Richard F. Branda and John W. Eatoil, "Skin Color and Photolysis: An Evolutionary Hypothesis," *Science*, 201 (1978):625–626.

While dark skin pigmentation has enjoyed a selective advantage in the tropics, the opposite is true in northern latitudes, where skins have generally been lightly pigmented. This lack of heavy amounts of melanin enables the weak ultraviolet radiation of northern latitudes to penetrate the skin and stimulate formation of vitamin D. Dark pigmentation interferes with this. Without access to external sources of vitamin D, once provided by cod liver oil but now more often provided in vitamin D fortified milk, individuals incapable of synthesizing enough of this vitamin in their own bodies were selected against, for they contracted rickets, a disease that seriously deforms children's bones. At its worst, rickets prevents children from reaching reproductive age; at the least, it interferes with a woman's ability to give birth if she does reach reproductive age (see Figure 11.2).

Given what we know about the adaptive significance of human skin color, and the fact that, until 700,000 years ago, hominines were exclusively creatures of the tropics, it is likely that lightly pigmented skins are a recent development in human history. Darkly pigmented skins likely are quite ancient. Human skin is more liberally endowed with sweat glands than is the skin of other mam-

These photos of people from Spain, Scandinavia, Senegal, and Indonesia illustrate the range of variation in human skin color. Generally, the closer to the equator populations live, the darker the skin color.

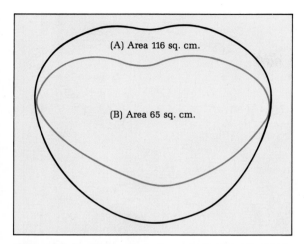

Figure 11.2   The outline of a normal pelvic inlet (A) is compared with that of a woman with rickets (B), which would interfere with her capacity to give birth. Rickets is caused by a deficiency of vitamin D. In the absence of artificial sources of the vitamin among people living in northern latitudes, lightly pigmented people are least likely to contract rickets.

mals; in combination with our lack of much in the way of body hair, this makes for effective elimination of excess body heat in a hot climate. This would have been especially advantageous to early hominines on the savanna, who could have avoided confrontations with carnivorous animals by carrying out most of their activities in the heat of the day. For the most part, carnivores rest then, being active from dusk until early morning. Without much hair to cover early hominine bodies, selection would have favored dark skins; hence all humans appear to have had a "black" ancestry, no matter how "white" some of them may be today.

One should not conclude that, because it is newer, lightly pigmented skin is better, or more highly evolved, than heavily pigmented skin. The latter is clearly more highly evolved to the conditions of life in the tropics, although with protective clothing, hats, and sunscreen lotions, lightly pigmented peoples can get along there. Conversely, the availability of supplementary sources of vitamin D allows heavily pigmented peoples to do quite well away from the tropics. In both cases, culture has rendered skin color differences largely irrelevant.

The inheritance of skin color is not well under-

Racism: A doctrine of racial superiority by which one group asserts its superiority over another.

stood, except that several genes (rather than variants of a single gene), each with its own variants, must be involved. Nevertheless, its geographical distribution, with few exceptions, tends to be continuous, like that of other human traits (see Figure 11.3). The exceptions have to do with the movement of certain populations from their original homelands to other regions, and/or the practice of selective mating. For example, there have been repeated invasions of the Indian subcontinent by peoples from the north, who were then incorporated into the Hindu caste system. Still today, the higher the caste, the lighter its skin color. This skin color gradient is maintained by strict in-group marriage rules. In the United States, statistical studies have shown that there has been a similar trend among African Americans, with African-American women of higher status choosing to marry lighter-skinned males, reflecting the culture's emphasis on light skin as a status symbol. It is quite possible that the "black pride" movement, which places positive value on features common among those of West African descent, such as dark skins, tightly curled hair, and broad flat noses, is leading to a reversal of this cultural selection factor.

THE SOCIAL SIGNIFICANCE OF RACE: RACISM

Scientific facts do not seem to change what people think about race. **Racism** can be viewed solely as a social problem, although at times it has been used by politicians as a purportedly "scientific" tool. It is an emotional phenomenon best explained in terms of collective psychology. Racial conflict results from long-suppressed resentments and hostilities. The racist responds to social stereotypes, not to known scientific facts.

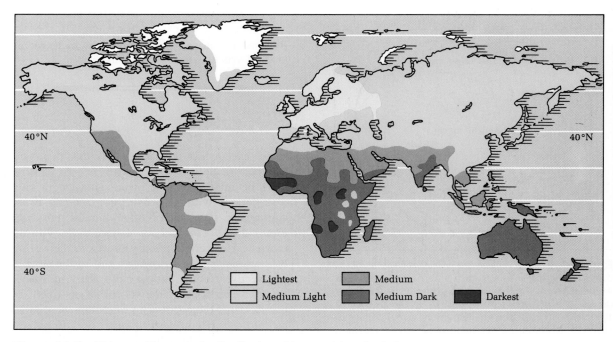

Figure 11.3   This map illustrates the distribution of human skin color before 1492.

RACE AND BEHAVIOR

The assumption that there are behavioral differences among human races remains an issue of contemporary society, not easily argued away. Throughout history, certain "races" have been attributed certain characteristics, which assume a variety of names— "national character," "spirit," "temperament"—all of them vague and standing for a number of concepts totally unrelated to the biological concept of race. Common myths involve the "coldness" of the Scandinavians or the "martial" character of the Germanics or the "indolent" nature of Africans. These generalizations serve to characterize a people unjustly; German citizens do not necessarily advocate genocide, nor do Africans necessarily hate to work. The term "race" has a precise biological meaning, but in popular usage, as we have already seen, the term often acquires a meaning unrelated to that given by scientists, often with disastrous results.

To date, no innate behavioral characteristic can be attributed to any group of people that the nonscientist would most probably term a "race" that cannot be explained in terms of cultural prac-

tices. If the Chinese happen to be especially successful mathematicians, it can probably be explained in terms of emphasis within their culture on abstract concepts, learned ways of perceiving the universe, and their philosophies. If African Americans are not as well represented in managerial positions as their fellow citizens, it is because for a long time they were given neither the necessary training nor the opportunity (nor is the problem fully rectified today). The list could go on, and all such differences or characteristics can be explained in terms of culture.

Similarly, high crime rates among certain groups can be explained with reference to culture and not biology. Individuals alienated and demoralized by poverty, injustice, and inequality of opportunity tend to display what the dominant members of society regard as antisocial behavior more frequently than those who are culturally well-integrated. For example, American Indians, when they have been equipped and allowed to compete on an equal footing with other North Americans, have not suffered from the high rate of alcoholism and criminal behavior exhibited by Indians living under conditions of poverty, whether on or off reservations.

RACE AND INTELLIGENCE

A question frequently asked by those unfamiliar with the deficiencies of the race concept is whether or not some races are inherently more intelligent than others. Intelligence tests carried on in the United States by European-American investigators among people of European and African descent have often shown that European Americans attain higher scores. During World War I, a series of tests known as Alpha and Beta IQ tests, were regularly given to draftees. The results showed that the average score attained by European Americans was higher than that obtained by African Americans. Even though many African Americans scored higher than some European Americans, and some African Americans scored higher than most European Americans, many people took this as proof of the intellectual superiority of "white people." But all the tests really showed was that, on the average, European Americans outperformed African Americans in certain social situations. The tests did not measure "intelligence" per se, but the ability, conditioned by culture, of certain individuals to respond to certain socially conditioned problems. These tests had been conceived by European Americans for comparable middle-class European Americans. While people of color coming from similar backgrounds generally did well, European Americans as well as people of color coming from other backgrounds to meet the challenge of these tests were clearly at a disadvantage. It would be unrealistic to expect individuals unfamiliar with European-American middle-class values and linguistic behavior to respond to a problem based on a familiarity with these.

Many large-scale intelligence tests continue to be administered in this country. Notable among these are several series in which environmental factors are held constant. Where this is done, African and European Americans tend to score equally well.[3] Nor is this surprising; since genes assort themselves independently of one another, there is no reason to suppose that whatever alleles

may be associated with intelligence are likely to be concordant with the ones for skin pigmentation. Intelligence tests, however, have increasingly become the subject of controversy. There are many psychologists as well as anthropologists who believe that their use is overdone. Intelligence tests, they say, are of limited use, since they are applicable only to particular cultural circumstances. Only when these circumstances are carefully met can any meaningful generalizations be derived from the use of tests.

Notwithstanding the foregoing, there continue to be some who wonder whether or not there are any significant intellectual differences between human populations. On a purely theoretical basis, it could be assumed that just as we see a spectrum of inherited variations in physical traits—skin color, hair texture, height—there could be similar variation in innate intellectual potential of different populations. It is likely that just as there are genes affecting the development of blue eyes, curly hair, or heavily pigmented skin, there are others affecting the development of intelligence. One proponent of this view is the North American psychologist Arthur Jensen. Basing his conclusions on statistical data from tests given to African and European Americans, Jensen has argued that such intellectual differences exist.

From a number of studies it is now clear that there is indeed an appreciable degree of hereditary control of intelligence. First, there is a general tendency for those pairs of individuals who are most genetically similar (identical twins) to be most similar in intelligence, even when reared in different environments. Furthermore, the scores on IQ tests of biological parents and their children are correlated and tend to be similar, while foster parents and their foster children show little of this tendency.

Equally clear are the effects of environment on intelligence. A number of studies consistently show that, in the United States, children reared in rural areas on the average get IQ scores about fifteen points lower than children from urban areas; that children deprived of frequent verbal and tactile interaction with adults get significantly lower IQ scores than those who aren't; that children in large families score lower on IQ tests than children who have few brothers and sisters; that in large families, the later born have lower IQ scores than the first

---

[3] Peggy R. Sanday, "On the Causes of IQ Differences Between Groups and Implications for Social Policy," in *Race and IQ*, ed. Ashley Montagu (New York: Oxford University Press, 1975), pp. 232–238.

born; that special training can raise IQ scores by as much as thirty points; and so forth. So, like all inherited traits, intelligence is expressed as an interaction between genes and environment.

That one's IQ is to some degree heritable is at the root of an all too common fallacy, the subject of the following Original Study by Stephen Jay Gould.

ORIGINAL STUDY

THE HEREDITARIAN FALLACY[4]

The hereditarian fallacy is not the simple claim that IQ is to some degree "heritable." I have no doubt that it is, though the degree has clearly been exaggerated by the most avid hereditarians. It is hard to find any broad aspect of human performance or anatomy that has no heritable component at all. The hereditarian fallacy resides in two false implications drawn from this basic fact:

1. The equation of "heritable" with "inevitable." To a biologist, heritability refers to the passage of traits or tendencies along family lines as a result of genetic transmission. It says little about the range of environmental modification to which these traits are subject. In our vernacular, "inherited" often means "inevitable." But not to a biologist. Genes do not make specific bits and pieces of a body; they code for a range of forms under an array of environmental conditions. Moreover, even when a trait has been built and set, environmental intervention may still modify inherited defects. Millions of Americans see normally through lenses that correct innate deficiencies of vision. The claim that IQ is so-many percent "heritable" does not conflict with the belief that enriched education can increase what we call, also in the vernacular, "intelligence." A partially inherited low IQ might be subject to extensive improvement through proper education. And it might not. The mere fact of its heritability permits no conclusion.

2. The confusion of within- and between-group heredity. The major political impact of hereditarian theories does not arise from the inferred heritability of tests, but from a logically invalid extension. Studies of the heritability of IQ, performed by such traditional methods as comparing scores of relatives, or contrasting scores of adopted children with both their biological and legal parents, are all of the "within-group" type—that is, they permit an estimate of heritability within a single, coherent population (white Americans, for example). The common fallacy consists in assuming that if heredity explains a certain percentage of variation among individuals within a group, it must also explain a similar percentage of the difference in average IQ between groups—whites and blacks, for example. But variation among individuals within a group and differences in mean values between groups are entirely separate phenomena. One item provides no license for speculation about the other. A hypotheti-

Even though many disorders that are fully inherited, like nearsightedness, are routinely corrected for (in this case, with corrective lenses), the false notion is widely held that "nothing can be done" about undesirable traits involving a genetic component.

cal and noncontroversial example will suffice. Human height has a higher heritability than any value ever proposed for IQ. Take two separate groups of males. The first, with an average height of 5 feet 10 inches, live in a prosperous American town. The second, with an average height of 5 feet 6 inches, are starving in a third-world village. Heritability is 95 percent or so in each place—meaning only that relatively tall fathers tend to have tall sons and relatively short fathers short sons. This high within-group heritability argues neither for nor against the possibility that better nutrition in the next generation might raise the average height of third-world villagers above that of prosperous Americans. Likewise, IQ could be highly heritable within groups, and the average difference between whites and blacks in America might still only record the environmental disadvantages of blacks.

I have often been frustrated with the following response to this admonition: "Oh well, I see what you mean, and you're right in theory. There may be no necessary connection in logic, but isn't it more likely all the same that mean differences between groups would have the same causes as variation within groups?" The answer is still "no." Within- *and* between-group heredity are not tied by rising degrees of probability as heritability increases within groups and differences enlarge between them. The two phenomena are simply separate. Few arguments are more dangerous than the ones that "feel" right but can't be justified.

[4] Stephen Jay Gould, *The Mismeasure of Man* (New York: W.W. Norton, 1981), pp. 155–157.

INTELLIGENCE: WHAT IS IT?

A question that must now be asked is: What do we mean by the term "intelligence"? The answer, quite simply, is that which is measured by IQ tests. Unfortunately, there is no general agreement as to what abilities or talents actually make up the trait of intelligence, except that it is not a single scalable thing in the head comparable to one's height or blood type. Rather, it is made up of a great many talents or abilities. Furthermore, no matter how closely related these are (whatever they are), they must be independently inherited, just as height and blood type are independently inherited. Thus, the various traits that constitute "intelligence" may be independently distributed as are, for example, the previously discussed skin color and blood type (compare Figures 11.3 and 11.4).

The next question is: If we are not exactly sure what IQ tests are measuring, how can we be sure of the validity of such tests—that is, can we be sure an IQ test measures what it is supposed to measure? The answer, of course, is that we can't be sure. But even at best, an IQ test measures performance (something that one does) rather than genetic disposition (something that lies within the individual). Reflected in one's performance are one's past experiences and present motivational state, as well as one's innate ability. In sum, it is fair to say that an IQ test is not a reliable measure of innate intelligence.

At present, the case for significant differences in intelligence between human populations remains unproven. Nor is it ever likely to be proven, in view of what we saw in Chapter 8 as the major thrust in the evolution of the genus *Homo*. Over the past 2.5

Nelson Mandella, a South African leader, illustrates the point that individuals of exceptional ability can and do appear in *any* human population.

million years, in all populations of the genus, the emphasis has been on cultural adaptation—actively inventing solutions to the problems of existence, rather than passively relying on biological adaptation. Thus, we would expect a comparable degree of intelligence in all present-day human populations. But even if this were not the case, it would mean only that "dull" and "bright" people are found in all human populations, though in different frequencies. Thus, geniuses can and do appear in any population, regardless of what that population's "average" intelligence may be. The fact of the matter is that the only way to be sure that individual human beings develop their innate abilities and skills, whatever they may be, to the fullest is to give them the opportunity to do so. This certainly cannot be accomplished if whole populations are deprived of equal opportunity.

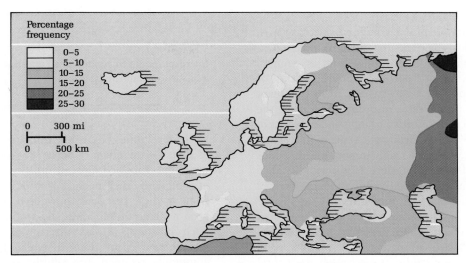

Figure 11.4 The east-west gradient in the frequency of blood Type B (shown above) in Europe contrasts with the north-south gradient in skin pigmentation (shown in Figure 11.3). Whatever genes are involved in the various talents that are lumped under the heading of "intelligence" must be independently assorted as well.

CONTINUING HUMAN BIOLOGICAL EVOLUTION

In the course of their evolution, humans in all parts of the world have come to rely on cultural rather than biological adaptation for their survival. Nevertheless, as they moved from their tropical homeland into other parts of the world, they did develop considerable physical variation from one population to another. The forces responsible for this include genetic drift and biological adaptation to differing climates.

Although much of this physical variation can still be seen in human populations today, the increasing effectiveness of cultural adaptation has often reduced its importance. For instance, the consumption of cod liver oil or vitamin D fortified milk has cancelled out the selective advantage of lightly pigmented skins in northern peoples. At the same time, culture has also imposed its own selective pressures, as we have seen in preceding chapters. Just as the invention of the spear thrower was followed by a reduction in overall muscularity, or just as the transition to food production was followed by worsened health and mortality, cultural practices today are affecting the human organism in important, often surprising, ways.

The probability of alterations in human biological makeup induced by culture raises a number of important questions. By trying to eliminate genetic variants for balanced polymorphic traits, such as the sickle-cell trait discussed in Chapter 3, are we also removing alleles that have survival value? Are we weakening the gene pool by allowing people with hereditary diseases and defects to reproduce? Are we reducing chances for genetic variation by trying to control population size?

We are not sure of the answers to all of these questions. If we are able to wipe out sickle-cell anemia, we also may be able to wipe out malaria; thus, we would have eliminated the condition that made the sickle-cell trait advantageous. Nor is it strictly true that medical science is weakening the gene pool by letting those with disorders for which there may be a genetic predisposition, such as diabetes, reproduce. In the present environment, where medication is easily available, such people are as fit as anyone else. However, if such people are denied access to the needed medication, their biological fitness is lost and they die out. In fact, one's financial status affects one's access to medication, and so, however unintentional it may be, one's biological fitness in North American society may be decided by one's financial status.

The effects of culture in enabling individuals to reproduce even though they suffer from genetic disorders are familiar. Perhaps less familiar are the cases in which medical technology selects against some individuals by removing them from the reproducing population. One example can be seen in South Africa. About 1 percent of South Africans of Dutch descent have a gene which, in its dominant form, causes porphyria, a disorder that renders the skin of its victims sensitive to light and causes skin abrasions. If these Afrikaners remain in a rural environment, they suffer only minor skin abrasions as a result of their condition. However, the allele renders them very sensitive to modern medical treatment, such as they might receive in a large urban center like Johannesburg. If they are treated for some problem quite unrelated to porphyria, with barbiturates or similar drugs, they suffer acute attacks and very often die. In a relatively quiet rural environment where medical services are less readily accessible the Afrikaners with this peculiar condition are able to live normal lives; it is only in an urban context, where they are more likely to receive medical attention, that they suffer physical impairment or loss of life.

Another example of culture acting as an agent of biological selection has to do with lactose tolerance: The ability to assimilate **lactose**, the primary constituent of fresh milk. This ability depends on the presence of a particular enzyme, **lactase**, in the small intestine. Failure to retain lactase into adulthood, although it is a recessive trait, is characteristic of most human populations, especially Asian, native Australian, and many (but not all) African populations. Hence, only 10 to 30 percent of Americans of African descent, and 0 to 30 percent of adult Orientals, retain lactase into adulthood, and so are lactose tolerant.[5] By contrast, lactase retention and lactose tolerance are normal for more than 80 percent of adults of northern European descent. Eastern Europeans, Arabs, and some East Africans are closer to northern Europeans in lactase retention than they are to Asians and other Africans. Generally speaking, a high retention of lactase is found in populations with a long tradition of fresh milk as an important dietary item. In such populations, selection has in the past favored those individuals with the ability to assimilate lactose, selecting out those without this ability.

[5] Gail G. Harrison, "Primary Adult Lactase Deficiency: A Problem in Anthropological Genetics," *American Anthropologist*, 77 (1975):815–819.

Lactose: The primary constituent of fresh milk.

Lactase: An enzyme in the small intestine which enables humans to assimilate lactose.

In developing countries, milk supplements are used in the treatment of acute protein-calorie malnutrition. Tube-fed diets of milk are used in connection with other medical procedures. Quite apart from medical practices, powdered milk has long been a staple of economic aid to other countries. Such practices in fact discriminate against the members of populations in which lactase is not commonly retained into adulthood. At the least, those individuals who are not lactose tolerant will fail to utilize the nutritive value of milk; frequently they will suffer diarrhea, abdominal cramping, and even bone degeneration, with serious results. In fact, the shipping of powdered milk to victims of South American earthquakes in the 1960s caused many deaths among them.

In recent years, there has been considerable concern about human activities which are having an adverse effect on the earth's ozone layer. A major contributor to the ozone layer's deterioration is the use of chloroflurocarbons in aerosol sprays, refrigeration and air conditioning, and the manufacture of Styrofoam. Since the ozone layer screens out some of the sun's ultraviolet rays, its continued deterioration will expose humans to increased ultraviolet radiation. As we saw earlier in this chapter, some ultraviolet radiation is necessary for the production of vitamin D, but excessive amounts lead, among other things, to an increased incidence of skin cancers. Hence a rising incidence of skin cancers can be predicted as the ozone layer continues to deteriorate. Although a ban on the use of chloroflurocarbons in aerosol sprays was imposed some years ago, the destruction of the ozone layer continued about twice as fast as scientists had predicted it would, even without the ban. Subsequently, an international treaty further limiting the use of chlorofluorocarbons was negotiated, but the effect of this is merely to slow down, rather than halt, further deterioration. Most immediately affected by the consequent increase in ultraviolet radiation will be the world's lightly pigmented peoples, but ultimately, all will be affected.

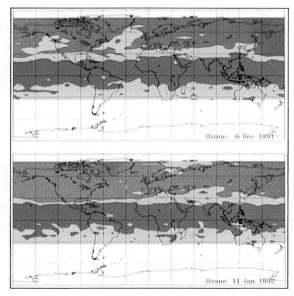

This National Aeronautics and Space Administration plot of total ozone distribution for January 1992 shows that the depletion of the atmospheric ozone layer continues possibly leading to increases in human skin cancers. Most severely affected will be lightly pigmented peoples.

Ozone depletion is merely one of a host of problems confronted by humans today that ultimately have an impact on human gene pools. In view of the consequences for human biology of such seemingly benign innovations, such as dairying or (as discussed in Chapter 9) farming, we may wonder about many recent practices; for example, the effects of increased exposure to radiation through increased use of X–rays, exposure to fallout from nuclear accidents and bomb tests, increased production of radioactive wastes and the like. To be sure, we are constantly reassured by various experts that we are protected by adequate safety regulations, but one is not reassured by discoveries, such as the one announced by the National Academy of Sciences in 1989, that what were accepted as safe levels of radiation were in fact too high, or the earlier discovery that the supposedly safe treatment of sinus disorders in the 1940s by massive doses of X-ray radiation produced a bumper crop of thyroid cancers in the late 1960s. It's not just increased exposure to radiation that we confront, but increased exposure to other known mutagenic agents, including a wide variety of chemicals. Pesticides are a case in point. In spite of repeated assertions as to their safety, there have been tens of thousands of cases of poisonings in the

United States alone (probably more in Third World countries, where controls are even less effective than in the U.S., and where substances banned from the United States are routinely used), and thousands of cases of cancer related to the manufacture and use of pesticides. All this on top of the several million birds killed each year (many of which would otherwise have been happily gobbling down bugs and other pests), serious fish kills, honeybee kills (bees are needed for the efficient pollination of many crops) and the like. In all, pesticides alone (never mind other agricultural chemicals) are responsible for an estimated eight *billion* dollars worth of environmental and public health damage in the United States each year.[6]

It is not that the experts who assure us of the safety of such things are deliberately misleading us.

[6] David Pimentel, "Response," *Science*, 252 (1991): 358.

The things we do often affect what we are in unexpected ways. Despite this, we often view innovations as harmless, until evidence convinces us otherwise. For example, power lines are generally viewed as harmless, so long as one does not touch them; nevertheless, recent studies are finding a correlation between certain kinds of cancers and residence in proximity to such lines.

(Although there are cases of that too, one notorious example being the case of asbestos. As early as 1902 it was included in a list of dusts known to be hazardous; by 1933 it was well-documented as a cause of lung cancer, yet in the 1960s, corporate executives denied ever hearing of the dangers.) For the most part, experts are convinced of the validity of what they say; the difficulty is that serious problems, such as those having to do with radiation or exposure to various chemicals, have a way of not being apparent until years, or even decades later. By then, of course, serious financial interests are at stake.

What is clear, then, is that cultural practices, probably as never before, are currently having an impact on human gene pools. Unquestionably, this is deleterious to those individuals who suffer the effects of negative selection, whose misery and death are the price paid for many of the material benefits of civilization we enjoy today. It remains to be seen just what the long-term effects on the human species as a whole will be. If the promise of "genetic engineering" offers hope of alleviating some of the misery and death that result from our own practices, it also raises the spectre of removing genetic variants that might turn out to be of future adaptive value, or that might turn out to make us immediately susceptible to new problems that we don't even know about today.

Chapter Summary

In humans, most behavioral attitudes are culturally learned or acquired. Other characteristics are determined by an interaction between genes and environment. The gene pools of populations contain various alternative alleles. When the environment changes, their gene pool gives them the possibility of the appropriate physical alteration to meet the change.

When a polymorphic species is separated into different faunal regions, it is usually polytypic; that is, populations differ in the frequency with which genetic variability is expressed. It appears that the human species has been polytypic at least since the time of *Homo erectus*.

Early anthropologists classified *Homo sapiens* into subspecies, or races, based on geographical location and such phenotypic features as skin color, body size, head shape, and hair texture. The presence of atypical individuals and the non-concordance of traits continually challenged these racial classifications. No examples of "pure" racial types could be found. The visible traits were found to occur in a worldwide continuum. No definite grouping of distinct, discontinuous biological groups has been found in modern humans.

A biological race is a population of a species that differs in the frequency of genetic variants from other populations of the same species. Three obser-

vations need to be made concerning this biological definition: (1) It is arbitrary; (2) it does not mean that any one race has exclusive possession of any particular allele(s); and (3) individuals of one race will not necessarily be distinguishable from those of another. As a means for understanding human variation, the concept of race has several limitations. First, race is an arbitrary category, making agreement on any particular classification difficult; second, humans are so complex genetically that often the genetic basis of traits on which racial studies are based is itself poorly understood; and finally, race exists as a cultural as well as a biological category. Most anthropologists now view the race concept as useless for an understanding of human variation, preferring to study the distribution and significance of specific, genetically based characteristics, or else the characteristics of small breeding populations.

Physical anthropologists have determined that much of human physical variation appears related to climatic adaptation. People native to cold climates tend to have greater body bulk relative to their extremities than individuals who live in hot climates; the latter tend to be long and slender. Studies involving body build and climate are complicated by such other factors as the effects on physique of diet and of clothing.

In the United States, race is commonly thought of in terms of skin color. Subject to tremendous variation, skin color is a function of four factors: transparency or thickness of the skin, distribution of blood vessels, amount of carotene and amount of melanin in a given area of skin. Exposure to sunlight increases the amount of melanin, darkening the skin. Natural selection has favored heavily pigmented skin as protection against the strong solar radiation of equatorial latitudes. In northern latitudes, natural selection has favored relatively depigmented skins, which can utilize relatively weak solar radiation in the production of vitamin D. Selective mating, as well as geographical location, plays a part in skin color distribution.

Racism can be viewed solely as a social problem. It is an emotional phenomenon best explained in terms of collective psychology. The racist individual reacts on the basis of social stereotypes and not established scientific facts.

Many people have assumed that there are behavioral differences among human races. The innate behavioral characteristics attributed by these people to race can be explained in terms of enculturation rather than biology. Those intelligence tests that have been interpreted to indicate that European Americans are intellectually superior to African Americans are designed by European Americans for European Americans from similar backgrounds. It is not realistic to expect individuals who are not familiar with European American middle-class values to respond to items based on knowledge of these values. African and European Americans both, if they come from different types of backgrounds, are thus at a disadvantage. At the present, it is not possible to separate the inherited components of intelligence from those that are culturally acquired. Furthermore, there is still no agreement on what intelligence really is, except that it is made up of several different talents and abilities.

Although the human species has come to rely on cultural rather than biological adaptation for survival, human gene pools still continue to change in response to external factors. Many of these changes are brought about by cultural practices; for example, the shipment of powdered milk to human populations which are low in the frequency of the allele for lactase retention into adulthood may contribute to the death of large numbers of people. Those who survive are most likely to be those with the allele for lactase retention. Unquestionably, this kind of selection is deleterious to those individuals who are "selected out" in this way. Just what the long-term effects will be on the human species as a whole remains to be seen.

Suggested Readings

Brace, C. L., and Ashley Montagu. *Human Evolution*, 2nd ed. New York: Macmillan, 1977.
Part 3 of this textbook serves as a good introduction to the nonracial approach to human variation.

Brues, Alice M. *People and Races*. New York: Macmillan, 1977.
This is a book about the physical differences that distinguish populations of geographically different ancestry. It does not take for granted a background in genetics or any other special field; everything necessary to understand the subject beyond a high school level is here.

Molnar, Stephen. *Human Variation: Races, Types, and Ethnic Groups*, 3rd ed. Englewood Cliffs, N.J.: Prentice-Hall, 1992.
Key questions examined here are: How does biological diversity relate to the classical racial divisions? Are these divisions useful in the study of our species? How would human environmental relationships affect humanity's future?

Montagu, Ashley, ed. *Race and IQ*. New York: Oxford University Press, 1975.
This book is a response to the claims of Jensen, Shockley, and others that there is a link between race and intelligence. Its aim, simply stated, is to debunk such claims. To do this, the editor has assembled articles by 15 authorities on various aspects of the problem.

Weiss, Mark L., and Alan E. Mann. *Human Biology and Behavior*, 5th ed. New York: Scott Foresman, 1990.
This recent textbook is notable for its chapters on variability, races, microevolution, traits of complex inheritance, and human adaptability. The authors use a minimum of jargon without oversimplification.

BIBLIOGRAPHY

Aberle, David F., Urie Bronfenbrenner, Eckhard H. Hess, Daniel R. Miller, David H. Schneider, and James N. Spuhler. 1963. "The Incest Taboo and the Mating Patterns of Animals," *American Anthropologist*, 65:253–265.

Adams, Richard E. W. 1977. *Prehistoric Mesoamerica*. Boston: Little, Brown.

Adams, Robert McC. 1965. *Land Behind Baghdad*. Chicago: University of Chicago Press.

Adams, Robert McC. 1966. *The Evolution of Urban Society*. Chicago: Aldine.

Al–Issa, Ihsan and Wayne Dennis, eds. 1970. *Cross-cultural Studies of Behavior*. New York: Holt, Rinehart and Winston.

Alland, Alexander, Jr. 1970. *Adaptation in Cultural Evolution: An Approach to Medical Anthropology*. New York: Columbia University Press.

Alland, Alexander, Jr. 1971. *Human Diversity*. New York: Columbia University Press.

Allen, Susan L. 1984. "Media Anthropology: Building a Public Perspective," *Anthropology Newsletter*, 25:6.

Amiran, Ruth. 1965. "The Beginnings of Pottery–Making in the Near East," in Frederick R. Matson, ed. *Ceramics and Man*. New York: Viking Fund Publications in Anthropology, no. 41.

Anderson, Connie M. 1989. "Neanderthal Pelves and Gestational Length," *American Anthropologist* 91:327–340.

Ashmore, Wendy, ed. 1981. *Lowland Maya Settlement Patterns*. Albuquerque, NM: University of New Mexico Press.

Barnett, H. G. 1953. *Innovation: The Basis of Cultural Change*. New York: McGraw-Hill.

Bar–Yosef, O. 1986. "The Walls of Jericho: An Alternative Interpretation," *Current Anthropology*, 27:157–162.

Bar–Yosef, O., B. Vandermeesch, B. Arensburg, A. Belfer–Cohen, P. Goldberg, H. Laville, L. Meignen, Y. Rak, J.D. Speth, E. Tchernov, A–M. Tillier, and S. Weiner. 1992. "The Excavations in Kebara Cave, Mt. Carmel." *Current Anthropology*, 33:497–550.

Bates, Daniel G. and Fred Plog. 1991 *Human Adaptive Strategies*. New York: McGraw-Hill.

Berdan, Frances F. 1982. *The Aztecs of Central Mexico*. New York: Holt, Rinehart and Winston.

Bernal, I. 1969. *The Olmec World*. Berkeley, CA: University of California Press.

Bicchieri, M. G., ed. 1972. *Hunters and Gatherers Today: A Socioeconomic Study of Eleven Such Cultures in the Twentieth Century*. New York: Holt, Rinehart and Winston.

Binford, L. R. 1972. *An Archaeological Perspective*. New York: Seminar Press.

Binford, L. R. and Chuan Kun Ho. 1985. "Taphonomy at a Distance: Zhonkoudian, The Cave Home of Beijing Man?" *Current Anthropology*, 26:413–442.

Blumer, Mark A. and Roger Byrne. 1991. "The Ecological Genetics and Domestication and the Origins of Agriculture," *Current Anthropology*, 32:23–54.

Boas, Franz. 1966. *Race, Language and Culture*. New York: Free Press.

Bodley, John H. 1985. *Anthropology and Contemporary Human Problems*, 2nd ed. Palo Alto, CA: Mayfield.

Bordes, Francois. 1972. *A Tale of Two Caves*. New York: Harper & Row.

Bornstein, Marc H. 1975. "The Influence of Visual Perception on Culture," *American Anthropologist*, 77(4):774–798.

Brace, C. Loring. 1981. "Tales of the Phylogenetic Woods: The Evolution and Significance of Phylogenetic Trees," *American Journal of Physical Anthropology*, 56:411–429.

Brace, C. Loring, Harry Nelson, and Noel Korn. 1979. *Atlas of Human Evolution*, 2nd ed. New York: Holt, Rinehart and Winston.

Brace, C. Loring, Alan S. Ryan, and B. Holly Smith. 1981. "Comment," *Current Anthropology*, 22(4):426–430.

Braidwood, Robert J. 1960. "The Agricultural Revolution," *Scientific American*, 203:130–141.

Braidwood, Robert J. 1975. *Prehistoric Men*, 8th ed. Glenview, IL: Scott, Foresman.

Braidwood, Robert J. and Gordon R. Willey. 1962. *Courses Toward Urban Life: Archeological Consideration of Some Cultural Alternatives*. Chicago: Aldine. (Publications in Anthropology Series, no. 32.)

Brain, C. K. 1968. "Who Killed the Swartkrnas Ape–Men?" *South African Museums Association Bulletin*, 9:127–139.

Brain, C. K. 1969. "The Contribution of Namib Desert Hottentots to an Understanding of Australopithecine Bone Accumulations." *Scientific Papers of the Namib Desert Research Station*, 13.

Branda, Richard F. and John W. Eatoil. 1978. "Skin Color and Photolysis: An Evolutionary Hypothesis," *Science*, 201:625–626.

Brinton, Crane. 1953. *The Shaping of the Modern Mind*. New York: Mentor.

Brothwell, D. R. and E. Higgs, eds. 1969. *Science in Archaeology*, rev. ed. London: Thames and Hudson.

Brown, Donald E. 1991. *Human Universals*. New York: McGraw-Hill.

Brues, Alice M. 1977. *People and Races*. New York: Macmillan.

Butzer, K. 1971. *Environment and Anthropology: An Ecological Approach to Prehistory*, 2nd ed. Chicago: Aldine.

Byers, D. S., ed. 1967. *The Prehistory of the Tehuacan Valley: Vol. 1. Environment and Subsistence*. Austin, TX: University of Texas Press.

Campbell, Bernard G. 1992. *Humankind Emerging*, 6th ed. New York: HarperCollins.

Carneiro, Robert L. 1961. "Slash and Burn Cultivation among the Kuikuru and Its Implications for Cultural Development in the Amazon Basin," in J. Wilbert, ed. *The Evolution of Horticultural Systems in Native South America: Causes and Consequences*. Caracas: Sociedad de Ciencias Naturales La Salle.

Carneiro, Robert L. 1970. "A Theory of the Origin of the State," *Science*, 169:733–738.

Cashdan, Elizabeth. 1989. "Hunters and Gatherers: Economic Behavior in Bands," in Stuart Plattner, ed. *Economic Anthropology*. Stanford, CA: Stanford University Press.

Cavalli–Sforza, L. L. 1977. *Elements of Human Genetics*. Menlo Park, CA: W.A. Benjamin.

Cavallo, John A. 1990. "Cat in the Human Cradle," *Natural History*, (February), pp. 53–60.

Chagnon, N. A. and William Irons, eds. 1979. *Evolutionary Biology and Human Social Behavior*. North Scituate, MA: Duxbury Press.

Chambers, Robert. 1983. *Rural Development: Putting The Last First*. New York: Longman.

Chang, K. C., ed. 1968. *Settlement Archaeology*. Palo Alto, CA: National Press.

Childe, V. Gordon. 1951 (orig. 1936). *Man Makes Himself*. New York: New American Library.

Childe, V. Gordon. 1954. *What Happened in History*. Baltimore: Penguin Books.

Ciochon, Russell L. and John G. Fleagle, eds. 1987. *Primate Evolution and Human Origins*. Hawthorne, NY: Aldine de Gruyter.

Ciochon, Russell L. and John G. Fleagle. 1987. "Ramapithecus and Human Origins," in Russell L. Ciochon and John G. Fleagle, eds. *Primate Evolution and Human Origins*. Hawthorne, NY: Aldine de Gruyter.

Ciochon, Russell L. and John G. Fleagle. 1993. *The Human Evolution Source Book*. Englewood Cliffs, NJ: Prentice-Hall.

Clark, Ella E. 1966. *Indian Legends of the Pacific Northwest*. Berkley, CA: University of California Press.

Clark, Grahame. 1967. *The Stone Age Hunters*. New York: McGraw-Hill.

Clark, Grahame. 1972. *Starr Carr: A Case Study in Bioarchaeology*. Reading, MA: Addison-Wesley.

Clark, J. G. D. 1962. *Prehistoric Europe: The Economic Basis*. Stanford, CA: Stanford University Press.

Clark, W. E. LeGros. 1960. *The Antecedents of Man*. Chicago: Quadrangle Books.

Clark, W. E. LeGros. 1966. *History of the Primates*, 5th ed. Chicago: University of Chicago Press.

Coe, William R. 1967. *Tikal: A Handbook of the Ancient Maya Ruins*. Philadelphia: University of Pennsylvania Museum.

Cohen, Mark N. 1977. *The Food Crisis in Prehistory*. New Haven, CT: Yale University Press.

Cohen, Mark N. and George J. Armelagos, eds. 1984. *Paleopathology and the Origins of Agriculture*. Orlando, FL: Academic Press.

Cohen, Mark N. and George J. Armelagos. 1984. "Paleopathology and the Origins of Agriculture: Editors' Summation," in Cohen and Armelagos, eds. *Paleopathology and the Origins of Agriculture*. Orlando, FL: Academic Press.

Cohen, Yehudi. 1968. *Man in Adaptation: The Cultural Present*. Chicago: Aldine.

Cole, Sonia. 1975. *Leakey's Luck: The Life of Louis Seymour Bazett Leakey, 1903–1972*. New York: Harcourt Brace Jovanovich.

Constable, George and the editors of Time-Life. 1973. *The Neanderthals*. New York: Time-Life.

Cook, S. F. 1972. *Prehistoric Demography*. Reading, MA: Addison-Wesley.

Coon, Carleton S. 1954. "Climate and Race." *Smithsonian Report* for 1953. pp. 277–298.

Coon, Carleton S. 1957. *The Seven Caves*. New York: Knopf.

Coon, Carleton S. 1971. *The Hunting Peoples*. Boston: Little, Brown.

Coon, Carleton S., Stanley N. Garn, and Joseph Birdsell. 1950. *Races: A Study of the Problems of Race Formation in Man*. Springfield, IL: Charles C. Thomas.

Coppens, Yves, F. Clark Howell, Glyn L. Isaac, and Richard E. F. Leakey, eds. 1976. *Earliest Man and Environments in the Lake Rudolf Basin: Stratigraphy, Paleoecology, and Evolution*. Chicago: University of Chicago Press.

Cornish, Andrew. 1987. "Participant Observation on a Motorcycle," *Anthropology Today*, 3(6):15–16.

Corruccini, Robert S. 1992. "Metrical Reconsideration of the Skhul IV and IX and Border Cave I Crania in the Context of Modern Human Origins," *American Journal of Physical Anthropology*, 87:433–445.

Cottrell, Leonard. 1963. *The Lost Pharaohs*. New York: Grosset & Dunlap.

Culatto, Elizabeth. 1992. "A New Take on Anthropoid Origins," *Science*, 256:1516–1517.

Culbert, T. P., ed. 1973. *The Classic Maya Collapse*. Albuquerque, NM: University of New Mexico Press.

Daniel, Glyn. 1970. *The First Civilizations: The Archaeology of Their Origins*. New York: Apollo.

Daniel, Glyn. 1970. *The Origins and Growth of Archaeology*. Baltimore, MD: Penguin Books.

Daniel, Glyn. 1975. *A Hundred and Fifty Years of Archaeology*. 2nd ed. London: Duckworth.

Darwin, Charles. 1936 (orig. 1871). *The Descent of Man and Selection in Relation to Sex*. New York: Random House (Modern Library).

Darwin, Charles. 1967 (orig. 1859). *On the Origin of Species*. New York: Atheneum.

de Laguna, Grace A. 1966. *On Existence and the Human World*. New Haven, CT: Yale University Press.

de Pelliam, Alison and Francis D. Burton. 1976. "More on Predatory Behavior in Nonhuman Primates," *Current Anthropology*, 17(3):512–513.

DeBeer, Sir Gavin R. 1964. *Atlas of Evolution*. London: Nelson.

Deetz, James. 1967. *Invitation to Archaeology*. New York: Doubleday.

Deevy, Edward S. Jr. 1960. "The Human Population," *Scientific American*, 203:194–204.

DeVore, Irven, ed. 1965. *Primate Behavior: Field Studies of Monkeys and Apes*. New York: Holt, Rinehart and Winston.

Dixon, J. E., J. R. Cann, and C. Renfrew. 1968. "Obsidian and the Origins of Trade," *Scientific American*, 218:38–46.

Dobzhansky, Theodosius. 1962. *Mankind Evolving*. New Haven, CT: Yale University Press.

Driver, Harold. 1964. *Indians of North America*. Chicago: University of Chicago Press.

Dumond, Don E. 1977. "Science in Archaeology: The Saints Go Marching In," *American Antiquity*, 42(3):330–349.

duToit, Brian M. 1991. *Human Sexuality: Cross Cultural Readings*. New York: McGraw-Hill.

Edey, Maitland and the editors of Time-Life. 1972. *The Missing Link*. New York: Time-Life.

Edey, Maitland A. and Donald Johannson. 1989. *Blueprints: Solving the Mystery of Evolution*. Boston: Little, Brown.

Edwards, Stephen W. 1978. "Nonutilitarian Activities on the Lower Paleolithic: A Look at the Two Kinds of Evidence," *Current Anthropology*, 19(1):135–137.

Ehrlich, Paul R. and Anne H. Ehrlich. 1970. *Population, Resources, Environment*. San Francisco: Freeman.

Eiseley, Loren. 1958. *Darwin's Century: Evolution and the Men Who Discovered It*. New York: Doubleday.

Ellison, Peter T. 1990. "Human Ovarian Function and Reproductive Ecology: New Hypotheses," *American Anthropologist*, 92:933–952.

Evans, William. 1968. *Communication in the Animal World*. New York: Crowell.

Fagan, Brian M. 1992. *People of the Earth*, 7th ed. New York: HarperCollins.

Falk, Dean. 1975. "Comparative Anatomy of the Larynx in Man and the Chimpanzee: Implications for Language in Neanderthal," *American Journal of Physical Anthropology*, 43(1):123–132.

Falk, Dean. 1989. "Ape-like Endocast of 'Ape-man' Taung," *American Journal of Physical Anthropology*, 80:335–339.

Falk, Dean. 1993. "Hominid Paleoneurology," in Russell L. Ciochon and John G. Fleagle, eds. *The Human Evolution Source Book*. Englewood Cliffs, NJ: Prentice-Hall.

Fedigan, Linda Marie. 1986. "The Changing Role of Women in Models of Human Evolution," *Annual Review of Anthropology*, 15:25–56.

Flannery, Kent V. 1973. "The Origins of Agriculture," in Bernard J. Siegel, Alan R. Beals, and Stephen A. Tyler, eds. *Annual Review of Anthropology*, vol. 2. Palo Alto, CA: Annual Reviews.

Flannery, Kent V., ed. 1976. *The Mesoamerican Village*. New York: Seminar Press.

Flannery, Kent V. and Joyce Marcus. 1976. "Formative Oaxaca and the Zapotec Cosmos," *American Scientist*, 64:334–383.

Fleagle, John G. 1992. "Early Anthropoid Evolution." Paper presented at the 91st Annual Meeting of the American Anthropological Association, San Francisco, December.

Forde, C. Daryll. 1963. *Habitat, Economy and Society*. New York: E.P. Dutton.

Fossey, Dian. 1983. *Gorillas in The Mist*. Burlington, MA: Houghton Mifflin.

Fox, Robin. 1968. *Encounter with Anthropology*. New York: Dell.

Fox, Robin. 1968. *Kinship and Marriage in an Anthropological Perspective*. Baltimore, MD: Penguin Books.

Frankfort, Henri. 1968. *The Birth of Civilization in the Near East*. New York: Barnes & Noble.

Frayer, David W. 1981. "Body Size, Weapon Use, and Natural Selection in the European Upper Paleolithic and Mesolithic," *American Anthropologist*, 83:57–73.

Freeman, Leslie G. 1992. "Ambrona and Torralba: New Evidence and Interpretation." Paper presented at the 91st Annual Meeting of the American Anthropological Association, San Francisco, December.

Fried, Morton. 1960. "On the Evolution of Social Stratification and the State," in S. Diamond, ed. *Culture in History: Essays in Honor of Paul Radin*. New York: Columbia University Press.

Fried, Morton. 1967. *The Evolution of Political Society: An Essay in Political Anthropology*. New York: Random House.

Fried, Morton. 1972. *The Study of Anthropology*. New York: Crowell.

Gamble, Clive. 1986. *The Paleolithic Settlement of Europe*. Cambridge, England: Cambridge University Press.

Garn, Stanley M. 1970. *Human Races*, 3rd ed. Springfield, IL: Charles C. Thomas.

Geertz, Clifford. 1984. "Distinguished Lecture: Anti Anti-Relativism," *American Anthropologist*, 86:263–278.

Gelb, Ignace J. 1952. *A Study of Writing*. London: Routledge.

Glob, P. 1969. *The Bog People*. London: Faber & Faber.

Goodall, Jane. 1986. *The Chimpanzees of Gombe: Patterns of Behavior*. Cambridge, MA: Belknap Press.

Goodall, Jane. 1990. *Through a Window: My Thirty Years with the Chimpanzees of Gombe*. Boston: Houghton Mifflin.

Goodall–Van Lawick, Jane. 1972. *In the Shadow of Man*. New York: Dell.

Goodenough, Ward. 1961. "Comment on Cultural Evolution," *Daedalus*, 90:521–528.

Goodenough, Ward H. 1990. "Evolution of the Human Capacity for Beliefs," *American Anthropologist*, 92:597–612.

Goody, Jack, ed. 1972. *Developmental Cycle in Domestic Groups*. New York: Cambridge University Press. (Papers in Social Anthropology, no. 1.)

Gordon, Robert. 1981. Interview for Coast Telecourses, Inc., Los Angeles.

Gould, Stephen J. 1981. *The Mismeasure of Man*. New York: W.W. Norton.

Gould, Stephen J. 1983. *Hen's Teeth and Horses' Toes*. New York: W.W. Norton.

Gould, Stephen J. 1985. *The Flamingo's Smile: Reflections in Natural History*. New York: W.W. Norton.

Gould, Stephen J. 1986. "Of Kiwi Eggs and the Liberty Bell," *Natural History*, 95:20–29.

Gould, Stephen J. 1989. *Wonderful Life*, New York: W.W. Norton.

Gould, Stephen J. 1991. *Bully for Brontosaurus*. New York: W.W. Norton.

Graham, Susan Brandt. 1979. "Biology and Human Social Behavior: A Response to van den Berghe and Barash," *American Anthropologist*, 81(2):357–360.

Graves, Paul. 1991. "New Models and Metaphors for the Neanderthal Debate," *Current Anthropology*, 32(5):513–543.

Greene, John C. 1959. *The Death of Adam*. Ames, IA: Iowa State University Press.

Greenfield, Leonard Owen. 1979. "On the Adaptive Pattern of Ramapithecus," *American Journal of Physical Anthropology*, 50:527–547.

Greenfield, Leonard Owen. 1980. "A Late Divergence Hypothesis," *American Journal of Physical Anthropology*, 52:351–366.

Grine, F. E. 1993. "Australopithecine Taxonomy and Phylogeny: Historical Background and Recent Interpretation," in Russell L. Ciochon and John G. Fleagle, eds. *The Human Evolution Source Book*. Englewood Cliffs, NJ: Prentice-Hall.

Hall, K. R. L. and Irven DeVore. 1965. "Baboon Social Behavior," in Irven DeVore, ed. *Primate Behavior*. New York: Holt, Rinehart and Winston.

Hallowell, A. Irving. 1955. *Culture and Experience*. Philadelphia: University of Pennsylvania Press.

Halverson, John. 1989. "Review of *Altimira Revisited and Other Essays on Early Art*," *American Antiquity*, 54:883.

Hamblin, Dora Jane and the editors of Time-Life. 1973. *The First Cities*. New York: Time-Life.

Hamburg, David A. and Elizabeth R. McGown, eds. 1979. *The Great Apes*. Menlo Park, CA: Cummings.

Harlow, Harry F. 1962. "Social Deprivation in Monkeys," *Scientific American*, 206:1–10.

Harris, Marvin. 1968. *The Rise of Anthropological Theory: A History of Theories of Culture*. New York: Crowell.

Harrison, Gail G. 1975. "Primary Adult Lactase Deficiency: A Problem in Anthropological Genetics," *American Anthropologist*, 77:812–835.

Harrison, G. A., J. S. Weiner, J. M. Tanner, and N. A. Barnicot. 1977. *Human Biology: An Introduction to Human Evolution, Variation and Growth*, 2nd ed. New York: Oxford University Press.

Haviland, W. A. 1970. "Tikal, Guatemala and Mesoamerican Urbanism," *World Archaeology*, 2:186–198.

Haviland, W. A. 1972. "A New Look at Classic Maya Social Organization at Tikal," *Ceramica de Cultura Maya*, 8:1–16.

Haviland, W. A. 1975. "The Ancient Maya and the Evolution of Urban Society," *University of Northern Colorado Museum of Anthropology, Miscellaneous Series*, no. 37.

Haviland, William A. 1991. "Star Wars at Tikal, or Did Caracol Do What the Glyphs Say They Did?" Paper presented at the 90th Annual Meeting of the American Anthropological Association, Chicago, November.

Haviland, William A. and Hattula Moholy-Nagy. 1992. "Distinguishing the High and Mighty from the Hoi Polloi at Tikal, Guatemala," in Arlen F. and Diane Z. Chase, eds. *Mesoamerican Elites: an Archaeological Assessment*. Norman, OK: University of Oklahoma Press.

Haviland, W. A. and M. W. Power. 1994. *The Original Vermonters: Native Inhabitants, Past and Present*. 2nd ed. Hanover, NH: University Press of New England.

Hawkins, Gerald S. 1965. *Stonehenge Decoded*. New York: Doubleday.

Hewes, Gordon W. 1973. "Primate Communication and the Gestural Origin of Language," *Current Anthropology*, 14:5–24.

Hodgen, Margaret. 1964. *Early Anthropology in the Sixteenth and Seventeenth Centuries*. Philadelphia: University of Pennsylvania Press.

Hole, Frank. 1966. "Investigating the Origins of Mesopotamian Civilization," *Science*, 153:605–611.

Hole, Frank and Robert F. Heizer. 1969. *An Introduction to Archaeology*. New York: Holt, Rinehart and Winston.

Holloway, Ralph L. 1980. "The O. H. 7 (Olduvai Gorge, Tanzania) Hominid Partial Brain Endocast Revisited," *American Journal of Physical Anthropology*, 53:267–274.

Holloway, Ralph L. 1981. "The Indonesian *Homo erectus* Brain Endocast Revisited," *American Journal of Physical Anthropology*, 55:503–521.

Holloway, Ralph L. 1981. "Volumetric and Asymmetry Determinations on Recent Hominid Endocasts: Spy I and II, Djebel Jhroud 1, and the Salb *Homo erectus* Specimens, with Some Notes on Neanderthal Brain Size," *American Journal of Physical Anthropology*, 55:385–393.

Howell, F. Clark. 1970. *Early Man*. New York: Time-Life.

Jennings, Jesse D. 1974. *Prehistory of North America*, 2nd ed. New York: McGraw-Hill.

Johanson, Donald and James Shreeve. 1989. *Lucy's Child: The Discovery of a Human Ancestor*. New York: Avon.

Johanson, D. C. and T. D. White. 1979. "A Systematic Assessment of Early African Hominids," *Science*, 203:321–330.

John, V. 1971. "Whose Is the Failure?" in C. L. Brace, G. R. Gamble, and J. T. Bond, eds. *Race and Intelligence*. Washington, DC: American Anthropological Association (Anthropological Studies no. 8.)

Johnson, Allen W. and Timothy Earle. 1987. *The Evolution of Human Societies, from Foraging Group to Agrarian State*. Stanford, CA: Stanford University Press.

Jolly, Allison. 1985. *The Evolution of Primate Behavior*. 2nd ed. New York: Macmillan.

Jolly, Allison. 1985. "The Evolution of Primate Behavior," *American Scientist*, 73(3):230–239.

Jolly, Allison. 1991. "Thinking Like a Vervet," *Science*, 251:574.

Jolly, C. J. 1970. "The Seed Eaters: A New Model of Hominid Differentiation Based on a Baboon Analogy," *Man*, 5:5–26.

Jolly, C. J. and Fred Plog. 1986. *Physical Anthropology and Archaeology*, 4th ed. New York: Knopf.

Joukowsky, Martha A. 1980. *A Complete Field Manual of Archaeology: Tools and Techniques of Field Work for Archaeologists*. Englewood Cliffs, NJ: Prentice-Hall.

Joyce, Christopher. 1991. *Witnesses from the Grave: The Stories Bones Tell*. Boston: Little, Brown.

Kay, Richard F. 1981. "The Nut-Crackers: A New Theory of the Adaptations of the Ramapithecinae," *American Journal of Physical Anthropology*, 55:141–151.

Kay, Richard F., J. F. Fleagle, and E. L. Simons. 1981. "A Revision of the Oligocene Apes of the Fayum Province, Egypt," *American Journal of Physical Anthropology*, 55:293–322.

Kay, Richard F., J.G.M. Theweissen, and Anne D. Yoder. 1992. "Cranial Anatomy of *Ignacius graybullianus* and the Affinities of the Plesiadapiformes," *American Journal of Physical Anthropology*, 89(4):477–498.

Kenyon, Kathleen. 1957. *Digging Up Jericho*. London: Ben.

Kleinman, Arthur. 1982. "The Failure of Western Medicine," in David Hunter and Phillip Whitten, eds. *Anthropology: Contemporary Perspectives*. Boston: Little, Brown.

Knauft, Bruce M. 1991. "Violence and Sociality in Human Evolution," *Current Anthropology*, 32:391–428.

Krader, Lawrence. 1968. *Formation of the State*. Englewood Cliffs, NJ: Prentice-Hall. (Foundation of Modern Anthropology.)

Kroeber, A. L. 1963. *Anthropology: Cultural Processes and Patterns*. New York: Harcourt.

Kuhn, Thomas. 1970. *The Structure of Scientific Revolutions*, 2nd ed. Chicago: University of Chicago Press.

Kummer, Hans. 1971. *Primate Societies: Group Techniques of Ecological Adaptation*. Chicago: Aldine.

Lancaster, Jane B. 1975. *Primate Behavior and the Emergence of Human Culture*. New York: Holt, Rinehart and Winston.

Lanning, Edward P. 1967. *Peru before the Incas*. Englewood Cliffs, NJ: Prentice-Hall.

Lasker, Gabriel W. and Robert Tyzzer. 1982. *Physical Anthropology*, 3rd ed. New York: Holt, Rinehart and Winston.

Laughlin, W. S. and R. H. Osborne, eds. 1967. *Human Variation and Origins*. San Francisco: Freeman.

Leach, Edmund. 1961. *Rethinking Anthropology*. London: Athione Press.

Leach, Edmund. 1982. *Social Anthropology*. Glasgow, Scotland: Fontana.

Leacock, Eleanor. 1981. *Myths of Male Dominance: Collected Articles on Women Cross Culturally*. New York: Monthly Review Press.

Leacock, Eleanor. 1981. "Women's Status in Egalitarian Society: Implications for Social Evolution," in *Myths of Male Dominance: Collected Articles on Women Cross Culturally*. New York: Monthly Review Press.

Leakey, L. S. B. 1965. *Olduvai Gorge, 1951–1961*, vol. 1. London: Cambridge University Press.

Leakey, L. S. B. 1967. "Development of Aggression as a Factor in Early Man and Prehuman Evolution," in C. Clements and D. Lundsley, eds. *Aggression and Defense*. Los Angeles: University of California Press.

Leakey, M. D. 1971. *Olduvai Gorge: Excavations in Beds I and II, 1960–1963*. London: Cambridge University Press.

Leavitt, Gregory C. 1990. "Sociobiological Explanations of Incest Avoidance: A Critical Review of Evidential Claims," *American Anthropologist*, 92:973.

Lee, Richard B. and Irven DeVore, eds. 1968. *Man the Hunter*. Chicago: Aldine.

Leeds, Anthony and Andrew P. Vayda, eds. 1965. *Man, Culture and Animals: The Role of Animals in Human Ecological Adjustments*. Washington, DC: American Association for the Advancement of Science.

LeMay, Marjorie. 1975. "The Language Capability of Neanderthal Man," *American Journal of Physical Anthropology*, 43(1):9–14.

Leonard, William R. and Michelle Hegman. 1987. "Evolution of P_3 Morphology in *Australopithecus afarensis*," *American Journal of Physical Anthropology*, 73:41–63.

Leroi-Gourhan, A. 1968. "The Evolution of Paleolithic Art," *Scientific American*, 218:58–70.

Lett, James. 1987. *The Human Enterprise: A Critical Introduction to Anthropological Theory*. Boulder, CO: Westview Press.

Levanthes, Louise E. 1987. "The Mysteries of the Bog," *National Geographic*, 171:397–420.

Levine, Robert Paul. 1968. *Genetics*. New York: Holt, Rinehart and Winston.

Lewin, Roger. 1983. "Is the Orangutan a Living Fossil?" *Science*, 222:1223.

Lewin, Roger. 1985. "Tooth Enamel Tells a Complex Story," *Science*, 228:707.

Lewin, Roger. 1986. "New Fossil Upsets Human Family," *Science*, 233:720–721.

Lewin, Roger. 1987. "Debate over Emergence of Human Tooth Pattern," *Science*, 235:749.

Lewin, Roger. 1987. "The Earliest Humans Were More Like Apes," *Science*, 236:106–163.

Lewin, Roger. 1987. "Four Legs Bad, Two Legs Good," *Science*, 235:969–971.

Lewin, Roger. 1987. "Why Is Ape Tool Use So Confusing?" *Science*, 236:776–777.

Lewin, Roger. 1988. "Molecular Clocks Turn a Quarter Century," *Science*, 235:969–971.

Lewis, I. M. 1976. *Social Anthropology in Perspective*, Harmondsworth, England: Penguin.

Livingstone, Frank B. 1973. "The Distribution of Abnormal Hemoglobin Genes and Their Significance for Human Evolution," in C. Loring Brace and James Metress, eds. *Man in Evolutionary Perspective*. New York: Wiley.

Lovejoy, C. Owen. 1981. "Origin of Man," *Science*, 211(4480):341–350.

Lowenstein, Jerold M. 1992. "Genetic Surprises," *Discover*, 13(12):82–88.

Marsella, Joan. 1982. "Pulling It Together: Discussion and Comments," in Stephen Pastner and William A. Haviland, eds. *Confronting the Creationists*. Northeastern Anthropological Association, Occasional Proceedings, vol. 1.

Marshack, Alexander. 1972. *The Roots of Civilization: A Study in Prehistoric Cognition; The Origins of Art, Symbol and Notation*. New York: McGraw-Hill.

Marshack, Alexander. 1976. "Some Implications of the Paleolithic Symbolic Evidence for the Origin of Language," *Current Anthropology*, 17(2):274–282.

Marshack, Alexander. 1989. "Evolution of the Human Capacity: The Symbolic Evidence," *Yearbook of Physical Anthropology*, 32:1–34.

Mason, J. Alden. 1957. *The Ancient Civilizations of Peru*. Baltimore: Penguin Books.

Matson, Frederick R., ed. 1965. *Ceramics and Man*. New York: Viking Fund Publications in Anthropology, no. 41.

McCorriston, Joy and Frank Hole. 1991. "The Ecology of Seasonal Stress and the Origins of Agriculture in the Near East," *American Anthropologist*, 93:46–69.

McGimsey, Charles R. 1972. *Public Archaeology*. New York: Seminar Press.

McHenry, Henry M. 1975. "Fossils and the Mosaic Nature of Human Evolution," *Science*, 190:524–431.

McHenry, Henry M. 1992. "Body Size and Proportions in Early Hominids," *American Journal of Physical Anthropology*, 87:407–431.

Melaart, James. 1967. *Çatal Hüyük: A Neolithic Town in Anatolia*. London: Thames and Hudson.

Mellars, Paul. 1989. "Major Issues in the Emergence of Modern Humans," *Current Anthropology*, 30:349–385.

Merrell, David J. 1962. *Evolution and Genetics: The Modern Theory of Genetics*. New York: Holt, Rinehart and Winston.

Michaels, Joseph W. 1973. *Dating Methods in Archaeology*. New York: Seminar Press.

Millon, René. 1973. *Urbanization of Teotihuacán, Mexico, Vol. 1, Part 1: The Teotihuacán Map*. Austin, TX: The University of Texas Press.

Molnar, Stephen. 1992. *Human Variation: Races, Types and Ethnic Groups* 3rd ed. Englewood Cliffs, NJ: Prentice-Hall.

Montagu, Ashley. 1963. *Human Heredity*, 2nd ed. New York: Signet Books.

Montagu, Ashley. 1964. *The Concept of Race*. London: Macmillan.

Montagu, Ashley. 1964. *Man's Most Dangerous Myth: The Fallacy of Race*, 4th ed. New York: World.

Montagu, Ashley. 1969. *Man: His First Two Million Years*. New York: Columbia University Press.

Montagu, Ashley. 1975. *Race and IQ*. New York: Oxford University Press.

Moscati, Sabatino. 1962. *The Face of the Ancient Orient*. New York: Doubleday.

Mowat, Farley. 1981. *People of the Deer*. Toronto, Canada: Bantam Books.

Murdock, George P. 1971. "How Culture Changes," in Harry L. Shapiro, ed. *Man, Culture and Society*. 2nd ed. New York: Oxford University Press.

Neer, Robert M. 1975. "The Evolutionary Significance of Vitamin D, Skin Pigment and Ultraviolet Light," *American Journal of Physical Anthropology*, 43:409–416.

Netting, R.M., R.R. Wilk, and E.J. Arnould, eds. 1984. *Households: Comparative and Historical Studies of the Domestic Group*. Berkeley, CA: University of California Press.

Oakley, Kenneth P. 1964. *Man the Tool–Maker*. Chicago: University of Chicago Press.

Olszewski, Deborah I. 1991. "Comment," *Current Anthropology*, 32:43.

Oswalt, Wendell H. 1972. *Habitat and Technology*. New York: Holt, Rinehart and Winston.

Otterbein, Keith F. 1971. *The Evolution of War*. New Haven, CT: HRAF Press.

Parker, Seymour and Hilda Parker. 1979. "The Myth of Male Superiority: Rise and Demise," *American Anthropologist*, 81(2):289–309.

Pastner, Stephen and William A. Haviland, eds. 1982. *Confronting the Creationists*. Northeastern Anthropological Association Occasional Proceedings, vol. I.

Patterson, Francine and Eugene Linden. 1981. *The Education of Koko*. New York: Holt, Rinehart and Winston.

Patterson, Thomas C. 1981. *Archaeology: The Evolution of Ancient Societies*. Englewood Cliffs, NJ: Prentice-Hall.

Peacock, James L. 1986. *The Anthropological Lens: Harsh Light, Soft Focus*. New York: Cambridge University Press.

Penniman, T. K. 1965. *A Hundred Years of Anthropology*. London: Duckworth.

Peters, Charles R. 1979. "Toward an Ecological Model of African Plio-Pleistocene Hominid Adaptations," *American Anthropologist*, 81(2):261–278.

Peterson, Frederick L. 1962. *Ancient Mexico, An Introduction to the Pre-Hispanic Cultures*. New York: Capricorn Books.

Pfeiffer, John E. 1977. *The Emergence of Society*. New York: McGraw-Hill.

Pfeiffer, John E. 1978. *The Emergence of Man*. New York: Harper & Row.

Pfeiffer, John E. 1985. *The Creative Explosion*. Ithaca, NY: Cornell University Press.

Piggott, Stuart. 1965. *Ancient Europe*. Chicago: Aldine.

Pilbeam, David. 1986. *Human Origins*. David Skamp Distinguished Lecture in Anthropology, Indiana University, South Bend, IN.

Pilbeam, David. 1987. "Rethinking Human Origins," in Russell L. Ciochon and John G. Fleagle, eds. *Primate Evolution and Human Origins*. Hawthorne, NY: Aldine de Gruytar.

Pilbeam, David and Stephen J. Gould. 1974. "Size and Scaling in Human Evolution," *Science*, 186:892–901.

Pimentel, David. 1991. "Response," *Science*, 252:358.

Pope, Geoffrey G. 1989. "Bamboo and Human Evolution," *Natural History*, (October), pp. 48–57.

Pope, Geoffrey G. 1992. "Craniofacial Evidence for the Origin of Modern Humans in China," *Yearbook of Physical Anthropology*, 35:243–298.

Premack, Ann James and David Premack. 1972. "Teaching Language to an Ape," *Scientific American*, 277(4):92–99.

Prideaux, Tom and the editors of Time-Life. 1973. *Cro-Magnon Man*. New York: Time-Life.

Rathje, William L. 1993. "Rubbish!" in William A. Haviland and Robert J. Gordon, eds. *Talking About People: Readings in Contemporary Cultural Anthropology*. Mountain View, CA: Mayfield.

Read, Catherine E. 1973. "The Role of Faunal Analysis in Reconstructing Human Behavior: A Mousterian Example." Paper presented at the meetings of the California Academy of Sciences, Long Beach, CA.

Read–Martin, Catherine E. and Dwight W. Read. 1975. "Australopithecine Scavenging and Human Evolution: An Approach from Faunal Analysis," *Current Anthropology*, 16(3):359–368.

Redman, Charles L. 1978. *The Rise of Civilization: From Early Farmers to Urban Society in the Ancient Near East*. San Francisco: Freeman.

Reid, J. J., M. B. Schiffer, and W. L. Rathje. 1975. "Behavioral Archaeology: Four Strategies," *American Anthropologist*, 77:864–869.

Renfrew, Colin. 1973. *Before Civilization: The Radiocarbon Revolution and Prehistoric Europe*. London: Jonathan Cape.

Rice, Don S. and Prudence M. 1984. "Lessons from the Maya," *Latin American Research Review*, 19(3):7–34.

Rindos, David. 1984. *The Origins of Agriculture: An Evolutionary Perspective*. Orlando, FL: Academic Press.

Romer, Alfred S. 1945. *Vertebrate Paleontology*. Chicago: University of Chicago Press.

Roosevelt, Anna Curtenius. 1984. "Population, Health, and the Evolution of Subsistence: Conclusions from the Conference," in Mark N. Cohen and George J. Armelagos, eds. *Paleopathology and the Origins of Agriculture*. Orlando, FL: Academic Press.

Rowe, Timothy. 1988. "New Issues for Phylogenetics," *Science*, 239:1183–1184.

Sabatino, Moseati. 1962. *The Face of the Ancient Orient*. New York: Doubleday.

Sabloff, J. A. 1989. *The Cities of Ancient Mexico*. New York: Thames and Hudson.

Sabloff, J. A. and C. C. Lambert–Karlovsky. 1973. *Ancient Civilization and Trade*. Albuquerque, NM: University of New Mexico Press.

Sabloff, J. A. and C. C. Lamberg–Karlovsky, eds. 1974. *The Rise and Fall of Civilizations, Modern Archaeological Approaches to Ancient Cultures*. Menlo Park, CA: Cummings.

Salthe, Stanley N. 1972. *Evolutionary Biology*. New York: Holt, Rinehart and Winston.

Sanday, Peggy R. 1975. "On the Causes of IQ Differences Between Groups and Implications for Social Policy," in Ashley Montagu, ed. *Race and IQ*. London: Oxford University Press.

Sanday, Peggy R. 1981. *Female Power and Male Dominance: On the Origins of Sexual Inequality*. Cambridge, England: Cambridge University Press.

Savage, Jay M. 1969. *Evolution*, 3rd ed. New York: Holt, Rinehart and Winston.

Scarr–Salapatek, S. 1971. "Unknowns in the I.Q. Equation," *Science*, 174:1223–1228.

Schaller, George B. 1963. *The Mountain Gorilla*. Chicago: University of Chicago Press.

Schaller, George B. 1971. *The Year of the Gorilla*. New York: Ballantine Books.

Schwartz, Jeffrey H. 1984. "Hominoid Evolution: A Review and a Reassessment," *Current Anthropology*, 25(5):655–672.

Semenov, S. A. 1964. *Prehistoric Technology*. New York: Barnes & Noble.

Sen, Gita and Caren Grown. 1987. *Development, Crisis, and Alternative Visions: Third World Women's Perspectives*. New York: Monthly Review Press.

Sharer, Robert J. and Wendy Ashmore. 1993. *Archaeology: Discovering Our Past*, 2nd ed. Palo Alto, CA: Mayfield.

Shaw, Dennis G. 1984. "A Light at the End of the Tunnel: Anthropological Contributions Toward Global Competence," *Anthropology Newsletter*, 25:16.

Sheets, Payson. 1993. "Dawn of a New Stone Age in Eye Surgery" in Robert J. Sharer and Wendy Ashmore, eds. *Archaeology: Discovering Our Past*, 2nd ed. Palo Alto, CA: Mayfield.

Shinnie, Margaret. 1970. *Ancient African Kingdoms*. New York: New American Library.

Shuey, A. M. 1966. *The Testing of Negro Intelligence*. New York: Social Science Press.

Simons, Elwyn L. 1972. *Primate Evolution*. New York: Macmillan.

Simons, Elwyn, L. 1989. "Human Origins," *Science*, 245:1343–1350.

Simons, E. L., D. T. Rasmussen, and D. L. Gebo. 1987. "A New Species of Propliopithecus from the Fayum Egypt," *American Journal of Physical Anthropology*, 73:139–147.

Simpson, George G. 1949. *The Meaning of Evolution*. New Haven, CT: Yale University Press.

Sjoberg, Gideon. 1960. *The Preindustrial City*. New York: Free Press.

Skelton, Randall R., Henry M. McHenry, and Gerrell M. Drawhorn. 1986. "Phylogenetic Analysis of Early Hominids," *Current Anthropology*, 27:21–43.

Smith, Bruce D. 1977. "Archaeological Inference and Inductive Confirmation," *American Anthropologist*, 79(3):598–617.

Smith, Fred H. and Gail C. Raynard. 1980. "Evolution of the Supraorbital Region in Upper Pleistocene Fossil Hominids from South-Central Europe," *American Journal of Physical Anthropology*, 53:589–610.

Smith, Philip E. L. 1976. *Food Production and Its Consequences*, 2nd ed. Menlo Park, CA: Cummings.

Smuts, Barbara. 1987. "What Are Friends For?" *Natural History*, 96(2):36–44.

Snowden, Charles T. 1990. "Language Capabilities of Nonhuman Animals," *Yearbook of Physical Anthropology*, 33:215–243.

Spencer, Frank and Fred H. Smith. 1981. "The Significance of Ales Hrdlicka's 'Neanderthal Phase of Man': A Historical and Current Assessment," *American Journal of Physical Anthropology*, 56:435–459.

Spradley, James P. 1979. *The Ethnographic Interview*. New York: Holt, Rinehart and Winston.

Spradley, James P. 1980. *Participant Observation*. New York: Holt, Rinehart and Winston.

Stahl, Ann Brower. 1984. "Hominid Dietary Selection Before Fire," *Current Anthropology*, 25:151–168.

Stanley, Stephen M. 1979. *Macroevolution*. San Francisco: Freeman.

Stiles, Daniel. 1979. "Early Acheulian and Developed Oldowan," *Current Anthropology*, 20(1):126–129.

Stirton, Ruben Arthur. 1967. *Time, Life, and Man*. New York: Wiley.

Stocker, Terry. 1987. "A Technological Mystery Resolved," *Invention and Technology*, (Spring), p. 64.

Stocking, George W. Jr. 1968. *Race, Culture and Evolution: Essays in the History of Anthropology*. New York: Free Press.

Straus, W. L. and A. J. E. Cave. 1957. "Pathology and the Posture of Neanderthal Man," *Quarterly Review of Biology*, 32:348–363.

Swadesh, Morris. 1959. "Linguistics as an Instrument of Prehistory," *Southwestern Journal of Anthropology*, 15:20–35.

Tague, Robert G. 1992. "Sexual Dimorphism in the Human Bony Pelvis, with a Consideration of the Neanderthal Pelvis from Kebara Cave, Israel," *American Journal of Physical Anthropology*, 88:1–21.

Tattersall, Ian. 1975. *The Evolutionary Significance of Ramapithecus*. Minneapolis: Burgess.

Thomas, David H. 1974. *Predicting the Past*. New York: Holt, Rinehart and Winston.

Thomas, David H. 1989. *Archaeology*, 2nd ed. New York: Holt, Rinehart and Winston.

Thompson, J. E. S. 1960. *Maya Hieroglyphic Writing: Introduction*. Norman, OK: University of Oklahoma Press.

Thorne, Alan G. and Melford H. Wolpoff. 1981. "Regional Continuity in Australasian Pleistocene Hominid Evolution," *American Journal of Physical Anthropology*, 55:337–349.

Tobias, Philip V. 1980. "The Natural History of the Heliocoidal Occlusal Plane and Its Evolution in Early Homo," *American Journal of Physical Anthropology*, 53:173–187.

Trinkaus, Erik. 1986. "The Neanderthals and Modern Human Origins," *Annual Review of Anthropology*, 15:197.

Ucko, Peter J. and Andrée Rosenfeld. 1967. *Paleolithic Cave Art*. New York: McGraw-Hill.

Ucko, Peter J., R. Tringham and G. W. Dimbleby, eds. 1972. *Man, Settlement and Urbanism*. London: Duckworth.

Vincent, John. 1979. "On the Special Division of Labor, Population, and the Origins of Agriculture," *Current Anthropology*, 20(2)422–425.

Voget, F. W. 1975. *A History of Ethnology*. New York: Holt, Rinehart and Winston.

Washburn, S. L. and Ruth Moore. 1980. *Ape into Human: A Study of Human Evolution*. 2nd ed. Boston: Little, Brown.

Weaver, Muriel P. 1972. *The Aztecs, Maya and Their Predecessors*. New York: Seminar Press.

Weiner, J. S. 1955. *The Piltdown Forgery*. Oxford, England: Oxford University Press.

Weiss, Mark L. and Alan E. Mann. 1990. *Human Biology and Behavior*, 5th ed. Boston: Little, Brown.

Wells, Calvin. 1964. *Bones, Bodies and Disease*. London: Thames and Hudson.

Wernick, Robert and the editors of Time-Life. 1973. *The Monument Builders*. New York: Time-Life.

Whelehan, Patricia. 1985. "Review of Incest, a Biosocial View," *American Anthropologist*, 87:678.

White, Edmond, Dale Brown, and the editors of Time-Life. 1973. *The First Men*. New York: Time-Life.

White, Leslie. 1949. *The Science of Culture: A Study of Man and Civilization*. New York: Farrar, Strauss.

White, Leslie. 1959. *The Evolution of Culture: The Development of Civilization to the Fall of Rome*. New York: McGraw-Hill.

White, Peter. 1976. *The Past Is Human*, 2nd ed. New York: Maplinger.

White, Randall. 1992. "The Earliest Images, Ice Age 'Art' in Europe," *Expedition*, 34(3):37–51.

White, Tim D. 1979. "Evolutionary Implications of Pliocene Hominid Footprints," *Science*, 208:175–176.

Whiting, John W. M., John A. Sodergem, and Stephen M. Stigler. 1982. "Winter Temperature as a Constraint to the Migration of Preindustrial Peoples," *American Anthropologist*, 84:279–298.

Willey, Gordon R. 1966. *An Introduction to American Archaeology, Vol. 1: North America*. Englewood Cliffs, NJ: Prentice-Hall.

Willey, Gordon R. 1971. *An Introduction to American Archaeology, Vol. 2: South America*. Englewood Cliffs, NJ: Prentice-Hall.

Wilson, A. K. and V. M. Sarich. 1969. "A Molecular Time Scale for Human Evolution," *Proceedings of the National Academy of Science*, 63:1089–1093.

Wittfogel, Karl A. 1957. *Oriental Despotism, A Comparative Study of Total Power*. New Haven, CT: Yale University Press.

Wolf, Eric. 1959. *Sons of the Shaking Earth*. Chicago: University of Chicago Press.

Wolpoff, M. H. 1971. "Interstitial Wear," *American Journal of Physical Anthropology*, 34:205–227.

Wolpoff, M. H. 1977. "Review of Earliest Man in the Lake Rudolf Basin," *American Anthropologist*, 79:708–711.

Wolpoff, M. H. 1982. "*Ramapithecus* and Hominid Origins," *Current Anthropology*, 23:501–522.

Wolpoff, M. H. 1993. "Evolution in *Homo erectus*: The Question of Stasis," in Russell L. Ciochon and John G. Fleagle, eds. *The Human Evolution Source Book*. Englewood Cliffs, NJ: Prentice-Hall.

Wolpoff, M. H. 1993. "Multiregional Evolution: The Fossil Alternative to Eden," in Russell L. Ciochon and John G. Fleagle, eds. *The Human Evolution Source Book*. Englewood Cliffs, NJ: Prentice-Hall.

PHOTO CREDITS

Illustrations for the cover and the part openers were created by Rebecca Ruegger. The illustration for Part III is based on a photo by Robert Frerck, Odyssey Productions.

The author is indebted to the following for photographs and permission to reproduce them. Copyright for each photograph belongs to the photographer or agency credited, unless specified otherwise.

p. 93 (top)	© E. R. Degginger/Color Pic, Inc.
p. 93 (bottom)	© Peter Drowne/Color-Pic, Inc.
p. 94 (left)	© M. Austerman
p. 94 (right)	© Watts/Anthro-Photo
p. 96	© Anita de Laguna Haviland
p. 98	© Gerry Ellis/The Wildlife Collection
p. 104	© Gerry Ellis/The Wildlife Collection
p. 113	© 1985 David L. Brill
p. 118	© Anthro-Photo
p. 121 (left)	© Ollie Ellison, Duke University
p. 121 (right)	© 1985 David L. Brill
p. 124	© 1985 David L. Brill; artifact credit, Peabody Museum, Harvard University
p. 125	© Irven DeVore/Anthro-Photo
p. 129 (top)	© Anthro-Photo
p. 129 (bottom)	© Anita de Laguna Haviland
p. 133	© Glynn Isaac/Anthro-Photo
p. 136	David L. Brill © 1985 by permission of Owen Lovejoy
p. 137	© 1985 David L. Brill; artifacts credit, Transvaal Museum, Pretoria
p. 139	© Institute of Human Origins
p. 140	© Tim White, Department of Anthropology, University of California at Berkeley
p. 141	Melville Bell Grosvenor, © National Geographic Society
p. 142	© 1985 David L. Brill; artifact credits, (left) *A. africanus*, Transvaal Museum, Pretoria; (right) *A. boisei*, National Museum of Tanzania, Dar es Salaam
p. 148	© National Museum of Kenya
p. 152 (all)	David L. Brill, copyright© The National Geographic Society
p. 153	© Anita de Laguna Haviland
p. 156	© E. R. Degginger/Color-Pic, Inc.
p. 159	Andy Freeberg/© 1991 Discover Magazine
p. 161 (both)	© 1993 Mary Ann Fittipaldi
p. 165	© National Museum of Kenya
p. 166	Negative No. 319781. Courtesy Department of Library Services, American Museum of Natural History
p. 168 (left)	© John Reader/Photo Science Library/Photo Researchers, Inc.
p. 168 (right)	© 1993 David L. Brill; artifact credit, Geologisch-Palaontologisches Institut der Universität, Heidelberg
p. 169 (left)	Transparency No. 626. Courtesy Department of Library Services, American Museum of Natural History
p. 169 (right)	© 1985 David L. Brill; artifact credit, National Museums of Kenya, Nairobi
p. 171	© National Museums of Kenya
p. 176	© 1985 David L. Brill
p. 177	© Geoffrey G. Pope, Anthropology Department, The William Paterson College of New Jersey
p. 180	© 1985 David L. Brill
p. 181	© Henry de Lumley/Museum National d'Histoire Naturelle
p. 185	© Leo de Wys, Inc./J. Kostich
p. 186	© 1985 David L. Brill; artifact credit, National Museum of Ethiopia, Addis Ababa
p. 189	© 1993 David L. Brill; artifact credit, Musee De L'Homme, Paris
p. 190 (left)	© E. R. Degginger/Color-Pic, Inc.
p. 190 (right)	© Zhou Guoxing, Beijing Natural History Museum

p. 191 © E. R. Degginger/Color-Pic, Inc.

p. 195 (both) © Alexander Marsack, New York University

p. 196 Negative No. 335658. Courtesy Department Library Services, American Museum of Natural History

p. 199 Photo courtesy of Dr. B. Vandermeersch. Item from Israel Antiquities Authority

p. 200 (left) © L.W.T. Lawrence, The South African Museum

p. 200 (right) © 1993 David L. Brill; artifact credit, Musee De L'Homme, Paris

p. 201 © 1985 David L. Brill; artifact credit, Musee De L'Homme, Paris

p. 208 (all) Courtesy Department of Library Services, American Museum of Natural History

p. 210 (both) © Anita de Laguna Haviland

p. 211 © Joe Ben Wheat, University of Colorado

p. 212 Peabody Museum, Harvard University. Photograph by J. Brain

p. 216 © W. Fitzhugh

p. 225 © Leo de Wys, Inc./Eric Schnakenb

p. 227 © Associated Press/Wide World Photos, Inc.

p. 228 (both) © Dr. W. van Zeist, Biologisch-Archaeologisch Institut, Rijksuniveriteit Gronigen

p. 234 © Pierre Boulat/Woodfin Camp & Associates

p. 238 Courtesy of The Oriental Institute of The University of Chicago

p. 241 © Ankara Archaeological Museum/Ara Guler, Istanbul

p. 242 (both) © British School of Archaeology in Jerusalem

p. 243 Peabody Museum, Harvard University. Photograph by Hillel Burger

p. 244 (both) © Allan H. Goodman, Hampshire College

p. 246 © Richard Hutchings/Photo Edit

p. 251 © Robert Feldman/Anthro-Photo

p. 254 © Anita de Laguna Haviland

p. 255 © Anita de Laguna Haviland

p. 256 © The University Museum, University of Pennsylvania/Paulus Leeser

p. 257 © Photo by Kevin Pope

p. 259 (both, top) © Ronald Sheridan/Ancient Art & Architecture Collection

p. 259 (bottom) Courtesy Department of Library Services, American Museum of Natural History

p. 260 © Leo de Wys, Inc./Steve Vidler

p. 264 © Anita de Laguna Haviland

p. 265 © William A. Haviland

p. 267 © William A. Haviland

p. 272 Victor R. Boswell, Jr., © National Geographic Society

p. 273 © Cultural Relics Bureau, Beijing, and the Metropolitan Museum of Art, New York

p. 277 © Tony Freeman/Photo Edit

p. 281 (top, left) © M. Shostak/Anthro-Photo

p. 281 (top, right) © Susan Van Etten/Photo Edit

p. 281 (bottom) © 1993 Peter Menzel

p. 282 © Lawrence Migdale/Tony Stone

p. 284 © Ron Haviv/Saba

p. 285 © Steve Elmore

p. 286 (top) © Beryl Goldberg

p. 286 (bottom, left) © Farrell Graham/Photo Researchers, Inc.

p. 286 (bottom, center) © Richard Wood

p. 286 (bottom, right) © E. R. Degginger/Color-Pic, Inc.

p. 291 © Robert W. Ginn/Photo Edit

p. 292 © Ron Haviv/Saba

p. 295 (top) © National Aeronautics and Space Administration

p. 295 (bottom) © E. R. Degginger/Color-Pic, Inc.

LITERARY CREDITS

INDEX

Terms in **boldface** type are defined in the running glossary definitions on the text pages shown with **boldface numbers.** Photograph and figure page numbers are in italic type.

Aboriginal Australians, 19
Absolute (chronometric) dating,
    48, 49–51, *50*
Acheulean tradition, *171*–177,
    172, 173, 176
Adapidae, 118–120, *119*
Adaptation, 65, *68–69*
  cold-climate, 191
  mutation and, 63–64
  sivapithecine, 127–130
  skin color and, 285–287
Adaptive radiation, 114
Adovasio, James, 34
Aegyptopithecus, 119, 120-*121*
Africa
  Australopithecine sites in, 134–136,
    135
  civilizations in, *252*
  domestication in, 234
  fossils found in, 37
  Homo erectus from, 167–168
African Americans
  race and attitudes toward, 283
  and sickle-cell anemia, 69–71
  skin color and, 287
Africans, human evolution studies
    by, *133*
Afrikaners, 294
Agar, Michael (Dr. Truck), *18*
Agriculture, 247. *See also*
    Domestication
  health and, 244–245
  innovation in, 257, *257*
  of Tikal Maya, 256
Alleles, 58, 279. *See also* Cell
    division
  for blood groups, *279*
  intelligence and, 289

porphyria and, 294
Allen, Susan L., 27n
Altered fossils, 36
Altimira Cave (Spain), 209
Amber, 33
American Association for the
    Advancement of Science, 124
American Indians
  Florida excavation of ancient
    society, 34–36
  Nez Perce, 6
  Omaha, 7
  sites of, 38
  Zuni, 7
American Sign Language (ASL),
    chimpanzee learning and, 101
Americas
  civilizations in, *252*
  domestication in, 234
Amino acid racemization dating,
    51
Analogies, 80
Anemia, sickle-cell, *61*
Animals
  adaptation of, 68–69
  anthropomorphism and, 56
  classification of, 80–81
  domestication of, 229, 233–234
Anthropoids, 83n
Anthropological linguist, 12, 13
Anthropologists, 5, *22. See also*
    anthropologists by name
Anthropology, 6
  applied, 8, 40, 95, 202
  and contemporary life, 27
  cultural, 9–19
  definition of, *5*
  development of, 6–8

discipline of, 9–19
  ethics and, 26
  forensic, 8, *10*
  and humanities, 24–26
  physical, 9
  and science, 19–20
  subfields of, 9, *11*
Anthropomorphism, 56
Apes, 91. *See also* Primates;
    Sivapithecines
  miocene, 121–122
  as primates, 79
  small and great, 93–95
Applied anthropology, 8, 40, 95
  stone scalpels and, 202
Arboreal, 83
Archaeological and Historical
    Preservation Act (1974), 40
Archaeological sites, 31
Archaeology, 11, 12–13, 30–53
  dating and, 47–51
Archaic cultures, 215–216
Archaic *Homo sapiens,* **185,**
    187–189, *190*
  culture of, 190–196
Architecture, Upper Paleolithic
    settlements and, 210
Arensburg, B., 198n
Arizona, University of, 12–13
Armelagos, George J., 245n, 246,
    257n
Arnhem Land (Australia), 23–24
Art
  African rock, 209, *210*
  in Australia and New Guinea, 211
  Upper Paleolithic, *208*–209, *210*
Artifact, 32–33
Aryan race, 283